The Chinese Origin of Physiocracy

Tan Min

The Chinese Origin of Physiocracy

上海交通大学出版社
SHANGHAI JIAO TONG UNIVERSITY PRESS

Springer

Tan Min
School of Economics
Shanghai University of Finance
and Economics
Shanghai, China

Translated by
Liu Xiangjun
School of Foreign Languages
Shanghai University of Finance
and Economics
Shanghai, China

ISBN 978-981-97-9702-8 ISBN 978-981-97-9703-5 (eBook)
https://doi.org/10.1007/978-981-97-9703-5

Jointly published with Shanghai Jiao Tong University Press
The print edition is not for sale in China (Mainland). Customers from China (Mainland) please order the print book from: Shanghai Jiao Tong University Press.

Funded by the Chinese Fund for the Humanities and Social Sciences

This Springer imprint is published by the registered company Springer Nature Singapore Pte Ltd.
The registered company address is: 152 Beach Road, #21-01/04 Gateway East, Singapore 189721, Singapore

Preface

It is in ancient Greece and Rome that Western economics has, for more than two hundred years since its creation as a science, been held to originate, among economists at large, including those of today's China. Although many scholars from France, Britain, the United States, Japan, and China published works intermittently, in the nineteenth century and the first half of the twentieth century, to prove that Physiocracy was influenced by Chinese thought to some extent, these influences were mainly limited to the fields of culture, politics, or art and rarely extended to economic theory.

In the history of economic theory, it was *Histoire des Doctrines Économiques* (1909), coauthored by the economists Charles Gide and Charles Rist, that openly admitted without prejudice, at a very early time, that the Physiocrats were influenced by Chinese thought. It is commendable that the two authors—both from France, a country that is the birthplace of classical political economy—could adopt so impartial and selfless an academic attitude, although their so-called influence of Chinese thought is only to link François Quesnay's *Tableau Économique* with Chinese characters while admitting that the Physiocrats followed the Chinese cultural tradition in terms of some concepts. The Japanese scholar Takimoto Seiichi's *History of European Economics* (1931) takes as its subtitle "The origin of modern Western economics in Chinese thought," which is in the history of theories the first work that unambiguously holds this view of the Chinese origin of Western economics. Unfortunately, the view is only expounded in the book's appendix, entitled "The origin of the fundamental thought of Physiocracy," and no profound and convincing argument is put forward. Joseph Schumpeter's important work of 1953 *History of Economic Analysis*, which is famous for its wealth of information, only mentions that *Despotism in China* by Quesnay, the founder of the Physiocratic School, "has given rise to speculations on the subject of Chinese influence upon the physiocrats" (Schumpeter, 1954a, p. 224). By "speculations," Schumpeter is, obviously, uncertain about the influence.

In China, many scholars have studied the issue since the 1930s. Among them, two economists have produced works worth mentioning, both appearing in the 1930s. The first is Tang Qingzeng's *History of Chinese Economic Thought* (Vol. 1), which devotes a whole chapter to the impact of Chinese economic thoughts on the West, especially the Physiocratic School. The pity is that his argument has nothing new, consisting of only a generalization of what some Chinese and foreign scholars had said before him. The second is Ly Siou-Y's paper "L'Influence de la Pensée Économico-Politique de la Chine Ancienne sur la Doctrine Physiocratique," published in Sun Yat-sen University's journal of *Social Research* (Volume 1, Issue 3), which is the second half of his doctoral dissertation completed in France, examining the influence from three perspectives: natural law, autocratic regime, and agricultural centralism. Although Ly fails to provide unique insights, this attempt is still commendable.

It can thus be seen that, before 1949, when the People's Republic of China (PRC) was founded, the "Eurocentrism" embedded in Western economics and originating from ancient Greece and Rome had persistently occupied an exclusively dominant position in the minds of Chinese and foreign economists. Since 1949, the study of the history of Chinese economic thought has gradually developed into an independent discipline, but some scholars of this discipline, while devoted to the exploration and summary of China's glorious cultural heritage, still regard it as an independent system unrelated to Western economics. Some even do not agree to use the general categories of modern economics to interpret Chinese traditional economic thoughts, arguing that doing so is copying the rules of the bourgeoisie. Others doubt the analytical comparability of Chinese economic thought and Western economic theories, believing that the comparison confuses the theoretical viewpoints of different modes of production. Under such circumstances, it is hardly feasible to say anything about the impact of China's economic thoughts on Western economics and to blame foreign economists who have no idea of ancient China's brilliant economic doctrines for continuing to adhere to their Eurocentric viewpoints.

In his *The Chinese Origin of Physiocracy*, a revised and expanded version of the author's doctoral dissertation completed in 1989, Dr. Tan Min explores the historical mystery of the influence of ancient Chinese economic thought on the Physiocratic School, which is a unique topic worth undertaking in spite of the difficulty of collecting and identifying a large amount of rare data at home and abroad. Its publication will undoubtedly draw the attention of both China's and foreign economists, because the breadth and depth of the issues discussed here are a great step forward compared to those of similar works by previous authors.

This work's outline goes as follows. The author first introduces the Chinese vogue that spread throughout Europe in the seventeenth and eighteenth centuries as the historical background to the subjective and objective bases for the origin of Physiocracy in ancient Chinese economic thought. Then, he compares all the unique contributions of this School, in terms of the natural order, *Tableau Économique*, *laissez faire*, agricultural primacy, single *impôt territorial*, population, and property ownership, with the corresponding ancient Chinese economic views, and points out in each of the seven aspects the Chinese influence on Physiocracy.

Although the author states that he "does not aspire to a complete answer to this question," his arguments for solving this mystery boast at least three strengths that are convincing and unprecedented.

First, this book no longer looks for the influence merely from the perspective of traditional Chinese culture, as some scholars did in the past, but directly digs into economic theories to find the Chinese origin of Physiocracy. The smaller the scope of exploration, the more possible it is to discover whether and to what extent there is a real connection between the two, and thus to make a more eligible judgement as to whether there is a Chinese source in the Physiocratic doctrines.

Second, a thorough analysis of all the basic ideas of the Physiocratic School and the corresponding Chinese thought to reveal the commonalities between the two, rather than comparing their similarities randomly, can effectively demonstrate whether the former have their origins in the latter. This comprehensive analysis makes it easy to discover, of all the Physiocrats' basic ideas, those that can be found in both the ancient West and ancient China, and those that can be commonly found in the latter but rarely in the former. It seems that no basic idea of the Physiocrats has been found uniquely belonging to the ancient West and having nothing to do with ancient China. That is, by examining all the basic doctrines of the School, one may readily find all the approximations from the ancient Chinese economic thought and merely part of such approximate samples from the ancient West. Through the above analysis, the author is able to argue forcefully that Physiocracy has its origin in ancient Chinese thought.

Third, the author often seeks the rationale behind Quesnay's arguments from the writings by the Physiocrats, Quesnay in particular, and has made many discoveries. Since Quesnay and his followers admired and sought to emulate the doctrines and institutions advocated in the Chinese classics, it is only natural that their theoretical views have their origins in China, whether their understanding of this Eastern country is correct or not. Indeed, it is difficult to refute the elaboration that the author has made in such an unprecedentedly effective way.

The above three salient points alone are already good reasons for the argument, convincing though not perfect, that Physiocracy has its origin in ancient China. They tend to be ignored only by a very small number of people with deep-rooted Eurocentrism. The Physiocrats have long been recognized in the West as among the founders of modern economics. And as both a theoretical system independent of Western economics and one of the pioneering elements of modern economic theory, ancient Chinese economic thought ought to share with ancient Greco-Roman thought the honor as one of the theoretical sources of Physiocracy. It can be said that Dr. Tan Min's research has lifted a layer of fog that has shrouded the history of economics for more than 200 years, so that people can finally understand that the pioneering ideas of ancient Chinese and Greco-Roman thought both played a role in the development of world economics in their own way. Furthermore, we can say from this work that while the economic thinking of ancient Chinese people has been one of the theoretical sources of Physiocracy, China, having been known as "the sleeping lion of East Asia" for more than two centuries, will certainly make its own new contribution to world economics in the near future. This work having such significance to the economists of both China and other countries, I find it a great pleasure to preface it.

Shanghai, China
October 1990

Hu Jichuang

Contents

List of Figures

Chapter 5

Chapter 1
Introduction

The topics discussed in this book, broadly speaking, fall under the comparative study of Chinese and Western cultures. It can be argued that examining the status, role, and influence of traditional Chinese culture within the global cultural landscape through a Sino-Western comparative lens has emerged as a global academic trend, capturing the shared attention of contemporary scholars across China and other nations. Most of these comparative studies, however, have so far focused on political and economic systems, philosophy, history, literature, and science and technology, with little attention devoted to economic thought. Thus the need for the present study.

1 The Necessity for This Study

A comparative study of Chinese economic doctrines and Western economic theories, from the perspective of the history of economic thought, has been conducted in two ways. First, treating ancient Chinese and Western economic thought as two completely independent theoretical systems in the analysis of their similarities and differences. This research has been pioneered and carried on primarily by China's economists with the aim of uncovering and collating the glorious achievements of ancient Chinese economic thought, so as to enrich the world's treasure trove of ancient economic thought, and to break down the Eurocentric bias that is so prevalent among economists. Second, examining the mutual influence and permeability between the two. In this latter case, the influence of Western economics on China's economic thinking mainly refers to the massive importation and gradual dominance of Western bourgeois economics since the end of the nineteenth century, and the spread and growing strength of Marxist economics before and after the May Fourth Movement of 1919. This recent historical trend has been recognized by China's economists. However, the opposite direction, that is, the influence of China's ancient economic thought on Western economics, especially on the formation of bourgeois classical

M. Tan, *The Chinese Origin of Physiocracy*,
https://doi.org/10.1007/978-981-97-9703-5_1

political economy, though touched upon by some Chinese and foreign scholars since the beginning of the twentieth century, has been rarely studied systematically, and remains an open question to this day.

In the history of Western economics, it has long been in the economic thought of ancient Greco-Roman tradition and medieval Europe that Western theorists search for the origins or developmental clues of modern political economy. Western economists, constrained by their national perspectives, tend to disagree about who are the pioneers of modern economic science, or about the origins of certain important economic theories, but they have never taken issue with the Eurocentric viewpoint that dominates all writings on the history of economics, so that the search for the non-European, especially Chinese, sources of modern economics has in fact become a no-go zone. Only a few Western economists have ventured into this field, skeptically or tentatively, lacking systematic and in-depth argumentation, so that their works fail to get widely disseminated, and to become part of Western orthodox or authoritative writings on the history of economics. Such works in the socialist countries, the former Soviet Union in particular, are essentially written within the framework of Marx's *Theories of Surplus-Value*, and fail to explore new questions beyond Marx's ready-made conclusions about the origins of political economy, let alone touching upon the above question itself.[1] In China, none of today's popular textbooks on the history of economic theory have yet discussed the relationship between ancient Chinese thought and Western economics. The Chinese scholar Hu Jichuang, in his *Prehistory of Political Economy*—though not in itself a work specializing in the relationship between the origin of Western economics and China—includes for the first time ancient China's economic thought within that of the world, so as to break the monopoly of ancient Greece as the starting point of the world's economic thought.

However, the emergence of Western economics as an independent science witnessed a very unusual period of cultural exchanges in which Western countries, especially France, imitated China. This special fact cannot but attract the attention of Chinese and Western people, including scholars devoted to the history of economic thought. It is noticed that at the time and even a while later, some famous European economists showed strong interest in citing China's economic data when they created their own economic theories. What is striking is that Adam Smith, in *An Inquiry into the Nature and Causes of the Wealth of Nations* (abbreviated as *The Wealth of Nations*), his masterpiece on the theoretical system of bourgeois classical political economy, directly refers to China's economic problems for more than 30 times. Many issues, such as China's wealth, consumption, population, land, ownership, agriculture, manufacturing, domestic commerce, foreign trade, land and water transportation, wages, profits, interest, currency, and political law, have been discussed, and some of the analysis is quite elaborate. What is even more frequent is his indirect discussions of the Chinese issue in the sections on the entire Asian or

[1] As the most prestigious historian of economics in the former Soviet Union, Rozenberg once mentioned that the Physiocrats idealized China and its emperors, only to mark the "feudal coat" of their system (Rozenberg, 1934–36). Here, Rosenberg failed to consider whether China had indeed had an impact on their economic doctrines.

Eastern world. The impact of this on the community of British economists is obvious. For example, Malthus, the founder of the British bourgeois vulgar political economy, has repeatedly talked about China's situation in his works; other representatives of vulgar economics, such as James and John Stuart Mill, are said to have provided Marx in their works with many sources of information about the Eastern despotic state (Bary, 1983).

Before the publication of *The Wealth of Nations* in 1776, China's influence on Europe had already begun to move to the final stage from the heyday of Chinese culture being eagerly pursued. As the dazzling aura of China's past image gradually dimmed, the decline of the Eastern feudal empire became increasingly apparent in the eyes of Europeans. In his discussion of China's economic issues in *The Wealth of Nations*, Smith is obviously more objective and sober than his predecessors, and critically analyzes and studies the various data about China from the bourgeois economists' perspective. In his view, China seemed to have stagnated for a long time. The reasons, he argues, are twofold. First, China was extremely contemptuous of foreign trade, which not only limited the country's sales through foreign markets to greatly increase its domestically manufactured products, but also gave it almost no chance to imitate the foreign countries already boasting a large scale of foreign trade to improve the productivity of its manufacturing industry. Second, there was a lack of capital and its accumulation in China's manufacturing sector. For example, its rulers emphasized agriculture in preference over industry and commerce, resulting in a large flow of social funds to the purchase or lease of land; the low status of Chinese craftsmen and manufacturing workers and their low labor prices made them unwilling to shift from agriculture to manufacturing; under the pressure of feudal bureaucrats, the Chinese people had no sense of security and formed the habit of hoarding gold and silver underground; and the high interest rate was brought about by the luxurious consumption of Chinese rich people. All of the above are regarded by Smith (1812) as important factors hindering China's capital accumulation (pp. 88–89). These two reasons are attributed to a more fundamental point that China "had probably long ago acquired that full complement of riches which is consistent with the nature of its laws and institutions" (p. 88). Therefore, the only way for China's going back to the path of economic growth, Smith (pp. 88–89) believes, was the breakup of its shackles of the feudal system.

However, when analyzing China's economic situation, Smith consistently insists in his book that China was the richest country in the world: "China has been long one of the richest, that is, one of the most fertile, best cultivated, most industrious, and most populous countries in the world" (p. 70); "China is a much richer country than any part of Europe" (p. 164); and China is "much richer, better cultivated, and more advanced in all arts and manufactures than either Mexico or Peru" (p. 349). These are just some of his many descriptions of China's rich natural resources, abundant human resources, good land and water transportation facilities and a broad domestic market, all of which were, in his eye, far better than those in Europe. This is why Robert Lekachman (1959, p. 89) later analyzed Smith's views of the countries of the world at the time in the following way: "To him, all European countries, except Holland, and the entire remainder of the world, except China, were underdeveloped."

That is, at that time in Smith's mind, only China and the Netherlands were counted as developed countries.

Smith's announcement that China was the richest country in the world, and his eagerness to study China's economic problems, are regarded as merely an effort to meet the needs of the British bourgeoisie's external expansion at the time, and are given no other explanation by future historians of economic thought. However, these viewpoints and ideological tendencies are notable clues to the investigation of the relationship between ancient Chinese thought and the classical political economy created by Smith. If we follow these clues, we will find that Smith received, cited, or absorbed ancient Chinese thoughts by way of the following three routes.

The first is his own access to various Chinese literature that was popular in Europe at the time. In this regard, L. A. Maverick, a Western scholar, suggests that Smith's *The Theory of Moral Sentiments* (1759) may be directly inspired by ancient Chinese moral and ethical thoughts for two specific reasons. First, the French Jesuit historian Jean-Baptiste Du Halde included the translation of an excerpt of *The Book of Mencius* in his *Description de l'Empire de la Chine* (1735), offering for the first time to the majority of European readers a more detailed introduction of the book, and "Mencius's doctrine of the perfectibility of man [...] may have moved Adam Smith in writing the *Moral Sentiments*" (Maverick, 1946, p. 25). Second, the treatise *Idée Générale du Government et de la Morale des Chinois*, published in 1729 by Silhouette, who was made Controller-General of France in 1759, was also influential in Europe (p. 27). Maverick (p. 32) quotes this work before he gives his own conclusion:

> One paragraph calls to mind the subsequent work of Adam Smith—the *Moral sentiments*: "The good man has for the basis of all his virtues, humanity. The love which one should feel for all men is not a thing foreign to man; it is the man himself. His nature causes him to love all, and that sentiment is as natural to him as is self-love; it is the quality that distinguishes him from other creatures; and it is the basis (*l'analise*) of all his laws. From this universal love springs justice." A full reading of Silhouette's discussion of "humanity" will well repay the student of Smith's ethics.

Smith's early book *Moral Sentiments* can be said to constitute the philosophical basis of his later *Wealth of Nations*, in which he mentioned that he had referenced some reports or travel notes of European missionaries and tourists to China. However, as mentioned earlier, when Smith wrote *The Wealth of Nations*, the attitude of Europeans towards Chinese culture had already undergone a significant change. The enthusiasm of regarding China as magical and worth imitating had been fading, giving way to calm observation, mixed with a growing suspicion and even scorn about its culture. Under this circumstance, the analysis and quotation of Chinese materials in Smith's book, though still bearing the obvious traces of Chinese culture being fashionable in Europe, are in general built upon a critical attitude of China's static state, somewhere between progression and regression. This makes it easy for people to form the impression that Smith was criticizing China, ignoring the fact that he might in the meantime have learned from the Chinese cultural tradition something that is beneficial to his theoretical system. Therefore, it is obviously not enough to judge the internal connection between his doctrine and Chinese culture solely by Smith's comments on Chinese materials.

The second is the influence from his British pioneers. Smith is generally held to have established the theoretical system of classical political economy by drawing on the British and French pioneers. In terms of the influence from Chinese culture, the British pioneers are prominent in two aspects. On the one hand, British deists such as Anthony Collins, Matthew Tyndal and Henry St. John Bolingbroke in the early eighteenth century "always used 'the argument from the Chinese' to attack the revealed religion, obviously enlightening people about the need to break the superstition and emancipate the mind" (Fan, 1981, p. 12). On the other hand, some British writers, novelists and poets of that period, such as Alexander Pope, Horace Walpole, Oliver Goldsmith, and Daniel Defoe, author of *Robinson Crusoe*, in their various literary works, praised China very much, used China as a theme, or at least paid tribute to Chinese culture, and some British political figures, such as Sir William Temple of Charles II, also expressed in their works their admiration of China (Fan, 1931, pp. 389–406; Fan, 1943a, pp. 1–21; Fan, 1943b, pp. 111–137; Zhu, 2005b, pp. 201–203). These British people, whether they were Smith's predecessors or his contemporaries, were all familiar to Smith, and some of them were very respectable in his eye. Their frequent reference to Chinese materials in their works, and their habit to draw on or absorb Chinese views to express their own ideas, undoubtedly had great influence on Smith. Among the key figures who had before Smith played an important role in the formation of the British classical political economy, David Hume was especially concerned about China. He declared in a positive tone that the disciples of Confucius are "nearly the only regular body of *deists* in the universe" (Hume, 1779, p. 79). For Smith, Hume was not only a close friend, but also the most respected elder. In fact, Smith was said to be a student of Hume. It can be seen that Hume's influence on Smith was extraordinary: the former's paying attention to China and obtaining nourishment from Chinese culture obviously left a mark on the latter's thought.

However, the influence of Chinese thought in the UK during that period was not as significant as it was in the European continent. For this difference, a variety of reasons have been revealed by some modern scholars. But whatever the reasons, the fact is that, in Britain, the popularity of Chinese culture was mainly witnessed in the field of literature, but not in philosophy: Confucius, one of the greatest Chinese philosophers, was viewed by the British as just an "honorable man." It is thus of secondary importance to search for the Chinese origin of Smith's economic theory from the Chinese materials that British pioneers were in contact with. In other words, Smith was more likely to be influenced by ancient Chinese thoughts through his non-British European predecessors. It is thus necessary to turn our eyes away from Britain to reveal the Chinese origin of Smith's theory.

The third is the influence from his French pioneers. Here, the pioneers mainly refer to the Physiocrats represented by Quesnay and Turgot. From 1764 to 1766, Smith traveled to the European continent, mainly France. During this time, he met famous people, such as Quesnay and Turgot, and discussed various issues with them. Rae (1895, p. 228), Smith's biographer, comments,

> [T]here never was a country where graver or more interesting problems, both economic and constitutional, offered themselves for study than France in the latter half of [the eighteenth] century, nor any political philosopher who enjoyed better opportunities than Smith of discussing such problems with the ablest and best-informed minds on the spot. Smith's residence in France [...] must have been an invaluable education to himself, supplying him day after day with constant materials for fresh comparison and thought.

It was under such conditions that Smith (Quoted in Rae, 1895, p. 216) claimed that Quesnay was the "ingenious and profound" creator of the Physiocratic School. Smith's praise was not as extremely reverential as that by Quesnay's disciples, but he "thought him [Quesnay] so clearly the head of the economic inquirers of the world that he meant to have dedicated the *Wealth of Nations* to Quesnay had the venerable French economist been alive at the time of its publication" (Rae, 1895, p. 216). Later, Smith (1812, pp. 537–538) again stressed in *The Wealth of Nations* that Physiocracy, "with all its imperfections is, perhaps, the nearest approximation to the truth that has yet been published upon the subject of political economy." He thus took great care to assimilate the part that is "as just as it is generous and liberal" (p. 538) of "the principles of that very important science" (p. 538). Because of this, some scholars comment positively on Smith's travel to France, especially his visit to the Physiocrats. Dugald Stewart (1811, p. 464) claims that it "must have enriched his mind with many new ideas [...]. But whatever were the lights that his travels afforded to him [...], they were probably useful in a still greater degree, in enabling him to perfect that system of political economy." Wan and Wu (1986, p. 16), two Chinese scholars, even think that "*The Wealth of Nations* would not have come into being without Smith's contact with the Physiocrats." "Had Smith remained in Glasgow all his days [...]," Rae (1895, p. 228) argues most cautiously, "it is a truism to say that [his] works would have been other and different from what we have."

That the Smithian doctrine is revealed to have inherited some elements from Physiocracy brings a broad prospect to the study of the relationship between Chinese thought and the doctrine, even Western economics as a whole. Because France, especially Paris, was the center of Chinese culture's spread throughout Europe at the time, and it was under this special historical condition that the Physiocratic School was born, the Physiocratic system was saturated with the influence of Chinese thought from the beginning, and the Physiocrats openly advertised their admiration of China. Smith was greatly influenced by the Physiocratic School in his first systematic formation of Western classical economics. If we can prove that the School has absorbed the thought that is embodied in the large number of materials from China, the connection between Smith's theories and Chinese thought will be convincingly established. In this regard, the British economist Blaug (1985, p. 33) mentions in his famous book on the history of economics, *Economic Theory in Retrospect*, that "Adam Smith's strange notions of Chinese economic development [...] were apparently derived from Quesnay, who believed that China practiced Mandarin despotism, esteemed agriculture, and allowed the natural order to prevail." It is only acknowledged here that Smith's insights on the Chinese economy came from Quesnay, but not whether Smith's own theory was influenced by China's economic thought. This has, however, already suggested to us that it was from Quesnay that Smith understood and absorbed

Chinese thought. Therefore, an in-depth study of the Chinese origin of Physiocracy becomes the key to ascertaining the influence of ancient Chinese thought on Smith's theory and on Western economics at large.

Furthermore, some important economic views of the Physiocratic School have had various degrees of influence on later economists. It is confirmed that Malthus's treatise, *An Essay on the Principle of Population*, together with most of his unique viewpoints, is attributed to the Physiocratic School (Semmel, 1965, p. 523). More scholars come to think that the Physiocratic concept of circular flow is one of the origins of Say's law, the Keynesian theory, and even Marx's simple reproduction pattern. A. Phillips (1955, p. 144) claims that the *Tableau Économique* marks the beginning of general equilibrium economic theories and should be credited as the precedent to those by Walras, Pareto, Cassel and Leontief. Leontief (1951, p. 9) frankly admits that he was inspired by Quesnay in his creation of the input and output table, which he labels as the American *Tableau Economique*. Henry George even publicly declares that the Physiocrats are his mentors. Such views have been not uncommon in the history of Western economics since the middle of the twentieth century. Correct or not, they all point to the conclusion that many economic doctrines of the Physiocratic School have been retained in the Smithian theories as a theoretical heritage, have indirectly spread with the expansion of Smith's doctrine, and have directly contributed to the development of several important economic theories of future generations. Therefore, the relationship between Physiocracy and Chinese thought is not only a historical issue that every economist who seeks to clarify the origins of modern economics cannot avoid, but is also significant to the development of Western modern economics.

In view of the above, we argue that the Chinese origin of Physiocracy, the focus of this book, should be taken as an important topic, and should be placed on the agenda of the history of economic theory.

2 The Origins of Physiocracy: An Important Subject

The key reason for our regarding the origins of Physiocracy as an important topic in the history of economics, in our research on the relationship between Physiocracy and Chinese culture, is first and foremost the significant impact of the Physiocratic system on the establishment of Western classical political economy and the development of Western modern economics. In other words, the significance of revealing the origins of Physiocracy is largely determined by its importance in the history of economics. Therefore, in order to deepen our understanding of the significance of the research on this topic, we first look at how economists, mainly those of the West, evaluate the historical position of the Physiocratic doctrines. This evaluation itself has gone through a historical process, reflecting the increasing emphasis of economists on Physiocracy and the consensus gradually built in the process.

Western economists generally recognize that the Physiocratic School[2] is the first group of economists with a complete and consistent theoretical system as its guide, except for the term "school." Some scholars point out unambiguously that the Physiocrats are "the first scientific school of political economy" (Higgs, 1897, p. 3), are "at once the first and the most compact school to be encountered in the history of economics" (p. 144), or are "the first modern school of economics" (Fox-Genovese, 1976, p. 9). Others put the word "school" in quotation marks, regarding for example the Physiocrats as "the earliest 'school' of economists in the fullest sense of the term" (Gide & Rist, 1915, p. 3), or "the first 'school' of political economy to emerge in the history of that science" (Spengler, 1968, p. 443), with the purpose of setting it apart from modern schools of economics. This latter view is shared by the Soviet scholar Rozenberg (1934–36), who argues that the use of the term "School" by Quesnay and his disciples cannot be understood in accordance with the universal sense adopted by Smith or Ricardo, because the Physiocratic School is similar to a political party, equivalent to a close political association, and is therefore nicknamed a sect by its opponents. In contrast, the American Austrian economist Schumpeter (1954a, p. 223), though noting that Quesnay and his followers are often referred to as a "Sect," still regards them as "a school [formed] by virtue of doctrinal and personal bonds, and always act[ing] as a group," and argues that Quesnay's disciples "absorbed and accepted the master's teaching with a fidelity for which there are but two analogues in the whole history of economics: the fidelity of the orthodox Marxists to the message of Marx and the fidelity of the orthodox Keynesians to the message of Keynes." In any case, the Physiocratic School is recognized by all economists as the first in the history of economics.

Roughly speaking, the Physiocratic School was active in around the 1760s.[3] Their theoretical writings and organizational activities reached their peak when Turgot was in power, which not only attracted the attention of the French intellectual circles, but

[2] It may be summarized from the discussion by the American economist Haney that the Physiocrats can be divided into two categories: the broad and narrow senses. The broad sense refers to those who opposed the philosophy of Colbertism or promoted the movement for *laissez faire*, and the narrow sense refers to those "Économistes" with Quesnay as their leader (Haney, 1911, p. 150). What is adopted in this book is the narrow sense of the Physiocrats.

[3] There are different opinions on the specific dates of the emergence and disintegration of the Physiocratic School. About its date of establishment, there have emerged two main arguments. One is for 1756, the year when Quesnay's first economic paper, "Fermiers," was published in the sixth volume of *l'Encyclopédie* (edited by Diderot). The other is for July 1757, when a debate between Quesnay and the elder Mirabeau began, after which Mirabeau was persuaded by Quesnay and became the first faithful follower of Quesnay's theories. As far as the date of the School's disintegration is concerned, there are even more different opinions. Some think that it should be 1772, in which the Physiocrats' journal, *Éphémérides du Citoyen*, was stopped, and Quesnay lost interest in studying political and economic issues and turned to geometry. Others argue for 1774, the year of Quesnay's death. 1776 has also been proposed, because it witnessed two important events: one was that Turgot was removed from the position of finance minister, indicating the failure of the agrarian reform, and the other was the publication of Adam Smith's *The Wealth of Nations*. Still, some others postpone the period until the outbreak of the French Revolution in 1789. Due to the above differences, the active period of the Physiocratic School is as short as fifteen or sixteen years, or as long as more than 30 years, but it is generally said to be more than twenty years.

also influenced many of the most powerful figures of the European countries, such as Catherine II of Russia, Gustav III of Sweden, Leopold II of Tuscany, Charles III of Spain, Joseph II of Austria, and Ferdinand I of Naples. But not long after, due to the Physiocrats' loss of power in the court, especially with the publication of Adam Smith's *Wealth of Nations* in 1776 and its rapid dominance in the European economic theory, the influence of the Physiocratic School declined dramatically. By the end of the eighteenth century, apart from the very few Physiocrats who were still active, the entire School had actually collapsed.

At the beginning of the nineteenth century, Western economists, especially those of the United Kingdom, launched a big debate about the validity of Physiocracy. The result, according to Ronald Meek (1962), a modern economist, was that "British political economy was finally purged of the Physiocratic elements" (p. 345). Since then, Physiocracy has been regarded by British economists as "an eccentric, ephemeral, and peculiarly French body of thought" (p. 345). This depreciation of the Physiocratic doctrines prevailed in the British community of economic studies for a long time, which shows to a certain extent the partisanship of some early British economists.

In this period, the community of French economists, which gave birth to the Physiocratic School, seemed to be rather silent. In fact, they just followed the British economists by striving to get rid of the influence of Physiocracy. A case in point was Jean-Baptiste Say, the founder of French vulgar political economy. In 1815, Du Pont, a member of the original Physiocratic School, wrote to Say, accusing him of forgetting to have grown up by first "sucking Quesnay's milk" but later attacking his own "milkmaid" (Quoted in Daire, 1846, pp. 394–424).[4] It was not until 1846 when the French economist Eugène Daire edited and published *Physiocrates*, a collection of the Physiocrats' works, that people's interest about Physiocracy was rekindled.

Daire included in his *Physiocrates* only those parts that fall within the scope of an economics of wealth and dropped the rest as "a very confused assembly of dissertations holding at once to the moral order, the political order and the material interests of society" (Quoted in Neill, 1948, p. 159). This editorial principle was criticized at the time for isolating the economic discourse from the rest within Physiocracy. In the eyes of those critics, Quesnay had a complete social philosophy that was unprecedented, and economics was only one of the main products of this social philosophy. But these disputes did not hinder the popularity of Daire's point of view (pp. 159–161).[5] Anyway, entangled in the editorial principle, the debate did not touch upon the status of Physiocracy in the history of economics.

---

[4] Du Pont wrote a letter to Say at the end of his life (he died in 1817), trying to persuade the latter that he was an economist like the Physiocrats (Quoted in Daire, 1846, pp. 394–424), which shows that at that time the Physiocrats regarded themselves as "economists."

[5] It is necessary to point out that when Marx analyzed the sources of physiocracy in *Capital* and *Theories of Surplus-Value*, his quotations come almost all from Eugène Daire's *Physiocrates*, and only occasionally from the Physiocrats' works, such as Turgot's *Reflections on the Formation and Distribution of Wealth* and Mercier de la Rivière's *L'Ordre Naturel et Essentiel des Sociétés Politiques*. According to Daire's editorial principle, Quesnay's *Despotism in China* was not included in this book, so Marx may not have read this article. This is probably a reason why Marx did not

The first person to give an in-depth research and a scientific evaluation of the economic theory of the Physiocratic School is Karl Marx, who profoundly and eloquently summarized the great achievements or great contributions of the School in the history of economics. Even Schumpeter (1954a, p. 232), an authority on bourgeois economics, has to acknowledge admiringly that "Karl Marx was the only first-rank economist to give Quesnay his due." However, in the mid-nineteenth century and beyond, Western economists did not accept Marx's scientific thesis on the historical status of the Physiocratic School. Oncken, a Swiss economist, when editing and publishing *Oeuvres Économiques et Philosophiques de Quesnay*[6] in 1888, said that the Physiocratic system was still expecting to receive the reputation of science, that is, the scientific value of Physiocracy was still not widely recognized by economists at that time.

In particular, Marx (1969, p. 64) commented on the Physiocratic School by affirming that "Adam Smith was strongly infected by the Physiocrats." This argument aroused a stir among a few prejudiced British economists.[7] Rae (1895, p. 201), in his *Life of Adam Smith*, asserted by quoting Morellet that Turgot and any other economist in France did not have "influenced or supplied any of Smith's ideas." Later, Edwin Cannan, when re-publishing Smith's *Wealth of Nations* in 1904, also emphasized, "In his exposition of physiocratic doctrine, Smith does not appear to follow any particular book closely [...], but he probably relied largely on his recollection of conversations in Paris [...]" (Quoted in Smith, 1937, pp. 628–629 [Note 3]). Although both Rae and Cannan noticed the close relationship between Smith and the Physiocratic School, which is evidenced in Rae's mention of Smith's reverence for Quesnay and his intention to "have dedicated the *Wealth of Nations* to Quesnay had the venerable French economist been alive at the time of its publication" (p. 216), and Cannan's account that Smith's library contained the Physiocrats' works (Quoted in Smith, 1937, pp. 628–629 [Note 3]), they still tried to devalue or deny the influence

mention China when he was investigating the source of the economics of Quesnay and other Physiocrats. Some bourgeois economists nicknamed Marx as a Eurocentralist. In fact, this is completely wrong. It can be found that, in his later years, Marx shifted the focus of research from the West to the East (Krader 1974). In this case, why did Marx not find from the numerous China-related remarks of Quesnay and other Physiocrats clues about the origin of Physiocracy beyond the Western tradition? It seems very likely that it is Daire's removal of the relevant remarks about China that led to Marx's failure to give a more comprehensive judgment on the origin. This is indeed a pity.

[6] It is generally held among Western economists that this collection by Oncken has replaced the one compiled by Daire, and has become the most authoritative and the most complete collection of Quesnay's works.

[7] As early as the late eighteenth century, shortly after the publication of Smith's *Wealth of Nations*, Du Pont declared that "whatever was true in Smith was borrowed from Turgot, and whatever was not borrowed from Turgot was not true; but he afterwards retracted that absurdly-sweeping allegation, and confessed that he had made it before he was able to read English" (Quoted in Rae, 1895, p. 203). Another Frenchman, Condorcet also claimed in his biography of Turgot that Turgot's *Réflexions* "may even be considered as the germ of the treatise on the *Wealth of Nations*" (Condorcet, 1787, p. 74). The French minister of finance Leon Say believed that "Turgot owed much of his philosophy to Smith, and Smith owed much of his economics to Turgot" (Quoted in Rae, 1895, p. 203). It can be seen that, generally speaking, French scholars consistently hold the view that Smith's economic theory has been influenced by the Physiocratic School, and few exceptions can be found.

of the Physiocratic School on Smith's theory. Viner (1865, p. 117), an American scholar, said, "[Those British] scholars interested in the sources from which Smith may have derived theories or concepts have made use of such information more for the negative purpose of excluding specific authors or groups of authors as influences on Smith than for the positive purpose of tracing such influence." This prejudice has not disappeared even now.

Even so, this kind of controversy still stimulated people to study the economic theory of the Physiocratic School and formed a research boom in the late nineteenth and early twentieth centuries. Many famous economists of this period devoted themselves to the study of physiocracy, leading to the so-called "revival of the Physiocratic doctrines." After this boom, Marx's high evaluation of the Physiocratic School came to be accepted by more and more Western economists. Higgs (1897), in his speech given at the London School of Economics in 1896, advocated that "the Physiocrats were the first scientific school of political economy" (p. 3), and believed that "nothing would be easier than to select sentences in which Adam Smith exhibits the influence of the Physiocrats" (p. 139). At the beginning of the twentieth century, several influential monographs of economic history attached great importance to the historical position of the Physiocratic School. The French economists Gide and Rist (1915), in their *Histoire des Doctrines Économiques*, regarded Quesnay and his disciples as "the real founders of the [political] science" (p. 2) and added, "It is true that their direct descendants, the French economists, very inconsiderately allowed the title to pass to Adam Smith, but foreign economists have again restored it to France, to remain in all probability definitely hers" (p. 2). The reason is, according to Gide and Rist, that "he (Smith) borrowed what was most characteristic and most suggestive in their teaching" (p. 55). In his *History of Economic Thought*, the American economist Haney (1911, pp. 133–157) also praised the Physiocratic School's economic doctrines as very systematic and crucial to the development of economic thought in the world, and argued that Smith borrowed a lot from the School. After that, Lewiński (1931, p. 65) summarized the contribution of the School as follows: "we are much indebted to the Physiocrats for having separated political economy from other sciences and for having tried to embrace for the first time in one system the whole economic process of production, distribution, and exchange." It is true that in the 1930s there were still a few economists who believed that Adam Smith had received little influence from the Physiocrats. Gray (1931, p. 98) was a case in point, who argued, "Almost certainly the similarities of Quesnay and Smith merely exemplify once more the wholly natural fact that independent inquirers do frequently, about the same time, arrive at substantially the same conclusions." But these same scholars, Gray (p. 118) noted, also realized that "[e]ven an admirer of Smith may have no scruple in finding in the Physiocratic group the real beginnings of modern economics."

Since the beginning of the 1940s, Physiocracy has been accepted in many works on the history of economic thought as "the first scientific system of economics in the strict sense."[8] Schumpeter (1954a, p. 372) listed Quesnay among "the brightest stars of economic analysis," and expresses his dissatisfaction with the little attention

[8] This evaluation is the term used by Oncken in the 1888 edition of the Quesnay collection.

Quesnay has received even today. This view was further developed in the hands of the British economist Meek (1962, p. 9) in the 1960s:

> The French Physiocrats are at once the most exciting and the most contemporary group of economists in the whole history of economic thought. The most exciting, because the birth of Physiocracy was in fact the birth of the science of economics in the broad general form in which it has come down to us today. The most contemporary, because the Physiocrats' major preoccupations, in both the theoretical and the practical fields, were strikingly similar to those of present-day economists.

He is surprised that the Physiocratic School fails to attract the full attention of the economists in the English-speaking world, which is one of the main reasons why he is committed to translating into English a large number of original works by the Physiocrats. He is a senior lecturer at the University of Glasgow in the United Kingdom, which used to be the place where Adam Smith learned and taught. Meek (p. 353) criticizes the negligence of the Physiocrats: "It is easy to exaggerate the extent of Smith's emancipation from Physiocratic notions. Taking the *Wealth of Nations* as a whole, Smith looks backward towards the Physiocrats almost as often as he looks forward towards Ricardo." These observations indicate that the attitude towards the Physiocratic School changed significantly at the time in the English-speaking world, the UK in particular.

The study of Physiocracy in the early twentieth century was largely due to the fact that "the Physiocratic doctrines scarcely [did] more than arouse historical curiosity" (Gide & Rist, 1915, p. 51),[9] that is, it was treated as a historical antique to appreciate and play with. Since then, with the deepening of research, many economists have begun to realize that the theory has not only its historical value for the establishment of economics as an independent science, but also many implications for a lot of economic theories that have emerged since then and are still popular today.[10] In the 1970s–80s, this trend became more obvious. There emerged in various works on the history of economic thought praise of Physiocracy: it "constitutes a watershed in the history of economic thought" (Quoted in Fox-Genovese, 1976, p. 110); "Quesnay's achievement is one of the most remarkable in the history of economics" (Eltis, 1975, p. 167); the analytical method of the Physiocrats, together with their new ideas and new concepts, has made a lasting contribution (Bhatia, 1978, pp. 49, 67) to the development of economic thinking; it is true that "[a]s a school the physiocrats enjoyed only brief glory[,] [b]ut their insights, and their obfuscations, became a part of nineteenth-century economics through the writings of Adam Smith and his followers" (Lekachman, 1959, p. 86); and so on. Many economists in this period not only took for granted the influence of the School on Smith, but also dug into the Physiocratic doctrines for the theoretical sources of many famous economists such as Say, Malthus, Henry George, Walras, Keynes, and Leontief. Samuelson (1962,

---

[9] Meek (1962, p. 34) also believes that the interest in their work beginning to be revived in the second half of the nineteenth century was "more antiquarian than anything else."

[10] Meek (1962, p. 34) points out, "It is only in our own time (the 1960s), with a renewal of interest in certain of the basic theoretical and practical questions upon which the Physiocrats concentrated, that their full stature as economists is gradually being revealed."

pp. 3–4), echoing Schumpeter, even claims that three of the world's four greatest economists are French, including Quesnay, who should be included in the great hall of fame, with the purpose to highlight the practical significance of Quesnay's creation of the *Tableau*. It can be seen that in the minds of Western contemporary economists, Physiocracy has not lost its theoretical vitality since its birth more than one hundred years ago.

The above discussions lead to the following conclusions about Western economists' understanding of the School. First, the historical position of the Physiocratic School as the founder of political economy, since Marx first proposed it decades ago, has been widely recognized by Western economists and has become the dominating view in the evaluation of Physiocracy in the various works on the history of economic thought. The difference only lies in specific ways of expression. Second, although there has been ambiguity and even prejudice for a long time, since the 1940s, the opinions of Western economists have basically converged in taking as a self-evident historical fact the influence of the Physiocratic School on Smith and even on the entire classical economics. Third, some basic principles of Physiocracy, including its analytical methods, after being absorbed and digested by generations of economists, have penetrated into various fields of economics and has become an integral part of modern Western economics.

At this point, based on the prevailing comments of Western economists, it is not difficult to confirm the Physiocrats' prominent position, their important role, and their far-reaching influence in the history of economics. Of course, what is described here is still the spread, instead of the source, of Physiocracy. However, its "spread" is intended to lead to its "source." Since it is certain that the Physiocratic School has made such a significant contribution to the creation and development of economic science, the exploration of the sources of the Physiocratic doctrines is obviously not insignificant, but crucial to a correct understanding of the origin and evolution of the modern economic science. This allows us to understand the unusual meaning of the source of Physiocracy from the relationship between its spread and its source. At the same time, our study of the source of Physiocracy is based on the following observations or reasons, which differ from the current popular ones that merely repeat the ready-made conclusions in the textbooks on the history of economics.

Firstly, in the large number of existing works about the Physiocratic School, the study of the origin of Physiocracy is still rather weak. This is reflected both in its little research achievement and, more notably, in its narrow research scope. As we all know, the mid-eighteenth century in which the Physiocratic School was active witnessed the Enlightenment, a famous movement in the European history, of which a striking feature is that its thinkers, in order to maintain rational freedom and oppose the Church's authority and feudal system at the time, eagerly sought for, absorbed and publicized new things and new ideas. To seek new ideological weapons to meet the needs of the struggle, they strived to get rid of the shackles of various traditional European concepts, especially those of Medieval Theology. There emerged thus a group of so-called philosophers who were eclectic and ready to embrace the whole world. Under the impetus of the Enlightenment, the Physiocrats established their system of economic doctrines with a strong color of the age in its source of thought, that is, they did not rigidly adhere to the French or European tradition, but were "internationally-oriented." In other words, in the special historical environment of the time, the Physiocratic School aimed to establish a new theoretical system that could distinguish the spirit of the times from that of the past, which prompted them to throw off the shackles of traditional European thoughts and consciously absorb from outside Europe all kinds of nourishment. At the same time, "France was the center of the intellectual movement of the Enlightenment" (Palmer et al., 2007, p. 349), which provided objective conditions for the Physiocrats' absorption of a wide range of foreign ideas, especially those from the ancient Chinese culture that was abundantly imported at the time. The background of the introduction of Chinese culture into France and the attitude of the Physiocrats to Chinese culture are to be further described below. Here we only point out that in the process of creating their theoretical system, the Physiocrats had not only a strong desire to find new sources of thought from outside Europe, but also the unique advantage, that is, the objective conditions satisfying the above subjective requirement of accessing a pool of foreign ideas, especially Chinese thought, in eighteenth-century France. Under this circumstance, it is obviously inappropriate to study the sources of Physiocracy while ignoring the traditional non-European ideas represented by Chinese culture at the time. This narrow vision, which is confined to European intellectual traditions and does not desire or dare to step beyond the threshold of Eurocentrism, not only distorts historical facts, but does little to help grasp the important sources of Physiocracy comprehensively and scientifically.

Secondly, it is far from adequate for the existing research of the origin of Physiocracy to focus only on the Physiocratic pioneers' writings having appeared since the mid-seventeenth century. It is not convincing to assert that only the theoretical views of these few pioneers—the ancient Greco-Roman and medieval sources of ideas, such as that of the theory of natural order, are to be discussed in detail later—constitute the origin of Physiocracy, because it is yet to be determined whether their theoretical views are based on individual independent ideas, or on other sources of Western thought. But what is certain is that these pioneers, as influential figures of the seventeenth and eighteenth centuries, were to varying degrees influenced by the imported Chinese culture. For example, the famous representatives Boisguillebert and Marshal Vauban are confirmed to have received the influence from *Nouveaux mémoires sur l'état présent de la Chine* by Le Comte, a missionary to China, and *Confucius Sinarum Philosophus* edited by four Jesuits to China. Another example is Richard Cantillon's *On the Nature of Commerce in General*, written in the early 1730s, which is generally believed to have the greatest impact on the formation of Physiocracy.[11] But Cantillon was Quesnay's contemporary, and as a Parisian banker born in Ireland, had repeatedly quoted information about China in his work. It is hard to say that his economic thoughts did not receive the influence of Chinese culture that was popular in Europe at the time. Of course, it was not until the latter half of the nineteenth century that Cantillon's above-mentioned masterpiece was brought

[11] Gide and Rist (1915, p. 46 [Note 2]), two French economists, claim, "His (Cantillon's) influence upon the Physiocrats has perhaps been exaggerated."

to light thanks to Jevons's high praise, and, because Cantillon's own life experience is not adequately revealed, the relationship between his economic thought and the Chinese vogue at that time is still a mystery. But we can conclude that it is not enough that we only trace the source of Physiocracy to its direct pioneers, who, in terms of both their times and their own writings, have reminded us that the formation of their ideological tendencies and theoretical perspectives has a significant connection with the prevailing Chinese culture around them.

Thirdly, anyone who pays a little attention to the history of Western economics will find that Western scholars, in their studies of Physiocracy, often describe some of its important economic theories as unique, unprecedented, or different from those of the Physiocrats' contemporaries. This actually implies that it is very difficult to trace such theoretical viewpoints to the traditional thinking of Europe, and they seem to be the Physiocratic creations that are detached from Europe. In fact, this is a Eurocentric view. If we abandon this point of view and take into account other sources of thought outside Europe, we will easily find that Physiocracy, which seems to be a sudden rise to Western scholars, has elements very similar to the imported foreign thoughts at that time, such as Chinese traditional thought. In this regard, we will cite a large number of arguments in the analysis below.

Fourthly, we must remember that although we emphasize the close relationship between Physiocracy and foreign cultures, especially that of China, we do not mean that what the Physiocrats assimilated is nothing but Chinese thought. As a typical representative of the French bourgeois classical political economy, Physiocracy must have its own Western origins, and it was mainly on the basis of its own culture that the Physiocrats absorbed various foreign cultures, Chinese thoughts included. This is beyond doubt. But the problem is that until now, in almost all the popular works on the history of economic thought, the study on the sources of Physiocracy is almost always restricted to the French or European origin, ignoring the historical fact that the Physiocrats were in close contact with Chinese culture in the process of forming their theoretical system. Therefore, the study of this book will focus on the Chinese origin of Physiocracy, with the purpose of restoring history to its original form, that is, striving to prove that the Physiocratic School, while establishing its theoretical system along the Western trajectory, referenced and assimilated a large number of ideas from China.

It can be seen from the above that it is important to propose and examine the influence of ancient Chinese thoughts on the Physiocratic School, both to carry forward the glorious achievements of ancient Chinese culture, and to enrich the history of economics itself. As far as only Western economics is concerned, studying the Chinese origin of Physiocracy will help to further understand why the Physiocratic School occupies such an important position in the history of economics and maintains its unique influence today, and to solve the relevant theoretical problems that have puzzled Western economists for a long time.

This topic, though still attracting little attention from the scholars of the history of economics, is nevertheless a new field of research. Luckily, a small number of people of insight have opened up this new field of study, a new academic path for later generations to continue to expand and explore. For a better understanding of the topic, below we first make a brief review of its research history and current situation.

3 Relevant Studies in Retrospect

In Chinese and foreign academic circles, the study of the influence of Chinese culture on the creation of Physiocracy has lasted intermittently for a century and gone through a rather bumpy process of development. At first, at the end of the nineteenth century, there was an upsurge of studying Physiocracy in the European continent, which lasted for several years. Some economists touched upon in varying degrees the relationship between a few representative Physiocrats and Chinese traditional culture. Instead of seeking the origin of Physiocracy in Chinese culture, they merely described this obvious connection on the surface. The monographs published during this period on the study of the Physiocrats were limited to the European continent. It was not until 1896 that an English book devoted to Physiocracy appeared in the British Isles. That is *The Physiocrats* by Henry Higgs. This 150-page booklet is composed of six lectures delivered at the London School of Economics, addressing itself as "a useful introduction" (Higgs, 1897, p. vii) to the Physiocrats. The author mentions that "the analogy of China so forcibly impressed the Physiocrats that they were seized with an enthusiasm even for the Celestial government, derided by de Tocqueville as *imbécile et barbare*" (p. 140). This argument is more a mockery than an exploration of the true Chinese influence on the Physiocrats.

At the beginning of the twentieth century, French scholars were the first to realize that Chinese culture did have an impact on Physiocracy and even on European philosophy in the eighteenth century. One of the most famous examples is Virgile Pinot, whose "Les Physiocrates et la Chine au XVIIIe Siècle" (1906–1907),[12] according to the information we have at present, is the first work that emphasizes in its title and specializes in the relationship between Physiocracy and China. In 1909, Gustave Lanson published a paper on the formation and development of the philosophical spirit in the eighteenth century, which highlights in its title the influence of the East and the Far East. In the same year, there appeared the article "Les Chinois de Turgot," which also specially discusses the relationship between the representatives of Physiocracy and China. These authors, regardless of the content of their papers, are pioneers in exploring the influence of Chinese culture on the Physiocratic School.

Among the notable books on the history of Western economic theories of that time, the first one to take this influence seriously is Charles Gide and Charles Rist's *Histoire*

[12] In 1932, Pinot published in Paris *La Chine et la Formation de l'Esprit Philosophique en France (1640–1740)*, a book also dealing with the relationship between the Physiocratic system and Chinese culture. However, the 1930s already saw the heated discussion on this subject, and it is not surprising that this book was published at that time.

des Doctrines Économiques (1909).[13] The two authors admit that the Physiocrats absorbed some useful thoughts from ancient Chinese culture, and link the *Tableau Économique* with Chinese characters, claiming that the Physiocrats imitated Chinese cultural traditions in some basic concepts. Unfortunately, these arguments are merely mentioned briefly in the book, including its Appendix.

The 1920s saw an increasing number of works concerning Chinese influences upon the Physiocratic School, among which the remarkable ones are still those by French economists, such as *China and the French Physiocracy* (1922) and *China, the Physiocrats and the French Revolution* (1929), both treatises foregrounding this issue. But the most typical of the period is *China and Europe: Intellectual and Artistic Contacts in the Eighteenth Century*, a book published in Berlin in 1923 by the German scholar Adolf Reichwein.[14] At the beginning of this work, Reichwein (1925) comes straight to the point by quoting Alphonse Paquet, a Western contemporary: "We Europeans are beginning to be educated by ancient China" (p. 3). This remark "summarize[s] the feeling of a small group of cosmopolitan thinkers and students of the East" (p. 3), which leads Reichwein to explore the "real inner relation" between Eastern and Western culture with fairness and "exactness" (pp. 3–11). While expounding the origin of Physiocracy, the author, mainly based on the writings of the representative figures of the Physiocratic School, proves with more than ten pages that the Physiocrats delved into ancient Chinese literature, and then asserts that the origin of Quesnay's theory is not the ancient Greeks as claimed, but the ancient Chinese (pp. 99–109). This is indeed an original idea, which has not been developed by predecessors in the systematic monographs on the history of cultural exchanges between China and the West. The problem lies in the fact that Reichwein is keen on textual research in an "accurate way," mainly enumerating materials and failing to make theoretical analysis on the relationship between Physiocracy and Chinese culture. The chapter entitled "The Physiocrats" in this book, according to Zhu Jieqin (1962, p. 1), is almost entirely a narrative of bourgeois objectivism. In addition, Reichwein discusses the influence of Chinese culture on the Physiocratic School from the perspective of general cultural exchanges between China and the West, but fails to make a special in-depth study on the origin of Physiocracy. Of course, this failure is determined by the nature of the book's topic, so we should not be too demanding.

In the 1930s, there emerged a climax in the research on the relationship between the Physiocrats and China. Almost all of the influential monographs on this subject were produced during this period. As far as European and American countries were concerned, the scholars engaged in this research went beyond the scope mainly limited to France and Germany in the past, and produced a number of high-quality

[13] In the less than forty years since its publication, this work has been reprinted six times in French and translated into various other languages, English, Japanese and Chinese included. Its Chinese version was published in 1986.

[14] This book was translated into English by J. C. Powell and published in London in 1925. In 1962, it was translated into Chinese by Zhu Jieqin and published in China by The Commercial Press.

English writings. At least three works—the first two in particular—deserve our attention.

The first is Geoffrey Hudson's *Europe and China*, which was published in London in 1931. This book examines the relationship between Europe and China from ancient times to 1800, much earlier than Reichwein's work elaborating their contacts only in the eighteenth century. Such a wide scope makes it inconvenient to devote a special chapter to the origins of Physiocracy. In the chapter "THE JESUITS IN PEKING," the author devotes several pages to the origins, and is convinced that the Physiocratic School was deeply influenced by Chinese culture. Hudson (1931, p. 326) specially points out,

> Because of the almost complete extinction of the cult of China after 1789 the great majority of European historians have failed to do justice to the influence of Chinese ideas in eighteenth-century Europe. They have dismissed the cult as a mere freak of fashion, or as a Utopian fantasy assuming the name of China but having no relation to the real China or its culture.

The above is no less than a criticism of European historians for their wrong ideas about the spread of Chinese culture to the West, and a warning to Western economists against their prejudice in their studies of China's influence on the Physiocrats.

The second is Mario Einaudi's *Physiocratic Doctrine of Judicial Control*, published by Harvard University in 1938, which examines the Physiocratic theories from the perspective of the political rather than economic science. Some basic political concepts of Physiocracy, especially those put forward by Quesnay, Einaudi (1938, p. 31) clearly points out, come from the study of Chinese system. Understandably, these political concepts are closely related to the economic viewpoints of the Physiocratic School, since economics was at that time not independent from politics or philosophy.

The third work worth mentioning is Blake Clark's *Oriental England: A Study of Oriental Influences in Eighteenth Century England as Reflected in the Drama*, which was written in Shanghai and published in Hong Kong in 1939. Its subtitle showing its focus, the book mentions that the Physiocrats absorbed some philosophical thoughts of Confucius.

It is from respectively the perspectives of general culture, politics and drama that the above three discuss the relationship between the origin of Physiocracy and Chinese culture. Although their investigation is, in terms of the collection and application of historical materials, not as remarkable as the aforementioned work by Reichwein, and although such materials come from English-speaking countries that have always been noted by their Eurocentrism, after all, they display a sign of change to seek the source of Physiocracy from China, a country outside Europe. This notable change is confirmed in the several monographs written in the late 1930s and early 1940s by L. A. Maverick, an American professor of economics at the University of California.

Maverick published a paper in the American Journal of *Economic History* in 1938, in which he openly puts forward the proposition of "Chinese influences upon the Physiocrats" from the perspective of the history of economic theory. He thinks that "[t]he influence of the Chinese upon the physiocrats was probably more extensive and more significant than has generally been appreciated" (Maverick, 1938, p. 54). Then he makes a general comparison between some basic economic viewpoints of Physiocracy and the Chinese laws and regulations that the Physiocrats came into contact with at that time, so as to prove that the similarities between them cannot be explained by coincidence alone, but are caused by "an actual borrowing on the part of the physiocrats" (p. 54). From this, he comes to a very meaningful conclusion: "Our twentieth-century heritage from [the Physiocrats] has retained deposits from the Orient. Western economists who study the economic and social thought of the Chinese may well regard it not as something alien and irrelevant to Western civilisation, but as having contributed directly to the development of Western thought" (p. 66).

In the same year, a French monograph was published in Paris, with a similar title: "China's Influence on the Emergence and Development of Physiocracy." It is a comparative study of Chinese economic thought and Physiocracy, pointing out that they are very similar in many important viewpoints, such as the concept of natural order, agricultural thought, legitimate despotism, and economic circulation theory. The differences in other issues are also analyzed, so as to prove that Chinese economic thought has an undeniable influence on Physiocracy, and Quesnay's creation of his initial theoretical system cannot be separated from his study and synthesis of Chinese thought.[15] This book, with 192 pages in total, can be regarded as the first academic monograph that has systematically investigated this subject in the history of economic doctrines. But somehow, in the 50 years since the publication of this work, we have never seen a book on the history of economic theory which cited or mentioned this work when analyzing relevant issues. Since we have not found the original book yet, it is hard to work out the reason.

Another work by Maverick, "The Chinese and the Physiocrats: A Supplement," was published in the same American journal in 1940 as the above one of 1938, and may well be regarded as a sequel. Its main purpose is to use all kinds of circumstantial evidence to explain how China, as an external force, exerted an indirect influence on the Physiocrats, especially Quesnay. The views put forward are a supplement to those in the previous paper. In 1942, he published "The Chinese Influence on Quesnay and Turgot" in a journal dedicated to oriental studies, which mainly restates the relevant arguments of the above two.

On the basis of these papers, Maverick published in 1946 his famous work *China: A Model for Europe*, which is now an essential reference book for scholars from the East and the West to study the relationship between China and the Physiocrats. It is divided into two parts.

The first mainly introduces the praise of Europeans for China's economy and politics in the seventeenth and eighteenth centuries: in the seventeenth century Europeans advocated imitating Chinese thoughts and in the eighteenth century they followed China's example. The analysis of Chinese influence on the Physiocrats can be mainly found in this part, which follows the basic argument in the previous papers but is

[15] The above introduction can be found in *Biography and Bibliography*, published in France in 1958, p. 383.

characterized by more extensive citations. Interestingly, in order to facilitate readers' direct comparison between ancient Chinese thoughts and Quesnay's Physiocratic doctrines, the author specially appends in this part his 46-page English translation of some excerpts of *Mencius* and Xü Guangqi's *Nong Zheng Quan Shu* (*The Complete Treatise on Agriculture*), accounting for almost half of this part (108 pages in total).

The second part is used for the introduction and complete translation of Quesnay's *Despotism in China*. This work has great reference value for studying how Quesnay and even the whole Physiocratic School learned from China. For a long time, this work had almost disappeared in the whole European and American academic circles. One of the important reasons is that since Quesnay first published it in *Ephémérides du Citoyen* (abbreviated below as *Ephémérides*) in 1767, it had not been republished for a long time, not to mention translated into English, except that its original French version was included in *Oeuvres Économiques et Philosophiques de Quesnay*, which was edited by Oncken in 1887. Under such circumstance, it was difficult for British and American economists to pay close attention to this work, let alone to spread it. Therefore, it was very significant for Maverick to "[supply] the first English translation" (Ch'ên, 1946, p. vii).[16]

In a word, the book, with no new ideas about the relationship between the Physiocrats and China, is of great historical value. It is in this sense that Maverick "has revivified a most important chapter in the history of cultural interchange between China and the West" (p. vii).

In Japanese academic circles of the 1930s, there appeared several works on the cultural exchanges between China and the West or the history of economic theories, in which many references were made to the relationship between the Physiocrats and China. The most representative is Goto Sueo's *The Westward Spread of Zhina's Thought in France* (1932)—"Zhina" is an offensive Japanese term against China. Twenty-four years later, the book was revised and reprinted with "Zhina" changed to "China" in its title.[17] It can be seen from this that the book had great influence in Japanese academic circles. Like Reichwein's, it focuses on the cultural contacts between the East and the West in the seventeenth and eighteenth centuries. The difference is only that Goto specializes in the cultural exchanges between China and France, and focuses on the influence of Chinese thought on France. Due to Goto's deliberate search for details and collection of abundant data, this magnificent

[16] In 1992, when the first edition of the present Chinese work was published, only the first and eighth chapters of Quesnay's *Despotism in China* were available in Chinese, the first chapter included in *The Continental States of Europe in the Seventeenth and Eighteenth Centuries*, translated by Li Guobin et al., published first by The Sanlian Press in 1959 and then revised by Gu Xiegao before it was published by The Commercial Press in 1986, and the eighth chapter in Quesnay's *Selected Economic Works*, translated into Chinese by Wu Feidan and Zhang Caoren and published by The Commercial Press in 1979. (Translator's note: It was not until 2018 that the first complete Chinese translation of the work was published by The Commercial Press. The translator is Tan Min, the author of the original Chinese version of the present work).

[17] This revised version was published in 1959. There is yet no Chinese translation of this book. Goto also authored *The Origin of Chinese Culture and Chinese Studies*, *The Communication between the East and the West*, and *A Biography of the Qian Long Emperor*, and translated into Japanese from a Western language *A Biography of the Kang Xi Emperor*.

work boasts more than 500 pages, the scope of which goes far beyond the 150-page Chinese translation of Adolf Reichwein's *China and Europe: Intellectual and Artistic Contacts in the Eighteenth Century*. It is reasonable to say that such a great work should provide more help for studying the influence of Chinese culture on Physiocracy. However, in terms of only its fourth and sixth parts on the influence of Chinese thought on Quesnay and Turgot, there are not many new things to offer. Besides, as a doctor of literary studies, Goto paid little attention to the analysis and textual research of economic thought, thus weakening the reference value of this work for the theme discussed here, although it still provides a lot of background information.

In addition, Ishida Mikinosuke (1941, p. 147), a Japanese scholar, states in his *Cultural Exchanges Between China and the West* that the influence of Chinese thoughts upon Western economic doctrines have enabled us to see the emergence of the so-called Physiocrats. What Ishida means is that the economic theory of the Physiocrats originated from the influence of China. However, such an important assertion is based only on the historical fact that Turgot was in contact with two Chinese youths, which is obviously too hasty.

Of all the Japanese writings in this period, the most striking is *History of European Economics*, published by Takimoto Seiichi in 1931. This book has an appendix, titled "Exploring the Origin of the Fundamental Thoughts of the Physiocrats: The Origin of Western Modern Economics lies in the Doctrines of China." The subtitle is very impressive. In Chinese and foreign historical treatises on economic theory, it is extremely rare to see such an explicit statement, proposed as a title, that the economic theory of Physiocracy originated from Chinese thought, although this formulation appeared in the appendix instead. It is a terrible pity to Japanese people, according to the author, that most people now think that economics in modern times originated in France or Scotland, but completely ignore China, which is an important mother country of the science (Takimoto, 1931, p. 39). However, his analysis lacks a comprehensive grasp and an in-depth exposition of the social background of the Physiocratic School accepting the influence of Chinese culture and the internal theoretical connection between Physiocracy and Chinese culture. Even if he puts forward some insights, he fails to demonstrate the argument. It is thus difficult for other economists to accept his conclusion that the core of Physiocracy originated in China. In fact, his conclusion is not only difficult to obtain the approval of the world, but has also aroused doubts and objections among some Chinese scholars, which even leads to the completely opposite argument that the economic theory of the Physiocratic School "has nothing to do with the agricultural primacy in ancient China" (Wang, 1957, pp. 279–280).[18]

In China, as early as 1912, Sun Yat-sen (1982, p. 510) made the proposition that "economics originated in China." Sun's intention, however, was only to emphasize that people should pay attention to and study ancient Chinese economic thoughts, and did not touch upon the origin of Western economics.

---

[18] This work was originally published in 1945 under the title "Zhongguo Jingji Yuanlun," literally meaning "An Original Theory of Chinese Economy."

One of the early works on the relationship between Physiocracy and Chinese culture in China is Li Yonglin's "The Relationship Between the Economist Turgot and Two Young Chinese Scholars" (1922). The paper quotes a lot of materials to prove that Turgot's famous work *Réflexions sur la Formation et la Distribution des Richesses* was written for two Chinese youths studying in France. This purpose of Turgot's, now known to many Chinese and foreign economists, but making the Chinese people "all surprised" (Li, 1922, p. 169) at that time, took so much effort to be confirmed in the early 1920s. We can thus see how difficult it was then to discuss in China the Chinese influence on the Physiocrats.

It was not until the 1930s that the situation in China changed: there emerged a sudden increase in the number of writings referring to or specializing in China's influence on the Physiocratic School. First of all, Yuan Xiangpu (1930) published "China's Contribution to Western Economic Thought" in 1930, in which he holds that ancient China's economic system and thoughts, like those of ancient Greece and ancient Rome, "have a great influence on Western economic thoughts, and should also occupy a position in the history of economic thoughts" (p. 1). Compared with this bold assertion, its argument is however thin and vague, and he only lists as "exceptionally decent" some Physiocrats' praises for ancient China. The following year, Li Guangzhong (1931) article "The Relationship Between the French Physiocrats and Chinese Political and Economic Thoughts" came out. This work was originally a summary of notes made for the above book by Reichwein: "the author didn't mean to publish the manuscript at first, but only for the sake of memorization" (p. 1), and published it later merely at the editor's demand. As only a paraphrase of Reichwein's work, it has nothing new. Moreover, this work lacks the scope and boldness of Yuan's article, and its "postscript" specifically states that the purpose of this article is only to sketch the cultural relationship between China and the West: "I dare not say that China's economic thought beats that of Europe or even the West" (p. 15). Even so, Guo Yuan (1934, p. 2), a Chinese economist of that time, still felt "really dissatisfied" with Li's use of causality to explain the influences of Chinese economic thought on the Physiocrats. In the early 1940s, Jian Bo specially added a note to his translation of the famous appendix of Takimoto Seiichi, claiming that his motive for the translation was by no means chauvinistically patriotic, parochially arrogant, or even nationalistic (Takimoto, 1931, p. 2). All this reflects the then special mentality of the Chinese scholars.

Besides the above two articles devoted to the special discussion on the Chinese origin of Physiocracy, there emerged in China's academic circles many works related to this topic in the discussions of the cultural relations between the East and the West or of the history of Chinese economic thought. Most of the authors paraphrased the existing materials or quoted the available views of Western scholars. Geng Danru (1934, p. 12) mentioned Quesnay as "the Confucius of Europe." Ch'ên Shou-Yi (1935a, p. 1) believed that Chinese culture "contributed considerable materials and viewpoints" to Physiocracy, and in another English article in the same year, he criticized Reichwein for his "incomplete" study of the Physiocrats: "Almost nothing is said of the Chinese sources of the economic thought of Quesnay and Turgot"

(1935b, p. 48).[19] He Bingsong (1935, p. 71) wrote an article entitled "A Study of the Spread of Chinese Culture to the West," claiming in a special section on Quesnay as the Confucius of Europe and an economist of Physiocracy that "Quesnay's economic theory mostly originated from China except for, for example, his creative method." Almost all of the above works were published in 1935, which indicates that the research on the relationship between Physiocracy and China entered a new period.

On the basis of the previous studies, there appeared in 1936 two weighty works written by Chinese scholars. One is the first volume of Tang Qingzeng's *History of Chinese Economic Thought*, in which a whole chapter is devoted to the influence of ancient Chinese economic thoughts in Western countries, especially on the Physiocrats. His comparative analysis leads to the following conclusion: "Indeed, ancient Chinese economic thought had a considerable influence in Western countries, especially on the Physiocratic School in France. [...] This influence was far more important than that from Roman doctrines, Christian thought, *The Bible*, etc. Therefore, it would be really ungrateful of the Chinese and foreign scholars who deal with the history of Western economic thoughts if they attached too much importance to Roman doctrines while disregarding ancient Chinese economic thoughts" (Tang, 1936, p. 366). Tang's book is characterized by analyzing and synthesizing the various opinions of predecessors on this topic before arriving at the above striking conclusion. Although it has not added anything new, its great influence on Chinese people cannot be underestimated.

The other work, less known but more important from an academic point of view, is Ly Siou-Y's French treatise: *Les Grands Courants de la Pensée Économique Chinoise dans L'Antiquité (du Vie au IIIe siècle avant J.-C.) et leur Influence sur la Formation de la Doctrine Physiocratique*. It is his doctoral dissertation written in 1936 when he was studying in the Law School of Dijon University, France. This work has not been published abroad. It consists of two parts. The first mainly discusses several key schools of ancient Chinese economic thought from the sixth to the third century BC, especially Daoism, which is put in the most prominent place. The following are sequentially the economic thoughts of Confucianism, Mohism and Legalism. This part is 50 pages long, accounting for more than half of the full text of 90 pages, and its contents are well known among scholars who deal with the history of Chinese economic thought. Apart from the preface and conclusion, there are still 30 pages left for the second part, which is on the influence of ancient Chinese political and economic thoughts on Physiocracy. This part is more interesting to us,[20] respectively on natural law, despotism and agricultural centralism, providing new materials but no new insights. The first and second parts are independent of each other, and there is almost no internal connection. Of course, as a doctoral dissertation, focusing on ancient Chinese economic thoughts may arouse the interest and attention of French

[19] Ch'ên Shou-Yi, a leading scholar on the history of cultural exchanges between China and the West, wrote the foreword to Maverick's *China: A Model for Europe*. Maverick (1946, p. viii.) claims that he "was happy to gain his help and friendship" in writing the book.

[20] This part (Ly, 1938, pp. 1–30) was later published in *Social Research*, with the new title "L'Influence de la Pensée Économico-Politique de la Chine Ancienne sur la Doctrine Physiocratique."

university professors. But as far as the subject we care about is concerned, the general theory of the former part is rather poor and of little significance. However, Ly's essay is the first one in which Chinese scholars have announced abroad directly in French that the importance of ancient China's influence "lies not only in its being the source of Physiocracy, but also in the history of economic science itself" (Ly, 1938, p. 3). It is a pity, however, that the author, after returning to China, almost disappeared from the academic scene and published no more work on the same subject.

In addition, Zhu Qianzhi's *The Influence of Chinese Thought on European Culture*, written in 1938 and published in 1940, contains a section under the heading of "The Physiocrats," which discusses issues such as the influence of Chinese thought on Physiocracy, "Quesnay: The Confucius of Europe" and Turgot's contact with Chinese culture. What is particularly commendable is that Zhu lists and quotes a large number of Chinese and foreign works related to the above subjects.[21] He not only concentrates on the relevant historical materials and viewpoints provided by various works at that time and before, but also summarizes them in different categories, making them clear to people at a glance. Moreover, he cites a lot of original works by the Physiocrats as proof. In this sense, the author has made considerable contributions, as a scholar from Chinese academia, to the study of Chinese influences on the Physiocrats, despite the fact that as a philosopher and historian, he tends to observe the Physiocrats' contact with Chinese culture from a philosophical perspective, and is thus unlikely to go deep into the field of economics to explore the true source of Physiocracy.

It can be seen from the above that in the 1930s, the academic circles in Europe, America, Japan and China all reached a climax in studying the connection between Physiocracy and Chinese culture. This unique phenomenon of Chinese and foreign scholars echoing each other with a common research topic can be described as a big event in the academic history of the world. Generally speaking, the climax was first brought about by French and German scholars, and then by British and American scholars, while Chinese and Japanese scholars played a role in adding fuel to the flames. The climax lasted until the mid-1940s, which saw the publication of Maverick's *China: A Model for Europe*.

Since then, the research of this subject has not seen a similar prosperous scene in the world. In European and American countries, from the late 1940s, some people began to doubt whether the Physiocrats were ever influenced by China, and thought that what Quesnay said about China was, to a great extent, the product of his own "mind," that is, a fiction. In the 1950s, Joseph Needham, who is famous for exploring the influence on the West from ancient Chinese culture and scientific and technological achievements, did not discuss the relationship between Chinese culture and the Physiocrats, which is really hard to understand. Schumpeter, in his *History of Economic Analysis*, which is known for its rich collection of data, only speculates that "ancient China, the home of the oldest literary culture of which we know" (1954a, p. 53), may boast more economic "trace[s] of analytic effort" (Ibid., p. 53) than any other place in the world. As for the statement that Quesnay's *Despotism in China* "has given rise to speculations on the subject of Chinese influence upon the physiocrats"

[21] See the list of reference books Zhu Qianzhi gives in the Preface to this book.

(Ibid., p. 224),[22] Schumpeter has never given his affirmation. By the 1960s, even Meek, a scholar who specializes in compiling and translating the works of the Physiocrats in order to attract the attention of economists in English-speaking countries, did not say a word about the influence from China. This is the same case with the following monographs devoted to the origin of Physiocracy, such as Elizabeth Fox-Genovese's *The Origins of Physiocracy: Economic Revolution and Social Order in Eighteenth-Century France* (1976), in which the author, though taking notice of the many comments on China in the works by the Physiocrats, thinks that the Physiocrats only "pretended to talk about" (Fox-Genovese, 1976, p. 11) China without receiving from Chinese culture any substantial influence in their formation of Physiocracy. It is not uncommon for Western scholars to seek the source of Physiocracy completely from the European tradition. This has continued to this day.[23]

The situation in Japanese academic circles was similar, and the research enthusiasm for this subject seemed to ebb even earlier. At the beginning, the call that the fundamental thought of the Physiocratic School originated from China was the loudest among Japanese economists, and it was most deplored by them that the disregard for this source was so widespread in the academic world of economists. But soon afterwards, in as early as the mid-1930s, their great passion quickly subsided. Though Goto Sueo revised and republished his work in 1956, the decline did not stop. Today, the above-mentioned work by Goto is still superior to other Japanese scholars' studies on the cultural exchanges between China and France, especially on Chinese influences upon the Physiocrats.

A view of some Soviet scholars needs to be mentioned too. In the Russian translation of the eighth chapter of Quesnay's *Despotism in China*, which is from the French edition of *Œuvres Économiques et Philosophiques de F. Quesnay* (1958), the translator specially adds in a note, "China is just a convenient means for Quesnay to describe his own thoughts, and his content has nothing to do with China's actual situation" (Quoted in Quesnay, 1979, p. 395 [Note 1]). This assertion completely rules out the possibility that Quesnay's thought was influenced by China. It not only shows that these Soviet scholars were ignorant of the past achievements of this topic, but also reflects the decline of its research in international academic circles at that time.

Starting from the 1940s, this subject in Chinese academia continued to be poorly researched for many years. Fortunately, in the late 1950s, some scholars again explored the influence of ancient Chinese economic thoughts on Physiocracy and

[22] Here, Schumpeter's "speculations" were based on Maverick's "Chinese Influences upon the Physiocrats" (1938). Mark Blaug, whose *Economic Theory in Retrospect* is as well-known as Schumpeter's above work, regards Maverick's *China: A Model for Europe* as a "fascinating study" (Blaug, 1985, p. 33), and uses the work to prove that "Adam Smith's strange notions of Chinese economic development (…) were apparently derived from Quesnay" (p. 33).

[23] Since the 1980s, a number of French scholarly works have been published on the Jesuits' arrival in China, including references to their relationship with the Physiocratic School. For example, in a work published in Paris in 1981, the author discusses the influence of the Jesuits in China on Quesnay (Geng, 1987, p. 23). But this is clearly not a discussion of the origins of Quesnay's economic doctrine.

even on European economic thoughts.[24] This was followed by another gap of over 20 years. In the early 1980s, Hu Jichuang enumerated for direct comparison 59 economic ideas from China and the West in the Chinese and English versions of his *Chinese Economic Thought Before the Seventeenth Century*,[25] and arrived at the conclusion that, by examining the achievements of ancient Chinese economic thoughts from a global perspective, we may easily find that Quesnay's most important doctrines contain ideas similar to those of ancient Chinese economic thought, which is rare when it comes to the European forerunners' ideas (Hu, 1984a, p. 1). This assertion inspires us to explore the origin of Physiocracy.

In the first half of the 1980s, the research of this subject was still rare.[26] Starting from the mid-1980s, the new trend of studying Chinese traditional culture came into being, and people re-noticed the special meaning of cultural exchanges between China and the West during the birth of modern economics,[27] although these works did not exceed the predecessors' research level.

From the late 1970s and early 1980s, driven by the prevalent comparative studies between Chinese and Western cultures, there emerged in Taiwan's academic circle many discussions on the relationship between Physiocracy and Chinese culture, which had been shelved for a long time. Wang Yi (1979, p. 5), for example, wrote *The Spread of Chinese Culture to the West in the Ming and Qing Dynasties*, with the main purpose of thoroughly understanding "China's role in the transformation of European ideology in the seventeenth and eighteenth centuries." The book particularly includes Quesnay's admiration for Chinese culture (pp. 151–153). Wang Zhongfu (1981, p. 132) talked about Quesnay's being "deeply influenced by Chinese theory," and Hou jiajü (1982, p. 239) affirms that the Physiocrats accepted and spread some economic thoughts of the pre-Qin Confucianism in China.

In recent years, Chinese scholars on both sides of the Taiwan Straits have rekindled their enthusiasm for studying the relationship between Physiocracy and Chinese

[24] See for example Zhu Qianzhi's "The influence of Chinese philosophy on European philosophy in the Eighteenth century," published in 1957 in *Philosophical Research*, and Hu Jichuang's *A History of Chinese Economic Thought*, published in 1962 by Shanghai People's Publishing House (Vol. I, pp. 510–514). The latter, though first published in 1962, was actually written in 1957 and delivered to the publisher by the end of that year.

[25] It was published in Beijing, first as a Chinese version in 1981 by China Social Sciences Press and then as an English version in 1984 by Foreign Languages Press. The former was entitled literally "The Brilliant Achievements of Ancient Chinese Economic Thoughts," and the latter, entitled "Chinese Economic Thought Before the Seventeenth Century," was thought highly of in James L. Y. Chang's (1986, p. 182) review in *History of Political Economy*: "Indeed, as one of the first scholarly works on comparative development of economic ideas between China and Europe, the booklet is a well-deserved addition."

[26] Li Jingneng (1979, p. 68) mentions that "the history of Western bourgeois economics in China dates back to 1766." In the paper, he only focuses on the relationship between Turgot and two Chinese youths, and on whether Turgot's writings had been introduced into China, without touching upon the influence of Chinese thought on the Physiocrats.

[27] See, for example, Shen Fuwei's *A History of Cultural Exchange between China and the West*, which was published by Shanghai People's Publishing House in 2017 and contains a section entitled "The Physiocrats' admiration of China," and Zhu Qianzhi's *The Influence of Chinese Philosophy on Europe*, which was republished by the Fujian People's Publishing House in 1985.

culture. Boasting no recognized representative monograph, they have nevertheless taken one step ahead of the counterparts in the Western academic circles that are still in silence, heralding and gestating a new breakthrough in the research of this important subject in the history of economic theory.

4 Difficulties of This Endeavor

A comprehensive review of the existing research on the Chinese origin of Physiocracy leads to the conclusion that, although there is no lack of incisive views in Westerners' works, their understanding of ancient Chinese thoughts is often rather superficial, and while the relevant writings of Chinese scholars are accurate in explaining their ancestors' thoughts, they seem unable to adequately explain how Chinese thought influenced Physiocracy, and are inferior to the Western scholars especially in the textual research of historical facts and the citation of materials. This situation calls for a new endeavor in comprehensively and deeply grasping the internal relationship between the Physiocratic system and Chinese cultural tradition, so as to give a more convincing explanation and a more scientific conclusion on the important subject of the Chinese origin of Physiocracy.

Specifically, we are to first sum up the Physiocratic system in the form of some basic arguments on the basis of a broad consensus of opinions from economists in China and abroad, and then investigate whether or to what extent the formation of each point has been influenced by ancient Chinese thoughts. Thus we are likely to completely and accurately understand and grasp the relationship between Physiocracy and Chinese cultural tradition, and to avoid all kinds of biased views.[28] According to this principle, we intend to take as the basic clues the Physiocrats' main theoretical viewpoints—namely on the natural order, the *Tableau Économique*, *laissez faire*, "net product," single *impôt territorial*, population, and property ownership—and examine their sources in turn, so as to ascertain what role the ancient Chinese thoughts have played in their origination. On the basis of the above separate analyses, we intend to carry out a general investigation into the relationship between the theoretical origin of Physiocracy and ancient Chinese thought before we give the conclusion.

[28] While examining the origins of Physiocracy, Takimoto Seiichi (1931, p. 3), a Japanese scholar, sums up six main points of the theory: firstly, believing in the natural law and emphasizing the natural order; secondly, prioritizing education and speaking very highly of *laissez-faire*; thirdly, focusing on agronomy and respecting agriculture; fourthly, adopting an integrated approach to learning; fifthly, reconciling the interests of the individual and those of the state; and sixthly, developing social thought. In fact, he only examines the first three points in relation to Chinese thought. In addition to the vagueness of this summary, some of the points, such as the *Tableau Économique*, have obviously been omitted. Even among the points cited, only some items are selected for comparison with Chinese thought. He is thus, in the absence of a more comprehensive comparative study, rather biased to conclude that the fundamental ideas that form the basis of the doctrine of Quesnay are almost entirely in line with ancient Chinese doctrines.

Of course, it is not easy to complete the above-scheduled mission. This difficulty can be further specified as follows:

The first, and the biggest, one lies in collecting reference materials about this subject. Firstly, as far as the historical value is concerned, the relevant materials are mostly found in non-Chinese works, among which those in French are the most abundant and important, followed by those in English and German, and last in Japanese. Although many have been translated between languages in different countries, Chinese versions are rare. It is indeed difficult to collect data from non-Chinese writings. Secondly, in non-Chinese materials, there are few discussions devoted to this topic. Many materials are scattered in all kinds of writings, and their collection is actually an arduous task. Thirdly, the research on this subject by scholars outside China, as mentioned above, are mainly concentrated in the 1920s–40s. Since then, with the decline of this research, relevant works have gradually been forgotten, and most of them have gone out of print. This is one of the reasons why we have for a long time found it so difficult to obtain some Western works on this subject. Fourthly, besides the published works, there are still some unpublished non-Chinese materials, some of which are valuable for the present research. Ly Siou-Y's French doctoral dissertation is a case in point. Thanks to the great help of P. Schmitt, the librarian of Dijon University, the author of this book is able to obtain this manuscript. It is still not known whether there are other similar non-Chinese materials.

Besides, in China, only two works by the Physiocrats—*A Collection of Quesnay's Works* and Turgot's *Réflexions sur la Formation et la Distribution des Richesses*—have Chinese translations. The Chinese versions of their other works, with no less reference value for investigating the source of Physiocracy, especially that of Quesnay's ideas, are extremely rare, or at most only sporadic. It is the same case with the English translation. Meek (1962, p. 9) said in the early 1960s that "since the time of Adam Smith no more than a few pages from the vast economic writings of the Physiocrats have been translated into English." This is still the case today. In France, few original works by the Physiocrats, except Daire's collection *Physiocrates* (1846) and Oncken's work *Oeuvres Économiques et Philosophiques de Quesnay* (1888), are systematically arranged for compilation and publication. This editing and publishing work is of great significance to our research topic. However, in the eyes of many Western scholars, the writings of other members of the Physiocratic School merely repeat Quesnay's opinions, and being so lengthy and repetitive, they are not worth editing and publishing. The popularity of this opinion is really a pity.

The second one is more challenging: how to identify and determine the Chinese cultural factors contained in various foreign ideas which were received and absorbed by the Physiocrats. Chinese culture, once introduced into Europe in that period, merged with Western culture in the process. In addition, many Westerners often added their own opinions and used Western traditional perspectives in understanding or explaining Chinese culture, which made the Western Chinese culture lose its original spirit as an independent cultural system to a certain extent. Under such conditions, in order to accurately judge the elements of Chinese thought in the Physiocratic doctrines, we must first investigate a large number of materials available to the Physiocrats at that time, and separate the contents that really belong to the

Chinese cultural tradition from those various bewildering explanations. This includes consulting, sorting out and identifying the vast literature and historical materials about the cultural exchanges between China and the West in Europe at that time, which is far beyond the ability of one person. In order to make up for this shortcoming, the author of this book makes full use of the available materials and focuses on analyzing the clear evidence that can confirm the influence of Chinese thought on the Physiocratic School, and for the fuzzy parts in the materials that cannot confirm the internal relationship between the two, the author chooses to compare some similar viewpoints from the Physiocrats and ancient China, providing at least some clues for future research.

The third is that, Quesnay, as the founder of the Physiocratic School, seldom revealed the sources in his writings. His intention was, according to Western scholars' research, to show his unfathomability and maintain his leadership in the School.[29] This makes it even more challenging for us to study this subject.

In short, the above difficulties have made many people doubt or flinch from the in-depth study of this subject. Happily, some others have blazed a trail in this direction. The author of this book is determined, as a Chinese scholar, to push forward this research with great effort, though he does not aspire to a complete answer to all the relevant questions.

[29] Reichwein (1925, p. 103), for example, points out, "It would rather seem as if he (referring to Quesnay) had deliberately kept silence, in order to appear independent and original." He adds that two other scholars Hasbach and Haller also held the same view that Quesnay did not reveal his sources for similar purposes (p. 164 [Note 3]).

Chapter 2
Europe's Chinese Vogue in the Seventeenth and Eighteenth Centuries

In order to facilitate an understanding of the Chinese origin of Physiocracy, it is necessary to first examine the Westward spread of Chinese culture in the seventeenth and eighteenth centuries, by discussing first the missionaries' activities in China, second the Rococo, serving as the cultural background for the spread, and third what the then enlightenment thinkers thought of China.

1 *L'Affaire des Chinois*

Anyone with a modicum of knowledge of the Sino-Western cultural exchanges in the past is certain to know about the publication of *The Travels of Marco Polo* in the late thirteenth century, which was widely celebrated in the Western world, and was read by almost all intellectuals. This travelogue, which depicts China as a paradise on earth, had been a major source of information on China for Europeans until the mid-sixteenth century, arousing their yearning for Chinese civilization. As a result, the desire to find China led to Columbus' adventurous voyage and his eventual discovery of the New World, and the quest itself became "the purpose and soul of centuries of travel" (Raleigh, 1910, p. 20), from which modern navigation geography originated. At that time, the Europeans greatly admired China's exquisite products, quoting the Chinese: "They [Chinese] say themselves that they have two eyes, the Franks one, and that the Moors are blind, so that they have the advantage of every other nation in the world" (Clavijo, 1859, p. 171).[1]

This quotation is tantamount to admitting that the Chinese were the best people in the world. During this period, the Western people's understanding of China was generally limited to a country with a large population, abundant products and a long history, without going much further, not to say deep into Chinese culture. It was not

[1] Clavius was a Spaniard who was sent to the East in the early fifteenth century. The Moors here refer to the Muslim Arabs who invaded Spain in the eighth century.

M. Tan, *The Chinese Origin of Physiocracy*,
https://doi.org/10.1007/978-981-97-9703-5_2

until the early 1580s that the Jesuits, represented by Matteo Ricci, came to China to preach one after another. It was only then that the prelude to a new chapter in the history of Sino-Western cultural exchanges was opened, which gradually reached its climax in the seventeenth and eighteenth centuries. It was *l'Affaire des Chinois* that the missionaries' activities in China revolved around.

In the late Ming and early Qing Dynasties, there was a controversy about Chinese Rites among the missionaries in China, which lasted for more than 100 years. At first, Matteo Ricci and others, after arriving in China in 1582, followed their pioneers and advocated preaching in the way that suited Chinese traditional customs. Other missionaries, however, argued that the Chinese practice of venerating Confucius and ancestors was idolatry and such heresy should be abandoned. This dispute led to a serious confrontation between those who opposed it and those who supported it, the former resorting to the Pope and the latter taking refuge in the imperial chair of Kang Xi. In 1773, the Pope ordered the dissolution of the Society of Jesus, which had been advocating the practice of missionaries following the local custom in China. The papal bull angered the Chinese emperor, leading to the expulsion of missionaries and the strict ban on missionary work in China. This was what the Europeans at that time called *L'Affaire des Chinois*.

L'Affaire brings to our attention the following points.

First, this religious incident, which focused on Chinese Rites, greatly stimulated the enthusiasm of Europeans in studying ancient Chinese civilization.

The controversy itself involved only the differences among the various sects within the Catholic Church. But its impact went far beyond mere religious matters. The Jesuits who took part in the controversy wrote many books on the subject. According to Henri Cordier's *Bibliotheca Sinica* alone, there were more than 260 books, with hundreds more unpublished. Some of these works were reprinted many times or translated into various languages, and were widely circulated in Europe. Even Englishmen, who seldom associated themselves with the Jesuits, published in their journals a series of articles relating to *L'Affaire*. Both sides of the controversy were active in promoting their respective views within Europe. For example, to criticize the views of some Jesuits, the missionaries in China requested Nicolas Malebranche, a French philosopher, to write the famous *Dialogue between a Christian Philosopher and a Chinese Philosopher on the Existence and Nature of God*. All this contributed greatly to the Westward spread of Chinese thought, which had such a special charm among the Europeans (Palmer, Colton & Kramer, 2007). Because of *L'Affaire*, as Reichwein (1925) puts it, China, once "held to be the original birthplace of human wisdom" (p. 152), became "the sole concern of public opinion" (p. 150) in almost all branches of science. Although what was significantly brought about by *L'Affaire* was considered by some people as merely a "dream about China," or even a "tragedy" that led to the confrontation between the East and the West in later centuries, they all recognized that the controversy, through the Jesuits, had made China's impact on Europe far greater than that of Europe's missionary activities on China. This is what we must first be clear about when discussing the relationship between Physiocracy and Chinese culture.

Second, the Jesuits' knowledge of Chinese culture gradually deepened in the Chinese Rites Controversy that lasted for more than a hundred years.

Matteo Ricci, having dressed in Confucian costume and buried himself in the study of "the Four Books and Five Classics" for fifteen years, claimed that he "knew quite well the learning of the ancient Chinese sages, and could recite some of the classics and get the gist in a rough way" (Quoted in Fan, 1981, p. 1). He used the Confucian classics to teach Catholicism, which was so convincing to some princes and officials of the Ming Dynasty that they took the lead in becoming Catholics. He earned for himself the title of *Xi Ru* (Western Confucian).[2] Thereafter both followers and opponents competed to find evidence from the Confucian classics. In the process of debating and cross-examining, both sides gradually deepened their knowledge and understanding of the ancient Chinese texts. At that time, many Jesuits lived in China for more than twenty years, some even as many as thirty or forty. Generally speaking, they had received one or two decades of specialized systematic training before arriving in China and had a very high level of knowledge. It was natural that after their arrival in China, their years of study and translation of Chinese texts[3] enabled them to become familiar with Chinese culture and traditions, and those who were smart and knowledgeable became known as "Confuciuses from the West."

These Jesuits' unremitting research on ancient Chinese culture unearthed a new academic treasure for the talented people of Europe. In his article of 1686—"Some Observations and Conjectures concerning the Character and Language of the Chinese"—Robert Hooke (Quoted in Needham, 1954, p. iii) remarks,

> TO MEN [he is speaking of the Jesuits in China] so qualified with *Mathematical* Knowledge, we owe the Discovery, of the before unknown Parts of the World, and from such we are to hope for the Perfection of that Knowledge, and the Discovery of the Rest. [...] We have hitherto not been admitted but to the Skirts, but this Discovery, when perfected, will lay open to us an *Empire* of Learning, hitherto only fabulously described; this will admit us to converse with the best and greatest of that *Empire*, that either are, or ever have been; this will Discover a new Indian Mine and Treasure, and make a new Trade to bring it hither.

The so-called "new Trade" refers to the cultural exchange that brought to Europe the "Treasure", the essence, of China's rich culture. Obviously, in the process of discovering and presenting this new "*Empire* of Learning," the visiting Jesuits had moved from their previous sketchy introduction to China to understanding the unique features of Chinese culture and conveying them to the Europeans in a more accurate way. This suggests to us that the continuous Westward transmission of Chinese culture in the era of the Physiocratic School made it possible for Europeans to get in touch with the treasures of Chinese culture.

After 1789, with the disappearance of the vogue for China, most European historians "dismissed the cult as a mere freak of fashion, or as a Utopian fantasy assuming

---

[2] See the section of "Matteo Ricci's Tomb" in Liu Tong's (2014) *Sketches of the Imperial Capital* (Vol. 5).

[3] Joseph de Prémare (Quoted in Fang, 1987, p. 1057), for example, in the preface to his *Treatise on the Spring and Autumn Annals*, says, "I have been buying every book in 'The Thirteen Classics,' 'The Twenty-one Histories,' the biographies of the first Confucians, and many books by the sages of other schools of thought, and have been reading them for more than ten years."

the name of China but having no relation to the real China or its culture" (Hudson, 1931, p. 326). In this regard, Hudson (1931, pp. 326–327), who specializes in this period of cultural exchanges between China and Europe, argues,

> Such an estimate entirely overlooks the facilities which the eighteenth century had for a knowledge of China. Besides the immense quantity of Chinese art objects [...], there were current a number of astonishingly accurate descriptions of China and its institutions, and tolerable translations of the most important works of Chinese philosophical literature.

Hudson's argument, it should be said, is objective and impartial.

Third, as the most important part in the Chinese culture transmitted to Europe by the Jesuits, the Confucian classics, especially the teachings of Confucius, constituted the focus of the controversy of Chinese Rites.

As early as the end of the sixteenth century, Michele Ruggieri, Matteo Ricci's forerunner, had already begun to translate *The Four Books*,[4] but the Latin translation that Ricci sent back from China in 1593 was better known to Europeans, and the people of the country [the then Italy], according to Zhu Qianzhi (2005b), read and delighted in it. However, the translation was still in fragments. Since then, many Jesuits in China had devoted themselves to the translation and commentary of Confucian classics, which became very popular. By the 1660s–70s, books such as Da Xue (*The Great Learning*), *Zhong Yong* (*The Doctrine of the Mean*), and *Lun Yu* (*The Analects of Confucius*) had been translated and published in China, and in 1687, Philippe Couplet brought these translations together in a volume under the Latin title meaning "Confucius, the Chinese Philosopher," together with the Chinese title *Xi Wen Si Shu Jie* (Annotated Four Books in Western Languages), published in Paris and reprinted in the same year. This translation is said to have been decreed and inscribed by Louis XIV himself. The book immediately attracted the attention of European scholars. The following year, it was reviewed in the Parisian newspaper *Le Journal des Savants* with the remark that the Chinese place a special value on virtue, wisdom, faith, righteousness, benevolence, courtesy, majesty and the fear of heaven and respect for the gods, which is unparalleled by any other nation, and is a major contribution of the Chinese (Fan, 1943, p. 3). Through this transformation from fragmented and piecemeal introductions to systematic and complete translations, the Confucian classics became a reliable basis for Westerners to draw on and cite Chinese Confucianism.

During this period, the doctrine of Confucius was particularly noted by European scholars. As early as 1615, in his *De Christiana expeditione apud Sinas suscepta*

[4] The Danish scholar Lundbeck (1988, p. 16) considers Michele Ruggieri to be the first Western translator of *The Four Books*, and testifies that after his return to Europe in 1590, Ruggieri provided information on China in his work of 1593. Zhu Qianzhi (2005b, p. 84), apparently unaware of Michele Ruggieri's above work, claims that Matteo Ricci was the first person to translate the Four Books. Wang Yi (1979), another Taiwanese scholar, believes that the first book to translate Confucianism into an European language is *Mingxin Baojian*, a book edited by Fan Liben, a scholar in the Ming Dynasty, which brings together the sayings of Confucius, Mencius, Xun Zi, Lao Zi, Zhuang Zi and Zhu Xi. It is dated 1592, 1593 and 1595 and was published in Manila. This translation was appended to his book by Navarrete and became quite popular in Europe. It is clear from this that the period around 1593 is the first time that the Confucian classics became known to Europeans.

ab Societate Jesu (*A Discourse of the Kingdome of China, taken out of Ricius and Trigautius*) (Zhu, 2005b, p. 74), the missionary to China Nicholas Trigault mentioned Confucius as the greatest Chinese figure whose teachings dominated religion, politics, morality and social life in China. In 1641, the French philosopher François de La Mothe Le Vayer published his *Vertu des Païens*, with a chapter entitled "De Confutius, le Socrate de la Chine" (Wang, 1979, p. 124), in which the philosopher states that "Confucius is the greatest of all virtuous people and the greatest of all philosophers; he is regarded by the Chinese as a 'demigod' and compared to the ancient Greek philosopher Socrates" (p. 166). In terms of the introduction to Confucius and his teachings, the aforementioned translation by Couplet was the most famous and influential. This book is entitled "*Confucius Sinarum Philosophus, Sive Scientia Sinensis latine exposita*" (Zhu, 2005b, p. 75), and is attached with a biography of Confucius, which includes a portrait of Confucius labeled with a Chinese note meaning "Confucius, the world's forerunner of Chinese learning." The modern Western scholar Reichwein (1925, p. 20) says, "Here we have, struck together for the first time, the three notes [...]: China—Confucius—political morality [...]; the Jesuit Father calls him '*Sapientissimus et moralis philosophiœ pariter ac politicœ magister et oraculum*' (Master and oracle most learned alike in moral and in political philosophy)." After that, the "three notes" were combined into a single concept that became inseparable in the European mind. Later on, in his widely circulated *Nouveaux mémoires sur l'état présent de la Chine* (Zhu, 2005b, p. 79), Louis Le Comte compared Confucius' philosophy with that of the ancient Western sages and praised Confucius' fourteen maxims as full of rationality, and even the famous Roman philosopher Seneca "hath spoken nothing better" (p. 140 [Note 1]). He sang high praise of Confucius' "rare qualities among ancient sages [...], and his being more a man who grasped the divine will to transform the New World than a pure philosopher trained by reason" (p. 140). During that period, writings on Confucius proliferated in various languages and editions in European countries. It became fashionable to study the doctrine of Confucius, and any discussion that required the invocation of an ideal model almost invariably resorted to Confucius. As Reichwein (1925, p. 78) puts it, throughout the first half of the eighteenth century, "Confucius was the one centre of interest" in Europe and "became the patron saint of eighteenth-century Enlightenment" (P. 77). This enormous wave of admiration for Confucius and his doctrine naturally spread to the Physiocrats and left deep traces in their system of economic theory.

It is necessary to add that it was because the Jesuits to China thought that the doctrines of Confucius and other pre-Qin Confucian scholars have many points in harmony with Catholic doctrines that they attached particular importance to the ancient Confucian classics. By this criterion, those other Confucian texts which, in their view, contradicted Catholic doctrines were rejected. The main target of their attack was the so-called post-Confucianism, especially that of the Song Dynasties. But as soon as Confucianism or Song Confucianism, whether Confucian or post-Confucian, was introduced into Europe, the intellectuals there ceased to pay attention to the narrow religious prejudices of the Jesuits and regarded Confucianism all as salvation elixir from the ancient civilization of the East, praised and accepted it without distinction, or, conversely, used "post-Confucianism" which preached atheism as a weapon to attack religious beliefs. He Zhaowu (1988, p. 113), a Chinese scholar, describes this phenomenon as follows: "The missionaries to China explained the ancient Chinese Confucian philosophy from the perspective of Western orthodox theology, while Western Enlightenment thinkers, through the missionaries' introduction, borrowed some of the views of Chinese Confucianism to carry out their own theoretical work against orthodox theology. We can summarize this phenomenon as a dialectic in the history of the exchange of ideas between China and the West." This point should be noted in advance, for it is significant for the later discussion of the origin of Physiocracy.

Fourth, French missionaries occupied a prominent place in the evolution of *L'Affaire des Chinois*.

In 1610, Matteo Ricci deplored the absence of French Jesuits in China, and in 1651 the French missionaries began to arrive in the Eastern country. For the next thirty years or so their power was still far from rivaling that of the Portuguese and Italian, who had been dominant. But the situation changed in 1687 when Louis XIV sent missionaries to China and they quickly became the mainstay of the Jesuits in the country. These first-rate missionaries, considered to be well versed in scientific knowledge, won the favor of Kang Xi and other emperors and became the staunchest defenders of Chinese rites. Not only did they increase dramatically in numbers, but, according to the French scholar Robert Chabrié, their writings were so rich that they were soon above all others (Zhu, 2005b, p. 73), and became the main source of knowledge about China that was spread to Europe at the time.[5]

For example, Le Comte, a French Jesuit, soon after returning to Europe from China, published two books in Paris, *New Records of China's Present Situation* (1696) and *On Chinese Etiquette* (1701). These works defended Chinese etiquette in front of the Europeans with detailed information from field studies, and became the target of fierce attacks by the opposing factions. As a result, they aroused many people's interest and were quickly translated into various languages and reprinted again and again. This indicated that the European stage of etiquette debate was transferred from Rome to Paris. Other examples are Du Halde's *Description de l'Empire de la Chine* (1735), *Lettres édifiantes et curieuses, écrites des missions étrangères* (1703–1776), and *Memoires Concernant l'historire, les sciences, les arts, les maeurs, les usages* etc., *des Chinois, par les Missionnaires de Pekin* (1776–1814), which spread widely and had great influence in Europe in the eighteenth century.

[5] On the basis of Louis Pfister's *Notices biographiques et bibliographiques sur les Jésuites de l'ancienne Mission de Chine: 1552–1773*, Wang Yi (1979, pp. 17–19) makes an analysis of the number of Jesuits in China and the changes in their writings in the two periods divided by the year 1687. Here we focus only on the change of the French Jesuits in China in terms of number. There were altogether 14 French Jesuits in China, 9.5% of the total number of Jesuits in China from 1552 to 1687, and 85, from 1687 to 1773, 39.5% of the total. In terms of writings, before 1687, the combined writings of the Portuguese and Italian members during this period account for almost 70% of the total, while those of the French members, though not counted here, are certain to take up only a small proportion. After 1687, the Chinese works of the French friars account for 64.2% of the total, which is 353, and 83% of the total, which is 745, if other types of writings are included, far exceeding those of the Jesuits from other countries.

Claimed to be three major works about China, they were compiled by French Jesuits, first published in Paris and then translated in various countries. In particular, Du Halde's book is considered to be a great synthesis of the various achievements of the European study of China in the past one hundred and fifty years, the pyramid of Western Sinology, and even a monument that is honored throughout the world (Ishida, 1941, p. 113). This masterpiece is one of the main sources of information on the influence of Chinese culture on Quesnay and other important Physiocrats, and thus deserves here a brief introduction. It was compiled on the basis of the reports of twenty-seven missionaries in China, just like an encyclopedia in China. Its first volume describes the geography of Chinese provinces and the era of each dynasty; the second deals with politics and economics, and introduces the four books and five classics of Confucianism, *Mencius* in particular, as well as *Xiao Jing* (*The Classic of Filial Piety*) and *Xiao Xue* (*The Lesser Learning*); the third includes religion, morality, medicine, and natural history; and the fourth is devoted to Manchuria, Mongolia, Tibet and Korea.

France became the center of European research on China, thanks to the concentration of the best of the French Jesuits in China and the constant stream of writings they sent back to France. In the eighteenth century, French intellectuals were even said to be more familiar with China than with some other European countries. It is true indeed that the scientific approach to the study of China, as is held by Édouard Émmannuel Chavannes (Beijing Sino-French Sinology Institute, 1943, p. 6), began in the eighteenth century and was developed by French Jesuit priests.

The above summary of the characteristics of *L'Affaire des Chinois* is of great significance for the following understanding of the times and the ideological background against which Physiocracy came into being.

2 The Rococo

In the seventeenth and eighteenth centuries, in addition to the visiting missionaries' written elaboration of their fieldwork and research of China, which aroused Europeans' yearning and admiration for ancient Chinese civilization, the massive European importation of Chinese artifacts, especially handicrafts, led to an unprecedented social trend in pursuit of Chinese objects and styles. This influence from China, though not explicitly recorded in writing, reflects the traditional spirit of Chinese culture in the unique artistic style of the imported products, visible in all their forms, patterns, colors and lines. Thus, in the course of the Westerners' search for oriental exotic products and their mass imitation of Chinese style, the spirit of Chinese culture imperceptibly permeated their daily life, forming in the history of Western culture the famous Rococo era, a special period with social customs quite different from those in the European tradition.

The Rococo is generally regarded as a new artistic liberation movement that emerged in Europe after the Renaissance. Its art is characterized by breaking the confinement of thought and artistic creation, that is, the limitations giving rise to stereotypes of living forms devoid of liveliness, so as to show an indulgent artistic style with a light and strange form. The art of Rococo emerged, firstly, in close connection with the trade between the West and China and, secondly, with France as its important birthplace. Occupying a negligible share of the Sino-European trade but boasting a strong Jesuit presence in China, France became an important cultural medium between China and Europe in the late seventeenth century. The importation of artifacts in trade and the strong advocacy in missionary writings stirred up Westerners' desire and fascination for the exotic Eastern lands, giving China a prominent place in European fashion. France, the home of *chinoiseries*, was the first to herald the birth of the Rococo movement. "There is a certain symbolical significance," Reichwein (1925, p. 22) rightly remarks, "in the fact that the first New Year's Day of the [eighteenth] century was celebrated at the French court with Chinese festivities. The Rococo was at the door."[6]

Indeed, during the Rococo period, European society reached feverish levels of interest in the collection and imitation of Chinese ceramics, lacquerware, silk fabrics and many other valuable objects. The popularity of porcelain in Europe could be seen in all social classes, up to the royalty and down to the common people, all competing to buy it. The rule of Louis XV even witnessed the so-called "daily necessities revolution": the destruction of silverware in favor of Chinese porcelain. The masters of imitation, to cater to fashion, were so deliberate that even every line and color was kept in strict accordance with Chinese porcelain. Thus a lyric got around, reading:

> Allons à cette porcelaine,
> Sa beauté m'invite, m'entraine.
> Elle vient du monde nouveau,
> L'on ne peut rien voir de plus beau.
> Qu'elle a d'attraits, qu'elle est fine!
> Elle est native de la Chine.

(Quoted in Hudson, 1931, p. 283)

Chinese lacquerware was another fashionable item in Europe at the time. The Chinese sedan chair, made of lacquer, became very popular in Europe, and even its color and its rules of sitting were all copied from China. The practice was spread to the most remote areas of Europe, including every small principality in Germany. The later Western carriage was the evolution of the sedan chair. Silk fabrics had long before been imported from China to the West, but it was not until the Rococo era that they became widespread. Copying the patterns, or floral designs, on Chinese

---

[6] The Chinese fashion had begun before the Rococo came. Some believe that the fashion began in the first half of the reign of Louis XIV, at the end of the sixteenth century, and reached its peak in the middle of the eighteenth century, while others think that the popularity of Chinese taste dates from the sixteenth century onwards. However, the consensus is that the Rococo first came into being at the height of Chinese fashion in Europe, at the end of the seventeenth century and the beginning of the eighteenth century. This was also the time when the French missionaries in China began to occupy a dominant position.

silk fabrics became an important part of European life, especially for women, to the extent that one had to wear everything Chinese-like, from head to foot, to keep up with the times. There was not a single thing in the dressing rooms of some princes and aristocrats that was not Chinese, and even the window screens were decorated with Chinese pictures. This period was indeed a time of great Chinese interest in the daily necessities of Europeans. No wonder the then British *World Magazine* was reported to have exclaimed that everything was now Chinese or China-like, and that none of the chairs, tables, cupboards, mirrors, or even the most mundane utensils, were immune to Chinese influence (Fang, 1931, p. 32).

In addition to daily necessities, other art forms of the Rococo era, as well as social customs in general, were also deeply steeped in the spirit of Chinese culture. The pursuit and imitation of Chinese architecture, for example, led to major changes in Western architectural forms. A missionary to China once said, "In the great variety and multiplicity, which the Chinese give to their buildings, I admire the fertility of their genius. Indeed, I am tempted to believe that, in comparison with them, we are poor and sterile" (Quoted in Reichwein, 1925, p. 57). Western architecture at that time followed the Chinese style, so that no garden without a "Chinese pavilion or railing" would dare to claim itself as fashionable. It was thought that there was nothing more exemplary of garden art than Chinese gardens, and when people built a garden, they only asked if it was Chinese or Chinese-British.

The popularity of *chinoiseries* could be found in almost every sphere of European social life during this period, especially in Paris, where various social places named after "Chinese" stood out, such as "Chinese cafés," "Chinese balls," "Chinese baths" and "Chinese masquerades." Chinese robes and gowns were popular among the princes and nobles, Chinese costumes were fashionable at court dances, and even Louis XIV appeared in costume as a Chinese at a grand ceremony in 1667. The king's favored concubines squandered a lot to satisfy their insatiable pursuit of Chinese things,[7] regarding as precious everything that came from China. Madame de Pompadour loved Chinese goldfish, which has since become a general social interest for Europeans. Chinese fans were also favored by court ladies, and it became fashionable for noblewomen to hold fans, which are still in vogue today (Reichwein, 1925, pp. 66–68). Theatrical literature with China as its theme was all over the place. *L'Orphelin de la Chine* ("The Orphan of China"), a French play adapted by Voltaire on the basis of "The Orphan of Zhao," a thirteenth-century Chinese play from the Yuan Dynasty, gained a huge success after its debut, and other dramatists from all over Europe used the above original Chinese play as the basis for their adaptations, which became a great event in the history of European theatre. Literary works were also kept in line with the prevailing social trends of the time and often used the name China to express the author's own thoughts and feelings: *The Chinese Spy*, a European author's book, was even used to encourage people to revolt against the government. All of these, which later Western historians labeled under the "Sinophilia" spreading all over Europe, are very indicative of the general spirit of European society at that

[7] The Marquise de Pompadour, mistress of King Louis XV, is said to have diverted 36 million livres from the national treasury to satisfy her Chinese pleasure cravings.

time. In short, the Rococo style is a direct imitation of China, and this imitation has been universally acknowledged by art historians in every respect. The striking fact of the Rococo period is that China occupied a prominent place in the trade-off of various influences. This is the Chinese cultural identity of the Rococo period.

The above examples demonstrate, vividly and concretely, that China was undoubtedly the model of Europe in the eighteenth century. "The vogue for China and Chinese objects [in the Rococo period]," Maverick (1946, p. 124) states, "may be looked at in a general way without considering particularly the economists [referring to the Physiocrats]." This understanding is wrong, because the Physiocrats lived in the heyday of the Rococo, when the imitation of China reached its peak. Such a cultural milieu had undoubtedly imbued them with the Chinese cultural spirit in an imperceptible way. In other words, we must explore the roots of the creation of Physiocracy from the cultural background of the time.

The emergence of the Rococo, its ideological aspect in particular, has philosophical implications. Reichwein (1925), one of the first Western scholars to pay attention to this significance, has repeatedly referred to the intrinsic link between the Rococo and the admiration for Chinese culture: "Pure matter of fashion as it may appear, there was, none the less, an inner significance in these external trifles" (p. 36). However, he is rather partial in attributing this "inner significance" entirely to the influence of Lao Zi's thought. He believes that Confucius' "severe political morality" is not in line with the Rococo's "gracious, charming society" (p. 26), and only Lao Zi (Lao Tzu) advocated *wu wei er zhi* (ruling by doing nothing): "In Lao Tzu's personality, the soul of the Rococo touches the soul of the Far East. ... [I]n all the precious things which Europe welcomed as '*la Chine*,' it was the soul of Lao Tzu which spoke" (p. 76). This understanding of the Chinese doctrines of Confucius and Lao Zi obviously results from Reichwein's ignorance of the fact that the doctrine of *wu wei* (inaction) can also be found in Confucianism, represented by Confucius, and that the Confucian system, which has been dominant since the Qin and Han dynasties, is actually a mixture of different doctrines. It is even more nonsensical for Reichwein to classify the doctrines by Confucius and Lao Zi as distinct from each other, belonging to northern and southern China respectively. This misunderstanding is later extended by others, who argue that the French court found the embodiment of their own Rococo spirit in Lao Zi's philosophy, which opposes reason, regulation and law, while the Physiocratic School, which was the ideological enemy of this irrational court, found their close relationship with Confucius, the ideological enemy of Lao Zi. In this way, Confucius' doctrine, which was admired by the Physiocratic School, is completely opposed to Lao Zi's thought. In the subsequent analysis in this book, we will show that the Confucianism accepted by the Physiocrats does not actually contradict Lao Zi's thought, but has absorbed the core of the latter in terms of certain important economic views.

3 China in the Eyes of Enlightenment Thinkers

The age of the Western Enlightenment is a time when Chinese culture was a hit throughout Europe. All the important European thinkers at the time, notably Leibniz, Wolff, Descartes, Voltaire, Montesquieu, Rousseau, Diderot and Holbach, showed admiration for Chinese culture in different degrees.

The German philosopher Leibniz (1646–1716) "was the first to recognize the great intellectual importance of Chinese culture for the development of the West" (Reichwein, 1925, p. 79).[8] He had been devoted at the beginning of his research career to the studies focusing on Confucius as "the king of Chinese philosophers" (p. 80). Even the reports from the missionaries that the French government sent to China in 1685 are considered as "the first fruits of Leibniz' urging for an interchange of cultures" (Maverick, 1946, p. 14).[9]

After he met in Rome some missionaries to China in 1689, Leibniz became increasingly eager for the knowledge of the Eastern country. He argued in *Novissima Sinica* (1697)[10] that "the Chinese Empire, which challenges Europe in cultivated area and certainly surpasses her in population, vies with us in many other ways in almost equal combat" (Leibniz, 1994, p. 46). He also pointed out in particular that "China is undoubtedly superior to us in practical philosophy, in political morality" (Quoted in Reichwein, 1925, p. 80), before he came to the following conclusion (pp. 80–81):

> [I]n view of the inordinate lengths to which the corruption of morals has advanced, I almost think it necessary that Chinese missionaries should be sent to us to teach us the aim and practice of natural theology, as we send missionaries to them to instruct them in revealed theology. For I believe that if a wise man were to be appointed Judge—not of the beauty of goddesses, but of the goodness of peoples—he would award the golden apple to the Chinese.

Leibniz had a sense of crisis and worried that Europe would lag behind China. Therefore, he urged missionaries in China to bring Chinese knowledge back to Europe, lest the Europeans be expelled from China one day and deplore the loss of such a good opportunity.[11] His remarkable achievements, namely binary arithmetic and monadic theory, are all related to his study and reference of Chinese culture. The principle of binary operation, he repeatedly emphasized, unveils the mystery of the oldest writing of existing science, the secret hidden in the 64 diagrams of *Yi*

[8] Maverick (1946, p. 112) praised Leibniz's pioneering work in a different way: "Leibniz was the first man who might claim the top honor; it was he who opened men's eyes to the example of China, and who urged the cultural academies then being set up in the various European capitals to make the securing of information about China one of their aims."

[9] Maverick (1946, p. 14) adds immediately, "He (referring to Leibniz) was influential in persuading the French government to take over from the weakening hands of Portugal the sponsorship of the Jesuit mission in China, and to send accomplished scholars to that mission."

[10] This book title has many Chinese translations, such as *Zhongguo Zuijin Shiqing* (Recent Events in China), *Zhongguo Zuixin Lishi Lijie* (Recent Historical Events in China and Relevant Comments), *Zhongguo de Xin Baogao* (New Report on China), and *Zhongguo Jinwen* (Recent Events in China) (Gorai, 1938, pp. 256–261; Zhu, 2005b, p. 229–224; Reichwein, 1962, p. 71).

[11] First mentioned in Leibniz's letter written in 1705, this was reiterated "at great length" in his letter to Bouvet on December 13, 1707.

Jing (*I-Ching* or *The Book of Changes*) that remained incomprehensible to people for thousands of years, which he claimed as a miraculous discovery (Leibniz, 1994, pp. 73, 133). This shows that "the ancient Chinese have surpassed the modern ones in the extreme, not only in piety (which is the basis of the most perfect morality) but in science as well" (p. 134). "His [Leibniz's] doctrine of Monads," as is pointed out by Reichwein (1925, p. 79), "coincides curiously in many points with Chinese ideas about 'the universal'," or as is held by Gorai Kinzo (1938, p. 187), is very similar to the social organization of Confucianism. Therefore, some German scholars believe that Leibniz's thought has two sources: Plato's theory and Chinese philosophy.[12] In fact, in Leibniz's view, ancient Chinese philosophy is more time-honored and more admirable than the Greek counterpart. He said,

> China is a great Empire, no less in area than cultivated Europe, and indeed surpasses it in population and orderly government. Moreover, there is in China a public morality admirable in certain regards, conjoined to a philosophical doctrine, or rather a natural theology, venerable by its antiquity, established and authorized for about 3000 years, long before the philosophy of the Greeks [...].

(Leibniz, 1994, p. 78)

He lashed out at the European scholars by claiming, "It would be highly foolish and presumptuous on our part, [...] scarcely out of barbarism, to want to condemn such an ancient doctrine" (p. 78). As his biographer G. E. Guhrauer says, Leibniz in that period longed for the European golden age of Chinese culture (Gorai, 1938, pp. 282–283).

Wolff (1679–1754), a disciple of Leibniz, was accused of apostasy and expelled from the University of Halle in 1721 for giving a lecture entitled "On the Practical Philosophy of the Chinese," which is an important event in the history of German philosophy.[13] He believed that Chinese philosophy is the oldest in the world, that there is nothing in European philosophy comparable to Chinese moral and political doctrines (Zempliner, 1962), that the most ancient Chinese monarchs are all philosophers (Gorai, 1938, p. 320), and especially that Confucius is a great genius, [...] the revivalist of Chinese holy wisdom (p. 322), and the representative of reason (p. 323), whose reputation is comparable to that of Jesus Christ or Muhammad (pp. 322–323).

---

[12] It may be conveniently added here that, in recent years, Julia Ching (1983, p. 118), an American scholar, while acknowledging that Leibniz himself had seriously studied Chinese thought, has tried to downplay the influence of Chinese thought on Leibniz, for example by describing the similarities between Leibniz's and Chinese thought as "coincidental," stating that the former "has not been significantly influenced, but at most partially influenced or corroborated, by Chinese philosophy," and placing the emphasis on their "differences" when similarities are found between the two. Ching thinks that this view of hers typically "reflects the views of modern Western scholarship." There seems to be a tendency in Western scholarship about the influence of Chinese thought: the closer they get to Leibniz's time, the more they recognize the relationship between the two, and the more distant the less, so that in modern times it has become common to highlight the differences between the two and even to undermine or obscure the influence of Chinese thought on Leibniz.

[13] The German historian Eduard Zeller pointed out that two very similar events in the history of German philosophy are the expulsion of Wolff from the University of Halle and the departure of Fichte from the University of Jena. Of these two, the former is particularly significant (Zhu, 2005b, p. 248).

Thus, he devoted himself to discovering the mystical wisdom, the deepest insights and the noblest thoughts in the Chinese classics, claiming that the principle underlying the ancient Chinese wisdom is fully compatible with his own (Zempliner, 1962; Gorai, 1938).

The Physiocrats had a high opinion of Wolff's philosophy and "honoured Wolff as a martyr alongside of Confucius and Christ" (Reichwein, 1925, p. 86). They learned from him something about ancient Chinese culture, such as the school system. Reichwein finds it "interesting to discover whether, through the school of the Physiocrats, it would be possible to trace back to Chinese models the first schemes for State schools devised by Turgot in his Ministry, and later by Condorcet, during the Revolution" (p. 87). This shows that the Physiocrats did not have to assimilate ancient Chinese thought by way of their own direct study of Chinese originals or primary sources, but that they could also draw on and assimilate the relevant findings of their predecessors and contemporaries. These research results were sometimes abstracted or summarized from the Chinese ideological sources, and then merged with other Western theories. Without analysis, it is difficult to find their sources. Thus, it must be noted that the Physiocrats' adoption of the research results from their predecessors is often regarded as a direct inheritance of traditional Western, rather than Chinese, thought. In fact, the Physiocratic School did absorb a lot of ancient Chinese philosophical ideas through direct contact with primary sources or research results of others. Before economics became an independent discipline, economic thought had always been a main part of philosophy, which was true in both China and the West. This is one of the reasons why we investigate the views about Chinese culture held by European Enlightenment philosophers in the eighteenth century.

Descartes (1596–1650), the founder of modern philosophy, was the pioneer of the Enlightenment, of which France was the center. His philosophical system, Lévy-Bruhl (1899, p. 1) notes, was not inherited but "initiated," or in figurative terms, emerged like "Proles sine matre creata" ("a son who does not need his mother to produce him") (Zhu, 2005b, p. 206). This suggests that the formation of Descartes' system was influenced by contact with foreign cultures, and not all of it came from traditional Western sources. "Though the precise influences may never be discovered," speculates Maverick (1938, p. 56), "it is not unlikely that Descartes [...] [was] affected by the Oriental currents." Furthermore, Zhu Qianzhi (2005b, p. 207), a Chinese economist, affirms that Descartes was "the first to come into contact with the East."

Western economists often associate with Descartes the origins of the Physiocratic system, especially its methodological features. Some argue that the Physiocrats applied Cartesian skepticism to the social sciences, and can thus be considered the purest Cartesian rationalists, affirming that Quesnay accepted many of Descartes' conclusions. Others criticize the Physiocrats as Cartesians in methodology, for their Physiocratic system has not made any new discoveries, but only consciously and purposefully honed this methodological weapon. Therefore, Quesnay's emphasis on "evidence" is considered as Descartes' "rational intuition;" Quesnay's similar mathematical or geometric methods in studying the *Tableau Économique* and his exploration of the physical laws of human life are said to be the same as, or to keep pace with, those used by Descartes in the natural sciences (Neill, 1949, pp. 534–548). Western scholars look to Descartes for the source of the ideas in Physiocracy, and many of them are, intentionally or not, dominated by an exclusive mentality centered on traditional European thought, but they do not know that Descartes' philosophical thoughts and methods themselves are likely to have been influenced by ancient China.[14] This has shaken the Eurocentric conception in the origin of modern economics.

Among the Enlightenment thinkers, Voltaire (1694–1776) was the greatest authority and the most famous representative of Chinese culture preachers. He regarded China as "the finest, the most ancient, the most extensive, the most populous and well-regulated kingdom upon earth" (Voltaire, 1901, p. 208). He believed that China's history was much older than the "Genesis" in the Bible, claiming that when the Europeans were barbarians, the Chinese nation had a high degree of civilization, so that no progressive man would believe the lies of the world history in the Old Testament as an inert authority. He even held that "Christ was merely a Socrates with oriental overtones" (Quoted in Zhu, 2005b, p. 283). It can be seen that in his hands, the knowledge from China was forged into a sharp weapon against Christianity itself. "They have," he said of the Chinese, "perfected Moral science, and that is the first of the sciences" (Quoted in Reichwein, 1925, p. 89). He marveled at the fact that Confucius preached in his writings "nothing but the purest morality" (Voltaire, 1901, p. 82), and "communicated the most rational ideas of the divinity, which human nature could conceive without the help of revelation" (p. 32). He thought that no maxims or teachings of Western nations can be compared with this pure morality. He took as his own Confucius' mottos "Do not do unto others as you would not have them do unto you" and "Repay wrongs with righteousness, and virtue with virtue," and believed that if Confucius' benevolence, righteousness, virtue and morality were practiced, there would be no war on earth. He adapted the script of *The Orphan of China*, a Chinese play, aiming at commending Confucian morality and proving that rationality and wisdom have natural superiority to blind brute force. In his eyes, Confucius was a wise teacher who believed only in reason and the people of China all believed in him; he was so respectful that he hung a portrait of Confucius in his home and revered him as a deity (pp. 81–82). He quoted Le Comte and other missionaries that "the Chinese had knowledge of the true God, when other nations were sunk in idolatry" (p. 32), that is, the Chinese had already practiced the most moral and pure religion at a time when Europe was in the grip of superstition and corruption. The so-called "pure religion," according to his interpretation, refers to the practice that Confucius made it possible for the world to acquire the purest knowledge of God, teaching people to be virtuous, so that they can follow universal rationality to build a peaceful and happy society without resorting to God's revelation (pp. 31–33). Facing this ideal state, he lamented, "It is a great pity that we should not have been as fortunate as the Chinese" (Quoted in Lévy-Bruhl, 1899, p. 188).

[14] Descartes himself said that his success was the result of leaving his country and having read a lot of books in the past. This is another clear rejection of the view that his ideas were all derived from the European tradition itself.

As a philosopher, he discovered a new spiritual and material world in the East: "What should our European princes do when they hear of such examples? Admire and blush, but above all imitate" (Quoted in Reichwein, 1925, p. 90). This leads to his famous assertion that differs significantly from modern Western perceptions: "If, as a philosopher, one wishes to instruct oneself about what has taken place on the globe, one must first of all turn one's eyes towards the East, the cradle of all arts, to which the West owes everything" (p. 90). This is indeed the origin of the viewpoint of "overall sinicization."

In *The Works of Voltaire*, remarks praising China and advocating the emulation of China abound. Especially in his work of 1760, his enthusiasm for the ancient and great Chinese civilization is overflowing everywhere: "With Voltaire's *Essai sur les mœurs* of the year 1760 admiration of China reached its zenith. The book is a perfect compendium of all the feelings of the time about the Far East" (Reichwein, 1925, p. 79). His study of China covers everything including politics, law, philosophy, history, literature, and even crafts and technology. In his view, China set an almost perfect example in all these fields of human civilization, and the only way out for the European countries was to copy it wholesale (Voltaire, 1901, pp. 19–38). In the eighteenth century, Voltaire put forward this typical idea of "overall sinicization," which is a far cry from the theory of "total Westernization" that was popular in China in the early twentieth century.

In terms of our present study, we can note that Voltaire and the Physiocrats shared many identical or similar views on China. It is a misunderstanding that some Western scholars, on the basis of individual arguments, regard Voltaire as the main opponent of the Physiocratic doctrines. In Voltaire's writings, there is not much that directly addresses Physiocracy, and his work *L'homme aux quarante écus* is an exception. In this story, the author ridicules the single *impôt territorial* proposed by the Physiocrats, saying, "The English, who are not much given to laughing, could not, however, help bursting out when they heard that men of intelligence among us had proposed this kind of administration" (p. 265). This is the main argument that has been used to set Voltaire against the Physiocratic School. Only a little analysis is enough, however, to show that this point is not reliable.

Firstly, Voltaire's arguments against the single *impôt territorial* have a certain element of speculation, or misinterpretation. He said, "It is certain that land pays everything, who is not convinced of this truth? But that a single man should be the proprietor of all the land is a monstrous idea" (Quoted in Ware, 1931, p. 616). The idea that "land pays everything" is recognized here as the theoretical basis of the Physiocrats' single tax theory. The connection between the single *impôt territorial* and the idea that "a single man should be the proprietor of all the land" was purely his personal concoction, and the Physiocrats did not say anything similar.[15] It was thus Voltaire himself, not the Physiocrats, who was absurd. Secondly, Voltaire's objections were mainly directed to the specific works or theories of individual members of the Physiocratic School, rather than to the entire theoretical system of Physiocracy. Thirdly, Voltaire praised the Physiocrats and their works as he gradually deepened his

[15] Ware (1931, p. 616 [Note 31]) points out that "Voltaire missed the point entirely."

understanding of the School. For example, he considered the Physiocrats' valuable journal, *Éphémérides du Citoyen*, and their excellent treatises on agriculture sufficient enough to teach and make happy the whole nation, and he himself admitted that he could not have written a better treatise on agricultural questions than those in the above journal. In particular, Voltaire held Turgot in high esteem as an individual, a philosopher, and a government official (Higgs, 1897, p. 116). Therefore, the failure of Turgot's reform deeply shocked Voltaire and dealt him a severe blow.

It is clear from the above that those who think Voltaire was opposed to the Physiocratic School cannot see the wood for the trees, and do not really understand the connection between the two. It is still a question to be explored as to what influence Voltaire's theory of total sinicization had on the formation of Physiocracy. Suffice it to say here that although Voltaire was born in the same year (1694) as Quesnay, the founder of the Physiocratic School, Voltaire was obviously more mature in terms of the breadth and systematization of Chinese thought. Quesnay was a latecomer who was familiar with Voltaire's work, which made it possible for him to make full use of the Chinese materials provided by Voltaire when creating a new economic theory.

Even Enlightenment thinkers like Montesquieu and Rousseau, who were unwilling to go with the flow, were unable to escape the influence of Chinese fashion in the creation of their doctrines amidst the praise of Chinese culture in French intellectual circles at the time.

Montesquieu (1689–1755) was an avid collector and researcher of various Chinese materials. Much of the Physiocrats' knowledge of Chinese culture were obtained through his paraphrases. His concept of fundamental rationality is said to have been influenced by Chinese thought, and to have had an influence on the formation of Physiocracy: "Just as Montesquieu sought for a 'spirit' or order which permeated or governed law, so the physiocrats looked for an underlying order in economic affairs" (Whittaker, 1960, p. 84).

Although he was negative about China's despotic government, he mentioned many advantages of Chinese culture in *The Spirit of the Laws*. For example, in Chap. 8 (entitled "A good custom in China") of Book 14, he says,

> The accounts of China tell us of the ceremony that the emperor performs every year to open the cultivation of the fields. By this public and solemn act one has wanted to rouse the peoples to their plowing.
>
> Moreover, each year the emperor is informed of the plowman who has most distinguished himself in his profession; he makes him a mandarin of the eighth order.
>
> (Montesquieu, 1989, pp. 237–238)

He argued that the Western monarchies should adopt Chinese emperors' edicts of exempting from taxation the provinces affected by natural disasters to show their kindness to the people (pp. 223, 225), praised "the spirit of the fine ordinances of the Chinese emperors" to oppose extravagance in favor of hard work and thrift (p. 102),and affirmed that the people were "infinitely happier" with the establishment of direct taxation in China than with the opposite system of the Roman government (pp. 226–227).

He also argued that the strengths of Chinese culture could remedy some of the shortcomings of despotic regimes, by stating, for example, that the Chinese legislators had established the most extensive rules of "civility," which was "a very proper means of inspiring gentleness, of maintaining peace and good order among the people, and of removing all the vices that come from a harsh spirit" (p. 317), so that "they are [...] the people in the world which most have tranquility as their purpose" (p. 617). He claimed that the Chinese legislators, i.e., Confucius and those who followed his teachings, "were more sensible when, as they considered men [...] in terms of the action proper to making them fulfill the duties of life, they made their religion, philosophy, and laws all practical" (p. 236), so in "the classics for the Chinese," "[t]he religious code replaces the civil code and fixes what is arbitrary" (p. 211). In this way, the Chinese despotism was subdued, while the Confucian classics were affirmed as doctrines binding on despotic power (p. 487).

Montesquieu discussed China with the purpose of advocating constitutional monarchy, or, in Reichwein's (1925, p. 94) words, "sought [...] to make China square with his own dogmas." It is doomed that his political ideal and China's political form are in serious conflict. However, from the study of Chinese materials, he found that Confucian political theory and ethics had a special status and charm in history, and that Chinese culture could be of great help in establishing the "national spirit" of France.

Montesquieu's exposition on the form of Chinese government had strong repercussions on Quesnay, which we will discuss specifically when we come to the Chinese origin of Quesnay's economic theory.

Rousseau (1712–1778) advocated the idea of "returning to nature," and his understanding of Chinese culture is mainly related to this advocacy. Many scholars believe that this idea benefited from oriental thought. In his commentary on Rousseau, Romain Rolland describes the pervasiveness of nature throughout Rousseau's life that "gave him an uncanny resemblance to the great mystic of the East" (Quoted in Zhu, 2005b, p. 301) and suggests that Rousseau "felt more than any other Westerner the ecstasy of the fullness of Eastern meaning" (p. 301). This "great mystic of the East," according to Reichwein (1925, p. 7), is Lao Zi, because "pure mysticism" is characteristic of Lao Zi (Lao Tzu): "It is the same sceptical attitude towards the institutions of customary right, of morality, of civilization generally, which links Lao Tzu with Rousseau," and "[e]ven more caustically and with Rousseau-like ruthlessness he (referring to Lao Zi) says: 'Give up Art, have done with gain, and there will be no more thieves and robbers'" (p. 8). Zhu Qianzhi (2005b), a Chinese scholar, points out that Rousseau, when he wrote his *Discours sur les Sciences et les Arts*, was very close to Diderot, and that Diderot already knew Lao Zi from Japanese writings, and had translated Lao Zi as Rossi, which reveals the way of Lao Zi's thought influencing Rousseau (p. 301). In another place, Zhu directly claims that "Rousseau's naturalism is close to the thought of Lao Zi" (p. 265).

However, Zhang Dongsun (1934, p. 157), a Chinese scholar, argues otherwise on the grounds that Lao Zi and Zhuang Zi's so-called "nature" means "letting things take their own course," rather than the natural world: Lao Zi and Zhuang Zi's doctrines of nature "are a far cry from Rousseau's idea of 'returning to nature' because Rousseau admits that there is a natural state, while Lao Zi and Zhuang Zi only ask for no artificial affectation, ignoring whether there is an inherent natural state in the outside world. [...] It must be emphasized that there is no 'naturalism' in the East [as in English]." We argue, nevertheless, that Lao's (1994, p. 241) description of an ideal situation as "a small country with few inhabitants" and Zhuang Zi's similar description are exemplary discussions of the primitive natural state of human society. Their exploratory delineation of the natural state of mankind is very similar to Rousseau's elaboration of "returning to nature" in terms of their basic ideas. Since Rousseau had easy access to Lao Zi's thought, especially since their core themes are basically the same, it is difficult to completely rule out the possibility of Rousseau's accepting the influence of Lao Zi's thought.

The fact that Chinese content or oriental implications can be found throughout the works by Leibniz, Voltaire, Montesquieu and Rousseau indicates that in the eighteenth century, the sentiment of European academia, even in literature, shifted to China:

> The year 1700 was, even for literature, the year of transition in which the affections of the learned world were turned towards China. "From this moment onwards, a clear conviction banished all uncertainty, and every one was forced to admire a people as old as it is wise, and as preeminent in religion as in wisdom," says a contemporary.[16]
>
> (Reichwein, 1925, pp. 78–79)

Among these "admirers," there was no one, apart from the important thinkers mentioned above, who did not express his attachment to Chinese culture. This is especially so with the old materialist encyclopedists.

Diderot (1713–1784), the chief editor of *l'Encyclopédie*, who wrote the entries on "China" and "Chinese philosophy" himself, said of the Chinese philosophers in general, "These peoples [...] are superior to all other Asiatics in antiquity, intellect, art, wisdom, policy, and in their taste for philosophy; nay, in the judgment of certain authors, they dispute the palm in these matters with the most enlightened peoples of Europe" (p. 92). In another place, he added, "[T]hey understand better than we the science of good sense and virtue; and if peradventure that science should happen to be the first of all sciences, they would be right in saying that they have two eyes and we have only one, and all the rest of the world is blind" (Quoted in Morley, 1886, p. 274).

Holbach (1723–1789), another contributor to *l'Encyclopédie*, claimed that China was the only example in the world that combined the fundamental law of politics with morality, that the people there regarded morality as their only religion, that reason displayed an incredible effect on the monarch and conquered China's conquerors, that the sage Confucius' morality, which is based on eternal truth, could resist the storm and make the savage conquerors have no choice but to show respect for it, that in China, both the monarch and the ministers were enthusiastic about people's education, and that from this kind of good habit, we can understand that all Chinese monarchs with virtues were actively improving customs, expelling evil virtues and

[16] Here the "contemporary" refers to Clerc (1769, p. xiii).

establishing moral domination (Quoted in Gorai, 1938, pp. 362–363). He praised the ancient Chinese emperor's choice system which took the qualification of a great monarch as the standard and chose a virtuous citizen as his successor (p. 364), and asserted that China's industrial development was unmatched by that of other countries (p. 363). In a word, China was a shining example of the combination of politics and morality, and European governments must take China as a model (p. 366).

Helvetius (1715–1771), also based on the opinion of Chinese scholars, realized that "the creation of God is nothing more than the sanctification of man's ignorance" (Zhu, 2005b, p. 269 [Note 1]), and stated, "I confess, just like them, that theology, that is, theology of God or that elusive entity, is not a special science" (p. 269 [Note 1]), which means that the atheistic or natural theistic viewpoint of anti-theology is derived from Chinese thought. This is why Pinot, a modern Western scholar, when discussing the formation of the French philosophical spirit, says that "in 1740 or so, the universality of the Bible came to an end, and that Chinese atheism inflicted on it a fatal wound" (p. 266).

Furthermore, the Enlightenment scholar La Mettrie (1709–1751), in his *Histoire naturelle de l'âme* (1745), openly declared that a true natural theist or atheist will always "do unto others as he would have them do unto him," turning the famous maxim of Confucius into a motto of anti-theism. He suggested that the definition of natural law is based on how we feel: It tells us not to "do not do unto others as we would not have them do unto us." This is the same as Voltaire's call for everyone in the world to obey the maxim to eliminate war and usher in the happiest epoch on earth. This maxim, according to Helvetius, is subordinate to the supreme law of public welfare. Morelly, too, in his *Code de la Nature*, published anonymously in 1755, regarded this maxim as the "first principle" of civil and international law, or the "fundamental principle of rights" (Peking University's Department of Philosophy, 1979, pp. 191, 258, 550, 794). Confucius' quotations were thus enshrined as a golden rule by Enlightenment thinkers, which, though seeming inconceivable to modern Western scholars, was prevalent in the eighteenth century European intellectual circles.

Of course, there were at that time also some representatives who defended European traditions to the exclusion of Chinese culture. The French writer Grimm saw that "the Chinese Empire has become … the object of special attention and of special study" (Quoted in Reichwein, 1925, p. 96), but did not agree that "this country became in a short time the home of wisdom, virtue, and good faith, its government the best possible and the longest established, its morality the loftiest and most beautiful in the known world; its laws, its policy, its art, its industry were likewise such as to serve for a model to all nations of the earth" (p. 96). He "saw in China-worship something excessive and in bad taste" (p. 96). Earlier, in his *Dialogues des Morts*, Fénelon had adopted the form of a debate between Confucius and Socrates, defending the ancient Greek tradition and expressing his objection to the commonly recognized strengths of China (pp. 96–98). In fact, these objections were a reflection of the deep and widespread influence of Chinese culture on the West during that period. Until the French Revolution, the remark that "China is a lovely place, it will make you like it" had been a common refrain in popular songs. Even the famous leader of the Revolution, Saint-Just (1767–1794), had a copy of *Biography of Confucius* in his collection, and quoted it in his writings (Yang, 1945, p. 31). This can be seen as a remnant of the fervor to revere China.

To sum up, the influence of Chinese traditional culture on the European Enlightenment can be understood from two aspects. On the one hand, the Sino-Western cultural exchange reached its peak in the eighteenth century, which coincided with the rise of the European Enlightenment. Marx (1966, p. 398) argued, "Men make their own history, but they do not make it just as they please; they do not make it under circumstances chosen by themselves, but under circumstances directly encountered, given and transmitted from the past." In their effort to seek theoretical bases and practical examples to oppose the church authority and the feudal system, the Enlightenment thinkers happened to encounter the era when Chinese thoughts and things were sweeping across Europe. Hence, from the then prevalent Chinese culture, they "conjur[ed] up the spirits of the past to their service and borrow[ed] from them names, battle cries and costumes in order to present the new scene of world history in this time-honoured disguise and this borrowed language" (Marx, 1966, p. 398). This is a more obvious and easily recognized aspect of the influence of Chinese culture on the West.

On the other hand, the influence is more subtle and not easily perceptible without in-depth study. This is because many traditional Chinese cultural codes, systems and ideas were sifted, absorbed and digested by the Enlightenment thinkers and incorporated into their theoretical system. This system has been inherited and developed by future generations of thinkers, so that the elements of Chinese culture, which have been integrated into traditional Western culture, have been deposited deeper and deeper into its cultural structure, making it more difficult for modern scholars to identify them. Some Western scholars have recognized the influence of Chinese culture in this regard. Hudson (1931, p. 276), for example, points out that, in the seventeenth and eighteenth centuries, objectively speaking, "[t]he Chinese suggestions provided the chief inspiration of the new style, a style which over a large field of the arts departed entirely from the main lines of European tradition" (p. 312), and that, subjectively speaking, "in contemporary France there grew up a school which saw in this [Chinese] system the model of political perfection, and proposed in Europe '*inoculer l'ésprit chinois*'" (p. 236).[17] Thus, he claims, "Destined in the nineteenth century and after to be violently invaded, overwhelmed and radically transformed by the progressing civilization of the West, Old China in the eighteenth reached out and cast a spell over its future conqueror, leaving indelible traces in the cultural tradition of Europe."

In the following, we will explore such "traces" of ancient Chinese civilization in the economic theories of the Physiocratic School.

[17] The proposition of '*inoculer l'ésprit chinois*' originally came from Bertin, Louis XV's minister, and was accepted by Louis XV himself, when the king wanted to abolish bad policies.

Chapter 3
François Quesnay and A. R. J. Turgot: Two Admirers of China

The Physiocratic School took Quesnay as its theoretical guru and acknowledged leader, and its other members did no more than accept, absorb, exegete and propagate his ideas in an accessible form, so as to make them widely popular. Therefore, when we investigate the Chinese source of the Physiocratic system, we actually explore mainly that of Quesnay's theories, referring to as a supplementary reference the viewpoints of other important members of the School.

This investigation must also take into account the views of another important representative of Physiocracy, A. R. J. Turgot, who, though never acting as a member of the School, treated Chinese culture in the same way as the School as a whole.

1 Quesnay: "The Confucius of Europe"

I. Quesnay and his disciples

Quesnay (1694–1774) was born into a rural family[1] and the first book he read was *Maison Rustique*, which aroused his keen interest in agronomic techniques. Many Western scholars of the history of economic thought see in this life experience a certain inevitable connection to his later formulation of Physiocracy. The fact that he turned his attention to China, an agricultural country, in search of his ideal kingdom had something to do with this background, in addition to the influence from the Chinese vogue.

Another important experience in his early years is his arrival in Paris in 1711 at the age of 18, when he began a five-year apprenticeship with the famous engraver Pierre

[1] There are various accounts of the occupation of Quesnay's father in Western scholarship, such as lawyer or rural lawyer, merchant and sometimes tax collector, magistrate and small landowner, but it is more common to say that his father was a farmer. What is certain is that Quesnay himself grew up in the countryside, with a plot of land or a small farm, and that he actually lived a rural family life in his youth.

M. Tan, *The Chinese Origin of Physiocracy*,
https://doi.org/10.1007/978-981-97-9703-5_3

de Rochefort. During that period, the various art-and-craft industries in Paris came under the influence of the Rococo, and the imitation of Chinese artistic styles became the object of intense competition among craftsmen. It is not difficult to imagine the effect this fashionable frenzy had on Quesnay when he served his apprenticeship. It is interesting to note that the first edition of Quesnay's *Tableau Économique*, printed in Versailles in 1758, was so beautifully engraved that some even suggested that it might have been the work of Louis XV, even though Quesnay himself had already received special training in this art. Even the powerful Madame de Pompadour, who took up engraving as her hobby, was probably influenced by Quesnay, who later served as her physician. All of this shows that Quesnay's exposure to Chinese culture was not temporary, but lasted a long time.

However, it was only in 1749, when he moved to Versailles as a royal physician, that Quesnay really found himself at the heart of the Chinese vogue. During the 15 years he lived there, the Chinese fashions prevalent at the Court, and in particular Madame de Pompadour's fascination with Chinese relics, inspired his long-nurtured admiration for Chinese culture. Through Madame de Pompadour, he persuaded Louis XV to imitate the ancient Chinese ceremony of "ploughing the land" in 1756, proving that, 11 years before he wrote his *Despotism in China*, the French court had been discussing Physiocracy in relation to the Chinese tradition. Since then, he regarded the ceremony as a necessity for the ideal monarch, and used this image of the Chinese emperor to guide the dauphin of France, later King Louis XVI. What received publicity from painters and praise from poets was later called "[a] tribute to the fashionable craze for the 'Agricultural System', [...] the ceremony performed by the Dauphin at Versailles, 15th June 1768, when he publicly 'held the plough'—a toy bedecked with ribbons" (Higgs, 1897, p. 89). This good intention of Quesnay's to use the Chinese emperor as a model for the heir to the French throne had its due influence in other European countries. A notable example was that, on August 19 of the following year, Emperor Joseph of Austria conducted the ceremony in Moravia by ploughing the land himself.

Quesnay's obsession with China as an ideal kingdom strongly influenced other members of the Physiocratic School. There are numerous passages praising Chinese civilization or quoting the Chinese system, both in their respective treatises and in the *Journal de l'Agriculture, du Commerce et des Finances* and the *Ephémérides*—both were the organs of the School. In his *The Natural and Essential Order of Political Societies* (1767),[2] Mercier de la Rivière endeavored to find examples from China to develop Quesnay's theory. Thus his opponent Mably accused him of "exhibit[ing] a predilection for the government of China" (Quoted in Higgs, 1897, p. 105), and commented harshly on the above book, "The rhapsodies of some writers over the agriculture of China have bewitched the author to such a point that he wished to

[2] According to Oncken's Note, the elder Mirabeau recalled, "I saw the author of *L'ordre naturel et essentiel des societes politiques* spend six whole weeks, clad in a dressing gown, working in the doctor's (Quesnay's) study, writing and recasting his book, and in the end disown his father and mother" (Quoted in Maverick, 1946, p. 137).

copy their government" (p. 109).[3] Indeed, such criticisms reflect the Physiocrats' deep respect for China.

The Abbé Baudeau (Quoted in Gide & Rist, 1915, p. 36 [Note 3]), a Physiocrat, argued, "The Chinese are the only people whose philosophy seems to have got hold of this supreme truth, and they regard their emperor as the eldest son of God." Incidentally, modern economists have always tended to regard the Physiocrats' idealization of the Chinese emperor in a negative light, dismissing it as steeped in feudalism, as the most absurd idea, or at best as a propaganda device aimed at proving that such an ideal state already existed in the world, and that it was sufficient for Europe and France to follow suit (Rozenberg, 1934–36). In fact, in the middle of the eighteenth century, when the Church and the feudal monarchies in Europe were still extremely powerful, this so-called "propaganda" often had a certain enlightenment significance. At that time, China was in the "prosperous age of Kang Xi and Qian Long," and its people were safe and secure, indeed worthy of the envy of war-ridden European countries. Western thinkers idealized China and its emperors, which prompted those countries to absorb or adopt many aspects of China's social and political system, science and technology, as well as philosophical thought. Therefore, it is not credible to dismiss the School's glorification of China's emperors as "absurd," or to attribute it simply to the "paucity" of knowledge about China at the time. Some of the Physiocratic views may seem to be "absurd" today, but if we put them into the specific historical environment at that time, we will find that underneath their superficial "absurdity," there is some hidden historical progress that modern scholars often fail to take note of.

Du Pont de Nemours, another member of the School, published in 1767 a collection of the papers by Quesnay and his disciples. Its title, place and date of publication were indicated on Page 575 of its first edition as follows:

> La Physiocratie: ou Constitution Essentielle du Gouvernement le Plus Advantageux au Genre Humaine, Peking, 1767.[4]

This collection is regarded as a classic by the Physiocrats, and Du Pont's inventive use of "Peking" as the address for the publication of such an important work was quite deliberate. The intention was not only to cater to the Chinese fashion in Europe, but also to cast an unfathomable layer of mystery over Physiocracy in order to elevate its status in French intellectual circles. The so-called "Physiocracy" and "Physiocrats" are the terms that originated from this title. For a long time, people have thought that Du Pont was the inventor of this title. In the late nineteenth century, Oncken first disagreed, arguing that *Physiocratie* had been adopted before Du Pont, by the Abbé Baudeau, or possibly by Quesnay himself. Not long after, Higgs (1897, p. 65 [Note 2]) agreed, saying that "there is more reason for the belief that it was due to Quesnay." It is also inferred that Du Pont's indication of "Peking" as the address of the first edition of his book, was no doubt at the behest of Quesnay, who always emphasized

---

[3] For more information about Mably's criticism in his *Doutes proposés aux Philosophes économistes sur l'Ordre naturel et essentiel des Sociétés politiques* (1768), see Higgs (1897, pp. 104–111).

[4] The addresses of the 1768 reprint of this book are given as Leyden, Holland, and Paris, France.

China (Einaudi, 1958, p. 271). Later, when the members of the Physiocratic School described the definition of the Physiocrats, they also, as Gide and Rist (1915, p. 3 [Note 1]) put it, "possessed not a little of the dogmatism of the Chinese." As can be seen here, Quesnay and his disciples used some very distinctive forms to express their reverence and yearning for China.

Quesnay was particularly impressed by the teachings of Confucius. He wrote a ten-page outline of Confucius' life under the title "The Life of Confucius," which was originally included in his manuscript, *Despotism in China*, but was somehow removed when the manuscript was officially published. This outline is valuable for investigating the intellectual sources of Quesnay's theories. Suffice it to repeat Fox-Genovese's (1976) summary[5] embedded with Quesnay's description of Confucius.

> Confucius, writes Quesnay, invoking by analogy the intellectual constellation of his own day, belonged to the generation succeeding that of Thales and including Pythagoras, Solon, and by slight extension, Socrates. In comparison with the Greeks, his doctrine did not spread widely during his lifetime. But his "glory only increased with the passage of the years, and it subsists in its entirety in the greatest Empire of the world which attributes to it its duration and splendor." Unlike the Greeks, Confucius did not indulge in sterile speculation. Confucius concentrated on humans as they exist, and recognized in them one main principle. He limited his work to inspiring mortals with "the respect, the fear, the recognition" which they owed that guiding force, to persuading them "that it knows all, that it knows even the most secret recesses of the heart, that it never leaves virtue without reward or crime without punishment." Such, Quesnay insists, was the basic precept through which Confucius attempted "to reform the morals of the human race."
>
> Having established the religious and human focus of Confucius' thought, Quesnay adds some biographical facts and psychological insights. From the tenderest years Confucius displayed "the wisdom that ordinarily is only the fruit of maturity." The games and amusements of childhood never distracted him. Indeed, his "grave, modest and serious air" earned him the veneration of all who came in contact with him and paralleled Quesnay's own sobriety. And like Quesnay, in later years Confucius made great strides in the study of the past. Having, through his studies, "acquired the most profound knowledge, he proposed to reestablish the form of government on wise principles, and to reform, by this path, the morals and the customs of the various little kingdoms which then composed the Chinese Empire." Through exhortation and example, Confucius sought to lead men to the path of morality. Indeed, the resplendence of his own virtues, the profundity of his "lumières," and his integrity all contributed to the recognition of his worth. He accepted several official positions, "but with the only intent of spreading his doctrine and working for the reformation of men."
>
> Throughout a long career, the actions of Confucius never contravened his maxims. "By his gravity, his modesty, his sweetness and his frugality, by his scorn of terrestrial pleasures, and by a continual vigilance on his own conduct, he was himself an example of the precepts he advanced in his writings and his discourses. ..." And again: "Never did one hear him speak advantageously of himself, and the praises that he received from others he listened to only with repugnance." Just as Confucius attributed his own wisdom "to the great legislators Yao and Xun," so would Quesnay place his maxims in the mouth of the great Sully.
>
> The great Chinese philosopher always worked to reestablish human nature in its original purity, to counteract and eradicate the errors introduced by a history of superstition and false reasoning. "Human nature, he frequently said to his disciples, came to us from heaven very

[5] The quotation within this summary is taken by Fox-Genovese from EMHL, Winterthur MSS, group 2, series E, "Histoire sommaire de Confucius," in Quesnay's *Le Despotisme de la Chine* (pp. 60–63, 66–67).

pure, very perfect: subsequently, ignorance, the passions, the bad examples corrupted it; and to be perfect, it is necessary to reascend to the point from which we are descended."
(pp. 74–75)

The above description of Confucius, according to Fox-Genovese (p. 75), is actually what Quesnay described himself, at least with the hope of possessing those virtues, of which the intent was explicitly expressed. Here, Fox-Genovese parallels Quesnay and Confucius in several places, namely, (1) the former's "sobriety" matched the latter's "grave, modest and serious air," (2) both made great achievements in their "later years," and (3) Quesnay was to Sully as Confucius was to Yao and Shun (Xun).

In addition to the record in "The Life of Confucius," Quesnay's (1946) writings reveal in many places his admiration and high esteem for Confucius: "The Chinese regard him as the greatest of all scholars, the greatest reformer of the laws, of ethics, and of the religion of their empire, which had fallen from its ancient splendor" (p. 161); Confucius was a "celebrated philosopher, who endured with immovable courage all the opposition and oppression" (pp. 161–162); Confucius was a "wise master" with a high reputation for wise legislation, who "caused candor, uprightness, and all the civil virtues to prevail among the people" (p. 162); "the highest veneration is shown in China for this philosopher" (p. 162);"he is regarded as the first teacher and scholar of the empire [and] his works have [extreme] authority" (p. 162); and even Kublai Khan, the Tartar emperor, "paid [Confucius] the same honors he would have rendered to a king" (p. 163). Quesnay often asked his disciples to quote his views without naming him. Therefore, the comments of other members of the Physiocratic School about Confucius can also be seen as a transmission or repetition of Quesnay's own thoughts. At that time, in their minds, not knowing Confucius was considered as great a sin as not knowing Socrates or Plato. So Du Pont (Quoted in Ly, 1938, p. 9), in response to a criticism of the theories of the School, said rhetorically, "Don't you know Confucius?" In this way, he acted as a de facto defender of Confucius' doctrines.

A French scholar once gave the following analysis: The Physiocrats were undoubtedly influenced by Chinese culture; they regarded Confucius as the ideal scholar, and believed that only their master Quesnay was a comparable figure (p. 11). This is exactly what happened. The Abbé Baudeau called Quesnay "the great legislator, the Confucius of Europe" (p. 9) and, when talking about Quesnay's *Tableau Économique*, said that this "Confucius of Europe" had discovered the basic order of France (p. 11). Mirabeau wrote to Rousseau that the discovery of the "net product," which they owe to "the venerable Confucius of Europe," would one day change the face of the world (p. 11). Even the organization of the Physiocratic School itself was believed by its members to be similar to the Confucian school of Confucius. Such praises, in comparing Quesnay to Confucius, or in considering him as the successor of Confucian orthodoxy, reached an unparalleled level in the much-quoted speech delivered by Mirabeau (Quoted in Reichwein, 1925, p. 104) at the time of Quesnay's death:

The whole teaching of Confucius aimed at restoring to human nature that first radiance, that first beauty, which it had received from Heaven, and which had become obscured by

> ignorance and passion. He, therefore, exhorted his countrymen to obey the Lord of Heaven, to honour and fear him, to love their neighbours as themselves, to overcome their inclinations, never to make passion the measure of action, but rather to subject it to reason, and not to do, or think, or say, anything contrary to reason. It would be impossible to add anything to this splendid diadem of religious morality; but the most essential part still remained to be done—to bind it upon the brows of earth; and this was the work of our master, whose keen ear caught from the lips of our common mother Nature the secret of the 'net product.'

This speech is more a tribute to a master of Chinese Neo-Confucianism than to Quesnay, reflecting an important feature of Quesnay's doctrine as a way to continue the work of Confucius. We know that those missionaries to China, who were well versed in the Confucian classics, were honored by Chinese scholars with the title of "Western Confuciuses." This is, however, very rare. Rarer still are those Western intellectuals who have been described in the West as "the Confuciuses of Europe." Quesnay is such a rare example in Europe.

Quesnay's title, "the Confucius of Europe," reveals the image he occupied in the minds of his disciples. His earlier works on economic philosophy discuss some of the basic ideas of Confucius' doctrines, but he never explicitly stated that his ideas came from Confucius' works. Reichwein (1925, p. 104) points out, "Everything except his method Quesnay owes to the models he had before him; to Chinese tradition in particular he is indebted for certain basic ideas." This is evident from his *Despotism in China* (1767). However, it may "be inferred with some certainty that he became acquainted with translations of Chinese literature at a much earlier date" (pp. 104–105). If Quesnay was already familiar with the Confucian texts, why did he not reveal this secret until his last work? The explanation for this is that Quesnay was careful not to reveal his source at the beginning, in order to preserve his theoretical originality, while his final decision to reveal the real source was, as Reichwein (p. 109) says, a political necessity: "This enthusiastic profession of faith of Quesnay's in the Chinese State had a definite political object. He wished to set the crumbling French monarchy on a new and sound, i.e. on a natural, basis, and hoped that such a profession would gain him a better hearing in an age which idealized China."

Quesnay's acceptance of the above title is bound to involve a considerable departure from Europe's own ancient Greek traditions. Admittedly, members of the Physiocratic School gave Quesnay other laurels, such as "the greatest genius of our age" and "the Moses of our day." He was more often called "the Modern Socrates," because his appearance was especially similar to that of the ancient Greek philosopher Socrates. And he was also compared to Prometheus, the god of the ancient Greek mythology who benefited mankind (Higgs, 1897, p. 47; Einaudi, 1958, p. 267). However, according to Quesnay's own works, he seldom quoted the ancient Greco-Roman philosophers, and his quotation turned out insignificant even if he did occasionally. Moreover, when comparing Confucius' doctrine with that of ancient Greek sages, he had a clear tendency to belittle the latter in favor of the former. For example, he commented that Confucius' *Analects*, with its discussion of good government, virtue, and good works, is full of principles and virtuous words, "which surpass those of the Seven Sages of Greece" (Quoted in Reichwein, 1925, p. 105). This tendency in Quesnay's thinking was apparently appreciated by his disciples. The

Abbé Baudeau's aversion to ancient Greek politics is typically manifested in his remarks paraphrased here: He believed that justice and good will were often lacking in the Greek republics, that they were ignorant of the laws of the natural order, and that their history is a record of constant destruction of peace and human happiness. This unrest and violence of the Greek nation, in his view, was the evil of the principle of its "'mixed' states," forbidden to "righteous thinkers," which, though once considered the "masterpiece" of Greek philosophers and statesmen, was still preached or experimented with in the Physiocrats' times (Reichwein, 1925, p. 105). Accordingly, Reichwein (p. 105), among many other Western scholars, states, "it was not [...] the ancient Greek, but the ancient Chinese, philosophy which stood godmother to his [Quesnay's] work. In the first place it is important to establish the fact that he [Quesnay] rated Chinese philosophy high above the Greek."

In fact, the idea that Chinese philosophy is superior to Greek philosophy was popular in the vogue for China throughout Europe in the seventeenth and eighteenth centuries, and was advocated by a number of important thinkers at that time. Leibniz (1994, p. 78) believed that Chinese philosophy was established "long before the philosophy of the Greeks." Voltaire (1901) also said that Chinese philosophy does not talk about gods and monsters, and there are no spokesmen of God like the Greeks who claimed to be inspired by God. However, the Physiocratic School represented by Quesnay expressed more clearly and prominently the argument that Greek philosophy is inferior to Chinese philosophy.

In the following, we will make a preliminary analysis of *Despotism in China*, Quesnay's representative work on Chinese culture, in order to have a general understanding of the scope of his knowledge about China and the sources that he accessed or mastered.

II. *Despotism in China*

Quesnay's *Despotism in China*, consisting of eight chapters, was published in four serial installments from the spring of 1767 in the *Ephémérides*. In 1887, Oncken included it in its entirety in the collection *Oeuvres Économiques et Philosophiques de Quesnay*. His opinion of the work is revealed in the following comment by Mably he cited in the "Note by Oncken":

> Generally speaking, the essay did not attract much attention, nor does it rank among the best works of the author. However, for the history of the physiocratic system, it is noteworthy, for it shows that Quesnay's political opinions took their final form later than his economic opinions.
>
> (Quoted in Maverick, 1946, p. 137)

Regardless of whether the above opinion is correct or not, the Physiocrats at the time showed a high degree of enthusiasm for the publication of this masterpiece. Du Pont, prior to the publication of the first part of this work, had a special publication notice informing readers: "The March number of the *Ephémérides* will begin the work *Le despotism de la Chine*, by the author of the *Tableau Économique*, writing under the name of monsieur A" (p. 138). Before this, the Abbé Baudeau, editor of the *Ephémérides*, had noted, in a review of Martin Hubner's *Essai Sur L'histoire du Droit*

Naturel, that it praised China, which was however insufficient, and then Baudeau introduced Quesnay's work by saying, "Happily we have in our hands something to make up for this lack, a treasured contribution from the hand of the master, under the title *Le despotism de la Chine*, which we shall communicate to our readers" (p. 138 [Note]). When he published Quesnay's work, he added another note: "We hasten to place before our readers this valuable work, as we promised them" (p. 138), and advertised that each chapter was "equally interesting, which [the author] has written [...] with the greatest care" (p. 138). Baudeau briefly described the contents of each chapter, and especially emphasized that the eighth chapter is the most important one, which summarizes all the previous chapters, and "contains a parallel between the natural basis for the proper government of nations, and the principles of government as that science is taught and practiced in China" (p. 138). These notes reveal the substance of Quesnay's deliberate emulation of China, for which he drew fierce attacks from his opponents. Baudeau's defense was that "[his fellow-physiocrats] had not intended to say that China was perfect, merely that it came nearer to that ideal than did any other government" (p. 129). This interpretation adequately reflects the exalted position of China in the minds of the Physiocrats. Oncken underestimated the place of *Despotism in China* in Quesnay's writings, apparently without taking into account the great influence of Chinese culture on Quesnay and the other Physiocrats.

Contrary to Oncken's opinion, the French scholar Pinot, in his 1906–1907 essay "Les Physiocrates et la Chine au XVIIIe Siècle," spoke highly of *Despotism in China*, especially its eighth chapter, as the first systematic revelation of the political and economic theories of the Physiocratic School, which had previously been scattered throughout Quesnay's writings (Pinot, 1906–1907, pp. 200–214).

Quesnay's *Despotism in China*, when examined for the origins of Physiocracy, has attracted special attention from future generations of scholars. Daszynska-Golinska (Quoted in Ly, 1938, p. 12), a French author, pointed out in his "La Chine et le système Physiocratique en Fance," "Quesnay is steeped in Chinese civilization in his *Despotism in China*, which gives people the impression that all the theories of the Physiocratic School are the products of Chinese philosophy." Maverick (1946), the American scholar who first translated *Despotism in China* into English, argues too that this work is "the apex of the movement of admiration for China" (p. 111). In another place, he explains that although the work does not represent Quesnay's major contribution to economics, it is "concerned with Chinese influence upon western economic and political thought, [and] deserves the position as the high water mark of the movement" (p. 115). Schumpeter (1954a, p. 224), later in his famous *History of Economic Analysis*, on the basis of Maverick's assertion, says that Quesnay's work "has given rise to speculations on the subject of Chinese influence upon the physiocrats." But the following preliminary introduction of the work shows that this Chinese influence is, far from a mere "speculation," an obvious fact.

Despotism in China is divided into a foreword and eight chapters. The basic contents of the whole book are briefly described as follows (Quesnay, 1946, pp. 139–304).

The "FOREWORD" begins with the term "despotism," which means that the monarch alone holds the power of the country. From this point of view, a despotic monarch can be "legal," or "arbitrary or illegal." In the latter sense, the despotic monarch exists in a dictatorship, who almost always has "a derogatory title," meaning a tyrant; in the former sense, the despotic monarch refers to the emperor of China, where "the Chinese constitution is founded upon wise and irrevocable laws which the emperor enforces and which he carefully observes himself." The following chapters revolve around the proposition of Chinese authoritarian politics in the former sense.

The first chapter, "INTRODUCTION," consists of five sections.

The first, "Western knowledge of China," explains the legends that China "surpassed the most polished states of Europe." The seemingly unbelievable accounts that "there should exist a people so ancient, learned and civilized" on the other side of the world were confirmed by the reports of missionaries to China, so that "[d]oubts gave way to belief; astonishment and admiration followed." It was known then that China, like Europe, exhibited "the same wisdom, the same intelligence, and the same variety as on our own, but with the difference that it seem[ed] to have assembled in the country above, almost all the products which one [might] find scattered about the rest of the world."

The second, "Origin of the Chinese Empire," affirms the long history of China. In response to some Western scholars' assertion about the Egyptian origin, the author questions, "Even though the identification of the Chinese with the Egyptians may be established, why may one not suppose that the latter came from China, or, rather than that, that both the former and the latter had a common origin?" He denounces as absurd "superficial writers" those in the West who think that the great deeds of Yao and Shun "do not merit the attention of scholars." He describes the earliest Chinese emperors as "all very good rulers," and claims at the same time that "[t]here are no people more submissive to their sovereign than the Chinese," thus forming through strict ethical precepts "the reciprocal duties of the ruler and his subjects." He especially praises the extraordinary learning taught by Confucius.

The third, "Extent and prosperity of the Empire," states that China, whose territory is equal to that of the whole Europe, was "the most beautiful in the world, the most densely populated, and the most flourishing kingdom known." It was rich in produce, had deep and fertile soils, harvested several times a year, was irrigated by many rivers, lakes and canals, and had excellent and well-maintained roads and bridges. The author also sees that there were still many poor families in China, and expounds his views on the relationship between population proliferation and wealth growth, and between the economy and wages in the field of distribution.

The fourth, "Classes of citizens," mentions that the Chinese aristocracy had no hereditary system, and that "the most illustrious family in China, and the only one in which nobility [might] be transmitted by heredity," was that of Confucius, which was "the most ancient in the world, for it [had] been preserved in a direct line for more than two thousand years." Among the commoners, "the husbandmen [held] first rank," followed by the merchants, as well as the artisans and common laborers.

The fifth, "Military forces," gives a brief account of China's military organization, military defense, soldiers, equipment, and military service. In particular, China's navy and shipping were "unimportant" because of the lack of "formidable" neighbors by sea and its limited foreign trade, but "it must be agreed that on the rivers and on the canals they ha[d] a skill that we lack[ed]," and it was particularly "amazing and incredible" that "they almost def[ied] the forces of nature, boldly navigating waterways that would frighten other people."

The second chapter, "FUNDAMENTAL LAWS OF THE EMPIRE," consists of nine sections.

The first section, "The natural law," is to be discussed later.

The second, "Sacred books or canons of the first order," discusses firstly the "mystical" *I-Ching* (*The Book of Changes*) and its "enigmatic lines;" secondly, *Shang Shu* or *Shû King* (*The Book of Documents*), a book that "tells of ancient times" and "includes excellent precepts and good rules for the public welfare;" thirdly, *Shi Jing* (*The Book of Odes* or *The Classic of Poetry*); fourthly, *Chun Qiu* (*Spring and Autumn Annals*), which is a "purely historical" book; and fifthly, *Li Ji* (*The Book of Rites*). These five books are collectively known as "The Five Classics."

The third, "Canonical books of the second order," briefly introduces the six Chinese classics, including *Da Xue* (*The Great Learning*), *Zhong Yong* (*The Doctrine of the Mean*), *Lun Yu* (*The Analects*), *Meng Zi* (*Mencius*), *Xiao Jing* (*The Classic of Filial Piety*), and Zhu Xi's *Xiao Xue* (*The Lesser Learning*). It is pointed out that "the Chinese do not distinguish at all between morality and politics; the art of living well is … the art of governing well, and the two sciences are one and the same."

The fourth, "Chinese learning," argues that although the Chinese were very fond of learning, they had achieved little in the "fields of pure speculation," such as mathematics, geometry, natural philosophy and physics, because these disciplines were not "actuated by a desire for gain." Their "principal study turn[ed] in the direction of the more useful sciences," away from grammar, the history and laws of the state, ethics and politics, which seem to be more directly necessary for people's conduct and social welfare. In China, instead of those "speculative" sciences, "those [sciences] of the natural laws […] reached the highest degree of perfection." The scant study of the natural laws and the poor governance in other countries made China "preferred" in the world.

The fifth, "Education," describes the proliferation of Chinese schools in cities and villages, and the fact that "[t]he instruction of the people [was] one of the principal functions of the mandarins." It also introduces the sixteen maxims that were an amplification of Emperor Kang Xi's edict of 1691, such as "teach[ing] the young people how much they should respect the fundamental laws of nature," and discusses the official Gazette of the Empire, a government publication that communicated news of official decrees throughout the country. In short, in China, the books containing the basic laws of the country were directly accessible to everyone, and even the emperor had to obey them: "One emperor attempted in vain to abolish them, but the laws triumphed over tyranny."

The sixth, "Studies of the scholars," introduces the system of "the imperial examination" in China.

The seventh, "Ownership of wealth," states that the ownership of property in China was "quite secure" and that the inheritance of property was carried out in accordance with "the natural order of the right of succession."

The eighth, "Agriculture," describes China's agricultural crops, farming and distribution of income. Special mention is made of the fact that agriculture in China was always respected, and those who lived by agriculture always "merited the special attention of the emperors."

The ninth, "Commerce viewed as serving agriculture," based on the assumption that the large amount of agricultural products in China would inevitably lead to a quite "flourishing" commerce, affirms that commerce depends on agriculture and has an important economic function in society; points out that China was a self-sufficient country with little foreign trade; and refutes the reports of Western merchants about the fraudulent trade of the Chinese, stressing that such fraudulent behavior was "even more inconceivable in a nation so civilized as China."

The third chapter, "POSITIVE LEGISLATION," consists of three sections.

The first section, "The laws are based on ethics; the canons; M. de Montesquieu," assures that Chinese laws were based on ethical principles; that Chinese ethics and politics were one science; that all positive laws of the empire had as their sole purpose the maintenance of rule; that there was no authority above the laws; that these laws were found in the sacred works known as the Five Classics; that these classics combined religion, state rule and positive law into one; and that the main task of monarchs and scholars was to delve into the natural law that governs them. The author then quotes as an illustration the Chinese situation described in Montesquieu's *The Spirit of the Laws*.

The second, "The absolute power of the Emperor is tempered," states that the decisions of the Chinese administrative agencies had the force of law when they were approved by the ruler, and that the decrees of the ruler himself, if they did not violate customs or infringe on the public welfare, were immutable laws that were valid forever. At the same time, this section also claims that, according to Chinese laws, "the custom of remonstrating with the emperor" was always encouraged, and that even the actions of the emperor himself, if he violated the law and the state system, were not immune from condemnation, let alone those of the officials at all levels.

The third, "Courts of the Empire," mainly introduces China's central official system, that is, the six ministries of officials, taxation and finances, rituals, soldiers, justice and industry, and their functions.

The fourth chapter, "TAXATION," describes China's good tax system and its financial expenditure.

The fifth chapter, "AUTHORITY," argues that the absolute power of the Chinese emperors meant that the laws and basic rules of governance must be properly observed. "[T]he constitution of the government of China [was] based upon natural law in such an irrefragable and so emphatic a manner" that the Chinese emperor, who was given such exalted titles as "Son of Heaven" and "Holy Emperor," could not abuse the people's obedience and treat them cruelly, but should love his subjects like a father according to the "General Maxims for the Economic Government of an Agricultural Kingdom." China maintained "such marvellous order" because good law solved all problems.

The sixth chapter, "ADMINISTRATION," consists of three sections.

The first section, "Tribunals," describes China's civil law system, mentioning in particular the tribunals' enforcement of the principles of justice through a system of supervision at all levels, and arguing that nothing could be more praiseworthy than this way of dispensing justice.

The second, "Penal laws," describes the main provisions of Chinese criminal laws, arguing that, compared with those of the West, "the penal laws in China [were] very lenient," and quotes as an example the remark of Navarrete, a missionary who had been imprisoned in China: "Especially admirable about the Chinese prisons [was] the fact that we were gently treated and with as much respect as though we were of distinguished rank."

The third, "Mandarins of the Empire," introduces the way Chinese officials were selected, their duties, and the system of rewards and punishments. It is stated that Chinese people had to pass the imperial examination to obtain official positions, so the officials were all learned; that the "only" duty of the official in office was to protect the people, and he must always be ready to listen to the people; that it was also the main duty of the official to "lecture to the people;" that the official could not serve in his own hometown; and that the death penalty was imposed on officials who took bribes of up to eighty ounces of silver.

The seventh chapter, "ASSERTED SHORTCOMINGS OF THE GOVERNMENT OF CHINA," consists of five sections.

The first section, "The assertions of M. de Montesquieu," refutes Montesquieu's criticism of China's despotic system.

The second, "Intruding religions," refers mainly to Daoism and Buddhism in China, but argues that the Chinese government should be forgiven for its tolerant attitude toward these sects, since in the country, the restriction of various religious beliefs was always seen as "a ridiculous act of authority."

The third, "The religion of the scholars," deals with the controversy over Chinese rites that was raging in Europe, focusing on the understanding of the meanings of "Tien" and "Shang-ti" in Chinese classics. One side thought that the two terms were materialized, and therefore suspected Chinese religion to be atheistic; the other side held that the terms were the same as those in the Christian doctrine, and should be understood not as "the visible and material heaven" but as "the sovereign lord of heaven, the author of all things, a god who sees all, who governs the world with wisdom and justice." Quesnay clearly favors the latter view.

The fourth, "Taxes other than on land," states that in addition to land taxes, China was said to have an illegitimate system of taxes, such as custom duties, tolls, and poll taxes. This, if true, was a failure of the state to be "sufficiently enlightened as to its true interests; for in an empire, the wealth of which springs from the soil, such impositions are destructive to taxation itself and to the revenues of the nation." The author argues that "[t]his truth, however difficult to grasp by reasoning, may be indisputably demonstrated by mathematics." He believes that this defect need not be attributed to the Chinese government itself, but was "only a mistake of administration, … for it may be corrected without involving any change in the constitution of that empire."

The fifth, "Overpopulation and unequal distribution of wealth," puts forward an important argument about the relationship between wealth and population in light of China's overpopulation: population tends to exceed wealth, but in fact "it is only the amount of the wealth which sets a limit to population," so that the poverty caused by overpopulation cannot be blamed on "the very constitution of a good government," as in China. Therefore, as an overpopulated country with good institutions, China had no alternative but to establish colonies.

The eighth chapter, "COMPARISON OF CHINESE LAWS WITH THE NATURAL PRINCIPLES UNDERLYING PROSPEROUS GOVERNMENTS," consists of twenty-four sections. It begins by stating that all of the above chapters have "shown the political and moral constitution of the great empire of China, based upon a knowledge of the Natural Law, of which it is, the outgrowth." Then, this chapter emphasizes that the information cited above completely follows the accounts of those Western historians and travelers having been to China, most of whom were in agreement with each other, and that what they had seen and heard is therefore completely trustworthy. It is stated finally that these "clear facts serve as a basis" for the conclusion of this last chapter, "which is but a systematic digest of the Chinese doctrine, worthy to be used as a model for all states." Derived directly from the theory of China as an example, the views of Quesnay himself, as summarized in this chapter, are obviously of greater reference value for our future concrete examination of the origins of various basic economic theories in Quesnay's system. They are to be cited later, and thus only the titles of the sections are copied here for reference:

1. Constitutive laws of nations
2. Tutelary authority
3. Diversity of the governments conceived by men
4. Assurance of the rights of the nation
5. The natural laws establish a bond between the sovereign and the nation
6. The constitutive laws of the nation are not of human origin
7. The right of taxation is securely founded
8. The natural law
9. The demonstration of the fundamental laws of a government will suffice to assure the natural law
10. Necessity for the study and teaching of the natural and fundamental laws of nations
11. Various types of nations
12. Agricultural nations
13. Government of agricultural nations in their primitive simplicity
14. Community of goods, their natural and peaceful distribution; personal liberty; ownership of the necessaries produced daily
15. Wars of nation against nation
16. The defense of nations is secured by armies; the armies require wealth; wealth is made secure by the armies
17. Establishment of an agricultural nation wherein the required conditions exist naturally

18. Institution of a tutelary authority
19. Positive legislation
20. Public revenue
21. Exclusive selfish interests should be discouraged
22. Reduction in the cost of justice
23. The law of nations
24. Accounting for public funds

From the above, it can be seen that Quesnay's masterpiece, *Despotism in China*, covers almost every field of Chinese politics, society, economy and ethics. These intellectual materials from China provide clear directions and concrete clues for us to understand and examine the Physiocratic system represented by Quesnay.

Now we come to the source of the main materials that Quesnay used to write the above book. According to his own account, Quesnay seemed to have consulted mainly Du Halde's *Description de l'Empire de la Chine*, supplemented by the works of other travelers that were not cited by Du Halde, that is, a list of more than ten reference works included in the notes at the end of the first section of Chap. 1. In addition, there are still some frequently cited important reference books that are not included in this list, such as Rousselot de Surgy's *Mélanges Intéressans et Curieux*. Some Western scholars, after careful examination, have concluded that Surgy's collection is Quesnay's primary source of information on China, and claimed that in the first seven chapters of Quesnay's work, almost all of the quoted material comes from the collection, and Quesnay only occasionally compressed and changed some relevant parts and introduced some simple transitional paragraphs. Pinot even thinks that Quesnay was too biased in favor of China and distorted the facts as described by Surgy. Maverick (1946, p. 127) shares Pinot's view, but disapproves of his exaggeration of Quesnay's prejudice. In fact, all knowledge of China at that time, spread by whomever it was, came mainly from the reports of Western missionaries to China, supplemented by references to the many accounts of merchants or travelers to the country. Quesnay (1946, p. 143) himself admitted, "We have scarcely anything to rest upon except the reports of missionaries." Therefore, for our research, what matters is not whose works that Quesnay cited came from, but how his use of the popular Chinese materials influenced his theoretical system.

2 Turgot: Author of *Refléxions*

Turgot (1727–1781) is another key representative of Physiocracy.[6] Marx (1969, p. 54) claims that "[with] *Turgot* [the Physiocratic system is] most fully developed,"[7] while some other Western economists regard him as more of a politician and economist than a pure economist like Quesnay. Such clues, along with his long political career as a government official, may lead us to conclude that his reception of the influence from China is unique to a certain extent.

I. Turgot's direct contact with Kao and Yang

The Jesuits' arrival in China was followed by numerous Chinese scholars going to study in Europe. According to historical records, the earliest Chinese student was Emmanuel de Sequeira, born in Xiangshan, Guangdong Province. He went to Rome with the Italian priest Martino Martini in 1654 to "explore the origin of things" and returned to the East in 1671. Shortly afterwards, the French missionary Philippe Couplet returned to Europe in 1681 with 400 Chinese books, and invited Shen Fuzong and other young Chinese priests to accompany him on a trip to the West in order to translate the Chinese texts. It is said that the Sinology in France began here. In 1707, in order to clarify the controversy over rites, the Qing court sent Fan Shouyi to Europe along with a Frenchman named Antonio Francesco Giuseppe Provana. Fan returned to China in 1719 and wrote *Shen Jian Lu*, the first Chinese-authored European travelogue. Since then, the number of Chinese students studying in Europe increased gradually until the eighteenth century, when cultural exchanges between China and the West were at their peak, which was also the prerequisite for Turgot to have direct contact with Chinese students.

Moreover, since the 1680s, it had been the national policy of France to encourage visits to China and strengthen contacts with the Eastern country. First, Chancellor of the Exchequer Colbert actively worked out a plan to send French missionaries to China, and then his successor Marquis de Louvois put it into practice. The first batch of missionaries arrived in China in 1687. This national policy in the time of Louis XIV had aroused great interest among the French in the arrival of Chinese in France. In 1702, Huang Jialue,[8] a Chinese native of Xinghua, Fujian Province, was sent to Paris by Jesuits in China, and was hospitably treated. The researchers of the

---

[6] In the works on the history of Western economic doctrine, Turgot is generally seen as a "fellow traveler" of the Physiocrats rather than one of them, since Turgot himself repeatedly stated that he refused to join any sectarian group. This wish is best illustrated by the following statement he made to Mirabeau: "I am not an encyclopœdist, for I believe in God: I am not an *économiste*, for I should wish to have no king" (Quoted in Higgs, 1897, p. 75).

[7] Upon this point, Oncken disagrees, arguing that Turgot, together with all the other Physiocrats, failed to understand the true spirit of Quesnay's doctrine, which is refuted by Rozenberg (1934–36).

[8] In the various early materials, Huang Jialue has been called "the certain Huang," or simply "Huang," and there are many omissions in the record of his deeds in France. In 1985, D. Eliseff, a researcher at the Institut Supérieur d'Études Experimentales, published *I, Huang Jialue, the Chinese translation of the Sun King*, a literary and historically-based monograph, in which he published some of the results of Huang's research in France, attracting the attention of academics.

then Royal Library of France took the opportunity to set up a group mainly devoted to the study of China, including some Sinologists who later became renowned in their time. Even Louis XIV ordered E. Fourmont, who had language ability, to learn Chinese from Huang, in order to write an introductory Chinese book suitable for the French, and revive Chinese language studies (Fang, 1987, p. 12).[9]

This policy of paying attention to China was followed by Louis XV and Louis XVI. Louis XV's Preceptor, Cardinal de Fleury, a famous politician who had held real power for 17 years since he succeeded the Duke of Bourbon in 1726, was a Jesuit by birth and his pro-China attitude was clear. Henri Léonard Bertin, Louis XV's minister, was an active advocate of Chinese culture. Inspired by the Chinese materials sent back by the Jesuits in China, Bertin copied the Chinese in many matters and led King Louis XV to love many aspects of China, including its relics and customs (Sacy, 1970). It was under the administration of Bertin that Turgot's contact with the two Chinese students took place, which was in fact made possible by direct personal recourse to Bertin. Louis XVI, having been influenced in his early years by the Chinese culture instilled by Quesnay and others, paid special attention to the theories of the Physiocrats with the Chinese ideal as their banner. Therefore, as soon as he ascended the throne in 1774, he appointed Turgot to take charge of the country with a view to carrying out the policy advocated by the Physiocrats.

The emphasis on China, which had been part of the policy of successive French administrations, must have made a deep impression on Turgot, who had long been a bureaucrat. Born into a family of high-ranking government officials, Turgot graduated from the seminary at an early age, and soon afterwards realized his wish by moving into judicial and administrative work. He was originally appointed as a judicial officer, and then visited the south and west of France in 1755 and 1756 with Gournay, the Intendant du Commerce. In 1761 he was appointed Intendant of the Généralité of Limoges, a post he held for 13 years until 1774, when he became Contrôleur Général des Finances of France. As a man of eminence with a long-term political experience, under the control of the national policy of attaching importance to China at that time, he would often look to China for theoretical and practical lessons to learn when studying economic problems and formulating economic policies.

Many of those close to Turgot were also passionate followers of Chinese culture. One of them was Voltaire, an advocator of total sinicization, with whom Turgot was always on good terms. He wrote to Voltaire when he took office as Intendant of Limoges, expressing his great respect for Confucius: "It is to Limoges that I am sent. I should have much preferred Grenoble, whence I could have made little pilgrimages to the shrine of Confucius in order to learn of the High Priest" (Quoted in Say, 1888, p. 71). What a devout follower of Confucius!

The greatest influence on Turgot's understanding of China at that time, however, came from Poivre. Poivre had been to India and Canton, China, between 1740 and 1756, and on his return he gave two addresses on agriculture for the Academy of Lyons in 1763 and 1764, based on what he had seen and heard during his travels.

[9] On the status of Fourmont in Western Sinology, Fang Hao (1987, p. 12) says that "he is the teacher of all the early French scholars of Sinology, and is called the founder of modern Sinology."

These addresses were first circulated in manuscript form, and then published in 1769 as the *Voyage d'un Philosophe*. Turgot mentioned these two manuscripts in 1765, so the situation of China described in the two certainly attracted his attention. In his articles, Poivre (Quoted in Maverick, 1946, pp. 43–44) placed great emphasis on the government's function of protecting agriculture, arguing that China had such a wise government that ruled according to a rational plan:

> Agriculture flourishes in China more than in any other country in the world; yet it is not to any process peculiar to their labour, it is not to the form of their plough, or their method of sowing, that this happy state, and the plenty consequent on it, is to be attributed; it must chiefly be derived from their mode of government, the immovable foundations of which have been laid deep, by the hand of reason alone, coëval almost with the beginning of time, and from their laws, dictated by nature to the first of the human race, and sacredly preserved from generation to generation, engraved in the united hearts of a great people.
>
> ...
>
> The whole attention, in general, of the Chinese government is directed towards agriculture.

That is why Poivre (Quoted in Reichwein, 1925, p. 92) openly appealed to Europeans: "China offers an enchanting picture of what the whole world might become, if the laws of that empire were to become the laws of all nations. Go to Peking! Gaze upon the mightiest of mortals; he is the true and perfect image of Heaven."

Poivre's description of ideal China, and in particular China's agriculture-oriented thought, had enthralled the Physiocratic School. For a theorist and policy implementer like Turgot, however, the influence of China seemed to have been more evident in his reforms. During his administration in Limoges, he "reformed the method of collecting the Taille, substituted a money payment for the forced labour of the Corvée, brought about the free circulation of corn within the Généralité, and established a system of poor relief" (Ashley, 1898, pp. v–vi). In the two years he served as Contrôleur Général des Finances of France from 1774 to 1776, he introduced a series of important reforms, such as "the establishment of freedom in the internal corn-trade, [and] the substitution for the Corvée of a tax to which the privileged classes were also to contribute" (p. vi). At the same time, he suggested, according to Léon Say (1888), that Louis XVI should respect frugality and lead by example, and take caring for civilians as the guiding ideology of financial reform, hoping that the king would compare the poor state of the seized with that of the privileged classes, which means that the privileged class must pay taxes. The above reform measures and their guiding viewpoints were in line with the basic spirit of China's successive economic reforms since the Middle Tang Dynasty. For Turgot, a French reformer who was familiar with China and devoted to collecting information about China, this phenomenon cannot be explained by mere historical coincidence. The national school plan drawn up by Turgot during his tenure as Contrôleur Général des Finances of France was very likely a result of his acceptance of China's precedent through the school proposal of the Physiocrats. Therefore, we may well speculate that some specific contents of Turgot's economic reform were inspired by China to a certain extent. This is by no means a fanciful statement. The truthfulness of this speculation is especially reflected in the direct contact between Turgot and the two Chinese students.

In 1763, Turgot was informed of the presence in Paris of two young Chinese who had completed their training as Christian priests and were waiting to return to China. The two were Kao Lei-se and Yang Teh-wang.[10] Having always had a keen interest in China, Turgot saw this as a great opportunity to learn about the real situation in China and to acquire all kinds of knowledge about the country. He persuaded Bertin to invite in the name of the government the two young men to stay for another year, so that they could learn about French science, agriculture and industry (Kao and Yang had been mainly studying theology), with a view to taking to China the situation of France, and to better collecting and understanding similar materials in China before sending them back to France. Turgot's proposal was adopted by Bertin, who also paid close attention to Chinese affairs, and asked Louis XV to approve it. It can be seen that this matter attracted great attention in France at that time.

During the extended period, Kao and Yang went to central France on the orders of Louis XV to inspect the workshops of the textile, printing and dyeing, and metal-working, as well as those of weapons manufacturing, paper making and the use of acids,[11] and often reported directly to Bertin their inspection results, especially the similarities and differences between Chinese and French technologies. At the same time, some French professors offered physics, natural history, chemistry and other courses, and instructed them in painting and copper plate engraving for their

[10] Kao (1733–1780) and Yang (1780–1787) were both born in Beijing, their parents being Christians. They were known to Westerners as Louis Ko and Etienne Yang. They studied at a church school in Beijing, and in July 1751 they were allowed to go to France, first to Guangdong and Macao, and then in January 1754 to France on an Indian company ship with a man named Louis Teheng. After arriving in France, he studied French and Latin at the Collège royal de La Flèche, as well as theology and logic. When the Jesuits were dissolved in 1763, Kao and Yang were able to continue their studies with an annuity of 750 livres, thanks to the appeal of some French authorities. In January 1765, Kao and Yang set sail for China, first arriving in Guangzhou in mid-June and then in Beijing in January of the following year, where they were well received by the missionaries. It is said that their return to China was not impeded by the Qing government, thanks to the good offices of the aforementioned Chen, who had returned three years earlier. Kao remained in contact with the Jesuits in France afterwards, and eventually died in Beijing. Yang went to Jiangxi as a missionary and died there (Li, 1922, pp. 166–180).

[11] Maverick (1946, p. 46) points out, "In 1764, Poivre received in Lyons these two young priests, Ko and Yang (Kao Lei-se and Yang Teh-wang), and took them through textile and dye plants. He also took them to the recently vacated college of the Jesuits, where, in the library, he showed them the thirty-two manuscript volumes of the great history of China, which Father de Mailla had prepared a generation before, and which was ultimately to be published in the decade of the 1780's. He wrote to Bertin, suggesting certain lectures about the chemistry of dyes, from which he thought the young men might profit." In another place, Maverick (1940, p. 315) mentions that, in the meantime, Poivre "had given them many samples of industrial products."

Poivre mentioned the two in his address delivered to the Academy of Lyons in 1764. In 1765, the two Chinese sailed to China. A year later, he was appointed Intendant of the Isle de France (Mauritius, in the Indian Ocean) and the neighboring island of Reunion, and acted, because of his rich knowledge of the East, as the "outpost of France in the exchange of industrial and scientific information." When Kao and Yang returned to China, they took with them industrial samples, as gifts from Louis XV to Emperor Qian Long, and later a shipment of Gobelin tapestries, together with the pensions or honoraria for the two young men, were entrusted to Poivre (pp. 44, 58). It is said that part of the gifts can be specified as lamé, decorative glass, ceramics, hand-held printing presses, electrical instruments, telescopes, hidden boxes, microscopes, gold watches, etc.

future correspondence upon their return to China. These professors were amazed at the two Chinese students' ability to explain and experiment on natural phenomena, which exceeded that of ordinary French students. That is why future generations of scholars, when studying this rare event in the history of Sino-French cultural exchange, mention that Kao and Yang had "extraordinary intelligence." In fact, these investigations and studies were basically arranged according to Turgot's intention. The two Chinese youths also attended the weekly gathering of the Physiocratic School, were received by Quesnay and his friends, and were often invited to give lectures. For the French, they were not students from abroad, but specialists and scholars. Reichwein (1925, pp. 102–103) regards Kao as "a Chinese *savant*, [...] who for thirteen years was a prominent figure in the scientific world, and from whom Quesnay must have learnt many particulars." All this was inseparable from the active efforts of Turgot. The French government's plan to exchange for China's industrial and agricultural materials and products through Kao and Yang, according to Poivre's letter to Bertin, was advocated by Turgot, and his expectation was very urgent. Therefore, the French of that period often referred to Kao and Yang as "les Chinois de Turgot" (Maverick, 1946, p. 45).

The significance of Turgot's association with Kao and Yang lies not only in the famous economist's direct contact with the two Chinese, but also in the fact that it gave birth to an important economic work that attracted much attention.

II. *Réflexions*

Réflexions sur la Formation et la Distribution des Richesses (abbreviated as *Réflexions*) enjoys a high reputation in the history of economic theory. Ashley (1898, p. xii) points out in the "Introduction" to his English translation of the book that "the fundamental Physiocratic ideas [...] find in the *Reflections* their briefest and most lucid expression," and, more notably, that Physiocracy, as elaborated in the work, has contributed to the production of the *Wealth of Nations* "in raising questions in Adam Smith's mind, which left to himself he would never have put, and in providing him with a phraseology which of himself he would never have hit upon" (p. xiii). Cossa (Quoted in Higgs, 1897, p. 94) argues,

> [T]his work states in a clear and taking form the common doctrines of the Physiocrats, but it also marks a step forward in the history of our science, since Turgot achieved in it a complete separation of economics from jurisprudence. It therefore deserves to be entered in red-letter, as the first scientific treatise on social economics.

Schumpeter (1954a) also thinks that "Turgot's theoretical skeleton is ... distinctly superior to the theoretical skeleton of the *Wealth of Nations*" (p. 248), and even that this book "looks as Marshall's *Principles* would look" (p. 248). These evaluations, correct or not, show that *Réflexions* occupies a very important position in the history of economic theory.

For our study here, it is even more important to note that the book was originally written for two Chinese students. Turgot (1898, pp. 110–111) himself wrote to Du Pont shortly after the completion of *Réflexions*, stating that "I have drawn up some questions for the two Chinese I have mentioned to you; and to enable them to see their object and meaning, I have prefaced them by a sketchy sort of analysis of the labours of Society and of the distribution of riches." Later, in a letter to Fucker, Turgot also referred to *Réflexions*, which was "made in response to the desire of the two Chinese in France to make them acquainted with certain questions concerning the economic state of their country and its institutions" (Quoted in Li, 1922, p. 172). About four years later, in a letter to Caillard, he again said, "You must make sure that the preface to the German translation of this work will include the following: 'This pamphlet is not intended for publication at all, but as an introduction to the questions of the economic state of China, to be presented to the two Chinese who wish to have a general idea of the answer to these questions'" (p. 172). In this way, Turgot repeatedly emphasized that *Réflexions* was written with the motive of satisfying the two Chinese, lest the world should forget it.[12]

Turgot wrote two things for the Chinese students at the time. One is an instruction on the study of China, the so-called *Questions sur la Chine* (abbreviated as *Questions*), which consists of 52 questions to be answered by the two Chinese students after their return to China, based on the study of the economic situation and economic system of their own country, so that French people could have a comprehensive and systematic grasp of economic information about China. It is said that, after writing this collection of questions, Turgot "read it aloud once to Kao and Yang for their attention" (p. 171). *Questions* was soon known to Quesnay as well.

The other is the well-known masterpiece, *Réflexions*. This work was at first a brief analysis to help the two Chinese students understand the set of questions, so Turgot called it the "Preface" to *Questions*. *Réflexions* and *Questions* are thus obviously complementary to each other. It is only in the hands of future generations of economic scholars that *Réflexions* is listed as a separate object of study, and the original sister text, *Questions*, is ignored. *Réflexions* was written for Kao and Yang, and its content should clearly be familiar to them.[13] According to Turgot, it was "presented" to them. Therefore, it remains not a mystery—as is mistakenly believed by Li Jingneng (1979, p. 68)—that it was through Kao and Yang that *Réflexions* and *Questions* were introduced into China.

The problem lies in the fact that both of them had returned to China as Christian priests and had been engaged in missionary work, so in their connection with Europe, they need to first or mainly answer the questions raised by the Christians.[14]

---

[12] Just because Turgot himself emphasized this fact strongly, it is specially noted in many extant works on the history of economics that the work is written for two Chinese. Schumpeter (1954a, p. 247), for example, states in his *History of Economic Analysis* that it "was written for the benefit of two Chinese students."

[13] It has been suggested that Kao and Yang were involved in the preparation of Turgot's *Réflexions* (Zhang, 1983b, p. 33). For this claim, however, no conclusive evidence has been found in relevant influential monographs.

[14] As Kao and Yang were about to return to China, the Jesuits asked the following questions to be answered in the form of regular reports upon their return to China. These questions were related to the following: (1) public law, including Chinese chronology, history, religion, politics, police, army and treasury revenues; (2) Genesis, the Flood, the early history of mankind, the state of population distribution and the origin of language and writing; (3) private law, including the laws of China for

In addition, Turgot's economic theory of Physiocracy, as the theoretical embodiment of capitalist social economy, "lacked an economic basis for a foothold" in the feudal society of China during the Qian Long era. As a result, when *Réflexions* was introduced into China, it was not at all clear that it had any resonance in Chinese society.

Undoubtedly, the writing of *Réflexions* should be dated after the completion of *Questions* and before Kao and Yang left France and returned to China in January 1765. However, the extant French original of *Réflexions* and its translations into other languages all date its completion to November 1766. In his introduction to the first part of this work, published in the November 1769 issue of the *Ephémérides*, Du Pont (1898, p. 1) stated that *Réflexions* was written by Turgot "three years ago, very hastily and for a particular purpose," that is, in 1766, not before January 1765. Yet no one in Western academic circles disputes the date of Kao's and Yang's departure for China in January 1765. Thus, this leaves an obvious gap between the writing date of *Réflexions* and the date of return of its two young receivers or the original readers. There are two explanations for this, one being that the January 1765 return date of the two Chinese youths is wrong,[15] and the other being that *Réflexions* was written in November 1766. Only one can be true.

The question is raised because it involves an important debate in the history of economics: Who influenced whom, or who gave greater influence to the other, between Turgot and Adam Smith? We know that Smith accompanied the Duke of Buccleuch on a two-year tour of France and returned in October 1766. During this time he befriended the Physiocrats and established close relations with Turgot in particular. Closely related to this historic contact between Smith and French economists is the fact that modern scholars generally admit that Smith was greatly helped by the Physiocrats. However, there are many dissenters, especially some economists in English-speaking countries, who believe that Smith's contacts with Turgot have had an important impact on Turgot's economic theory, one of their arguments being that *Réflexions* was written in November 1766, that is, after they got to

---

the maintenance of personal and social order; (4) the habits of the people and scientific industries, including the clothing, food and housing of the people, the industries and businesses that benefited the people, and the customs, habits and sciences.

In his first detailed report on Chinese antiquity, written after his return to China, Kao describes the origins and development of Chinese literature and science, the ancient classics such as *The Analects of Confucius*, *The Great Learning*, *The Middle Mean*, *The I-Ching*, *The Book of Poetry*, *The Book of Filial Piety*, *Zuo Zhuan*, *The Rites of the Zhou* and *The Book of Rites*, the history books of Sima Qian, Ban Gu and Sima Guang, the origins of China, the geography, politics, customs, population, scholarship and religion of Yao, Shun and Yu, and so on. In particular, the report introduces the theories that conform to the Westerners' understanding, such as that arguing for China as a colony of ancient Egypt.

[15] Recently, some Chinese scholars have pointed out that Yang and Kao's return to China in 1765 may have been erroneous, on the grounds that *Questions* and *Réflexions* prepared by Turgot for their investigation back in China were written in 1766, so their return could not have been earlier than 1766 (Wu, 1989, p. 148 [Note 3]). However, it is also possible to argue that Turgot could have written his *Questions* and *Réflexions* no later than 1765, since Kao and Yang returned to China in 1765. It seems that more evidence is needed to clarify this issue.

know each other. In fact, it is not credible to assert that Turgot was more influenced by Smith just because *Réflexions* was written after his contact with Smith. However, the conclusion that the first draft of *Réflexions* had been completed as early as January 1765, before Turgot and Smith met, if verified, would be useful to solve the above dispute and to study the theoretical sources in the founding period of the economic science. Strangely, in the past two hundred years, no one in western scholarship, including that of France, has pointed out this obvious gap.

Let us now look at the main points of *Questions* and those that intrinsically connect it to *Réflexions*.

Questions (Turgot, 1844, pp. 310–321; Quoted in Maverick, 1946, pp. 47–58) consists of four parts, with a total of fifty-two questions (and some accompanying "observations").

The first part, "Wealth, Distribution of the Lands, and Agriculture," covers the first thirty questions. This is in terms of economics the most important part of the whole work. It mainly asks about the "rich" class in China, involving those who own a great amount of land and houses, large enterprisers, large merchants, and big money-lenders, as well as the classification of their properties; the relationship between officers and the rich, and the standard of salaries of high ranking officials; the distribution of land and the method of cultivation; the annual income from land, the sale of land, and the relationship between the sale price of land and its annual income; the proportion of arable land for rice to that for wheat; interest rate standards; annual per capita food consumption standards; daily wage rates for workers and their differences between Beijing and the rest of the country; the land tax system; the free trade of food and the average annual price of grain in Beijing, and so on.

Four observations are inserted in this part. First, it is pointed out that a large amount of capital for operating industry and commerce can be invested in joint ventures, and profits can be distributed according to the investment ratio of each person: "It is therefore possible for a country to have a great deal of industry and commerce without there being any great fortunes or an excessive inequality among the fortunes" (Maverick, 1946, p. 47). Second, it is considered that those engaged in agriculture, industry and commerce should not specialize in military or other administrative duties, otherwise they would have to abandon their jobs that give them subsistence, thus reducing the income of the nation: "There are none but the landlord who receives an income without working, and the lender of money who receives interest, who can, without disturbing either their fortunes or the system of productive work, devote themselves to all sorts of occupations, to the study of science, and to the public functions of war, justice and administration" (p. 48). However, China's imperial examination system also provided opportunities for the children of wealthy farmers or wholesalers to fill official positions, "so that it is not absolutely necessary … that there be landlords or money lenders who receive a large income without work" (p. 49). Third, the French criteria for distinguishing categories of property are put forward for reference in classifying the wealthy in China. Fourth, Turgot explains the method of calculating the average annual price of rice.

The second part, "The Arts," covering Questions 31–45, is divided into three aspects: Paper-Making, Printing and Textiles, all of which are very specific and technical. At the same time, Turgot expresses his desire to obtain Chinese samples or models of these technological machinery and products. In fact, his interest in Chinese arts production is by no means limited to the above aspects. In his collection, we find on the back of a book the words "On the Utility of Bronze" written by a Chinese writer. Turgot is eager to know the Chinese technology in an amazingly detailed way. In Chinese printing, for example, he asks in detail whether the paper is wet before printing; whether the ink used for printing is the same as that used for writing; whether the ink is soaked in oil; whether the ink is applied directly to the tablet, or applied with a brush, or with a fur ball; in the course of roll-over printing on the back of paper, whether the tablet and paper are placed under a press, or whether the paper is placed on top of a blackened tablet and then applied with a brush or a wooden stick to a blackened tablet, etc.

The third part, "Natural History," covers the next four issues. The main purpose is to understand the types, distribution and reserves of minerals in China, and to give very detailed instructions on the specific matters of collecting and sending mineral samples.

The fourth part, "Questions on a Few Points of History," covers the last three questions. The first is about the history of the Jews in China and the holy scriptures they use. The second is about the language, physiognomy and skin color of Miao people and their similarities and differences with the Chinese in the surrounding provinces. And the third is whether the Tartars, who have been nomadic, adopt Chinese customs, farming and arts after their assimilation, and especially whether the late emperors Kang Xi and Yong Zheng have a more Chinese way of living and thinking than their predecessors.

The above discussion shows Turgot's unique sensitivity to and scrutiny of the various projects related to China, reflecting his familiarity with the knowledge of China that was being introduced to the West at that time. The Chinese materials he made use of went beyond the few famous monographs that were then popular in Europe, and included lesser-known materials, such as the memoirs of the former Abbé de Verthamont (Quoted in Maverick, 1946, p. 55), and the introduction to China by P. Antoine Thomas. In particular, he attached great importance to acquiring first-hand information about China, such as that from Poivre, who had been to China, and especially to establishing close contact with Kao and Yang. In a word, Turgot's enthusiasm for Chinese things matches Quesnay's and has its own characteristics. Its main feature is the practical spirit displayed throughout *Questions*. As Maverick puts it, Turgot, like Leibniz before him, urged the French government to "secure reliable, factual information about that remote land (China), over which so many rosy mists had been spread" (Maverick, 1946, pp. 112–113).

Réflexions, that is, the preface to *Questions*, if investigated alone, seems to have little to do with China except that the price comparison between silver and gold in China is mentioned in Section 46 of Part 101 (Turgot, 1898, p. 41). However, it is not difficult to find many things in common between *Réflexions* and *Questions*.

Firstly, the two works are consistent in basic structure. The research object of *Réflexions* is the formation and distribution of wealth, and the first part of *Questions* is mainly about China's income of the rich, land income, interest income from lending, tax system, official salary, wages and so on, which belong to the field of wealth distribution.

Secondly, both study the formation and movement of capital. In *Réflexions*, Turgot proposes five methods of applying capital (pp. 50–65). These five are all dealt with in *Questions*: whether there were many people in China who owned large amounts of land, houses or estates; or renters of land who provided agricultural advances; or many very rich entrepreneurs who employed large numbers of workers to work and produce large quantities of goods; or many very rich merchants who engaged in big business. In particular, Turgot devotes in *Réflexions* considerable space to discussing the fifth method of using capital, i.e., "the loan upon interest" (p. 65), and in line with this, he repeatedly mentions in *Questions* the issue in China. He regards debtors and landlords as suitable for the military and political positions of the state without affecting the country's production of wealth, and able to "give heed to motives more noble, such as the love of glory, the desire for esteem, and the love of the public good" (Maverick, 1946, p. 48). The esteem for the moneylender and interest collector here is fully consistent with that in *Réflexions*, which dismisses those who hated moneylenders and interest collectors as "moralists, more rigid than enlightened" (Turgot, 1898, p. 68).

Thirdly, both deal with land differences and land cultivation methods. In terms of land differences, Turgot repeatedly argues in *Réflexions* that "[t]he diversity of soils and the multiplicity of wants lead to the exchange of the products of the land for other products" (p. 3). He notes in *Questions* the variety of rice in the southern provinces and wheat in the northern provinces of China, as well as the eating habits of the Chinese people, thus asking the question about the exchange of agricultural products. In *Questions* he also shows a keen interest in China's long-standing practice of setting taxes according to land distinctions. In terms of land cultivation methods, he lists in *Réflexions* five different ways in which landowners made land provide income (pp. 17–25). This is expressed in various forms in *Questions*: whether most of the land under cultivation in China was worked by the landowners themselves or by tenants who paid annual rents to the landowners; whether slave farming was used in some areas; whether it was common to lease land to tenant farmers who paid one half or one third of their harvest; whether the landowners provided advances and supplied livestock for these tenants; whether it was customary to lease land to the tenants who made advances and had their own animals for farming, and who paid a certain amount of silver or grain to the landowners each year; whether the landowner leased the land permanently; whether tenancy practices varied from place to place in China, depending on the land's fertility and the distance from it to markets and commercial areas; whether horse farming was used in provinces where tenant farming was established; what was the maximum area of land that could be cultivated by a single person in China and the area of land owned by a single farmstead; whether the land was finely divided; whether the buying and selling of land was common, and so on. In a word, each of the farming methods envisaged in *Réflexions* was to be verified, either positively or negatively, in the Chinese example. This method of research, which was devoted to finding the basis of economic theory in China, may seem strange to later generations, whereas it was commonplace in France at the dawn of political economy. The subtleties of this approach are praiseworthy.

Fourthly, the two are mutually complementary in coverage. *Questions* contains only those questions that still have doubts or need to be further confirmed, omitting those that have been confirmed and praised, such as the prioritization of agriculture, which is integrated into *Réflexions*. In his analysis of the formation of wealth, Turgot in *Réflexions* gives primacy to the work of the farmers and repeatedly emphasizes it (pp. 7–9), while in *Questions*, in addition to his emphasis on "wealth—distribution of land—cultivation," Turgot does not specifically raise the question of whether or not China was emphasizing agriculture. This reflects the fact that the idea of emphasizing agriculture in China was deeply rooted in French theoretical circles and became an indisputable fact, so there was no need to reintroduce it as an issue. Another case in point is his inclusion into *Réflexions* (p. 41) of China's gold-silver exchange rate (twelve ounces of silver for one ounce of gold) of that time, which can be categorized as the discussion of currency.

In short, we can find through the above analysis that many of the economic theories put forward in *Réflexions* are related to the study of China to varying degrees: to be verified by Chinese examples, to be inspired by Chinese problems for further development, or to directly absorb nourishment from ancient Chinese thoughts. At least, the views put forward are very similar to Chinese thoughts. Ishida Mikinosuke (1941, p. 148), a Japanese scholar, is quite right in saying that *Réflexions* has been the most deeply influenced by China. The "Introduction" to the English translation of the book also says that the book was written because "China was commonly regarded by the French economists of the time as the peculiar home of enlightened government; and these young men were expected to keep their European patrons informed upon the internal affairs of their country" (Ashley, 1898, p. viii). In other words, *Réflexions* was prompted by the *Zeitgeist* of admiration for China. However, this work was written in a hurry, providing only a theoretical framework, and many economic viewpoints are not fully developed, so that their relationship with Chinese thought is obscured to some extent. Fortunately, it is only by comparing them with those in *Questions* that we can catch a glimpse of their true relationship. In any case, the fact that Turgot paid so much attention to the two Chinese students and understood through them certain economic issues is a clear indication that he was deeply influenced by China or attached great importance to Chinese issues, and *Réflexions*, as a masterpiece of Turgot's study of Chinese issues, has perpetuated this Chinese influence in the history of economic thought.

3 Reasons for the Admiration

From the above analysis, we now have a better understanding of the Physiocratic admiration of China, especially that of Quesnay and Turgot, two key representatives of the Physiocratic School. Obviously, their attitude to take China as a model in everything was not merely a personal preference or an impulse, but had its own deep political and economic reasons. Such reasons, touched upon in the previous discussion, are still scattered and yet to be sorted out. It is necessary to make further explanations here. In our view, for the Physiocratic admiration of China, at least the following political and economic reasons are worth noting.

First, in France, the reasons that led to the emergence of the Physiocratic School were the same as those that led to its reverence for China.

For the Physiocratic system, "the starting-point is in France, in a predominantly agricultural country, and not in England, a predominantly industrial, commercial and seafaring country" (Marx, 1969, p. 50). Since the Physiocrats based their doctrine on an agrarian socio-economic base, it was not difficult for them to find their intellectual soulmates in China, a country that had been an agrarian country for thousands of years. Moreover, during that period, due to France's mercantilist policy of developing industry and commerce at the expense of the farmers, the whole agriculture was devastated and in extreme decline. Therefore, the Physiocratic School broke with mercantilism from the very beginning and was born in sharp opposition to it. In order to forge a theoretical weapon against mercantilism, the Physiocrats were very likely to look for materials from the Chinese arsenal of thought, which had always insisted on adopting the guiding principle of prioritizing agriculture before industry and commerce. This was especially so at a time when the European intellectual circles could not provide ready-made weapons to criticize mercantilism due to the lack of tradition in this area. "[A]ll the theoretical outlooks which emerge in history," Engels points out, "are to be comprehended only when the material conditions of life of the respectively corresponding epochs are understood and the former are derived from these material conditions" (Marx & Engels, 1966, p. 509). In terms of the material conditions of life that gave rise to the theoretical system of the School, although the bourgeois society of France had already begun to incubate from the feudalist system at that time, the economic characteristic of being mainly agricultural still had great similarities with that of China as a feudal agricultural country, which brought about many common points in attaching importance to agriculture and rejecting mercantilism.

Second, it was precisely because Quesnay and his disciples were convinced that they were sincerely preserving and consolidating the feudal system, that they regarded without fear as a treasure trove of ideas the various prevalent Chinese materials that still belonged to the feudal system of thought.

The Physiocratic system was actually the first systematic understanding of capitalist production, but within the Physiocratic School and among those who interacted with it were many disciples of the aristocracy and feudal dignitaries. Therefore, whenever the School put forward demands on behalf of the bourgeoisie, it always used the "feudal signboard" (Marx, 1992, p. 436) and presented itself as the spokesman of the feudal class. This is what Marx (1969, pp. 51–52) called the contradiction between the feudal appearance and the bourgeois essence in the Physiocratic system. In fact, the distinction between the appearance and the substance of the Physiocratic system has only been understood since Marx proposed it, but Quesnay himself could not have understood it, so that admitting that Quesnay accepted Chinese thought in appearance would be tantamount to saying that Quesnay accepted it in its entirety.

Whether the Physiocratic system with the appearance of feudalism could survive in the long run actually depended on which mode of production it represented. This is however another issue. Our concern here is mainly about how much Chinese thought the system absorbed.

Third, Quesnay's political purpose for top-down reforms by enlightened monarchs, and his resemblance to Confucius in many aspects, naturally led to the Physiocratic enthusiasm about China.

After about 1740, the system of enlightened despotism became the prevailing system in Europe. Quesnay, like many other Enlightenment thinkers in eighteenth-century France, championed an enlightened despotism and advocated top-down reforms by enlightened monarchs to prevent the storms of revolution. Initially he hoped that many of his own reforms could be implemented from the top down through Louis XV, but after this hope was dashed, he pinned his hopes on the dauphin, imagining that the future heir to the throne could become his own believer and realize his claim. For this political purpose, the legends of China's complete enlightened despotism and the various qualities and ideals of an enlightened Chinese emperor undoubtedly gave Quesnay great encouragement, and created in him a strong desire to learn about the political and economic system and all other knowledge about China. Driven by this strong desire, he collected and collated all kinds of Chinese materials with special enthusiasm, and after researching, discovering, and summarizing them, he left us his *Despotism in China*. This work is not only a meticulous depiction of the Chinese political and economic system, but also a true expression of his political beliefs.

It is indeed noteworthy that, at a time of profound economic change, when capitalist relations of production were replacing feudal relations of production, Quesnay's political attitudes and the basic tendencies of his economic rhetoric closely resembled those of his mental image of Confucius. The end of the Spring and Autumn period in China when Confucius was active is an era of alternating old and new feudal lord economy. On the one hand, he was politically very conservative, advocating self-restraint and benevolence and striving to maintain the old aristocratic hierarchical order. On the other hand, he reflected the demands of the emerging landlord class that was undergoing rapid formation in economic thinking. This dual characteristic of being politically conservative while adapting his economic views to the needs of the new era is very similar to that of Quesnay, who, in his political philosophy, remained steeped in the prejudices of the feudal age, but essentially proclaimed in his political economy the establishment of a bourgeois system of production on the ruins of feudalism. Therefore, the fact that he was called by his disciples "the Confucius of Europe" indeed reflects the real implication that Quesnay was deeply influenced by Confucius.

Fourth, the Physiocrats, in an effort to find a way out of the deep financial and economic crisis, which France was facing at the time, by drawing on the development models of other countries in formulating their reform programs, naturally turned their attention to China, which had been longed for at the time.

Here, it should be pointed out that, firstly, the Europeans of the Age of Enlightenment often regarded the past of Europe as a barbaric era and a dark age, and did not pay much attention to absorbing nourishment from the thoughts of their ancestors. The Physiocratic School was certainly no exception. Besides, the School's being based in Paris, the center of the Enlightenment, increased its members' urgency to seek practical reference from outside Europe, especially from ancient China. Secondly, at a time when the Physiocrats were troubled by the severe financial and economic crisis in their own country, the numerous reports about the prosperity that ancient China had enjoyed for thousands of years were indeed very attractive to them. China had been a feudal kingdom with a vast territory since the Zhou Dynasty at the latest, and boasted a history of two to three thousand years, during which, except for a few short divisions, it had maintained a long period of sustained socio-economic prosperity. According to the Marxist principle of the relationship between existence and consciousness, on the basis of such sustained economic prosperity and development in China, certain economic thoughts or theories would inevitably be formed and used as a guide, and such theories and ideas were sufficient to become a valuable source for the Physiocratic School to draw on. Thirdly, the theoretical program designed by the School to cure the morbid French society and economy actually reflected the demands of the emerging bourgeoisie at the end of feudal society, but this did not prevent some of the theories in their program from being directly inspired by ancient Chinese thought. Marx (Quoted in Engels, 1977, p. 275) pointed out,

> Since political economy [...] is in fact nothing but the scientific insight into the economy in the period of capitalist production, principles and theorems relating to it, for example, in the writers of ancient Greek society, can only be found in so far as certain phenomena—commodity production, trade, money, interest-bearing capital, etc.—are common to both societies. In so far as the Greeks make occasional excursions into this sphere, they show the same genius and originality as in all other spheres. Because of this, their views form, historically, the theoretical starting-points of the modern science.

In this sense, since China already has a three-thousand-year history of commodity-currency relations, and ancient Chinese economic thought had been a world leader until the seventeenth century, what Marx said about the contributions of the ancient Greeks to modern bourgeois economic science is equally applicable to the influence of ancient Chinese thought on the Physiocratic system.

Chapter 4
The Natural Order

We have discussed above the vogue for China in Europe, the background to the emergence of Physiocracy, and the Physiocrats' admiration of Chinese culture. In the following chapters, we will focus on all the major theoretical points that possibly link the economic theories of the Physiocrats with ancient Chinese thought. Examined in this chapter is the origin of the doctrine of natural order, that is, the philosophical foundation of Physiocracy, in terms of the Physiocratic concept of natural order itself, its origin in European traditional ideas of natural laws, and the influence from ancient Chinese doctrines.

1 The Physiocratic Concept of Natural Order

Before analyzing the sources of the Physiocratic concept of natural order, we need to have a proper understanding of the basic features of this concept and its place and role in Physiocracy.

I. **Physiocracy: "the science of the natural order"**

Physiocratie, the original French word for physiocracy, is a combination of the Greek words for nature (ψύбιs) and domination (κρατέω). The new word means the domination of nature, that is, human society must obey the laws of nature in order to achieve the highest welfare. This particular term is said to have been coined by Quesnay himself, due to his love of the Greek language and his long medical research and practice—he was thus very familiar with the physiological mechanisms of the human body. Besides, the French word for physiology, *Physiologie*, is very similar to *Physiocratie*. However, at its peak, the Physiocratic School was known as the "Economists." Although Du Pont first introduced *Physiocratie* as the name for their theoretical system in 1767 when he edited an anthology of Quesnay's writings, the term was not generally accepted at that time.

M. Tan, *The Chinese Origin of Physiocracy*,
https://doi.org/10.1007/978-981-97-9703-5_4

Later, Smith (1812), in *The Wealth of Nations*, which was first published in 1776, contrasted the theories of Quesnay and his disciples, who "represent[ed] the Produce of Land as either the sole or the principal Source of the Revenue and Wealth of every Country" (p. 524), with the mercantile system, which valued "the industry of the towns" (p. 525). Unlike the mercantilists, the Physiocrats "under-valued" (p. 526) urban industry and focused solely on agriculture, whose theory was thus called "the agricultural system(s)" as opposed to "the mercantile system" (pp. 524–546). With the popularity of Smith's doctrine, the term *Physiocratie* became synonymous with "the agricultural system." Only Western economic writings still use the original terminology in form, although the content is often based on Smith's interpretation of the term as "agricultural system" or the theory of "emphasizing agriculture." But the economic literature in China and Japan even formally retains the agricultural emphasis of Smith's interpretation, calling Quesnay's group *Zhongnong Xuepai* (literally meaning "the School of Emphasizing Agriculture") or *Zhongnong Zhuyi Zhe* (literally meaning "Agriculture Emphasizers"), and their theoretical system *Zhongnong Zhuyi Tixi* (literally meaning "the system of emphasizing agriculture"). It is no wonder that some Chinese and Japanese scholars have argued that it is wrong to regard Quesnay's theories as emphasizing only agriculture, stressing that such misunderstandings are very dangerous, and have therefore either argued against calling Physiocracy the agricultural system (Idei, 1929, p. 16), or proposed that *Physiocratie* be literally translated as natural political doctrines (Guo, 1934, p. 1).

The Chinese terms for Physiocracy and the Physiocratic School, for all their literal emphasis on agriculture, have been used to this day, and have become commonplace terms that do not need to be changed. However, when we use them, we must not be limited by their literal bias towards agriculture, but should fully understand their original meanings. The so-called Physiocracy, according to Du Pont's definition, is "the science of the natural order" (Quoted in Gide & Rist, 1915, p. 5), or, as Mercier de la Rivière suggests in the title of his work, "[t]he natural and essential order of political societies" (Quoted in Maverick, 1946, p. 137).

II. **The basic features of the Physiocratic concept of natural order**

Since the end of the nineteenth century, the voluminous writings on the theories of the Physiocrats have almost invariably referred to their concept of natural order. Some are penetrating theories while others are divergent views. This has to do with some vague notions of the Physiocrats' own expression of the idea of natural order, as well as the later scholars' excessive exaggeration of the so-called mysterious or confusing aspects of this idea (Taylor, 1955, p. 79),[1] so that some people claim that the Physiocrats never gave a clear definition of the concept (Lin, 1979, pp. 39–40). Eugène Daire, for example, included within a collection of the Physiocrats' works only those parts that fall within the scope of an economics of wealth and dropped the rest as "a very confused assembly of dissertations holding at once to the moral

[1] Taylor's (1955, p. 79) original statement is: "There is some confusion of ideas in the physiocratic conceptions of *lois naturelles*, *droit naturelles*, and *l'ordre naturel*, but not so much confusion, I think, or so much mystery, as has often been supposed."

order, the political order and the material interests of society" (Quoted in Neill, 1948, p. 159). It is evident that the failure to clarify a certain confused state of scholarly interpretation of this concept will directly affect the exploration of its origin, and the comparative analysis of its similarities and differences with traditional Chinese and Western thought.

Our in-depth and detailed analysis of the concept is based on Quesnay's interpretation,[2] supplemented by the expositions of other Physiocrats and the studies of later economists. The basic features of the concept are thus laid out below.

Firstly, the Physiocratic concept of natural order reveals the natural laws that govern human society.

Du Pont once praised Quesnay as "a man of exceptional genius [...], [who] applied his whole intellectual strength to an investigation of the physical laws which govern society" (Quoted in Gide & Rist, 1915, p. 8 [Note 1]). The logic of Quesnay's (1888; 1946) thinking is that, like the material world, there exist objective laws in human society that are not subject to the will of the people, namely, the natural order, which is governed by the supreme laws of nature. However, the natural order of society is different from the laws of the material world. It is not absolutely binding, and people can accept or reject it by their own will, thus establishing the positive order of society, which is manifested in various political and economic systems, laws and regulations of different times and various countries. The positive order is often influenced by irrational motives and is prone to conflict with the most favorable justice of society and the immutable laws of the natural order. If people understand the natural order and act according to its criteria to develop the positive order, the society is in a healthy state; if the positive order violates the natural order, the society is in a state of disease. In the words of Quesnay, the natural order is the supreme law of all man-made legislation, of all civil, political, economic and social conduct, while man-made laws are merely laws concerning the administration of the natural order, made by the supreme power. Such a law can only be established if it is declared to be the natural law upon which the most favorable order of the people united into society is based, and the natural rights of each individual are extended in proportion to the degree to which the best possible law constituting the most favorable order is indeed obeyed.

Quesnay's (1888; 1946) emphasis on the dominant role of natural laws forming the ideal state of society resulting from people's total obedience to such laws constitutes a major hallmark of his idea of natural order. Such natural laws, in the Physiocratic view, are first and foremost objective, in that these fundamental laws are absolutely not created by man, but must be obeyed by any human authority, or in that man cannot create and establish the natural order, just as he cannot create himself. The second point is that these natural laws are supremely good, because they are steadfast, indestructible, and generally of the most excellent character, and may therefore serve as the fundamental laws of the most perfect rule, and of all positive laws. The third is that they are universal, and apply to all ages and to all human powers. The last is that they are unchanging or eternal. The Physiocrats believed that the fundamental

[2] For Quesnay's own interpretation, see his "Le Droit Naturel," and the eighth chapter of his *Despotism in China*.

structure of society and the natural form of domination are established before the promulgation of the positive laws of equitable distribution, and that the rights of mankind are not founded in history, but are rooted in the nature of mankind.

In short, the so-called "natural order" or "natural law," as advocated by the Physiocrats, is perfect, and is not subject to the will of man. The Abbé Baudeau (Quoted in Gide & Rist, 1915, p. 10) once said, "Its fiat was 'unique, eternal, invariable, and universal.' Divine in its origin, it was universal in its scope, and its praises were sung in litanies that might rival the *Ave Maria*."

Secondly, God plays the decisive role in the creation of the natural order.

Quesnay (1946, pp. 270–281) attributed the ideal natural order to the perfection of God, the Creator of nature. He believed that God himself is the creator of laws, and is therefore above all laws, and that the laws He has made are correct, complete and supreme, so that all men must obey them. He also repeatedly mentioned that the natural laws are unchangingly enacted by the Creator, and that the basic laws of society are rooted in the supreme will of the creator.

This was confirmed by other Physiocrats. Mercier de la Rivière (Quoted in Gide & Rist, 1915, p. 8 [Note 2]) said, "Its (natural order's) laws are irrevocable [...]. They are just the expression of the will of God." "The natural order," Du Pont (p. 8 [Note 1]) also claimed, "is merely the physical constitution which God Himself has given the universe." As a matter of fact, the theological concepts of "God" and "the Creator," though casting a religious veil over the natural order of the Physiocrats, did not restrict their in-depth study of the objective socio-economic laws, and God's role in them was only manifested in the creation or formulation of the basic natural laws in the "first" period of society. In other words, once the laws of nature were created, the role of God ceased to exist, and the question that remains is how people perceive and obey these natural laws. This is a key point in our understanding of the Physiocratic idea of natural order, as the following analysis also proves.

Thirdly, the natural order denies religious revelation in favor of the light of reason.

Quesnay (1946) formulated the idea of natural order with the proposition that the supreme law of nature is "clearly distinguished by the light of reason" (p. 275). Like the other Enlightenment thinkers of that period, he understood reason to be the nature of man. In his view, the superiority of man over other animals is rooted in human reason, which in turn derives from the natural order (p. 279). From this premise, the object of study shifted from the religious notion that God had created the natural order to the purely secular realm of human understanding of the natural order. In this new field of study devoid of the will of God, Quesnay gave full play to his imagination and creativity.

Quesnay (pp. 273–278) believed that the necessity of man's knowledge of the natural order lies in the stability and prosperity of the empire, which can be achieved by no other way but recognizing this supreme law. In other words, if in such a state the government is illuminated by the light of reason, the positive laws which are injurious to society and to the monarchy will be abolished. This is the main meaning of "the light of reason." But, just as Neill (1949) has said, Quesnay "was not a rationalist" (p. 546). Quesnay sought a reason deepened, developed and completed by the study of natural law. In his view, "ignorance" is the most harmful flaw to mankind, even a sin; a rational man must overcome ignorance to obtain knowledge and develop reason with a certain degree of clear understanding of natural laws, which is indispensable to the best possible rule (pp. 534–548). Human reason, therefore, is only the capacity and talent necessary to acquire knowledge of the natural order, and is not equivalent to that knowledge itself.

As to the ways or means of acquiring knowledge of the natural order, Du Pont (Quoted in Gide & Rist, 1915, p. 9) said, "[Quesnay] must have seen that man had only to examine himself to find within him an inarticulate conception of these laws. In other words, introspection clearly shows that men are unwittingly guided by an 'inherent' knowledge of Physiocracy." For Quesnay, this introspective enlightenment can only be perfected by those who are "wise." Ordinary people need only be inculcated, through education, with the thought-provoking truths that can only be accurately and clearly understood through the use of reason. Therefore, "[t]he first political establishment of the government [...] will be the instituting of schools for teaching this science" (Quesnay, 1946, p. 271), through the public and private education of the natural order, and the deeper the people know this knowledge, the more the State will be governed by the natural order, and the more the positive order will be perfected, so as to prevent the emergence of tyrants and the distortion of the laws of nature and the fundamental laws (pp. 271–273). In this way, the natural order's fundamental or "supreme legislation [...] is manifested to men through the light of reason, cultivated through education and the study of nature" (p. 277).

It follows that the Physiocrats, on the one hand, emphasized the natural order as the objective laws that make all human reason unconditionally subordinate to them, and on the other hand, believed that the study of these objective fundamental laws leads to a theory which, though not promulgated in the form of a law, is nevertheless valid and reveals some unshakable laws from which statesmen and entire nations can draw examples. In other words, in these same laws may be found the original principles and the unchanging source of positive law and rational distribution (Quesnay, 1888; 1946). Though in speaking of the origin of an objective natural order, they introduced the religious idea of God's creation of all things, when they went on to discuss the intelligibility of this order, they excluded entirely, by their belief in "the light of reason" or "light of wisdom," the existence of religious revelation.[3] This is why Reichwein (1925, p. 107 [Note]) regards it as "the kernel of Quesnay's doctrine, that man can, by learning, acquire a knowledge of the natural laws, and is only by virtue of such knowledge capable of good actions." Harry Landreth (1976, p. 26) argues,

[3] In their discussion of how to acquire the knowledge of the "natural order," Gide and Rist (1915, p. 9) put forward the following question: "Will a divine voice by means of a supernatural revelation show us the way of truth, or will it be Nature's hand that shall lead us in the blessed path?" Their answer is that the Physiocrats seem to have ignored this question. In fact, Quesnay's large number of relevant discussions show that he did not "fail" to pay attention to God's revelatory role, but that he used instead the mundane light of reason to replace the revelatory role. That's why we cannot find in Quesnay's discussions the traces of "God's voice" or "the Creator's hand." This is exactly a distinctive feature of Quesnay's idea of natural order that is different from the past religious explanations.

> The Physiocrats' unique idea was their concept of the role of natural law in the formulation of policy. They held that natural laws governed the operation of the economy and that, while these laws were independent of the will of man, man could objectively discover them as they could the laws of the natural sciences. This idea contributed significantly to the development of economics and the social sciences.

This view is currently shared by many scholars of economics.

In fact, the Physiocrats' advocacy of a prominent role for national education in the understanding of the natural order has had a great impact in Europe and has become an enduring legacy, regarded by Hudson (1931, p. 325) as having "led the way in the eighteenth century in demanding that education should be secularized and that it should be made universal."

Fourthly, the natural order unifies physical and moral law.

This is unique to Quesnay's theory of natural order. In Chapter V of his *Natural Right*, Quesnay (1962, p. 53) states,

> Natural laws are either physical or moral.
>
> I am here taking physical law to mean *the regular course of all physical events in the natural order which is self-evidently the most advantageous to the human race.*
>
> I am here taking moral law to mean *the rule of all human action in the moral order conforming to the physical order which is self-evidently the most advantageous to the human race.*
>
> These laws taken together constitute what is called *natural law*.

Two years later, in the first section of the eighth chapter of *Despotism in China*, Quesnay (1946, pp. 264–265) restates this view in a slightly altered form:

> The constitutive laws of nations are the laws of the Natural Order that are most advantageous to the human race. These laws may be either physical or moral.
>
> The physical constitutive law underlying government is understood to mean the regulated progress of every physical event in the Natural Order that is evidently the most advantageous to the human race. The moral constitutive law is understood to mean the regulated progress of all moral action in the Natural Order that is evidently the most advantageous to the human race. These laws together form what is called the Natural Law.

Quesnay (Quoted in Gide & Rist, 1915, p. 8 [Note 1]) is said to have predicted long ago that "natural laws extended far beyond the bounds hitherto assigned to them." His inclusion of the moral order in the sphere of natural laws is a remarkable sign of his breaking the traditional boundaries. This means that in the moral sphere, as in all other natural spheres, there are objective laws which are completely independent of the will of man, and that the violation of moral laws is also punishable by nature. This idea was described by the Physiocratic School as Quesnay's "great discovery" and marked a "turning point" in the civilized world. The principle of moral law, or moral order, gained such importance among the Physiocrats because they believed that Quesnay had discovered similar laws governing human society in the moral order, following the great laws of harmonious order that governed the material world discovered by Newton and other natural scientists. The Western scholar Thomas P. Neill (1949, p. 537) claims, "The Physiocrats [...] thought that they had discovered a new science, that it was an elucidation of natural law, and that its scope extended to all of man's dealing with man and with nature. It was therefore a moral science governing man's social activity."

Modern scholars have described Quesnay's combination of physical and moral laws as natural laws as "a unique approach," "a revolutionary method" and "a radical departure from tradition." Only in the interpretation of the interrelationship between physical and moral laws do they differ among themselves. In general, however, most of them affirm the following two points. First, by proposing the concept of moral order, the Physiocrats took the lead in bringing the study of objective laws from the field of natural sciences to that of social sciences, especially the economic science. "Political economy as it emerged from this [eighteenth] century," Taylor (1955, p. 71) says, "was [...] a product of [the] interweaving and blending of scientific and ethical idea." Second, in the name of studying moral laws, the Physiocrats explored the laws of nature in the socio-economic field, which was promoted and inspired by the exploration of the laws of nature in the natural sciences.

Fifthly, the various factors of the natural order are organically interdependent.

Quesnay made in the seventh chapter of *Philosophie Rurale*[4] an exemplary remark about this organic nature of the natural order: All things act, only by the interconnection of the various relations and activities in nature. It is said that the elements are in a state of struggle with each other, but at the same time, they support and promote each other. The order and course of this marvelous institution is finally determined by the Creator, and the great laws which regulate all things, are continuous in every part and govern the whole (Mirabeau & Quesnay, 1764). Du Pont considered this doctrine "very novel indeed" (Quoted in Gide & Rist, 1915, p. 2).[5]

The two modern scholars Gide and Rist (1915) argue that, because of this doctrine, the Physiocrats not only "must be regarded as the forerunners of the organic sociologists" (p. 7), but also should be credited to have creatively applied this doctrine of social organism to the analysis of the economic field (pp. 5–12). Based on this principle, Quesnay (1888; 1946) argued that the study of human economic activity should take into account all the aspects that are mutually adapted and mutually reinforcing, as well as their role and different characteristics in the economic organization, and take away all the administrative irregular intervention to pursue the cause and result of the natural order, the relationship between which can only be achieved by the path of simplification. He claimed that, to describe all the elements involved in making up the economic institution, with the aim of understanding the purest truths, it is first necessary to become acquainted with the whole process of this institution's reproduction. The problem here, therefore, is to dissect the institution, to show, by means of anatomy, all its parts, the interrelations of its parts, and the results

[4] *Philosophie Rurale* was published by Mirabeau, but it is generally believed to have been written under Quesnay's direction, with the sixth chapter exclusively credited to Quesnay himself.

[5] In the same place of their book, Gide and Rist (1915, p. 2) think that Du Pont "cannot be said to have exaggerated" in his comment, and corroborate this point by adding a note: "Professor Hector Denis, speaking of the Physiocratic doctrine, remarks that its imperfections are easily demonstrated, but that we seldom recognise its incomparable greatness."

of the interaction of its parts, in order to show the organization of this institution.[6] In assessing Quesnay's doctrine of natural order, Hasbach argues that "his real originality lies in his organic theory of economic life" (Quoted in Higgs, 1897, p. 46). Taylor (1955, p. 77), a modern economist, also argues, "In their (the Physiocrats' and Adam Smith's) schemes of doctrine, political economy became a development of the eighteenth-century notion of a harmonious, 'natural' social order."

Besides the related organic concept, Quesnay attached great importance to "order:" "[L]ove of order," one of his disciples said, was "the ruling passion of his heart" (Quoted in Reichwein, 1925, p. 104). Quesnay's concept of "order" implies harmony or equilibrium. When he advocated a physiological and anatomical approach to the analysis of the organism of socio-economic processes, his concept of natural order could be expressed both as the interrelatedness of the parts of the organism forming a whole, and as the equilibrium of everything in the whole in motion. Society is ideal and healthy only when it is in equilibrium. The idea of equilibrium is thus directly deduced from his doctrine of the organic order of nature.

Sixthly, the natural order has the utilitarian goal of seeking the highest welfare.

For Quesnay (1888; 1946), the natural order is a God-given order for the well-being of mankind, and it is man's duty both to study and understand it and to conform his daily life to it. Since the natural order is in the best interests of mankind, it is only by truly obeying it that we can achieve the greatest possible benefit. In this context, "benefit" refers mainly to material benefits. He said that in order to adapt to the natural order, it is better to subsume the scope of the natural rights of man in the various kinds of material things which he may enjoy, and vice versa, and that the rights suitable to the various kinds of material things which man may enjoy must be considered in the light of the order of nature and the order of justice. The purpose is to maintain the stability and prosperity of the Empire from time to time, to increase sufficiently the wealth necessary for the tutelary authority and to safeguard the interests of the people such as property, liberty and security.

The overriding purpose of Quesnay's natural order is to maximize the happiness of the people. "His (Quesnay's) definition of natural law," Mourant (1949, p. 133) points out, "appears [...] to be more definitely utilitarian in its implication. [...] [T]heir (the Physiocrats') interest is entirely with the development of a social system that will lead to the happiness of man based on more purely utilitarian considerations." Rousseau (1997, p. 270) treated the Physiocratic theory of natural order as a "utopia," but future scholars were to see in Rousseau's description the need to discover the precise nature-made system of institutions, which is necessary to obtain the greatest good for

[6] The so-called "anatomy" mentioned here refers to a method of abstraction. In the second "Dialogue on the Work of Artisans," Quesnay (1962, p. 204) says "that in nature everything is intertwined, everything runs through circular courses which are interlaced with one another. The fact that these different movements are necessarily interconnected means that things can be understood, differentiated, and examined only through the medium of abstract ideas [...]. It is only through the medium of such abstractions that we can examine and appraise the mutual relations between these different classes of men and work in the social order, and give them the designations which conform most closely to their functions, in order to express ourselves in exact terms in the detailed working-out of economic science."

the nation as a whole, and is therefore related to the existing state of things. "The ideal end of all political societies," Du Pont said, "is the same, namely, to make all of their members as prosperous and happy as possible" (Quoted in Taylor, 1955, pp. 83–84). In this light, this utilitarian goal of maximizing welfare is also a fundamental part of the theory of natural order.

Above we have summarized six main features of the concept of natural order. Except for the second, that is, the origin of natural order in terms of God's will, which is limited by Quesnay's times, the other five have different degrees of positive significance for the development of social sciences, especially the economic science, and are not without novelty and uniqueness. Of course, when the natural order is treated as a general concept, it is difficult to trace its origins, especially outside the European tradition. Still, the above excavation of the basic features of the natural order is not without reason, at least in giving us a more comprehensive grasp of the concept, and in making it easier to conduct a finer and deeper comparative analysis of its origins, so as to make a judgment as scientific as possible.

III. **The position and role of the natural order in Physiocracy**

On this issue, there are two opposing views among Western economists. One view is represented by the two French economists Gide and Rist (1915, p. 5), who argue, "The essence of the Physiocratic system lay in their conception of the 'natural order.'" The other is held, for example, by the British economist Meek (1962, p. 373), who strongly opposes the above view, stating, "it would be [...] wrong to suggest [...] that their ideas about 'natural law' somehow lay *at the basis* of their economic analysis, so that their economics must be said to have been derived from their philosophy." He corroborates his argument by quoting Schumpeter: "[N]either the theological nor the naturalist element was really the point from which they started. They merely expressed the results of economic analysis in this theological or naturalist form *after* they had established them" (Meek, 1962, pp. 373–374; Schumpeter, 1954a, pp. 49–50).

The latter view, in fact, inherits the editorial principles of the mid-nineteenth century, when Eugène Daire included within a collection of the Physiocrats' works only those that fall within the scope of an economics of wealth and dropped the rest as "a very confused assembly of dissertations holding at once to the moral order, the political order and the material interests of society" (Quoted in Neill, 1948, p. 159). At the time of the Physiocrats, however, economics had not yet been separated from other disciplines, especially from philosophy. The concept of natural order was mainly a philosophical category, which permeated the various theories of the Physiocrats and formed the philosophical basis of their economic theory. Even Meek (1962, p. 33) himself admits that the Physiocrats' "attempts at a synthesis of economics, politics, and philosophy were accompanied by the invention of the name 'Physiocracy' [...] to embrace all the elements of the wider doctrine." Thus, to deny the guiding role of the idea of natural order in the economic analysis of the Physiocrats, or to regard their concept of natural order as merely a way of expressing the results of economic analysis, is an opinion that risks being detached from the historical conditions of the time.

Back to the Physiocrats themselves. Quesnay (1946, p. 277), when discussing the so-called "light of reason," which reveals the basic laws of the natural order, emphasized in particular, "It is only by this free exercise of reason that men may make progress in economic science, which is a great science, for it is the one that underlies the government of nations." This was confirmed by Du Pont, who, in his "Preface" to Quesnay's *Natural Right*, claims, "What makes the economic science fulfil its fundamental task is, above all, the knowledge of order, and of metaphysical and natural laws. [...] In the supreme law of nature lies the fundamental principle of economic order" (Quoted in Quesnay, 1979, p. 289 [Note 1]). In assembling the writings of the Physiocrats, he also stated that "the science of economics is nothing but the application of the natural order of government to society" (Quoted in Neill, 1948, p. 164). As late as 1815, in a letter to Say, he stressed that "physiocracy 'sets forth with certitude' [...] the natural laws which are most advantageous to men assembled in society" (p. 164). All this shows that in the mind of the Physiocrats, the natural order is undoubtedly the essence of their economic theory, or "the underlying principle on which their economic doctrines were built" (Roll, 1923, p. 128).

The position and role of the natural order in Physiocracy, whether the order is described as the "central idea" or "philosophical basis," have been recognized by most economists. At the same time, the economic theory of the Physiocratic School is inseparable from the exposition of the natural order, which is the unanimously recognized fact in many popular textbooks on the history of economic theory of the East and the West. Therefore, to take the origin of the natural order as one of the focuses of this book is very important for grasping the various basic economic principles of the Physiocrats and searching for the main sources of their entire economic theory. The following is a comparative study of the similarities and differences between the Physiocratic concept of natural order, in terms of first the traditional European concepts, and then the ancient Chinese doctrines, in order to investigate the main sources of the concept.

2 European Traditional Views of Natural Laws

In the writings of Western scholars in general, it is taken as self-evident that the Physiocratic theory of natural order, whenever mentioned, is always associated with the European traditional view of natural law. Disputes arise only in determining the specific views of natural law in European history that this theory of natural order has inherited. Some people believe that it is mainly derived from the views of the Stoic and Roman jurists, or the doctrines about the Stoic and Christian universal salvation. Others trace it back to Plato or Aristotle in ancient Greece, or assert that it is mainly rooted in the medieval philosophy established on the basis of natural laws. Still others only mention that this theory is derived almost entirely from the generally known rational tradition of the Physiocratic era, or specifically state that it first originated in the ancient Greek and Roman conceptions of natural laws and later, by way of Grotius and Locke, became known to the Physiocrats in modern times. The above assertions, however, are only general conclusions that are often based on an individual or partial interpretation of the theory of natural order, or even drawn from the similarities on the literal level. To find the specific source of this Physiocratic theory, we now begin with an overview of the origin of the traditional European natural laws and their main contents.

I. **The origin and purport of traditional natural laws**

Natural laws are one of the oldest in Western civilization,[7] which can be traced back to the Babylonian notion of celestial lawgivers' "legislating" natural phenomena for non-human beings. For jurists in general, however, the legal discourses of ancient Greek philosophers are often cited as the starting point for the formation of the concept of natural law. The natural philosopher Heraclitus had already made the distinction between natural law and man-made law. Later Socrates, in response to the sophistry of the principle that "man is the measure of all things," proposed that "God is the measure of all things." He divided law into uncodified constitution and statute law, the former being the code of human behavior in the world, which is the legislation of God, and the latter being the code of citizen behavior, which is the legislation of man. If there is a conflict between the two, the latter should be discarded in favor of the former. Socrates is therefore called the founder of the doctrine of natural law. Plato in his later years recognized the existence of natural law, but it was still second to the politics of the wise man with the philosopher as king. Aristotle, unlike Plato, advocated the "rule of law" over the "rule of man" and made the distinction between natural law and human law, using natural law as the basis for the formulation of human law, because the latter is variable while the former is permanent. Besides, the natural law that he said reflects the "order of natural existence" that regulates the relations between husband and wife, between father and son, and between master and servant.

Strictly speaking, Zeno of Citium, the founder of the Stoic school of philosophy, is the first to propose the theory of natural law in the ancient Greek era. He believed that natural law is a universal and supreme law, and that its validity far exceeds that of the laws enacted by various states. Conversely, human law should conform to the kind of immutable natural law that represents reason and governs the whole world. At the heart of this School's thought of law is the theory of natural law, which universalizes the concept of natural law.

Roman jurists basically used the Stoic concept of natural law to build their legal theory. They are regarded as having merely regurgitated the natural law theories of the Greeks, without much originality in jurisprudence, but their specific interpretations, through popularization and systematization, constitute a more complete theoretical system of natural law. At the end of the Roman Republic, Cicero first put forward

---

[7] The following accounts of the thought of traditional Western natural law, unless otherwise noted, are based on the following works: Zhang Hongsheng's *History of Western Legal Thought*, The Editorial Board of the History of Western Legal Thought's *Selected Sources on the History of Western Legal Thought*, Shen Zongling's *Modern Western Legal Philosophy*, and Schumpeter's *History of Economic Analysis* (pp. 73–143, "Chap. 2 The Scholastic Doctors and the Philosophers of Natural Law").

the doctrine of natural law in a more systematic way. He believed that the essence of natural law lies in pure reason, and reason is the manifestation of justice, so justice is the principle of natural law, and all laws come from this principle; that natural law embodies the will of God, which is the master of all things; that natural law is of a universal and eternal nature, boasting authority above the legislation of all human societies, and "is a kind of permanent and immutable applicable law of the state in all times;" and that the disobedience of natural law is no different from the denial of pure reason, i.e., self-betrayal.

During the Roman Empire, there was a jurisprudential debate about the relationship between natural law, civil law and *jus gentium*. It was generally agreed that law emerged from natural law, that is, the eternal and universal divine law, and that this traditional doctrine of natural law was embodied in the Justinian Code, completed in 529 A.D. The Code takes natural law as the most basic law, which is the sum of all rules, and this sum comes from the nature of all things, that is, reason, so that natural law determines not only the behavior of man but also that of animals. The universal law is the sum of the rules established by natural reason for all peoples, and is common to all men. Civil law is the positive law made by each nation itself, named according to the country in which it is located. The above division of law, based on the theory of natural law, was established in codified form in ancient Rome.

Broadly speaking, the Greco-Roman jurists still considered natural law as arising from nature. By the Middle Ages, natural law was equated with God's revelation, and reason became a special instinct given to man by God. This is typified by the legal thought of Thomas Aquinas. He divided law into four types: eternal, natural, human and divine law (Aquinas, 1959, pp. 113–117), and thus placed all the laws governing the cosmic and social order within the theological system. Through the cumbersome arguments of scholasticism, he thought that eternal law is permanent, that divine law, i.e. the Bible, is the source of all law, and that natural law and human law are both changing (pp. 117–147). This, on the one hand, places the status and role of natural law under those of eternal and divine law, and on the other hand, traces the origin of human law to God's law, thus subordinating the former to the latter. This gives a theological veneer to the theory of natural law.

The medieval doctrine of natural law developed to its peak in the hands of Aquinas. Since then, feudal jurists only continued to chew on the dogma of the so-called Thomism. The theologians and scholastics, in particular, took these dogmas to heart and did not dare to step out of line. It was not until the beginning of the modern bourgeois revolution that the doctrine of natural law broke through the fences of antiquity and the Middle Ages and underwent a revolutionary change. This change marked the culmination of the development of the concept of natural law in Europe in the seventeenth and eighteenth centuries, and is mainly manifested in the following two aspects.

First, the bourgeois jurists interpreted natural law as the expression of human reason, which is different from the ancient Greek and Roman jurists who believed that natural law arose from nature, and from the medieval scholastic jurists who equated natural law with God's revelation.

Grotius, a Dutch jurist known as the founder of modern natural law theory, argued that "natural law is the correct law of reason" and that human nature "is the source of natural law." Spinoza, another representative of the early Dutch bourgeois school of natural law, agreed that natural law has its origin in reason, and believed that this is an unshakable moral principle. Among the British thinkers, Hobbes based his view of natural law on the theory of human nature and advocated that man is born evil, believing that people are all "selfish." Locke, however, advocated the theory of born goodness and emphasized the role of "reason." The French Enlightenment thinker Rousseau (1997, p. 41) believed that "Man is born free, and everywhere he is in chains," using the "will" to explain natural law. The various concepts put forward by these representative figures all belong to the category of so-called "human nature," using human reason to justify the doctrine of natural law. The cult of "rationality" during this period, in contrast to the concept of "rationality" in ancient and medieval doctrines of natural law, was, in the words of Schumpeter (1954a, p. 141), "something fundamentally new."

Second, the proliferation of non-legal sources and the expansion of new fields of study had, since the seventeenth, and especially the eighteenth, century, undermined the framework of the legal system, in which the doctrine of natural law had for a long time taken the form of jurisprudence, with all non-legal materials playing the secondary role.

Now, the "jurisprudence of nature" ceased to play the dominant role in the rule and coordination of all, and became merely a specialty within the new complex. Schumpeter comments on the significance of the new trend in this period by claiming (1) that "the natural-law system of thought disintegrated or, at least, underwent a transformation" (p. 141), and (2) that the concept of natural law is fundamentally important to "the origins and early history of all social sciences" (p. 107), that is, "the historical origin of all social science is in the concept of Natural Law" (p. 428). It cannot be denied that it was a very common phenomenon for the emerging social sciences of the seventeenth and eighteenth centuries to rely on the ancient concept of natural law to develop their theoretical doctrines, and the economic science was no exception. Schumpeter's claim that "the historical origin of all social science is in the concept of Natural Law" does not at all take into account other sources of thought outside Europe, and is thus typically Eurocentric.

As a complement to the above discussion, the American economist Taylor (1955, pp. 41–42) has given an overview of the century-by-century evolution of traditional natural law thought in modern times:

> [I]n the seventeenth century it (the idea of "laws of nature") attained a somewhat new prominence, a new and more definite shade of meaning, and a new fruitfulness for scientific thought, which have made it a main element in the scientific mentality of the last three centuries. In the eighteenth century, the idea pervaded all disciplines, including the "moral" or psychological and social as well as the "natural" sciences. In the course of the nineteenth century, its sphere gradually became limited in effect, for many minds, to the natural sciences. Students of the social sciences became conscious of difficulties in the way of its use in their field, of which the eighteenth-century mind had been less acutely aware.

In the twentieth century, however, the so-called revival of natural law or neo-Thomism emerged in the West in an attempt to resurrect the natural law in medieval theology, arguing that the classical natural law of the seventeenth and eighteenth centuries had "abused" or "deformed" the concept of natural law:

> He (God) had only been, from the XVIIth Century on, a superadded guarantor for that trine, self-subsistent absolute: Nature, Reason, Natural Law, which even if God did not exist would still hold sway over men. So that finally the human Will or human Freedom [...] was to replace God in actual fact as supreme source and origin of Natural Law.
>
> (Maritain, 1951, p. 83)

This denigrating statement truly describes the rationalist characteristics of natural law doctrine in the Age of Enlightenment. The historical transmutation of natural law thought after the end of the eighteenth century is beyond the scope of this book and need not be discussed here.

II. Similarities and Differences between the idea of natural order and the traditional concept of natural law

The Physiocratic idea of natural order and the Western traditional concept of natural law obviously converge in two points: first, the affirmation of the existence of a divine legislator; second, the emphasis on the immutable, universally applicable and flawless nature of natural law or natural order, instead of the actual laws and regulations made by man.

Apart from these two points, there are some meanings of the concept of natural order that at first glance appear to be similar to those found in traditional natural law doctrines, but a little analysis will easily reveal their dissimilarities. Some differences are so great that the former is even completely outside the scope of the latter. Below, we focus on these differences.

First of all, the natural law in the Physiocratic system of natural order refers to the law of nature in the general sense, instead of the simple jurisprudential sense of the traditional natural law. Having been used since ancient Greece, the terms "logos" (a transliteration of the Greek word *λόγος*), "law" and "order," though touching upon the inherent laws of the movement of nature, have not explicitly stated the nature of the natural laws governing human society. Generally speaking, the term "natural law" was rarely used by the ancient Greeks, except during the authoritarian period of antiquity, when the term was prevalent among the Stoics. It was not used much either in the Middle Ages, for the order of civil society was maintained more by customary law than by statutory law. Therefore, Western historians, in their study of the conceptual origin of natural law, has suggested that the term is derived from two main sources: one came from the ancient Babylonians, and was later adopted by the Jews in Christianity to strengthen the concept of God as a divine legislator in the universe; the other was from the sixteenth and seventeenth century analogy based on the practice of authoritarian monarchs adopting statutory laws to rule their countries (Zilsel, 1942, pp. 276–279). The former is already familiar to us. The point is that the latter emphasizes that the "law of nature" is a concept derived by analogy from the practices of human society. Besides, it was not until the early seventeenth century, affirms Mason (1962, p. 172), that the famous philosopher Descartes first "use[d] consistently the term and the conception of 'laws of nature,'" which provides a new way of studying the sources of the Physiocratic idea of natural order without having to stick to the traditional doctrine of natural law.

Secondly, one of the fundamental points of the Physiocratic idea of natural order is the unity of objectivity and intelligibility of the law of nature or the supreme law. In the Physiocrats' view, the unity is achieved through human reason, i.e. "the light of reason" or "the light of wisdom." This is a distinctive feature of the Physiocratic idea of natural order in comparison with the ancient and medieval concepts of natural law. On the surface, the traditional doctrine of natural law is full of rational concepts. But the so-called "rationalism" in European history is, according to Schumpeter (1954a, p. 113), a "protean word," with completely different meanings in different historical periods. In ancient Greece, rationality could mean "natural reason" or "cosmic reason," without any need to consider objective laws independent of human will. This is very different from the Physiocratic idea, which advocates the use of human reason to gain knowledge about the objective laws of nature, so as to better understand and obey them. In the Middle Ages, reason meant "God's reason" or "divine reason," and humans had only to be divinely inspired to know natural law. Such a purely religious concept is even more different from the rational thought of the Physiocratic School, which aims to reveal the laws of nature. Many Western scholars, when referring to the origins of the Physiocratic idea of natural order, rarely link it directly to the medieval notion of theological natural law. Schumpeter (1954a), a modern economist, is no exception: he refutes those historians' "pointing to a theological bent in Quesnay's thought" (p. 232), and states explicitly that "no economic proposition of Quesnay's rests upon any theological premises" (p. 233).

Of course, in the era of the Physiocrats, the advocacy of human reason was a common characteristic of Enlightenment thinkers. But it should be pointed out that the Physiocratic sense of human rationality is based on the premise of acknowledging the existence of an objective order, and its aim is to understand and thus better observe the objective basic law, which was a very unique viewpoint among the Physiocrats' contemporaries. Neill (1949), a modern scholar, argues that Quesnay cannot be simply labeled as a "rationalist" (p. 546) because he is "an independent thinker who stands above any one method or any system" (p. 545). At the same time, even if the rationalist trend popular in Europe in the seventeenth and eighteenth centuries had a profound influence on Quesnay's doctrine of natural order, it should be noted that the trend prevailed in the era of ancient Chinese thought sweeping all over Europe. Therefore, the formation of this rational trend of thought, in addition to its basis in Europe's own spiritual and material conditions, was also influenced by traditional Chinese thought, the possibility of which can never be ruled out if we examine the materials of early thought. We will discuss this point later when we come to the similarities between the Physiocratic idea of natural order and ancient Chinese thought.

Thirdly, the Physiocrats put forward the proposition of moral order or moral law, along with that of physical order, in their doctrine of natural order. This is a new perspective that differs from all traditional concepts of natural law and from modern discourse of natural law. Its significance lies in the fact that it transferred the study of objective fundamental laws from natural sciences to moral sciences that govern the behavior of human society, that is, social sciences, especially the economic science (Landreth, 1976, p. 26). This shift to the banner of "moral law" is quite strange today, but under the historical conditions at that time, must have had its own precursor intellectual materials to refer to. These materials obviously lacked Europe's own sources of thought. The reasons are as follows. In ancient Greece, morality was only a criterion of judgment inseparable from law. The Roman jurists essentially inherited the idea from ancient Greeks that moral and legal norms were one and the same, and were developed under new conditions. In the Middle Ages, Aquinas' (1959, pp. 117–119, 147–149) discussion of morality and its relation to law was pervaded by the religious thought that God determines everything. This shows that the traditional conception of natural law seldom investigates the objective fundamental laws of social science in general from a purely moral point of view. Besides those in ancient Europe, modern natural law scholars see no need to distinguish between morality and law, and they make the separation only on the grounds that morality must be governed by a "court of the heart" as opposed to the law's being governed by a "court outside the heart." They have never formulated the notion of moral law as explicitly as the Physiocrats, and have never given to the notion a special meaning of exploring objective laws in the socio-economic sphere. In order to ascertain the real origin of this meaning, other sources of thought outside Europe must be taken into account.

Fourthly, another essential feature of the idea of natural order is its organic nature. As we have mentioned, Quesnay placed great emphasis on the "order" of things. Literally, even in the writings of the ancient Greek philosophers, there was no lack of such words as "order" or "universal order," although they were mostly incidental references. By the time of the Roman Empire, a special discourse on the idea of "order" began to appear. The Christian thinker Saint Augustine stated that order is the most proper arrangement of the different parts, each in its proper place, that this order or true harmony is derived from God's eternal and just judgment, which is what he referred to as natural law, and that the so-called "natural order" is nothing more than the guidance of the supreme God of the Bible (Rotelle et al., 1991–2019). In the Middle Ages, Aquinas believed that "a threefold order" of natural, divine and political order could be found in man (p. 109), proclaiming "the pre-eminence of natural powers conferred [...] by God" (p. 177). These ancient and medieval conceptions of "order" were either general and irrelevant, or were bound by the fact that, constrained by the religious idea that God determines everything, their perception of order was limited to the different parts that were "arranged" or "placed" in the most appropriate place, and their "orderly rule and obedience" or "orderly command and observance" were begotten only by the will of God, without recourse to human rationality. These theories of "order" or "natural order," although literally identical to Quesnay's term "natural order," do not embody the organism in the Physiocratic idea of "order." Just as Needham (1956, pp. 291–292), a modern Western scholar, argues, the organic principle is a new intellectual product in the West that emerged only in the seventeenth century and that it reflects originality outside the mainstream of European intellectual development of that time. Therefore, when we examine Quesnay's doctrine of organic natural order, we must turn to other sources of thought outside of Europe.

Fifthly, the Physiocratic thought of natural order consists in maintaining property, freedom and security, and aims at achieving the highest welfare. Different from the references to "public welfare" or "common welfare" in ancient and medieval natural law doctrines, the Physiocratic view of welfare is based more on material interests, in particular on the maximum growth of material wealth of the nation as a whole. The Physiocrats were convinced that the natural order is in the best interests of mankind and that everyday life has to be adapted to the knowledge of the natural order that man has acquired in order to achieve the greatest possible benefit. These utilitarian views are unique both in European history and in the natural law thinking of the Physiocrats' contemporaries.

In short, the above discussion shows that the Physiocratic thought of natural order, in terms of its various aspects, is not entirely derived from the traditional European conception of natural law, as is generally claimed by Western scholars. These aspects are either beyond the scope of the traditional natural law of pure jurisprudence, or incompatible with traditional concepts, or not touched upon in the discussions of traditional concepts such as moral order and organic principles. Some of these aspects, even though widespread in Europe in the seventeenth and eighteenth centuries, were already under the influence of Chinese thought at that time, so their true origin needs to be verified in a broader context.

Among the elements of the Physiocratic idea of natural order that are basically the same as those of the traditional natural law, apart from the belief in the existence of a creator, which is a religious remnant, the most significant is to explain the regular changes in the universe by means of eternal and consistent order and law. The origin of this is generally traced back to ancient Greek philosophers, after which it was simplified and systematized by ancient Roman jurists, and later deified by medieval scholastics. Thus, in the view of many Western scholars, the notion of order or law in this sense is purely Greek in origin. As A. C. Crombie says in his "The significance of medieval discussions of scientific method for the scientific revolution," "It seems to me that it was the Greeks who invented natural science as we know it, by their assumption of a permanent, uniform, abstract order and laws by means of which the regular changes observed in the world could be explained by deduction" (Quoted in Needham, 1969, p. 42 [Note]). In *The Edge of Objectivity*, by quoting Einstein, Charles Coulston Gillispie (Quoted in Needham, 1963, p. 142) also argues, "no Oriental civilization graduated beyond technique or thaumaturgy to curiosity about things in general. Of all the triumphs of the speculative genius of Greece, the most unexpected, the most truly novel, was precisely its rational conception of the cosmos as an orderly whole working by laws discoverable in thought." In a similar vein, Schumpeter (1954a, p. 114) claims by inference, "Just as we may look upon the physical universe—in the way first made fashionable by the Stoics—as a logically consistent whole that is modeled upon an orderly plan—so we may look upon society as a cosmos that is possessed of *inherent* logical consistency."

In fact, these views are one-sided, presented only from a European standpoint without taking into account identical or similar streams of thought outside Europe.

Needham (1963, p. 144), who has long studied the history of Chinese science and civilization, strongly objects that "it is nonsense to say that the assumption of a permanent, uniform, abstract order and laws by means of which the regular changes in the world could be explained, was a purely Greek invention," for, if we look at the whole world, there are other non-European sources of thought with the same meaning, outside the traditional natural law view of ancient Greece. Quesnay himself, according to the Physiocrats' writings, seldom quoted Greek philosophers, and even considered Confucius' *Analects* to be sufficient to make the author surpass the seven Greek sages (Quoted in Reichwein, 1925, p. 105). Quesnay's disciple Baudeau (Quoted in Gide & Rist, 1915, p. 34 [Note 2]) also claimed with contempt that "[t]he Greek republics never became acquainted with the laws of the order." This makes us even more skeptical about the popular argument that the Physiocratic thought of natural order is completely derived from the traditional concept of natural law. With their doctrine of natural order divorced to a large extent from the ancient Greek tradition in Europe, where did the Physiocrats draw their new nourishment? This is the focus of the following section.

3 The Influence from Ancient Chinese Doctrines

In the eighteenth century, when the Physiocratic School was born, the cultural exchange between China and the West was at its peak, and the whole Europe, especially the French intellectual circles, was under the strong influence of traditional Chinese culture. It is against this background that we compare the Physiocratic theory of natural order with ancient Chinese thought. It is entirely possible that the Physiocrats, in expounding their theory on natural order, drew heavily on the precursor materials from ancient China along with those from the European tradition. From the writings of Quesnay and his disciples, it appears that they received this external thought not primarily through direct reading of ancient Chinese texts or their translations, but rather through the introductions of other Westerners. Such introductions either came directly from the mouths of Westerners to China, such as missionaries, officials, travelers, and merchants, had been passed on to Europe and then processed, or had been integrated into Western scholars' own doctrines. Thus in the following comparative study, we will not only cite ancient Chinese texts as evidence, but also analyze Western scholars' understanding of the relevant Chinese texts during that period according to some basic meanings of the idea of natural order, so as to confirm what nutrition the Physiocratic theory of natural order has absorbed from ancient Chinese doctrines.

I. The universal law embodied in Dao and Li

1. Introduction to Dao and Li

In China's traditional culture, the belief in universal laws has a very long history, and is typically embodied in the concepts of Dao (Tao) and Li (reason). The term

Tao originally referred to a specific road, but later extended to "orbit" and "law," such as the orbit of celestial bodies as in "the Way of Heaven," and the law of man's compliance as in "the Way of men,"[8] so that the related things and their rules took on an abstract philosophical meaning. Broadly speaking, the evolution of Dao followed two directions, Daoist (Taoist) and Confucian.

The former originated from Lao Zi (1994), who gave the following explanation:

> There was something formless yet complete,
> That existed before heaven and earth;
> Without sound, without substance,
> Dependent on nothing, unchanging,
> All pervading, unfailing.
> One may think of it as the mother of all things under heaven.
> Its true name we do not know;
> 'Way' is the by-name that we give it.
> (p. 174)

Lao Zi's statement that "Tao gave birth to the One; the One gave birth successively to two things, three things, up to ten thousand" (p. 195) means that "Dao" ("Tao") is the universal law or the essence of all things that the movement and change of things must follow. Another important part of Lao Zi's theory of Dao is his view of nature, which is embodied in the following statement: "The ways of men are conditioned by those of earth. The ways of earth, by those of heaven. The ways of heaven by those of Tao, and the ways of Tao by the Self-so" (p. 174). In this way, the dominant meaning of "life" is replaced by the natural attributes of "Dao." Therefore, Dao "was always and of itself so" (p. 205). As for all things, Dao's requirement is:

> Rear them, but not lay claim to them,
> Control them, but never lean upon them,
> Be chief among them, but not manage them.
> (p. 205)

Denied is thus the supreme position of God the Creator.

The latter, that is, the Confucian tradition of Dao, is based on the *I-Ching*, in which a typical statement is the following taken from the section of "Xi Ci" (The Great Appendix. Section I.): "that which is antecedent to the material form (Tao) exists, we say, as an ideal method, and that which is subsequent to the material form ('Qi') exists, we say, as a definite thing" (Legge, 1963, p. 377). That is, the Dao has no form and contains the meaning of laws and standards, and "Qi" has a form, referring to heaven and earth and all concrete things. Another statement tells of the constitution of Dao by "[t]he successive movement of the inactive and active operations" (p. 355), which embodies the universal law of movement and change of

---

[8] It is recorded, for example, in the chapter of "Lord Zhao" of *Zuozhuan* that: "The Way of Heaven is far away, while the Way of men is near at hand, and it does not have access to the former. How can we know anything of it?" (Durrant, 2016, p. 1553).

all things in heaven and earth, that is, "the course (of things) in heaven and earth" (p. 353). In other early Confucian texts, in addition to Dao, alternative words are used to express the meaning of laws, such as the categories of "law" and "[being] constant" in the following statements: "Heaven [...] [t]o every faculty and relationship annexed its law" (Mencius, 1875, p. 312)[9] and "[t]he course of Nature is constant" (Xunzi, 1994, p. 14).

In the section of "Xi Ci" of the *I-Ching* is also mentioned the importance of understanding universal laws: "He who knows the method of change and transformation may be said to know what is done by that spiritual (power)" (Legge, 1963, p. 366).[10] That is, the first prerequisite for good governance is intensive human study in order to exhaust the subtleties of the Dao of Heaven. Likewise, Lao Zi recognizes the intelligibility of Dao, and regards knowing, cultivating and keeping Dao as the highest way of human cognition, virtue and ruling the world. Because Dao is the general law and source of the development and change of all things in the universe, and has the supreme status, the understanding of it is different from that of the general specific things, and requires higher rational capabilities, that is, to "wipe and cleanse your vision of the Mystery till all is without blur" (Lao, 1994, p. 153), which means to use far-reaching thinking to observe. This way of perceiving things, which rejects the senses, is in fact a kind of rational intuition of a mystical nature. However, it has something in common with the aforementioned Confucian view in its emphasis on getting to know universal laws through profound rational observation.

Admittedly, for Chinese scholars, Confucianism and Daoism, as two schools of thought, have significant differences in terms of their understanding of universal laws and other issues. However, from the perspective of the Chinese cultural tradition as a whole, the similarities between Confucianism and Daoism in terms of many issues, such as the importance of universal laws and the understanding of such laws, together constitute a number of basic characteristics that distinguish ancient Chinese culture from the European counterpart. Moreover, since the two Han Dynasties, there had been a growing tendency for Confucianism to draw nourishment from Daoism and the teachings of other schools of thought. By the end of the sixteenth century, what Western missionaries to China saw was mainly the incorporation of various schools of thought from the pre-Qin period, and Confucianism, in particular, became a mixture

[9] The original text, in which Mencius mentions "Tao" and "law" in parallel, goes as follows:

"It is said in the Book of Poetry,
'Heaven in giving birth to the multitudes of the people,
To every faculty and relationship annexed its law:
The people possess this normal nature,
And they [consequently] love its normal virtue.'

Confucius said, 'The maker of this ode knew indeed the constitution [of our nature].' We may thus see that to every faculty and relationship there must belong its law, and that since the people possess this normal nature, they therefore love its normal virtue."

[10] Also stated in "Xi Ci" of the *I-Ching* is the following: "The (operations forming the) Yî are the method by which the sages searched out exhaustively what was deep, and investigated the minutest springs (of things). 'Those operations searched out what was deep:' therefore they could penetrate to the views of all under the sky. 'They made apparent the minutest springs of (things):'—therefore they could bring to a completion all undertakings under the sky" (Legge, 1963, p. 370).

of views from all schools. Even though there were still many differences between the various schools of thought, it was clear to the vast majority of Westerners at the time, including the Physiocrats, that it was not the specific differences that were of interest or concern, but rather the basic ideas that characterized Chinese culture. Therefore, our discussion of Confucianism and Daoism in this book only focuses on those views that are representative of the Chinese cultural tradition, rather than on the differences between the two. This arrangement applies to all the following discussions.

Li appears in as early as the pre-Qin texts, as part of the Chinese expressions for *tiaoli* ("orderly"), *tianxia zhi li* ("the heavenly reason"), *shun xing ming zhi li* ("reason for all things"), and *wu zhi li* ("things' reason"). Han Fei Tzŭ (1939, p. 192) used Li and Dao (Tao) in conjunction, believing that "everything has its unique principle and Tao disciplines the principles of all things," which means that Li is a special law of things, and is different from the universal law of Dao. In the Qin and Han dynasties, the discussion of Li basically followed the views of the pre-Qin period. The only difference is the tendency to associate Li with benevolence, righteousness and morality. Just as Dong Zhongshu (1975) claimed, the virtue of man can be turned into Li (reason) and Yi (righteousness). Here, Li embodies the sense of law with strong idealism. However, what is generally called Li or *tianxia zhi li* ("the heavenly reason") is based on natural phenomena and refers to objective laws.

Since the Han and Wei Dynasties (202 BC–266 AD), Confucian scholars have adopted both Daoism and Buddhism, which prepared for the emergence of Neo-Confucianism. This new doctrine sprouted in the middle of the Tang Dynasty, and took it as its own duty to inherit Confucian orthodoxy. In the Song Dynasties (960–1279), Confucian scholars mainly focused on the clarification of righteousness and reasoning, with that of human nature and heavenly ordinances occupying a supplementary place, so "the study of Li, or Neo-Confucianism" became the name for this specialized learning. In the early Northern Song Dynasty, Zhou Dunyi created the "Taiji diagrams" and Shao Yong (2016) the "Congeniality diagrams," both to illustrate the inner laws and regularity of the composition and cyclic changes of the universe. Zhang Zai (1966) believed that all things embody Li, each acting according to its own rules and regulations. In the late Northern Song Dynasty, Cheng Hao and his brother Cheng Yi elevated to the highest position in their doctrines the category of Li from its subordinate status since the pre-Qin period. In their view, Li, as the original and universal law of the universe, is not only the highest principle of nature and the derivative of all things, but also the highest principle of society, which is embodied in "the three bonds in prince-minister, father-son, and husband-wife relations, and the five constant virtues for family members." Their doctrines were later inherited and developed by Zhu Xi. Thus emerged the Cheng-Zhu School.

Zhu Xi (2006), a master of Neo-Confucianism in the Southern Song Dynasty (1127–1279), believed that Li can be used to refer to all the terms about the origin of the universe, the universal law or the master of all things in the past, such as "heaven," "emperor," Dao and "Taiji." By Li, he meant the universal law of movement and change of all things in heaven and earth, that is, there is Li in all things, and Li exists nowhere but among things. The so-called "things" governed by Li are all-embracing, including all natural and social phenomena, as well as all psychological phenomena and norms of moral conduct. In the case of natural things, Zhu Xi (2006) argued, there is a Li for each, up above, covering *Wuji* and *Taiji*, and down below, including the smallest grass, tree and insect. For him, *tianli* ("the heavenly reason") is the umbrella term for the four virtues of benevolence, righteousness, rites and wisdom, and the principles of human relationships between ruler and minister, between father and son, between brothers, between husband and wife, and between friends. He also elaborated on the process of recognition from "things" to Li, which means "to know the reason of things," that is, to know things and discover their laws through subject-object contact (Quoted in Li, 1986).

After Zhu Xi, Neo-Confucianism continued to be advocated by the feudal rulers and dominate Chinese ideology for a long time. In the cultural exchanges between China and the West in the seventeenth and eighteenth centuries, it became an important subject of study for missionaries to China and then for many Westerners, including the Physiocrats.

2. **Disputes among the missionaries in China**

As we know, Matteo Ricci first established the Jesuit missionary guidelines in China, advocating in their preaching Catholicism the adoption of Confucian and Mencian teachings and the patriarchal idea of reverence for one's ancestors. This missionary approach was widely echoed among the Jesuits: Le P. Intorcetta even believed that "if Confucius had been born today and understood the doctrine of Christianity, he must have been the first to convert to Christianity" (Quoted in Zhu, 2005b, p. 141). These missionaries looked for vestiges of Christian doctrine in the pre-Qin Confucian classics, all to facilitate their missionary activities, though at the risk of distortion. Other missionaries, who claimed to be defenders of the purity of the Word, criticized the Chinese rites for their "heresies" against Christian doctrine. The so-called "heaven" or "god" in Chinese classics, for example, is also different from the Creator in the Western religion that has a will and is the master of all things in heaven and earth.

The opposition between these two views, that is, the controversy of the rites, not only brewed the so-called *L'Affaire des Chinois*, which would later become a sensation in Europe, but also stimulated Westerners to carry out in-depth study of ancient Chinese doctrines, such as those of Dao and Li. However, research during this period was always confined to a Catholic theological perspective. The Jesuits had been divided in their theological evaluation of the "ancient Confucian" view of heaven and earth, but when they now discussed the "modern Confucian" doctrines of the Song Dynasties, they formed a unified camp against the Confucian Neo-Confucianism under the banner of religious theology. Ricci, for example, strongly rejected the essence of Song Confucianism, which was incompatible with Catholic teachings, because "these Confucian scholars do not believe in the immortality of the soul or the existence of ghosts and gods, but only respect heaven and earth, which nurture and sustain mankind, and do not hope for happiness in heaven" (Bernard, 1936, p. 252). This rejection was shared by many other missionaries in China. Their arguments boiled down to one point, that is, the highest categories of Dao, Qi, "Taiji," and especially Li, that were advocated by the Song Confucian scholars, have neither will nor self-reliance and tend towards atheism, which is obviously contrary to the

Catholic concept of the Creator as the master of all things, and therefore cannot be the origin of all things in heaven and earth.

The dispute of Western missionaries in China on the ancient Chinese doctrines of Dao and Li, and especially their criticism of Song Confucianism, were originally an internal debate within their church, but the influence of this debate extended far beyond. The controversy is extremely important to our study in that it introduced the Chinese doctrines of Dao and Li to Europe in a way that was easily understood by Westerners, thus drawing widespread attention from European intellectual circles.

3. **The spread and influence of Chinese Neo-Confucianism in Europe**

The above controversy around Chinese classics mainly appeared in the seventeenth century, and many of the disputed views reached Europe through various channels, taking the fresh form of an unfamiliar and fascinating study of ancient Chinese culture. Ch'ên Shou-Yi (1935a, p. 19) says, "The wisest thing the Westerners did was to accept the 'ancient meaning' of Confucianism and to abandon the so-called 'post-Confucian' system of scriptural theory and thought. Since Confucianism and Catholicism seldom came into direct conflict, the original Confucianism could be used as a preparation for the Chinese to accept Catholicism without [...] the obstruction of the naturalistic tendency in Confucianism after the Song Dynasty." This assessment is, in fact, valid only for a small number of missionaries in China. The majority of Westerners were not aware of the distinction between Pre-Qin and Neo-Confucianism, viewing Confucianism all as a distinct culture, and were even more inspired by the latter.

Dao and Li, as universal laws, constitute a fundamental part of traditional Chinese thought. They were appraised by the missionaries in China by theological standards, who opposed using these terms to replace the status of the Creator. However, some missionaries still revealed the thought of natural laws contained in the two and explored the consistency between Confucianism and Catholicism. Bouvet (1699) said in his memorial to Louis XIV at the end of the seventeenth century that the fundamental maxim of Catholicism is the perfection of the laws of nature, which, in a fundamental sense, are embodied in Confucianism, because Confucianism and the laws of nature are scarcely different from, if not identical with, each other. He thought that the fundamental meaning of Catholicism and Confucianism is the same. In the 1729 volume of *Lettres édifiantes et curieuses, écrites des missions étrangères*, published in Paris, it is also argued that the Chinese classics contain the principle of natural law, and it is speculated that this principle has been taught to the ancient Chinese by the descendants of Noah. This inclusion of the ancient Chinese classics into the sources of Judaism is obviously nonsense, but it reflects the fact that European missionaries were already aware of the traditional Chinese idea of natural law. Ricci (2016, p. 95) once admitted that there is something sophisticated about this Chinese idea, saying, "I am sure that there initially must have been very profound reasons for the teachings concerning the Supreme Ultimate." The missionaries in China, however, had to be careful to distinguish between "ancient Chinese sages" and "modern Chinese scholars," i.e., the Song and Ming philosophers, when speaking of Confucianism. But this difference was ignored by ordinary Westerners, who highly valued the Neo-Confucianist natural law concept, whether they were detractors or partisans. Their enthusiastic discussions and their research, in turn, had a profound influence on the wide spread of the Chinese concept of natural law in Europe. The attitudes of the two prominent thinkers, Malebranche and Leibniz, towards Chinese philosophy are given here as typical examples.

At the beginning of the eighteenth century, the French philosopher Malebranche (1980), at the request of missionaries to China, wrote "Dialogue between a Christian Philosopher and a Chinese Philosopher," subtitled "On the Existence and Nature of God," which aimed to correct the Chinese Confucian scholars' misconceptions on the nature of God in order to support the missionaries' debate and facilitate their preaching. He referred to the Chinese term of Li as being infinitely closer to the Western idea of God and acknowledged that the Chinese doctors were very knowledgeable. These insights stemmed from the fact that Chinese philosophers saw Li as supreme, or understood it as the immutable order, the eternal law, norm and justice itself. This was thought to bear some resemblance to the Christian philosophers' concept of God. But a further analysis of this, in his view, revealed a major difference between the two philosophies. There are two eternal existences in Chinese philosophy, one is Li and the other is Qi, and the former cannot exist on its own but in the latter. The spirit of man, according to Confucianism, is nothing but material purified or fit to be reasoned with and thus made wise or able to think, and it is apparently for this purpose that they believe that reason is the light that shines on all men, and that it is in reason that we see all things. These were seen as incompatible with the Christian concept of "God" and as errors and strange myths that must be rejected. It was in this sense that he asserted that Chinese philosophy is atheistic, arguing that it has much in common with Spinoza's "treacherous" atheism.

To make his conclusion convincing, he cited at the end of his treatise the evidence that some Jesuits to China gave for Chinese atheism. However, his assertion was criticized by the Jesuits who sought to use Chinese Confucianism, especially pre-Qin Confucianism, for missionary purposes, accusing his thesis for blithely crediting atheism to a Chinese philosopher and ridiculing the expansion of reason seen in his God. His thesis, they pointed out, was full of pantheistic and even atheistic ideas.

The basic point of Malebranche's treatise on Chinese philosophy (essentially Chinese Neo-Confucianism) was to emphasize the fundamental difference between Chinese and Western (Christian) philosophy, especially in terms of the former's Li. This view later had a rather subtle influence on the Physiocratic theory of natural order. More precisely, in a negative way, it provided the Physiocrats with a source of reference for extracting the essence of the Chinese system of philosophy. At the same time, other Westerners introduced and promoted China's Neo-Confucianism in a praiseful tone, thus influencing the later Physiocrats in a positive way. An early outstanding representative of this was the German philosopher Leibniz.

Leibniz's admiration for Chinese culture has been discussed in Chap. 2 of this book. Here we focus on his knowledge and understanding of Chinese Neo-Confucianism. From the account of the missionaries, Leibniz (1994, pp. 79–83) observed the following in particular:

> The first principle of the Chinese is called Li [...]. This great and universal cause is pure, motionless, rarified, without body or shape, and can be comprehended only through the understanding. From the Li qua Li emanate five virtues: piety, justice, religion, prudence, and faith.
>
> [...] [T]heir Li is the law which directs all things and is the intelligence which guides them. It is the Law and universal Order, according to which Heaven and Earth have been formed; the origin, source and principle of all which has been produced. [...] It has dominion over all; it is present in all things, governing and producing all as absolute master of Heaven and Earth. [...]
>
> [...] It is not only the principle of the physical basis of Heaven and Earth and other material things, but also the principle of the moral basis of virtues, customs, and other spiritual things. [...]
>
> [...]
>
> [...] [I]t also possesses Truth and Goodness par Excellence [...].
>
> In conclusion: [...] the Chinese also attribute to the Li all manner of perfections [...]. It is the supreme power, the supreme good, the supreme purity. It is supremely spiritual and supremely invisible [...].
>
> Consequently [we can say] that the Li of the Chinese is the sovereign substance which we revere under the name of God[.]

With regard to "Heaven" and "Dao," he pointed out, "Father Longobardi mentions that the Chinese say that the Li is the Grand Void, the immense capacity (or Space) [...]. In the same way we explain the immensity of God" (p. 81). Here, "space" is understood "not as a substance which possesses parts upon parts, but as the order of things [...]. This order of things among themselves arises from their relationship to a common principle" (p. 82). Thus,

> the order of Heaven is the being of sovereign goodness which is imperceptible. And [...] the Li [is] the natural order of Heaven, insofar as all things are governed by weight and measure and conform to their condition [through the operation of the Li]. This order of Heaven is called Tien-tao, and according to Father de Sainte-Marie, Confucius in the Chung-Jung says that the Tien-tao is the same as the Li, the determinate order of Heaven in its course and its natural operations.
>
> (p. 102)

In his letter to Malebranche, Leibniz named the laws governing the natural and moral worlds as Dao (Tao), similar to the Confucian Dao. He pointed out, "The Chinese say yet other great and good things of Heaven, of the Spirit of Heaven, of the order of Heaven, all of which are most fittingly said of the true God" (p. 102).

He believed that the Chinese term "Xangti" (Shang-di) is the same as Li: "[I]t would be better to say that the Xangti, or that which the Chinese revere principally, is the Li which governs Heaven, rather than say that it is the material Heaven itself" (p. 104). He praised the ancient Chinese sages for their rightly "[r]egarding the Spirit which governs Heaven as the true God, and taking it for the Li itself–that is, for order or for sovereign reason" (p. 105). He thought that "Taiji" ("Taijie" or "Taikie") is not different from Li, either. He explained "Taiji" as "that which has attained the ultimate degree of perfection and consummation–because it operates effectively and exercises its virtue in the production of things, and gives them that ability which includes pre-established order by virtue of which everything proceeds thereafter by its own natural propensity. Consequently, after creating natural objects God needs only thereafter to proceed in his ordinary course" (p. 98). He also quotes Longobardi's metaphor by claiming "that the Li is the 'cause of understanding and the guiding norm of all nature'; but that the Taikie is 'nature's womb, containing in itself, potentially, all possible things'" (p. 100). The difference between the two is only in form.

In a word, all these Chinese terms, different in name but identical in reality, can be classified under the category of "universal spirit," which is called, in Leibniz's own words, "Li or Order; as operative in Creatures it is called Taikie or that which consummates creation and establishes things; as governing Heaven, the principle creation is called Xangti, or King-on-High or Tien-Chu, Lord of Heaven" (p. 109).

Leibniz's interpretation of Chinese Neo-Confucianism was based on the accounts of the missionaries who opposed it, but reached a conclusion different from theirs. What is more, he argued that Western scholars had only just emerged from barbarism, that Chinese philosophy was already an ancient doctrine, and that it would be "the height of arrogance" to condemn it simply because it seemed incompatible with scholasticism. This view is in direct opposition to that of Malebranche. But seen in another way, the different schools they represented jointly contributed to the spread and development of ancient Chinese thought in Europe, showing clues to its possible influence on the universal laws in Physiocracy.

Both Malebranche, who opposed Chinese philosophy, and Leibniz, who defended it, recognized that the Chinese terms of Li and Dao mean the eternal and universal laws that govern everything in heaven, earth and the spiritual world, and are not subject to individual will. The difference is only that one believed that China's laws are purely materialistic and atheistic, while the other believed that they reflect the will of God. Since then, the use of Western concepts such as laws to explain the Chinese terms like Li and Dao had been generally accepted by Western scholars in the eighteenth century. At the same time, the Chinese doctrine of Li and Dao as an independent and self-contained system of thought, with its spread in Europe, was bound to break through the narrow jurisprudential scope of traditional Western natural law, and to enrich and flesh out in a broader field, with its unique and profound content, the original laws of nature. Needham (1954, p. 18) argues that "the Chinese proved themselves able to speculate about Nature at least as well as the Greeks in their earlier period." Since the understanding of the laws of nature by ancient Chinese is in no way inferior to that of ancient Greeks, but is even more distinctive, the popularity of ancient Chinese doctrine in Europe in the eighteenth century undoubtedly played an important role in the development of Western natural law from its traditional limits to its highest point during the same period.

Wearing the philosophical glasses of Spinoza, Malebranche (1980) judged the Chinese Li to be atheistic, but he also revealed that there is a certain similarity between the Christian God and Li in the sense of eternal law, and that Li, in the sense of instructing people to understand all things, is reason, wisdom, and the light that shines on all men. So some people ridiculed him for seeing in God an expansion of reason. Leibniz openly declared that the Chinese Li is identical with the Christian God. In his mind, Chinese philosophy is natural theology, and he advocated in the *Novissima Sinica* that "Chinese missionaries should be sent to us to teach us the aim and practice of natural theology, as we send missionaries to them to instruct them in revealed theology" (Quoted in Reichwein, 1925, p. 80). This parallelism of the Chinese theology of nature and the Western theology of revelation is very enlightening in terms of explaining Li. From the so-called ubiquitous natural Li in China, he saw a natural religion without "revelation," which seems to be more meaningful than the "revelation" of Western religions. Even if Chinese philosophy were to be interpreted by the word "revelation," as it was put in 1688 in an article of the Parisian newspaper *Le Journal des Savants*, it would be "only the revelation given by nature" (Quoted in Fan, 1943a, p. 3), rather than by God, thus excluding the position of the Creator altogether. Wolff (Gorai, 1938), a disciple of Leibniz, though admitting that ancient Chinese were ignorant of the Creator of the universe [...] and revelatory religion (p. 326), was an admirer of Confucianism, praising it as the only principle of the Chinese, which is the revelation of reason, and arguing that the only task of the ancient saints in China was to develop their reason into a state of perfection (p. 328). Thus his lectures on Chinese philosophy shocked the pietists of religious theology, although the theological disguise of his thought was much more thickly veiled than Leibniz's. It is clear from this that Leibniz's study of Neo-Confucianism of the Song and Ming Dynasties led him away from Western theology and onto a new path of rationalism.

Malebranche and Leibniz are both important intellectual pioneers who had a direct influence on Quesnay. Their disagreement on Chinese philosophy is mainly manifested in their judgment on the theological nature of Song Confucianism. But regardless of whether they judged Chinese philosophy to be atheistic or naturalistic, the ideas themselves, as systematically quoted and introduced by them, provided fresh and rich spiritual food for later Western scholars, especially the Enlightenment thinkers. That the Enlightenment scholars openly advocated Chinese atheism as a powerful weapon to attack religious theology was possibly very unexpected to Malebranche himself. Still, the Chinese deism was easier to accept. It is more covert, promoting rational power under the cover of "God," so that many Western scholars adopted this doctrine. Hume (1779, p. 79) praised the disciples of Confucius as "nearly the only regular body of *deists* in the universe." Voltaire believed that "in China alone had 'Theism,' the true religion of the philosopher, 'been raised to the position of a national cult" (Quoted in Reichwein, 1925, p. 89), and that this religion, under the promotion of the Chinese government, "was formed upon the plan of Nature, and instituted on the principles of mere Reason" (Quoted in Fan, 2015, p. 204). They even went so far as to declare that Europe did not need Christianity and the church, but should follow the Chinese "early Confucianism" (Ch'ên, 1935b, pp. 44–74). It can be seen that the advocates of natural religion and the opponents of apocalyptic religion used China as their talisman and standard.

In the whole course of its spread from China into Europe, China's Neo-Confucianism (originating mainly from the Song Dynasties) met with both support and resistance, the convergence of which formed the rationalist wave opposing the European Christian theology. Zempliner (1962), a Czech scholar, remarks analytically that it was not coincidental that the European philosophy of the seventeenth and eighteenth centuries showed interest in the Chinese philosophy, which was closely related to the mutual perpetuation of the natural theology in Germany, and the rationalist and anti-Christianity theories in France; he believes that the attraction of the Chinese philosophy lay first and foremost in its innate relationship with the then emerging rationalist metaphysics. This analysis helps to confirm the role of Chinese thought in propelling to a certain extent the European Enlightenment. Or just as Zhu Qianzhi (2005b, p. 354) puts it, ancient China paralleled ancient Greece in providing the origin for the rationalism in eighteenth-century Europe.

With so much space devoted to China's doctrine of Dao and Li, the disputes of the missionaries in China about the doctrine, and its spread and influence in Europe, we seem to have deviated from the subject under discussion. These discussions, however, form the necessary background to explore the Physiocratic theory of natural law. Otherwise, the study here would be an isolated one, and it would be difficult to draw conclusions about the origin of the Physiocratic theory of natural law. We will see below what kind of internal connection there is between this Physiocratic theory and the Chinese doctrine of Dao and Li.

4. **The connection between the Physiocratic and ancient Chinese doctrines of natural law**

In their system of natural order, the Physiocrats put forward the proposition of natural law. First, it focuses on human society rather than nature. Second, it is relative to positive law. Both points can find their model of application in China, as is seen from the research by the Physiocrats.

The former can especially be seen in Quesnay's (1946) discussion of Chinese despotism: he argued that Marco Polo's early "account of the antiquity of the monarchy, the wisdom of its laws and government, its fertility, its wealth, its flourishing trade, the prodigious number of the inhabitants of that empire, the learning of the people, their politeness, their taste for the arts and sciences" (p. 142) was all true and credible. The existence of such an "ancient, learned and civilized" (p. 142) people and "such a powerful empire, one that surpassed the most polished states of Europe" (p. 142), in a place far from Europe, could not but fill him with "astonishment and admiration" (p. 143). He concluded from such reports about China that "the Chinese constitution is founded upon wise and irrevocable laws, which the emperor [...] carefully observes himself" (p. 141). These "wise and irrevocable laws," as the foundation of the nation's civilizational prosperity, naturally inspired Quesnay to recognize and focus his attention on the natural laws of human society.

The latter can be summarized from Quesnay's detailed examination of China's "fundamental laws" and various governmental laws and regulations, based on his knowledge of Chinese sources, mainly missionary reports. In his view, the most important of China's "basic laws" were natural laws, and all other statutes, such as the positive laws (uniting ethics and politics), the tax law, the civil law (including a system of supervision at all levels), the criminal law, and the law of mandarins (for rewarding and punishing officials), had to embody and safeguard the natural laws. The Chinese ruling system was therefore "based upon natural law in such an irrefragable and so emphatic a manner" (p. 225). He appreciated China's emphasis on natural laws as distinct from man-made laws, and for this reason he carefully studied the Chinese concept of natural law.

He explored the issue from a religious point of view, and gave the following observation (pp. 178–180):

> The primary concern of the Chinese religion is the supreme being; they worship him as the principle of all things, under the name of Shang-ti, which means sovereign or emperor; or Tien, which means the same thing. According to the Chinese expositors, Tien is the spirit that presides over heaven, and they regard heaven as the most perfect work of the author of nature. The aspect of heaven has always drawn the veneration of men heedful of the beauty and the sublimity of the natural order; it is there that the immutable laws of the creator are manifested the most clearly. But these laws should not be attributed simply to one part of the universe, for they are the general laws of all its parts. This word is also taken to mean the material heaven, and the meaning is dependent upon the subject to which it is applied. The Chinese say that the father is the Tien of a family; the viceroy, the Tien of a province; the emperor, the Tien of the empire.
>
> All the canonical books, and especially the one called Shu Ching, present the Tien as the creator of all that exists, the father of peoples; he is an independent and omnipotent being who knows even the innermost secrets of our hearts; he it is who rules the universe, who foresees, postpones, hastens, and determines at will all happenings here below; his holiness is the equal of his omnipotence, and his justice, his sovereign charity; nothing that man does moves him, but virtue; the poor in the thatched cottage, the king on the throne [...] enjoy equally his justice, and receive punishments suited to their crimes. Public calamities are warnings that he employs to rouse men to the love of virtue; but his mercy and his clemency surpass his severity; the surest way of turning away his indignation is by reforming evil ways.
>
> It is said, furthermore, in these same books, that the Shang-ti is infinitely enlightened; that he [...] has given us our intelligent spirit, with its capacity for thinking, that differentiates us from the beasts; that he loves virtue so much that it is not sufficient that the emperor [...] unite the priesthood with royalty; that more is necessary—the emperor must be virtuous and penitent. [...] [O]ne must not believe, however, that he is too elevated to think of things here below, for he himself examines all our actions; and his tribunal for judgment of us is established in the depths of our consciences.
>
> ...
>
> The emperor [...] is the only one who is permitted to render formal worship to the Shang-ti; the Shang-ti has adopted him as his son: the emperor is the principal heir to his grandeur on earth. He clothes the emperor with his authority, entrusts him with his commands, and heaps benefits upon him.
>
> No one but the most elevated person in the empire is fit to sacrifice to the master of the universe [and to] draw the benedictions of heaven upon his people.

Quesnay quoted the relevant records in Chinese history books reported by the missionaries, describing in detail the solemn rituals, devotional attitudes, and penitential words of these emperors during the years of floods and droughts when they prayed to heaven for blessings, so as to prove that the Chinese emperors' religious rituals of worship and sacrifice to heavenly emperors, which lasted for many centuries, were not tainted by idolatry forbidden by natural laws, but reflected their love for their subjects (pp. 179–186). Quesnay also noted that the Chinese classics seldom touch upon "theological subtleties" (p. 185), such as the immortality of the soul and punishment in the afterlife, arguing that the Chinese were guided in their doctrine by "the light of reason" (p. 185).

Quesnay discussed these so-called Chinese religious issues under the heading of "The Natural Law," which Maverick finds "noteworthy" (p. 178 [Note *]). In our view, what is noteworthy is not the connection between natural laws and religious issues, which has been the tradition in the West since the Middle Ages, but rather the fact that Quesnay's analysis of the so-called religious issues in China shows his unique understanding of the concept of natural law. It is clear that Quesnay approached Chinese natural law from a theistic perspective: he took the side of the missionaries to China in favor of ancient Confucianism and accepted the views of Leibniz. In his *Despotism in China*, which includes a section devoted to the "natural law," he repeatedly cited as his authority the accounts of the French missionary Le Comte, who, in his famous *Nouveaux mémoires sur l'état présent de la Chine*, made it clear that, for 2000 years, "the Chinese had knowledge of the true God" (Quoted in Voltaire, 1901, p. 32).[11] Voltaire (1901, pp. 31–38), a contemporary of Quesnay, was convinced that Confucianism recognized the existence of God through his study of the meanings of the Chinese words "Tien" (heaven) and "Shang-ti" (God) and, like Quesnay, made strenuous efforts to defend the purity of the orthodox Chinese doctrine, refuting the arguments that disparaged this doctrine as idolatry and promotion of superstition. This suggests that their understanding of Chinese religion was derived from essentially the same source.

On the premise of affirming Chinese religion as theistic, Quesnay's above interpretation of the concept of natural law in Chinese religion is novel in the following aspects.

First, Quesnay argued that the Chinese natural law is the unchanging, general law of the Creator for the entire universe, the law of the so-called "Tien" and "Shang-ti." By using "Tien" to represent the Creator in Western religions, Quesnay easily arrived at a view similar to Leibniz's natural theology. When Quesnay said that the Chinese, who were aware of the beauty and excellence of the natural order, always revered "the aspect of heaven," he was in fact replacing a personalized God with a natural heaven. Furthermore, in his *Natural Right*, Quesnay (1888, pp. 359–377) mentioned that the role of the Creator is only to establish the laws of nature in the "first" period of society, meaning that once the laws of nature are established, the involvement of the Creator is no longer necessary. This is similar to Leibniz's (1994) interpretation of the Chinese Li as the natural product of all things to emerge under the domination of the pre-determined order of "reason" created by God, after which God does not need to use special power.

Second, Quesnay praised the Chinese idea of the emperor acting as the Son of Heaven, who represented "heaven" and obeyed the laws of nature. In other words, it was not the emperor's personal will, but the "mandate of heaven," i.e., the demands

[11] In another place, Le Comte also says that Confucianism is nothing more than a "fine atheism," which seems to contradict the views quoted here. In fact, his basic tendency was to argue that "the Chinese had knowledge of the true God" rather than atheism, which is why his *Nouveaux Mémoires sur l'État Présent de la Chine* was in the Controversy of Rites accused of favoring China and thus banned.

of the natural order, that exercised supreme power. This understanding of Chinese natural law as the creation of "heaven" differs from the traditional Western concept of natural law, which, as enacted by the Creator, can only be divinely ordained but not humanly explained—this is the basic characteristic of apocalyptic religions. "The Chinese, the Physiocrats believed, had so far been alone in appreciating this truth" (Martin, 1963, p. 230), so that they regarded the emperor as the Son of Heaven. The reason is, according to the Abbé Baudeau, that the Chinese spoke of "the order or voice of heaven and reduce[d] all government to a single law to conform to the voice of heaven" (Quoted in Martin, 1963, p. 230). This remark is a footnote to the aforementioned so-called "supreme truth."[12] Since a secular ruler can act according to the laws of nature in the name of the "Son of Heaven," the so-called "Heaven" becomes an abstract concept, which cannot have a revelatory function. According to Quesnay's understanding, "heaven" or "God" endows man with the spirit of reason, values his virtue, and, in return, man is able to move "heaven" with goodness, and only the most virtuous are qualified to act as the "Son of God." The emphasis on human reason and virtue here is anathema to apocalyptic religion. Thus, in discussing the concept of natural law in China, although it is judged to be theistic, Quesnay often deviated from the traditional Western religious position. In particular, he affirmed that the Chinese seldom talked about theological issues such as the immortality of the soul and punishment in the afterlife, but used "the light of reason" as their guiding philosophy, which excludes divine revelation from the Chinese idea of natural law. Quesnay's above interpretation of Chinese natural law conforms with his own idea of natural law in the emphasis on the light of reason to negate religious revelation.

Third, Quesnay believed that it was mainly through the self-improvement of their inner virtues that the Chinese people sought to "move heaven," that is, to know the laws of nature. This is close to the description of Mercier de la Rivière (1846), his disciple, that the observation of the natural order can only be made through a process of introspection, that is, self-examination, in which one discovers the clear concepts of these laws, and to the claim by Du Pont that Quesnay had seen that man can only think for himself and find within himself the ineffable conception of these laws (Quoted in Daire, 1846, pp. 335–424). The Physiocrats' view that the supreme law of nature is not the opinion of any ordinary man, but of a rational minority like them, is the same as the argument that only the good and virtuous in China can know the law of nature, or that only the most noble can represent the natural order. Martin (1963, p. 231), a Western scholar, points out, "The Physiocrats were therefore left with the task of discovering the law of nature and persuading the rulers of France to conform not to their own wishes but to the dictates of Heaven." The use of "the dictates of Heaven" clearly reveals the fact that the Physiocratic idea of natural law is steeped in the traditional notion of the emperor as the representative of "heaven" or as the son of heaven in ancient Chinese doctrine.

---

[12] Baudeau says in the introduction to his *Philosophie Économique*, "The Chinese are the only known people, whose philosophers were, from the earliest ages, penetrated by that supreme truth, which they call simply Order, or the Voice of Heaven" (Quoted in Reichwein, 1925, p. 109).

Fourth, Quesnay (1946, pp. 190–191) argued that the Chinese attached great importance to the study of the laws of nature, which they had perfected to the highest degree. He deplored the fact that other countries had neglected the study to a large extent, and claimed that China, not the other countries, should therefore be emulated. On the basis of this assessment, Quesnay, in expounding his own doctrine of the natural order, apparently followed the example of China, and made the study of the laws of nature an important part of his theory. His idea of acquiring knowledge of the laws of nature through research can probably be traced back to the ancient Chinese view that "the investigation of things leads to knowledge."

Closely related to the above is the fifth point that Quesnay emphasized the Chinese education of the basic laws of nature. In this regard, it is obvious that Quesnay's theory of natural law is a direct inheritance of ancient Chinese thought. The ancient Chinese idea of education as a way to study and understand the laws of nature (that is, to cultivate Dao) emerged very early, as in the first sentence of *The Doctrine of the Mean*, which reads, "What Heaven has conferred is called THE NATURE; an accordance with this nature is called THE PATH *of duty*; the regulation of this path is called INSTRUCTION" (Confucius, 1869, p. 283). The traditional Chinese education and examination system, in particular, was a source of admiration for Westerners. Feynes, a visitor to China, claimed admiringly in his *Voyage fait par terre depuis Paris jusques à la Chine* (1636), "China is a country with the politics of the philosophers [...]. The Chinese universities are entitled to unparalleled honor in the world, because young men compete for admission to the universities to discuss the laws of the country and the people, with which they should be familiar in their future careers" (Quoted in Zhu, 2005b, p. 77). Du Halde, too, claimed vehemently, "China has numerous libraries and an incredible wealth of books, with schools and scholars all over the country [...]. Reading is the only way for the Chinese to gain respectability. [...] Scholars govern the cities, towns, and imperial ministries, and people can believe that China is the most intelligent country that values cultural civilization" (Quoted in Wang, 1979, p. 158). In short, in the seventeenth and eighteenth centuries, all Western scholars who spoke of the Chinese educational system used it as a model for Europe. Chantilly (pp. 158–159), for example, openly said, "I hope our kings will follow this good example." This call undoubtedly had a profound effect on Quesnay, and when he examined China's "fundamental laws," he included a special section on "education" after "natural law," in order to give it a larger space describing China's urban and rural education system, the duty of officials to teach the people, and the decrees of the emperor to teach young people to respect the basic laws of nature (Quesnay, 1946, pp. 193–200). In another place, he mentioned that China had a "continuous and admirable educational system. The government leaves no stone unturned to maintain education on a grand scale" (p. 157). It was the Chinese example that inspired Quesnay to draw the issue of education into his doctrine of natural order by arguing, "The first political establishment of the government, [...] will be the instituting of schools for teaching [the positive laws]. Every kingdom but China has been ignorant of the necessity for this provision, which is the basis of government" (p. 271). Thus, in his view, "[t]he prime object of the administration of a prosperous and lasting government should [...] be, as in the Chinese Empire, the profound study and the continual and general teaching of the natural laws, which in a high degree constitute the frame of the nation" (p. 281).

Quesnay's emphasis on the importance of state education for the study and observance of the laws of nature has no similar precursor in traditional European thought. The Western scholar Hudson (1931, pp. 325–326) states,

> In China education was essentially related to the state in a way without parallel in Europe under the *ancien régime*. The system of public competitive examination gave an open career through local graduation up to the Hanlin Academy, and made an education centred on social theory the sole key to civil office. Quesnay, like all the Sinophils of his time, was a great admirer of this system, and desired something like it for Europe; he held that the public welfare depended on the study of the 'natural order,' i.e. of the right constitution of human society, and that it was the first duty of a ruler to promote education in this.

Thus, the concept of education in the Physiocratic idea of natural order "had obvious reference to the Chinese model" (p. 325). This analysis is, indeed, to the point.

The above examination clearly shows that the Physiocrats' elaboration of natural law—namely, affirming the objectivity, perfection, universality and eternity of this law, stressing that human beings can know this law through their own "light of reason" without divine revelation, emphasizing the importance of universalizing the knowledge of this law through study and research, especially through education, and even asserting that this law was created by God—can almost always find its source in ancient Chinese thought. Some of this elaboration may be based on both the original Western ideas and the same or similar views from ancient China, which was the fashionable practice of Chinese culture-obsessed theorists in Europe of that period. Others are entirely taken from ancient Chinese thought. What has been discussed here, however, does not yet cover the complete picture of the Physiocratic theory of natural order. If we take into account other important aspects of the theory, such as the organic nature and the concept of moral order, and compare them with the relevant ideas in ancient Chinese thought, we will further find that traditional Chinese thought had a much greater influence on the Physiocratic theory of natural order, which may be above what the average person can imagine.

II. **Ancient Chinese organism**

Chinese thinkers generally have an organic view of the world, and it is the organic order of things that their terms of Dao and Li refer to. This interrelation between all things in the universe can be illustrated by the following: (1) the doctrine that "[t]he successive movement of the inactive and active operations constitutes what is called the course (of things)" (Legge, 1963, p. 355), which regards the alternation of *Yin* and *Yang* as the fundamental law of the universe; (2) the principle of "the five elements," that is, the world is made up of five substances: wood, fire, earth, metal, and water, all giving birth to and competing with each other in their reflection of the origin and diversity of all things in the world (1879, pp. 137–149); (3) the doctrine of "interactions between heaven and man;" (4) the *I-Ching*, a very typical work that depicts the simple-to-complex, well-ordered generation and development of the universe: "in (the system of) the Yî there is the Grand Terminus, which produced the two elementary Forms. Those two Forms produced the Four emblematic Symbols, which again produced the eight Trigrams" (1963, p. 373). The eight Trigrams emulate the eight basic natural things or phenomena of heaven, earth, thunder, wind, water, fire, mountain and marsh, and evolve into a system of 64 hexagrams covering all natural and human changes in the world. This organic principle of *Yin* and *Yang* and eight hexagrams was widely used in China's ancient fields such as medicine, alchemy, calendar, and astronomy. Shao Yong (2016), a scholar in the Northern Song Dynasty, used the system of 64 hexagrams to represent his cyclic view of history. As a statesman and economist of the State of Wu in the Spring and Autumn Period, Fan Li combined the astronomical knowledge of Jupiter's operation and the five elements, with a long period of agricultural experience of good and poor harvests, and developed a famous agricultural theory of economic cycle (Hu, 1962, pp. 176–180), which is the application of China's traditional doctrine of organic cycle in the field of economic thought.

In his *Science and Civilisation of China*, Joseph Needham (1956, pp. 279–298) makes a systematic study of the writings of many Chinese ancients throughout the ages. He believes that Chinese philosophy is a kind of "organic materialism" or "organic naturalism," the key terms of which are "order," "pattern," and "organism." In another place, he claims that the key word is always "harmony," and the ancient Chinese sought order and harmony in the whole of nature and regarded this as the ideal of all human relations. The use of "order" or "harmony" as the main feature of Chinese organic thought is not the creation of Joseph Needham. He is inspired by the famous French sinologist Marcel Granet, who believes that the universe and each part that makes up the whole have an alternating, recurring nature, a belief so dominant in Chinese thought that the view of order is always subordinated to that of interdependence. Needham is convinced of the reliability of Granet's insight and takes the concept of "order" as the basis of Chinese society. In his view, the Chinese Dao is the all-encompassing name for this order, which can be translated as "natural order" and which exerts its influence in an extremely organic manner and in all its effects, and "heaven" is better translated as "the order of the universe." Contrasting this idea of organic order with the traditional Western theory of natural law,[13] he sees two significant differences.

First, unlike Western thought of natural law, the Chinese concept of order does not involve God. Needham points out that the Chinese worldview is based on a very different way of thinking, that the harmonious collaboration of all things is based not on the directives of a supreme power outside themselves, but on the fact that they are all part of the unified system that makes up the universe and the organism, and they obey precisely the internal directives of nature. He further explains that the Chinese have long had a concept of "natural ladder," that man, heaven and earth each has its own level of organization, and that man is to conform to the basic laws of heaven and earth. Since the universe itself is a vast organism, with all its parts cooperating in an interdependent manner, each of these parts acts upon the others not through

[13] Joseph Needham claimed to have made this comparison by making a more thorough investigation, together with his collaborators, into East Asian conceptions of natural law and Western European culture.

mechanical impulses, but through the unanimous cooperation of the spontaneous dynamics of its own intrinsic nature. In this way, the negation of mechanical impulses leads to that of the existence of God the Creator. In other words, because the thinking of the Chinese throughout the ages has been "profoundly organic" and impersonal, they have failed to realize that there is a divine lawgiver who makes laws for all things.

In connection with the previous point is the second that the Chinese concept of order does not involve law. In Needham's view, the reflection of the cosmic organism in human society is the universal desire for mutual understanding, interdependence and solidarity in order to adapt to the social system, which cannot be based on decrees or laws of absolute obedience. The Chinese have long had the concept of "God," but this concept never includes creativity or quasi-legislative authority, and is not related to the individual in ancient times. That is why he regards the statement in *Lüshi Chunqiu* that celestial bodies operate according to "[t]he teaching that does not instruct, [t]he lesson without words" (Lü, 2000, p. 411) as a representative view from the "sublime and great" China, pointing out that it has nothing to do with the Western concept of a "heavenly legislator." He also thinks the so-called "greatest Chinese school of thought," i.e. the Song Dynasties' School of Neo-Confucianism, makes an attempt to form a set of organic philosophy, which takes everything as a component of the "Li" of the universe. "Li" is not a "law" enacted by a divine legislator, so that it is impossible to find any trace of the concept of natural law in Song Confucianism. Thus, the Chinese concept of order excludes that of law.

Joseph Needham's argument that the Chinese concept of order involves neither God nor law is a result of the comparison with the Western concept of natural law, which may not be relevant to the analysis of Chinese thought itself. But his conclusion that Chinese thought of order is marked by natural organism is correct. He points out that organism has been a traditional concept in China since ancient times, and in particular that the philosophy of Neo-Confucianism, which is a synthesis of Chinese philosophy around the twelfth century, is a philosophy more akin to organic philosophy than any European thought. This view has been gradually accepted by some Western scholars since the mid-twentieth century. The American scientist Capra (1975, pp. 17–19, 130–131) compares modern physics with Eastern philosophical thought, arguing that Dao and Qi in Chinese philosophy embody the embryonic form of the quantum field in modern physics, and that the *I-Ching*'s treatment of the movement and change as the innate features of things themselves is consistent with the dynamic model of the basic particles' interaction and mutual transformation. So he says that the changes induced by modern physics in the past decades seem to have moved unanimously toward a worldview similar to that of the East, in which all the phenomena of the universe are one indivisible and harmonious whole. Uritam (1975, p. 148), another American scientist, similarly claims that "some of the directions we see science taking today, some of the emerging views of the world as a unified whole were characteristics not foreign to traditional China. For the wholistic understanding of the unity, naturalness, orderliness, coherence, harmony, and interrelation of the cosmic organism was the goal that Chinese natural philosophy and science sought for millennia." These observations, like those held by Joseph Needham, affirm the organism of ancient Chinese thought and its influence on Western thought.

However, the above-mentioned spread of Chinese organism in the West has been largely limited to the field of natural sciences, or to Western scholars' discovery that certain trends in modern natural science can find their precursors in ancient Chinese civilization. As a matter of fact, just as in natural sciences, there are in social sciences clues that can be traced about the influence of ancient Chinese organism on the West.

In the history of European culture, the theory of natural organism, which is popular in the natural and social sciences of the modern West, did not emerge very early. If one trails back the origin, up to Leibniz, the thread seems to disappear. On the basis of this, Needham (1956, pp. 291–292) infers that Leibniz's monadology is the first organic theory to emerge in the West. We have mentioned Leibniz's monadology in Chap. 2 of this book when discussing the attitude of Western Enlightenment thinkers towards Chinese culture. The basic idea of this theory is to unite all separate things into a whole, so that they become an organic whole in which the parts are interconnected. In his view, the harmony and unity of the monadic organisms that reflect the manner of motion of all objects, is "pre-established," that is, preordained by God. In this regard, Lenin (1976, p. 377) gave a positive assessment by saying, "Leibnitz through theology arrived at the principle of the inseparable (and universal, absolute) connection of matter and motion."

Leibniz's principle of organism was not only unique in his time, i.e. at the turn of the seventeenth and eighteenth centuries, but also is so in the whole history of Western thought. Needham (1956), on the premise that "European organic naturalism in its modern form seems to begin with Leibniz" (p. 294), argues that "there may have been (...) two channels leading to Leibniz, not only the Neo-Confucian material which the Jesuits translated (...), but also far more ancient ideas which entered European thought through Jewish and Arabic intermediation more than a thousand years earlier" (p. 298). The latter route is supposed to have originated in Asia, first of all through certain inspirations from the school of naturalists in China in the third century B.C. Both of these channels are ultimately attributed to the influence of ancient Chinese thought, which is why many Western scholars have taken China as their guidance when referring to Leibniz's doctrines, including his organism.

Needham thinks that "Leibniz's monads were the first appearance of organisms upon the stage of occidental theorizing" (p. 292), and that "some of that originality which enabled him (Leibniz) to make contributions radically new to European thought was Chinese in inspiration" (pp. 291–292). In other words, "the philosophy of organism owes a great deal to Leibniz, and [...] his mind was stimulated by the Neo-Confucian version of Chinese correlativism" (p. 292).[14] This provides

[14] This view leads He Zhaowu (1988) to assert, "In any case, there can be no doubt that the beginning of modern scientific thought is to a large extent indebted to Leibniz's ideas, just as Leibniz's are to a certain extent indisputably to Chinese ideas" (p. 113). He Zhaowu thinks that this organicist idea "has been incorporated into modern Western scientific thought through Leibniz" (p. 112) in the westward spread of the Chinese Confucianism of the Song Dynasties and the organicism of Zhu Xi. In addition, He states, "In his opening the way for Western natural theism, Leibniz has essentially borrowed certain ideas from Chinese philosophy. This idea of natural theism soon flourished in

a clue to the introduction of traditional Chinese organic ideas into modern Europe: the economic organic theory of the Physiocratic School is nothing but an application of that organicist principle, which entered European thought with Leibniz, to the field of economics. The Physiocratic views of economic organism, such as the emphasis on all things being interrelated, the interrelationship being governed by the internal order, and the concept of the whole, are all very similar to those of Leibniz's natural organism. Even Quesnay's so-called view that the organic order was "initially" determined by the Creator can also find a basis in Leibniz's statement that the "pre-established harmony" (p. 292) was prearranged by God.

So far, no Western scholar has specifically studied the relationship between the Physiocrats and Leibniz, but a coincidence has emerged in the discussion of organism: on the one hand, Needham has pointed out that Leibniz's organic theory of nature reflects an "originality" that is outside the mainstream of the development of European thought in his time (pp. 291–292); on the other hand, Hasbach (Quoted in Higgs, 1897, p. 46) argued that "his (Quesnay's) real originality lies in his organic theory of economic life." Between these two "originalities" there may exist a continuity of the same organic point of view. Schumpeter (1954a), in the discussion of the so-called natural law philosophers before the Physiocrats, has obviously ignored the major influence of Leibniz's analysis of organic theory on the Physiocratic School when he claims that "the great name of Leibniz [is] left out advisedly" (p. 117), for he thinks that Leibniz has "made no contribution to our subject (the history of economic analysis)" (p. 117). Of course, it is also possible that the Physiocrats drew direct nourishment from the organic theory outside Leibniz, that is, from the Chinese thought prevalent in their time. But whether from the vertical channel inherited from their European predecessors or from the horizontal channel influenced by foreign ideas in the middle of the eighteenth century, the Physiocratic theories of economic organism can, in the end, be traced back to the ancient Chinese concept of organism, thus displaying an originality different from that of the traditional European thought.

III. The moral and ethical concepts of Confucianism and other related issues

As an important part of the entire Confucian doctrine, the moral and ethical concepts of Confucianism have occupied the orthodox position of Chinese academic thought for more than two thousand years. Confucian moral standards were the supreme doctrines of the feudal ruling class and constituted one of the main elements of Chinese feudal culture. But they also preserved a rich national cultural heritage for future generations. It can be said that Confucian morality is the basis of traditional Chinese thought, that is, it is always human-centered, revolving around man's practical needs, political governance and moral norms, and provides the basis for linking man and nature, pursuing the will of heaven with human affairs, and understanding human affairs with the will of heaven, so that the ethical outlook is fused with the view of heaven, and the moral code is enshrined as the principle and purpose of nature. In

France, forming the climax of the Enlightenment. (Leibniz [...] himself lived in Paris for a long time, and many of his writings were written in French.)" (p. 113). For more information, see He (1988, pp. 110–115).

contrast, the ancient Western view of nature is always nature-oriented, holding that nature is external to man and unaffected by human affairs, and that people have to understand nature only through an exploration of the causes and principles of the external world. The above basic difference between the two perspectives from the ancient world is summarized today as follows: the former is "blinded by man and is insensible to Nature," while the latter is "blinded by Nature and [is] insensible to man."[15] The difference was most strongly felt by Western scholars in the cultural exchanges between China and the West in the seventeenth and eighteenth centuries, when they faced the complete and systematic moral and ethical doctrines of Chinese Confucianism.

The early missionary writings that introduced Confucius and the Confucian classics to the West almost invariably referred to Chinese morality. Examples abound in terms of book titles, such as *The Political Morality of the Chinese*, *The Moral Theory of Confucius*, *The Government and Moral Concepts of the Chinese*, *Chinese Moral Philosophy and Governmental Legislation*, and *An Introduction to Political Morality in China*. During that period, Chinese morality was proclaimed to be derived "from the purest sources of natural reason" (Reichwein, 1925, p. 88), and in particular, Confucius' middle way morality was inherently rational in the hearts of all men, and was advocated as a substitute for Western morality, which was pedantic and useless (pp. 77–98). It was also claimed that "[t]he sum of his [Confucius'] writings seem to be a body or digestion of ethics, that is, of all moral virtues, either personal, œconomical, civil, or political, and framed for the institution and conduct of men's lives, their families, and their governments, but chiefly of the last" (Quoted in Temple, 1770, p. 323). These numerous introductions and propaganda about Chinese moral doctrines had an unprecedentedly great influence on the European intellectual circles in the eighteenth century: "A more or less generally accepted conception of the Chinese had gradually formed itself in the European mind, and this was continually being held up as a model. [...] [I]n the Chinese, people saw simply the virtuous human being. In China they thought they had discovered a wholly new moral world" (Reichwein, 1925, pp. 88–89).

Leibniz (1994) argued that China had an "extremely admirable morality" and "attained the most perfect moral standard" in the area of loyalty and filial piety, so that a "morally corrupt" Europe had the need to receive the Chinese teaching (Quoted in Reichwein, 1925, p. 80). Voltaire acknowledged that the Chinese "have perfected Moral science, and that is the first of the sciences" (p. 89), and praised the so-called Chinese "pure morality" (p. 89) as unparalleled among Western nations. Continuing with Voltaire's argument, Diderot (1975) said that the Chinese science of human morality ranks first among all sciences and praised the "truth" of Confucianism as a means of ruling the country and pacifying the world, which is by no means beyond the scope of ethics and political science. Holbach, citing the combination of Chinese politics and morality as what he considered as the only example in the world, claimed that European governments must take China as a model (Quoted

[15] Translator's note: This difference is a generalized adaptation of Xun Zi's (1994) criticism of Zhuang Zi's doctrines: Zhuang Zi "was blinded by Nature and was insensible to man" (p. 102).

in Gorai, 1938). Even Montesquieu (1989), who was critical of China's despotic system, believed that Chinese ethics and morality had a special place and charm in history and helped to establish the French national spirit. The opposition of Grimm and others to Chinese culture (Quoted in Reichwein, 1925, p. 96) reflected nothing but their defense of European traditions; their resentment was naturally aroused by the fact that Westerners at that time generally regarded Chinese morality as "the noblest and most perfect in the world." These statements concerning Chinese moral doctrine, whether openly positive or indirectly negative, all reveal the trend of the times. However, more often than not, some Chinese moral principles such as "do not do unto others as you would not have them do unto you" were widely quoted as the highest principles of morality and wise sayings, thus enriching the traditional Western thoughts.

It was not only from the mediation of the above comments, but much more from Wolff's elaboration on Chinese moral doctrines, that the Physiocratic theory of natural order was influenced by Chinese doctrines of morality and politics. Wolff pointed out clearly that there was nothing in European philosophy that could be compared with Chinese moral and political doctrines. In particular, he praised Confucius' doctrines on morality and the state, which he considered to be incomparably deeper and richer in thought than those of the Greek philosophers. Therefore, in his advocacy that the moral doctrines and state systems of the ancient Chinese were the model for his time, he formed his own unique system of philosophical thought by taking inspiration from Chinese philosophy (Zempliner 1962).

Wolff's moral views were to a great extent based on his understanding of Chinese moral doctrines: He thought highly of the fact that ancient Chinese had had good law, politics, and morality even before Confucius, that they lived in happiness because they had ruling philosophers who were sages on the inside and kings on the outside, and that these philosophers were role models and guides for their subjects to reach the highest perfection. His positive assessment of Chinese morality was that the Chinese engaged only in those actions and morals that were completely rational and thus based on human nature. Therefore, the Chinese could acquire high moral qualities without taking God as their creator; it was enough for them to know the power of human nature. The Chinese recognized that there was no limit to understanding the truth (Zempliner 1962).

On the basis of the Chinese unity of heaven and man, he arrived at the following: Ancient Chinese must have guessed, if not discovered, the laws of nature that are universally valid not only for the larger universe, but also for the smaller universe. This means, in Wolff's view, that in the Chinese mind, nature is the direct source of moral laws. The belief in a moral order for all things in the universe is typical of Confucian philosophy. According to Confucius, heaven is an impersonal moral force, i.e., the cosmic counterpart of human morality (Zempliner 1962).

By analyzing Chinese ethics and studying its inner laws, Wolff argued that the goal of ethics is to achieve perfection in one's actions and to become a perfect human being. Wolff claimed that after a thoughtful reading of the main books of the Kingdom of China, when he found the general basis for the various doctrines and opinions in their books, he felt that their arguments for teaching the Chinese to cultivate virtue are no less valid than his own. Wolff also relied on a quotation from *The Doctrine of the Mean* to show that the Chinese standard of action, according to Confucian morality, is kept in accordance with "heavenly reason," or "rational nature" (Zempliner 1962).

Wolff's support for Chinese morality was condemned by religious leaders as propagating atheism, but he argued that ancient Chinese were not atheistic, because it is impossible for a man to deny the existence of God when he does not know it at all. In other words, people who do not know God at all or do not believe in God at all can also have a high morality. So he declared that he would rather have the morality of the Chinese than the hypocritical Christian morality of the pietists (Zempliner 1962).

Wolff saw in the "rites" that governed the private life of the Chinese, as well as the life of society and the state, a deep, inner meaning to the Chinese moral code. The obvious examples he gave have led A. Zempliner, a scholar specializing in the origins of Wolff's philosophy, to acknowledge that the ancient Chinese model of moral obligation influenced the formation of Wolff's moral categories and his category of natural law (Zempliner 1962), or that Chinese philosophy contributed to the creation of Wolff's ethics and political science.[16] Some Western scholars have also linked Wolff with Leibniz, claiming that, to study the worldview of Leibniz and Wolff, one must first study Plato and Chinese philosophy.[17]

The connection between the Physiocratic theory of moral order and Wolff's practical philosophy has not yet attracted the attention of Western scholars devoted to Physiocracy, and the investigation in this regard is almost a blank. However, the above discussion is sufficient to prove that their basic formulations are very similar. More examples are: The main part of Wolff's practical philosophy is derived from China's ethics and political science, and Quesnay's concept of moral order presupposes that "Chinese ethics and politics are a science;" Wolff argued that there are natural laws to follow in Chinese morality, and Quesnay included moral order in the category of natural laws; Wolff took human nature as the only direct source of the Chinese moral law and recognized the need to know this law through reason, thus ruling out theological grounds, and Quesnay insisted on the proposition of human reason for the moral law, even though he still had the formal cloak of religious theology.

Mirabeau's assessment of his mentor Quesnay is quite similar to that of Wolff. As has been said, he regarded Wolff as a martyr to Confucius, and as the "father of philosophy" who exercised the greatest and most useful influence on German thought; correspondingly, he called Quesnay "the Confucius of Europe" and thought that the great achievement of Quesnay was to transform into practice Confucius' great teachings of religious ethics, such as "No rites, no action; no rites, no thought; no rites, no words." The near unanimity in these evaluations implies that there is some sort of succession between Quesnay's idea of moral order and Wolff's practical

---

[16] Zempliner (1962) adds too that the influence of Chinese philosophy on Wolff has so far been poorly studied in the history of philosophy, and that Wolff's contact with Chinese philosophy must not be seen as a simple and accidental event in his life and activities.

[17] See the preface to the book by C. G. Ludovici, "Commentary on the entire history of the development of the philosophy of Leibniz."

philosophy. Wolff had pointed out at an early time that the Chinese moral doctrine of bringing self and others to perfection already contains all the essentials of the natural law (Gorai, 1938, p. 330). Quesnay's subsequent prominent emphasis on the importance of moral order and moral law in his theory of natural order as a variant of the theory of natural law may well have been inspired by this view of Wolff. Of course, we cannot exclude the possibility that Quesnay's idea of moral order was influenced by the Chinese moral ethos in his time, or that it was the result of his reading of other popular discourses on Chinese culture and even the translations of ancient Chinese classics. However, since Quesnay's ideas are so similar to Wolff's, and since the Physiocratic School held Wolff's philosophy in high esteem, it may be appropriate to conclude that it was more from Wolff that Quesnay drew inspiration to form his unique theory of moral order.

The Western scholars who study the Physiocratic School have praised Quesnay's concept of moral order in various ways, calling this conceptual creation "unique," "revolutionary," and "very different" from traditional doctrines. Actually, Wolff had already developed a similar concept of moral law long before Quesnay. It is because these Western scholars do not understand the connection between Quesnay and Wolff that they allow Quesnay to stand alone. If we look at the source of their ideas, we can see that both Wolff's concept of moral law and Quesnay's concept of moral order have their origin in the moral and ethical doctrines of Chinese Confucianism.

If there is something unique about Quesnay's concept of moral order that surpasses Wolff's, it is that, through this concept, Quesnay is the first to discuss objective laws in the field of social sciences, especially the economic science. This is one of the Physiocrats' major contributions to economics. They introduced the concept of moral ethics into the category of natural order, which was significant to their creation of classical French political economy. The reason why they highly valued the concept of moral ethics, if traced back to its roots, is the strong influence from traditional Chinese thought.

Finally, it is worth mentioning that the Physiocratic theory of natural order and the Chinese Confucian doctrine have very similar purposes: the former aiming at seeking the highest welfare and the latter at ruling the country and pacifying the world. For example, it is stated in the section of *Da Xue* (*The Great Learning*):

> The ancients who wished to illustrate illustrious virtue throughout the empire first ordered well their own States. Wishing to order well their States, they first regulated their families. Wishing to regulate their families, they first cultivated their persons. Wishing to cultivate their persons, they first rectified their hearts. Wishing to rectify their hearts, they first sought to be sincere in their thoughts. Wishing to be sincere in their thoughts, they first extended to the utmost their knowledge. Such extension of knowledge lay in the investigation of things.
>
> (Confucius, 1869, p. 266)

According to Zhu Xi's commentary, the source of knowledge lies in "the investigation of things," i.e. studying objective things to gain knowledge of their laws, which is linked to the goal of ruling the country and pacifying the world. That is why the Japanese scholar Gorai Kinzo (1938, p. 35) argued that the study of the laws of nature is the starting point of Confucian politics and morality.

The starting point in Quesnay's idea of natural order is to study and research the laws of nature, and the end point is to obtain the greatest possible benefit. That is to say, the attainment of the highest possible welfare, like that of statesmanship, must be achieved by knowing and obeying the laws of nature. In his writings, Quesnay lists *Li Ji* (*The Book of Rites*) as one of the five classics of the Chinese "first level sacred books" and *The Great Learning* as the first of the six books in the "second level classics." He must have thus understood the basic spirit of the quote from *The Great Learning*: "WHAT the Great Learning teaches, is—to illustrate illustrious virtue" (Confucius, 1869, p. 264). Therefore, it is no coincidence that Quesnay's idea of the highest welfare and the Confucian concept of ruling the country and pacifying the world are identical in terms of their goals, methods of realization, and emphasis on the interests of the nation as a whole from a macro perspective.

It must also be pointed out that the Physiocrats, when discussing the highest welfare, including property, freedom and security, referred more to material benefits, whereas Confucians, when talking about ruling the country and pacifying the world, tended to attach more importance to ethical elements such as "sincere thoughts," "rectifying hearts," and "cultivating persons" (p. 266), advocating that "[f]rom the emperor down to the mass of the people, all must consider the cultivation of the person the root of *everything besides*" (p. 267). The latter seems to be incompatible with the former, but this is exactly what Confucianism impressed the Physiocrats, because, according to Quesnay's understanding, Chinese morality and politics are not different from each other and the two completely merge into one science. The political science had inherently included economics before the latter became a science on its own. With morality and politics merging into one, it is natural to affirm the guiding role of moral norms in dealing with economic issues. Quesnay's (1946, p. 190) belief that Chinese learning is more directly necessary for the well-being of society, and has especially in terms of natural laws reached the highest degree of perfection, is another manifestation of his admiration for the Chinese idea of moral-political integration.

Still another aspect of the Confucian doctrine that the Physiocrats most respected and repeatedly mentioned is embodied in the following quotations:

> (1) The great attribute of heaven and earth is the giving and maintaining life. What is most precious for the sage is to get the (highest) place [...]. What will guard this position for him? Men. How shall he collect a large population round him? By the power of his wealth.
>
> (Legge, 1963, p. 381)
>
> (2) If the people have plenty, their prince will not be left to want alone.
>
> (Confucius, 1869, p. 195)
>
> (3) First wealth, then education.[18]

Such advocacy that the rulers must first improve the people's material life occupies a very important position in the Confucian thought of governing the country and pacifying the world. Besides its emphasis on the production and development of

[18] This popular quotation is summarized from the following dialogue between Confucius and his disciple Yen Yew: "'And when they (people) have been enriched, what more shall be done?' The Master said, 'Teach them'" (Confucius, 1869, p. 202).

national wealth from a social point of view, like the highest welfare ideas of the Physiocrats, it also had a direct influence on some of their economic views, as will be seen in the further discussions. Thus, in the Physiocratic theory of natural order, the aim of achieving the highest welfare may have also drawn some nourishment from Chinese Confucianism.

4 Summary

In the preceding sections, we have examined the basic elements of the Physiocratic theory of natural order, and based on such examination, we have compared the theory with the traditional Western theory of natural law and ancient Chinese doctrines respectively. This comparative analysis shows that the Physiocratic theory of natural order has a close relationship with ancient Chinese doctrines, and the closeness even exceeds that of the former's inheritance from the traditional Western theory of natural law. All the important propositions of the theory of natural order, such as universal law or natural law, have clear and precise expositions in both the traditional Western theory of natural law and ancient Chinese doctrines, which are enough for the Physiocrats to learn from. The rationality in the theory of natural order, as the common product of the two sources of thought from China and Greece, is more affinitive to the Chinese origin that more emphasizes understanding social and natural law through practice and education than the Western origin. In terms of observing the laws of nature to achieve the highest welfare, although similar views can be found in both ancient Chinese and Western thought, the Physiocrats paid more attention to the former.

Furthermore, the so-called moral law or moral order has introduced the concept of morality into the natural order in the name of moral science, thus expanding the study of the basic laws of nature from natural to social sciences, mainly the economic science. This is new and unprecedented in the inherent system of Western traditional thought, but is rich and commonplace in Confucian moral doctrines. Likewise, the organic feature of the natural order displays its uniqueness outside the mainstream Western thought, and is consistent with the basic characteristics of traditional Chinese thought.

Only the emphasis on God's creation of the natural order seems to purely follow the Western tradition. This emphasis, however, in terms of the role played by the natural order in the creation of modern economic science, was the least important, and was soon abandoned. Even so, the Physiocrats found a classic argument for a theological explanation of the natural order in the ancient Chinese concepts of "heaven" and "God." In their view, the Chinese regarded the "obedience to the will of heaven" as the principle of all measures, and the emperor as the Son of Heaven, which indicates that the only supreme will in the exercise of supreme power is not the will of man, but that of God, that is, heaven. So the Physiocrats' advice to the French rulers was not to follow the will of individuals, but to obey the will of heaven as their own responsibility, and to worship the Chinese philosophy of providence.

The Physiocratic understanding of the theological properties of the natural order is not so much inherited from the Western tradition, especially the concept of natural law in the Middle Ages, as it is drawn from the interpretations of Chinese philosophy by the philosophers such as Leibniz and Wolff. Leibniz (1994) interpreted Chinese natural law as a pre-determined order instituted by God, after which God does not need to use special power. Wolff, also inspired by Chinese philosophy, argued that while moral laws are determined by God, the eternal, necessary, and unchanging nature of the laws themselves is such that these moral laws must continue to be valid in the absence of God, and that their laws can only be known through reason (Zempliner, 1962). This view was not so clearly expressed by the Physiocrats, but they understood the role of God in the natural order only as the creation of the fundamental laws of nature in the earliest period of society, implying that after the creation of the laws of nature, it was not necessary to consider the role of God, and the key was only how to recognize and obey those laws. This understanding is fundamentally similar in spirit to Leibniz-Wolff's interpretation of Chinese philosophy, which in fact depart from the traditional religious conceptions and place similar restrictions on the determinative role of God. Therefore, among the meanings of natural order, the emphasis on God's status as the creator is the most typical characteristic of the original Western concept of natural law, but the Physiocrats added a lot of Chinese cultural elements to this meaning, which brought about a certain variation of this Western notion.

By analyzing the source of the Physiocratic theory of natural order from different perspectives, we find that among all its basic elements, those that may have drawn nourishment from the history of Western natural law correspond to the same or similar precursor elements from the ancient Chinese doctrines. However, some important elements, such as moral law and organism, are rich in meaning in the ancient Chinese doctrines, but are rarely, if not never, mentioned in Western traditional thoughts. Moreover, those that can find their precursors in both Chinese and Western ancient sources seem to rely more on Chinese sources. On the one hand, this is because European scholars of that period were devoted to Chinese culture and put aside the culture of ancient Greece. On the other hand, under the stimulus of a large amount of imported Chinese culture, the Physiocrats took a more critical attitude toward the traditional culture of Europe, which was typically represented by Quesnay's argument that Greek philosophy fell behind that of ancient China.

One of Quesnay's contemporaries said that Quesnay did not have any original ideas (Reichwein, 1925, p. 106), which, when taken in conjunction with the various elements of his theory of natural order, is indeed true. However, his effort to absorb, digest, and organize the essence of the foreign cultural heritage in an independent system of natural order, without the prejudices of the European cultural tradition, is in itself a creative work. As a matter of fact, it is mainly for the convenience of analysis that we have broken the natural order down into individual constituents. We find that in the works of the Physiocrats, the various elements of natural order are actually interconnected and intermingled with each other, constituting a complete system of thought. As a whole, the theory of natural order takes on an appearance that is not identical with the simple combination of its individual elements. This appearance tends to blur people's vision and make them regard the theory as a purely Western product. Of course, it is impossible for the Physiocrats to cut off their own cultural traditions; their discussions of the natural order generally adopt the original Western concepts or terms,[19] thus appearing to be irrelevant to ancient Chinese doctrines. But the irrelevance is a complete illusion. As we have shown in the previous sections, an in-depth comparative analysis of this Physiocratic theory and traditional Chinese thought is sufficient to show that the two are inextricably linked in many aspects. This relationship, as Reichwein (1925, p. 29) says of the eighteenth-century Western society's eagerness to emulate Chinese artifacts, is embodied in the "curious cross-bred *Chinoiserie*, in which European ideas of form were coupled with Chinese motives."

In short, we can arrive at the following conclusion: one of the most important sources of the Physiocratic theory of natural order is the Chinese cultural tradition, and especially those unique parts of the theory that are held by Western scholars to be different from the European mainstream thought can almost always be found in ancient Chinese doctrines.

The above conclusion, though probably rather unfamiliar to modern scholars, was bluntly acknowledged two hundred years ago by the Physiocrats. This is best exemplified by Quesnay (1946), who, in the eighth chapter of *Despotism in China*, expressly states that he has studied "the political and moral constitution of the great empire of China, based upon a knowledge of the Natural Law, of which it is the outgrowth" (p. 264), and that he has made "a systematic digest of the Chinese doctrine, worthy to be used as a model for all states" (p. 264). The so-called "doctrine" here mainly refers to the understanding of the laws of nature, and may well be regarded as a "theory" of natural order. In his view, the Chinese example proves that "the laws which constitute the natural order are perpetual and immutable laws" (p. 303), so he concludes the book in a rhetorical tone:

> Are not the continuance, the extent, and the permanent prosperity of the Empire of China assured by observance of the natural laws? Does not this populous nation rightly regard other peoples that are governed by human wills and subjected to social obedience by force of arms, as barbarous nations? Does not this vast empire, subjected to the natural order, present an example of a stable, permanent and invariable government, proving that the inconstancy of transitory governments has no other basis or rule except the inconstancy of men themselves? [...] It is, then, not to special circumstances that one must attribute the perpetuity of its government, but to an inherently stable order.
>
> (pp. 303–304)

In Quesnay's eyes, China's theory and practice of the natural order were exemplary and superior to those of any other country in the world. Quesnay's disciples believed so, too. Baudeau, for example, preached, "The Chinese are the only known people, whose philosophers were, from the earliest ages, penetrated by that supreme truth,

---

[19] For the concept of "natural order," we can find in ancient Chinese texts not only the terms with corresponding meanings, such as "Dao" ("Tao") and "Reason," but also those with corresponding forms. It is stated in "The Discourses of the State of Zhou" of *Guo Yu*, "The *qi* of heaven and earth cannot lose its order. If its order is lost, the people will be in chaos" (Xü, 2002, p. 26). Here, "The *qi* of heaven and earth" is what Western scholars call the "natural order."

which they call simply Order, or the Voice of Heaven" (Quoted in Reichwein, 1925, p. 109).[20] In other words, the Chinese were the only people who had grasped the "supreme truth" of natural order. This means that in the eyes of the Physiocrats themselves, their theory of natural order was directly modelled on traditional Chinese thought.

Since then, as time went by, Westerners in general gradually forgot the historical background that Chinese culture had greatly influenced the Physiocratic School, and often regarded without analysis as products of Europe's own traditions those Chinese cultural deposits that had survived in the theory of natural order. Among the many Western scholars who have studied the Physiocrats in modern times, few have discussed "the arrangement in China, that country which was supposed to come closest to the ideal order of the Physiocrats" (Neill, 1948, p. 164). Only a number of theorists, who are devoted to the cultural exchange between China and the West, have made a more objective and impartial evaluation of the origins of the Physiocratic theory of natural order.

Reichwein (1925) mentions that "China had a special attraction for his (Quesnay's) realistic mind, because it was a living witness of the thing he was seeking and an assurance that the idea of a 'natural order' was capable of realization, nay, could even point to ways by which it might be realized" (p. 102). In another place, Reichwein adds,

> His attempts to fuse divine order with human order, natural order, as the right way or, in the Chinese phrase, the *Tao* of the world, with actual order—an aim of which the Chinese world perhaps offered the grandest realization [...]. Herein his mentality was akin to that of the Chinese; and from this intellectual kinship sprang his deep love for the Chinese conception of the State and its citizens.
>
> (p. 103)

Reichwein thus concludes, "to Chinese tradition in particular he (Quesnay) is indebted for certain basic ideas" (p. 104), such as the concept of natural order.

Reichwein is one of the earliest modern Western scholars to discuss Quesnay's theory of natural order in relation to Chinese cultural traditions, but he only deals with this topic from the eighteenth-century encounter between Chinese and European cultures, and does not discuss it specifically. His discussion is thus too brief.

Hudson (1931), in his *Europe and China*, also acknowledges that Quesnay's system of natural order is under "the influence of Chinese ideas" (p. 326) or "modified by Chinese conceptions" (p. 326 [Note 1]). However, he fails to clearly indicate where this influence or revision of traditional "Chinese conceptions" manifests itself.

Takimoto Seiichi (1931, p. 18), in "The Source of the Fundamental Thoughts of the Physiocrats," examines first and foremost the source of Quesnay's theory of natural law, that is, natural order, before he puts forward the following striking view: Different from most European scholars who speculated that Physiocracy originated in Greece and Rome, or had its genes embodied in the theories of Grotius, Pufendorf and Locke, Quesnay's theory conformed to the ideal of the Chinese archaic kingship entirely, and constituted almost unconditionally the fundamental thought of the

---

[20] Baudeau says this in the introduction to his *Philosophie Économique*.

liberal school of economics and of the French Revolution. This is probably the first time in the history of economic doctrine that Quesnay's theory of natural order was held to be derived entirely from ancient Chinese doctrine. This assertion, though very clear, is a rather weak argument, and is thus disdained even by some economists in China. In 1938, a French scholar published a book entitled *The Chinese Influence on the Emergence and Development of the Physiocrats' Doctrine*, in which, after comparing traditional Chinese economic thought with the Physiocrats' theories, he confirms that the two share the same concept of natural order. Given that the book has little influence and has hardly been mentioned, it is unlikely to offer any new insights about the origin of the Physiocrats' theory of natural order.

Different from the aforementioned scholars, we have in this chapter started from the basic elements inherent in the natural order rather than its general discussion, and then discussed them in the contexts of Chinese and Western cultural traditions respectively, in an effort to conduct a multi-perspective, multi-level and all-round research to grasp or deduce in a broader scope the sources of the Physiocratic theory of natural order. This is an arduous task without precedent. However, only in this way can we hope to avoid the drawbacks that may arise from rushing to judgment by grasping only a few isolated words or individual points of view of the Physiocrats, so that our conclusions on the origin of their natural order can be based on a more scientific basis.

The natural order occupies a pivotal place in the Physiocratic system, and, in the words of Quesnay, is "'the supreme rule of all human lawgiving, of all political, economic and social action.' [Quesnay] conceives it chiefly in terms of the economic life" (Hudson, 1931, p. 322). It is a central link that connects the major economic theories of the Physiocrats: their interpretation of almost all important economic principles has to resort to this basic concept, and even the name of the School itself has been given the meaning of "natural rule." Strictly speaking, the concept of natural order belongs to philosophy, but it played a very important role in the Physiocrats' creation of modern economic science, which reflects the characteristics of the times when economics was not completely independent from philosophy. That is why Martin (1963, p. 230) says, "The starting-point of the Physiocrats was that of eighteenth-century philosophy in general." "Quesnay indicates," Neill (1948, p. 164) says, "that economics, politics and sociology should all be part of social philosophy." This spirit of the times has had a profound effect on the history of economic science. The Western economist Taylor (1955) notes that "what has happened since the eighteenth century, in natural science as in economics, has been a serious modification, but hardly a complete abandonment, of the belief in an harmonious Order of Nature" (p. 63), and that, specifically, "[i]n their (the Physiocrats' and Adam Smith's) schemes of doctrine, political economy became a development of the eighteenth-century notion of a harmonious, 'natural' social order" (p. 77). Since the Physiocratic theory of natural order has such an important role in Physiocracy and in the whole history of economic doctrine, it is very meaningful to conclude, by sorting out the relevant historical facts, that this theory has traditional Chinese culture as one of its important sources.

Chapter 5
Tableau Économique

We have in Chap. 4 explored the origins of the natural order, the philosophical foundation of the entire Physiocratic system. From this chapter onwards, we will examine the relationship between the various important economic theories of Physiocracy and ancient Chinese thought. Most perplexing in this regard is the origin of the *Tableau Économique*, the focus of this chapter. After a look at the crucial position of the *Tableau* in Western economics, we will carry out an analysis about its Chinese and Western origins, before we make a comparison between the two.

1 Significance to Western Economics

"The *physiocratic* school," Marx pointed out, "left us in Quesnay's *Tableau Economique* [...] a nut on which all former critics and historians of political economy have up to now broken their jaws in vain" (Quoted in Engels, 1977, p. 291). Later Engels (1977, p. 21) noted again that this *Tableau* "has remained an insoluble riddle of the sphinx to all modern political economy." What Marx and Engels meant here is that the concepts contained in the *Tableau* concerning the production and circulation of a country's total wealth have remained incomprehensible to future generations of economists. As far as our studies are concerned here, the source of the *Tableau* is no less a "riddle of the sphinx." Before answering this question, we now give an overview of the evolution of the *Tableau*, as well as its position and influence in the history of economic theory.

First published in December 1758, Quesnay's *Tableau* describes the cycle of 400 livres of income between productive and unproductive (or, as Quesnay put it, "sterile") expenditure, and are accompanied by twenty-two "Remarques sur les Variations de la Distribution des Revenus Annuels d'une Nation," which are very similar to the fourteen "maxims of economic government" proposed by Quesnay in his previous "Grains" written for *l'Encyclopédie*. This is the first edition of the *Tableau*. The

M. Tan, *The Chinese Origin of Physiocracy*,
https://doi.org/10.1007/978-981-97-9703-5_5

second was created two or three months later, and the income base was changed from 400 to 600 livres, with twenty-three guidelines, entitled "Extrait des Oeconomies Royales de M. de Sully." The third edition was created in 1759, and its charts are roughly the same as those of the first and the second, with an income base of 600 livres. It differs from the first two in that the explanatory text on both sides of the chart has been removed, and a paragraph has been added above the chart under a heading which briefly sets out twelve "Objets a considerer." To the third edition is added an "Explication" and twenty-four maxims with detailed explanatory notes, entitled in the same way as the second. This is a fine edition in quarto, praised as "the mature zigzag" (Fox-Genovese, 1976, p. 259).

The above is the history of the original editions of the *Tableau.* All the three versions were printed in very small numbers and sent only to a few people who were close associates of Quesnay. In the course of time the three were either scattered and lost or mixed and indecipherable, and "for the next two hundred years or so, they remained shrouded in fog" (Chen, 1981, p. 150 [Note 1]). Even among the leading members of the Physiocratic School, understanding of the *Tableau* was not easy. Quesnay (1962), having learned that Mirabeau was "bogged down" (p. 115) in the *Tableau*, wrote to enlighten him: "It is true that it relates to so many things that it is difficult to grasp the way they fit together, or rather to understand it self-evidently" (p. 115). As can be seen, even Quesnay himself admitted that the *Tableau* was difficult to understand. Until 1766, almost eight years after the publication of the first edition of the *Tableau*, Du Pont was still unable to give a convincing explanation (Fox-Genovese, 1976, p. 268).

In order to make the *Tableau* easy to grasp, Quesnay published, in 1760, in a sequel to the sixth volume of his *L'ami des hommes*, "Le Tableau Oeconomique avec ses Explications," at the behest of Mirabeau. Only this *Tableau*, like the first three unpublished editions, adopted the complex zigzag schema, which is also called the "original *Tableau.*" In the 1763 edition of *Philosophie Rurale* co-authored by Quesnay and Mirabeau, this zigzag was replaced by a simplified one, but not without the basic pattern of the original *Tableau.* This was still difficult for the general public to understand. In 1766, Quesnay published "Analysis of the Arithmetical Formula of the *Tableau Économique* of the Distribution of Annual Expenditure in an agricultural Nation," accompanied by "Important Comments." This text introduced the new "Arithmetical Formula," a major revision of the "original *Tableau*", which is called "simple *Tableau*" or "abbreviated *Tableau*" because of its simple structure. The *Tableaus* listed in Quesnay's *First Economic Problems* (1766) and *Second Economic Problems* (1767) are all derived from this "Arithmetical Formula," which is the basic model for understanding the basic theory of the *Tableau* today. Most of the published types of the *Tableau* mentioned above, after being supplemented and revised, are included in *La Physiocratie*, a book edited and published by Du Pont in 1769, who expanded to 30, from the originally more than 20, economic management principles attached to the *Tableau*, and crowned them with the new title of "General Maxims for the Economic Government of an Agricultural Kingdom." In this way, during the 10 years since 1758, according to statistics, there were 11 "original *Tableaus*" and 5 "short *Tableaus*" designed by Quesnay, and there were about 46 in total, including the various ones by Mirabeau to illustrate Quesnay's *Tableau*. It is no wonder that Meek (1962, p. 28) says in his analysis of the economics of Physiocracy, "The subsequent history of the Physiocratic doctrine, in a sense, was the history of the gradual popularization, clarification, and elaboration of the *Tableau*."

In the eyes of the Physiocrats, the *Tableau* had a very high status. the Marquis de Mirabeau once regarded the *Tableau*, alongside "writing" and "money", as one of the "three great inventions which have principally given stability to political societies [...]. The third, is the Economical Table, the result of the other two, which completes them both by perfecting their object; the great discovery of our age, but of which our posterity will reap the benefit" (Smith, 1812, p. 539). He added elsewhere that the *Tableau* provides the rules of the "economic science, immortal base of our subsistence, of our morals, and of all in a word that can be truly called the fundamental science of the government of States" (Quoted in Fox-Genovese, 1976, p. 253); or in the Preface to *Philosophie Rurale*, that this *Tableau* serves "as the foundation and outline of the economic science, and as a guide to the rule of States" (Mirabeau & Quesnay, 1764, p. iii). The Abbé Baudeau also argued that Quesnay's "genius first begat the sublime idea of this *Tableau*. The *Tableau* gives us such a clear idea of the premier position of the science (the economic science) that all Europe is bound to accept its teaching, to the eternal glory of the invention and the everlasting happiness of mankind" (Gide & Rist, 1915, p. 18 [Note 2]). Another Physiocrat, Le Trosne (1728–1780), stressed, "Economic science, being a study of measurable objects, is an exact science [...]. What the science lacked was a convenient formula which might be applied to test its general conclusions. Such a formula we now have in the *Tableau économique*" (p. 19 [Note 2]). Among those who were not Physiocrats but their contemporaries was Nicolas-Gabriel Clerc (1769, pp. xiv–xv), who declared, "All kinds of social institutions will henceforth be tested by the touchstone of the *Tableau Économique*, and a careful study of this work will clear away the clouds that blind politics."

These remarks of praise, which flourished for a while, soon disappeared with the decline of the influence of the School itself. In fact, during the active period of the School, criticism of the *Tableau* was already frequent. Voltaire laughed at it, and even Turgot doubted its miraculous power. In particular, Linguet (1736–1794), who regarded the Physiocrats as "[t]he only economists [...] to deal with" (Marx, 1969, p. 345), commented, "The *Tableau* is an insult to common sense, to reason, and philosophy, with its columns of figures of *reproduction nette* terminating always in a zero, striking symbol of the fruit of the researches of any one simple enough to try in vain to understand it" (Quoted in Higgs, 1897, p. 150).[1] Thus he ridiculed the *Tableau* as the unbelievably grotesque idol of a fanatical faction and denounced it as quackery. Obviously, Quesnay's followers, despite their extensive propaganda for the *Tableau*, had no real insight into its underpinnings, and therefore failed to popularize and promote it effectively. By the time Smith published *The Wealth of Nations*, he only mentioned briefly the "Arithmetical Formula" that Quesnay used to show how the annual product of the land is distributed among the various classes,

[1] The *Tableau Économique* Linguet refers to here is the original zigzag version.

adding in the meantime "[t]he first of these formularies, which by way of eminence he (Quesnay) peculiarly distinguishes by the name of the Economical Table" (Smith, 1812, p. 533). For quite a long time after the Physiocratic School, other classical and vulgar economists, instead of continuing and developing the attempts already made by the *Tableau*, forgot it, or mentioned it simply as a strange work. It was disparaged at the beginning of the nineteenth century as a work of no brain power, and as an odd work, strange and difficult to understand, which is full of strange numbers, and is more problematic than the Physiocratic doctrine itself (Rubin, 1932, p. 89). As late as the nineteenth century, Dühring still claimed that the *Tableau* "could offer nothing but confused and arbitrary conceptions, ascending to mysticism" (Quoted in Engels, 1977, p. 302). These views led to the long oblivion of the *Tableau*, which thus became a century-old mystery in the history of economic doctrine.

The first person to solve this mystery is Marx, who pointed out, "Quesnay's *Tableau* was intended to portray how the total annual product of a country (concretely, France) circulates among these three classes and facilitates annual reproduction" (p. 295). What Marx analyzed was the "Arithmetical Formula" of the *Tableau*, that is, a short table with only five lines connecting six starting points or destination points, rather than the complex original zigzag. That is why he said, "Quesney's *Tableau économique* shows in a few broad lines how the annual result of national production, defined in terms of value, is distributed by circulation in such a way that, with other circumstances remaining the same, simple reproduction can take place, i.e. reproduction on the same scale" (Marx, 1992, p. 435). In this way, the answer to the "riddle" involving the reproduction and circulation of the total social capital contained in the *Tableau* is clearly displayed before people for the first time.

Marx (1990, pp. 737–738) spoke highly of Quesnay's *Tableau*: "It is one of the great merits of the Physiocrats that in their *Tableau économique* they were the first to attempt to depict the year's production in the shape in which it emerges from circulation." He praised the attempt greatly: "[This was] in the second third of the eighteenth century, the period when political economy was in its infancy—this was an extremely brilliant conception, incontestably the most brilliant for which political economy had up to then been responsible" (1969, p. 344). He also pointed out, "Doctor Quesnay has made of political economy a science; he has summarised it in his famous 'Tableau Economique'" (1913, p. 112).

Marx's scientific analysis and high regard for Quesnay's *Tableau* have been of great importance to Western economists' reunderstanding of its value. As early as 1895, the German scholar Stephan Powell wrote to Engels, believing that Marx's analysis of the *Tableau* brought for the first time the Physiocratic School back into the limelight. Since then, the *Tableau* has gained increasing prominence in the history of Western economics. Fox-Genovese (1976, p. 246), a Western scholar specializing in the origins of Physiocracy, points out, "[S]ince Marx's 'rediscovery' of the physiocrats, many economists of various persuasions have recognized the Tableau as a milestone in the development of economic thought." Phillips (1955, p. 137), another Western scholar, adds that, with respect to Quesnay's *Tableau*, "one need not search far to find words of praise from modern writers." However, Gray (1931), a modern economist, criticizes the *Tableau* as "an embarrassed footnote" (p. 106) in the history of economic thought though "it may be doubted whether it will ever be anything but a vast mystification" (p. 106). Most scholars, nevertheless, give it a very positive assessment. Newman (1952) thinks that Quesnay's *Tableau* constitutes, together with Turgot's *Reflexions*, "the cornerstone of modern political economy" (p. 34) and "is probably the earliest successful attempt to analyze a nation's wealth on a macro-economic basis" (p. 35 [Note 1]). Meek (1962, pp. 295–296) argues, "The *Tableau* is far from being the ideal and airy thing which it is sometimes made out to be: on the contrary, it is one of the most striking examples in the whole history of economic thought of the achievement of a harmonious unity between abstract theory and concrete investigation." Fox-Genovese (1976, p. 252) states, "The Tableau Économique represents a revolutionary break-through in economic analysis and reflects the historical reality of its conception." It is recorded in *The Encyclopedia Americana* (Vol. 23) that Quesnay's *Tableau* influences the subsequent generations of economists, for it emphasizes the interrelationship between all factors in the economic order and attempts to incorporate them all into input-output of the anticipatory model. Meek (1962) also adds that "the *Tableau* does constitute, from all points of view, Quesnay's most significant contribution to economics" (pp. 39–40), in terms of many issues of interest today, such as "general equilibrium analysis, the development of under-developed countries, the economics of control, and input-output analysis" (p. 39). Last but not least, Schumpeter's (1962, pp. 3–4) 1935 description of Quesnay as one of the four greatest economists of all time is also due to his creation of the *Tableau*. In short, it is almost unanimously recognized in the minds of many famous economists and in popular works on the history of economic doctrines that the *Tableau* has made an indelible and significant contribution to the establishment and development of economics.

The point here is that the mid-eighteenth century, when the *Tableau* was formed, is a time naturally reminiscent of the popularity of Chinese culture in France, and of Quesnay's own fervent reverence for the oriental culture. This opens up a new way of thinking for solving the mystery of the origin of the *Tableau*: besides the historical conditions of the West itself, the birth of the *Tableau* may also be related to the massive spread of Chinese culture in Europe at that time, and it may be regarded as another product of the contact between the Western and Chinese systems of thought in the eighteenth century.

Early Western scholars have left several confusing accounts of the above proposition, which has not only remained unverified, but also attracted little attention among economists. But for the research topic of this chapter, the above proposition, though in outline, provides valuable clues for further investigation. Now we follow these clues to take a look at several arguments about both the Chinese and Western origins of the *Tableau* before we make a comparative analysis of the two.

2 The Chinese Origin

Quesnay was reticent about what ideas he drew from his predecessors in the creation of the *Tableau Économique*, but some worthwhile clues are revealed from the opinions held by his followers or opponents, which can be roughly summarized into three arguments. The first is that the *Tableau* is a systematization and concretization of the ancient Chinese principle of natural order in the form of a diagram. The second is that the *Tableau* imitates the 64 diagrams of the Chinese classic *I-Ching*. And the third is that it is related to Chinese hieroglyphs or ideographs. All the three, though seeming incredible to modern economists, are crucial to solving the mystery of the origins of the *Tableau*. The following is a successive analysis of these three arguments.

I. The Chinese principle of natural order

As has been pointed out, the Physiocrats, including Quesnay himself, regarded Chinese as the only nation to have mastered the "supreme truth" of natural order, and demanded that all governments in the world, especially that of France, follow China's example. But it was Nicolas-Gabriel Clerc, a scholar outside the Physiocratic School, who explicitly linked the origin of the *Tableau* to the principle of natural order in China. Clerc, a contemporary of Quesnay, was a historian and a writer on education, and just like Quesnay, served as a royal physician. In 1769, eleven years after the publication of the *Tableau*, Clerc published *Yu le Grand et Confucius*, a book written to teach his students the fundamentals of government (Maverick, 1940, p. 317).[2] Clerc (1769, pp. xiv–xv) makes in this work special reference to the relation of the Chinese legislators' principles of natural order to Quesnay's *Tableau*:

> Of course, if we look at all the schools of thought included in the researches and writings of the Chinese legislators, we will find immutable insights never seen in Europe or in the existing world. Yet even these rare and great men merely recognized the basic laws of natural order, and taught them to others. It is like Columbus being content to inform the Spaniards of the American continent, but not interested in surveying its maps. This principle of natural order was discovered by Europe ten years ago, and France has produced the genius for its application. All kinds of social institutions will henceforth be tested by the touchstone of the *Tableau Économique*, a careful study of which will clear away the clouds that blind politics. The author, a clever supranationalist, has chosen solid arguments for his thesis and has thoroughly explored the rights of mankind. Since time immemorial, we have been concealed from the core of nature by the rags of Goths or barbarians, and from the real nature by forged ornaments. Now, relying on the vigorous advocacy of the author of the *Tableau Économique*, the rags are being stripped away and the counterfeit ornaments torn away.

[2] In the same place, Maverick (1940, p. 317) also briefly introduces Nicolas-Gabriel Clerc's *Yu le Grand et Confucius*, stating, "The book is written in a free and flowing style, and contains extensive advice on good government, an exposition of the natural moral order, thoughts on directed or purposeful evolution both social and individual, and many sections on education, on which subject the author has also written in other works."

> I am not surprised, therefore, to hear that the English give a prize of a thousand guineas to the man who translates this work.[3]

Maverick (1940, p. 317) summarizes the basic meaning of Clerc's above discussion by quoting him as follows: "[T]he Chinese discovered the law of the natural order, but did not work out all its details; it had remained for the genius (Quesnay) who ten years earlier had produced the *Tableau* to develop the principles, and, as it were, to provide charts and maps." In other words, Quesnay's *Tableau* is just a way of materializing the laws of natural order that the Chinese found in the form of a chart. Goto Sueo, a Japanese scholar, in his analysis of this quotation from Clerc, comes to a view that is roughly the same as Maverick's interpretation. Goto (1956, p. 389) points out that it is Quesnay's *Tableau* that Clerc referred to when he mentioned the European discovery of the principles of natural order ten years earlier. Where, then, did Quesnay discover this principle? Goto (ibid.) quotes Clerc to the effect that the shortcoming of the Chinese legislators was that they did not systematize the basic law of nature, whereas Quesnay described this law in detail. Thus, Clerc believed that Quesnay based his *Tableau* on Chinese thought, or rather, Quesnay systematized Chinese thought in his *Tableau*. In short, both Maverick and Goto affirm that Clerc regarded Quesnay's *Tableau* as a complete inheritance and development of the Chinese principle of natural order.

The natural order is indeed a theoretical cornerstone of the *Tableau*. Upon sending his first version of the *Tableau* to Mirabeau as a gift, Quesnay described his intent in a letter "to construct a fundamental Tableau of the economic order for the purpose of displaying expenditure and products in a way that is easy to grasp, and for the purpose of forming a clear opinion about the organization and disorganization which the governments can bring about" (Fox-Genovese, 1976, p, 257). A little while later, in his second letter to Mirabeau, he added that "it will be very easy to picture them [certain closely interwoven ideas] as a whole in their order and interconnection at a single survey" (Quesnay, 1962, p. 117). That is to say, the *Tableau* is nothing more than a simple and clear expression of the basic economic order of society. The institutions that bring poverty and ruin to the nations "[have] no connection with the order of the *Tableau*" (p. 131). Thus, the order in the *Tableau* is "the order of the regular circulation" (p. 120), the order of perpetual reproduction, expressing the same amount of income (Mirabeau & Quesnay, 1764). Here, "the same amount of income" refers to the income of the current year, which is always the same as that of the previous year, forming what is called the "order of perpetual reproduction," which is in fact the order of continuous simple reproduction. It is under conditions of simple reproduction that Quesnay's *Tableau* extracts the results of all administrative irregularities in order to trace the natural order of causes and effects (Mirabeau & Quesnay, 1764). It is an attempt to understand "the purest truths" through "the path of simplification." Recognizing that the "great law" which governs all things permeates the parts and governs the whole, Quesnay (1962), in his analysis of the

---

[3] Guinea is an old British gold coin. Clerc might not have seen Quesnay's first edition of *Tableau Économique*, created in 1758, so the *Tableau* discovered "ten years ago" may refer to the one created in 1759.

Tableau, repeatedly emphasized that "*the nation should be given instruction in the general laws of the natural order, which constitute the form of government which is self-evidently the most perfect*" (p. 231), or "according to the most constant rule of the natural order" (p. 153), should oppose all economic actions that are contrary to the natural order. The foundational position of the natural order in the *Tableau* is thus established.

Clerc recognized that the *Tableau* is based on the natural order, and like many others of his time, he used China as a model for observing the natural order. So, it was not unreasonable for him to infer that the *Tableau* implements the principles of the natural order of ancient China. The core of the natural order, which serves as the basis for the *Tableau*, is "that they [the Physiocrats] conceived these forms (the bourgeois forms of production) as physiological forms of society: as forms arising from the natural necessity of production itself, forms that are independent of anyone's will or of politics, etc. They are material laws" (Marx, 1969, p. 44). This central idea is embodied in the *Tableau*, which examines the reproduction and circulation of social wealth in order to study the regularities in it. In Quesnay's own words, the object of economics is to study the laws of nature that ensure the reproduction and continuity of human society, so that expenditure can achieve the greatest possible reproduction (Mirabeau & Quesnay, 1764). Clerc thought that the *Tableau* reveals "the core of nature" or "the real nature" that has long been concealed by man, and that is exactly the law of nature that is not subject to human will. In his view, the basic law of the natural order has already been recognized by the "Chinese legislators," thus forming their incomparable "immutable insights;" and Quesnay, although called "the genius" with the discovery of this law, is far behind these "rare great men" in China. This means that Quesnay's invention of the *Tableau* as a concrete demonstration of the principles of the natural order follows in the footsteps of the Chinese ancients.

Clerc's assertion was made two years after Quesnay's publication of *Despotism in China*. In that work, Quesnay's great admiration for the natural order in China must have drawn Clerc's attention to the theories of the Physiocrats, leading him to conclude that the principles of natural order in the *Tableau* came from China. Our analysis in the previous chapter has proved that the Physiocratic theory of natural order has indeed absorbed some elements of traditional Chinese culture as one of its important sources. Therefore, Clerc's central link between the birth of the *Tableau* and the inspiration of Chinese ideas through the principle of natural order should be said to be historically authentic.

II. *Yi Jing*

Clerc (1769, pp. xiv–xv) compared the Chinese legislators' unveiling the principle of natural order to Columbus's discovery of the New World, and compared the *Tableau Économique*, which concretizes and schematizes this principle, to the mapping of the New World by Columbus's successors. But for the Physiocrats, even the specific diagram of the *Tableau* itself resembles the 64 hexagrams of ancient China. The Abbé Baudeau once said, "This *Tableau* is able to explicate economic principles with a few numbers, as Fu Xi's 64 hexagrams the philosophical essentials" (Quoted in Zhu, 2005b, p. 316). This statement is further expressed by Baudeau in the following way: "It actually required several volumes to develop the basic truths, which the *Tableau économique* contains in four lines, just as those four lines were required to explain the sixty-four figures of the Fo-hi" (Quoted in Reichwein, 1925, p. 109). Not only did the Physiocrats have such an understanding, but their opponents at that time also compared the *Tableau* with the sixty-four hexagrams in *Yi Jing* (*I-Ching* or *Y-King*). Linguet, for example, in his *Reponse aux Docteurs Modernes* (1771), satirized the Physiocrats: "Confucius drew up a table, the *Y-King*, of sixty-four terms, also connected by lines, to show the evolution of the elements, and your *Tableau Oeconomique* is justly enough compared to it, but it comes three hundred years too late. Both alike are equally unintelligible" (Quoted in Higgs, 1897, pp. 149–150).[4] For this reason, Linguet published the *Tableau* alongside *Yi Jing* for comparison.

Among several arguments in Western scholarship for the Chinese origin of the *Tableau Économique*, that the *Tableau* is modeled on the 64 hexagrams of the *I-Ching* is particularly influential. Oncken, when editing *Oeuvres Économiques et Philosophiques de Quesnay* in the late nineteenth century, pointed out that "the composition of the *Tableau Économique* imitated the 'sixty-four hexagrams of Fu Xi'" (Quoted in Zhu, 2005b, p. 317). Reichwein (1925, p. 109) believes, on the basis of the Abbé Baudeau's statement, that Quesnay's *Tableau* "was the ingenious translation into mathematics of a Chinese doctrine." J. Hecht, another modern French scholar, says in a more explicit tone that the *Tableau* was certainly inspired by the *I-Ching* and the 64 hexagrams of Fu Xi (Quoted in Einaudi, 1958, p. 268). So, what exactly may the *Tableau* have been inspired by the *I-Ching*? Before discussing this question, we need to first introduce the history of the spread of the *I-Ching* to the West and the basic attitude of the Physiocrats towards this Confucian classic.

1. *Yi Jing*'s spread in Europe

Yi Jing (*I-Ching*), also known as *Zhou Yi*, consists of two parts: the *Jing* and the *Zhuan* (Biography). The former consists of mainly 64 hexagrams (*Gua*) and three hundred and eighty-four hexagrams (*Yao*). Each of the *Guas* and *Yaos* has its own description, that is, *Gua Ci* and *Yao Ci*, which were originally used for divination. Their origins vary. Legend has it that Fu Xi painted *Guas*, and Wen Wang composed *Cis*. The germination period may be as early as the Yin and Shang Dynasties. The latter contains seven kinds of explanation of the *Gua* and *Yao* hexagrams, a total of ten articles, collectively known as the "Ten Wings," which is, according to the old legend, the work of Confucius. In fact, the *I-Ching* is not a one-man work, but was formed gradually in the Spring and Autumn Period and the Warring States Period. It ranks first among the thirteen Confucian Classics, and the spread to Europe of this important Chinese ancient work began with the introduction and translation of Western Jesuits in China.

In about the 1680s, introductory texts on the *I-Ching* were already available in the West. After returning to Europe in 1682, the missionary to China Philippe Couplet

[4] Here, "three hundred years" may, according to our following analysis, mean that the annotated version of the sixty-four diagrams in the Ming Dynasty spread into Europe three hundred years later, so Linguet made a mistake by saying that "your *Tableau Oeconomique* ... comes three hundred years too late."

had an audience with the King of France and wrote a book entitled *To the King of France, Louis XIV*, the introduction of which, "Chinese Philosophy Explained," discusses the *I-Ching*'s 64 hexagrams and their meanings. Since then, the number of missionaries studying the *I-Ching* in China gradually increased. At the turn from the seventeenth to the eighteenth century, the Westerners engaged in this research, more out of missionary needs than otherwise, attempted to prove that the *I-Ching* has the concept of Catholicism, so as to achieve their purpose of "resorting to ancient Chinese to preach to the Chinese." Among them were the famous so-called "Figurists," of which Joachim Bouvet was the initiator, and Foucquet and Joseph de Prémare were important members.

The Figurists were all French Jesuits in China, who specialized in gleaning remarkable points from the *I-Ching* and other ancient classics and interpreting them in symbolic terms, in order to prove that these Chinese works contain primitive religious revelations. Bouvet, for example, argued that the mysteries of the Bible "are hidden in a prophetic manner in the valuable masterpieces of ancient China" (Quoted in Wang, 1979, p. 103) and that "we must compare the Bible with the ancient Chinese classics, especially the *I-Ching*, in order to rediscover with reference to each other the perfect philosophy containing heavenly teachings and beliefs" (p. 103). He regarded Fu Xi as the prophet who brought the primitive religions of mankind to China, and asserted that "there is no better way to show how the heart and soul of the Chinese are in harmony with the doctrine of Christ than studying the *I-Ching*, which contains the truth and is very difficult to understand" (p. 103). "The mystery of the numbers of the *I-Ching*," he also said, "seems to echo the mysterious mathematics of ancient Greek philosophers Pythagoras and Plato, and Egyptian Jewish philosophy, which have been handed down by the first ancestor to the descendants [...] and must be the mysterious revelation from the Creator" (pp. 103–104). Therefore, he believed that "the mystery of creation and the Trinity can be seen in the hexagrams" (p. 104). "The divine teachings of the great *I-Ching*," he argued, "can only be carried forward through the cooperation of Chinese and Western scholars. Both Chinese and Western human beings come from the same ancestors, originally brothers, and from the same Creator, adhering to the same sacred teachings, and sharing a common belief" (p. 102). It can thus be seen that he stressed the value of studying the *I-Ching* purely out of religious vision.

Foucquet also quoted the *I-Ching* to prove that the mystery of the original revelation had been taught around the world, and that "the most complete preservation of this ancient secret is in China" (p. 105), arguing that "the character *Yi* is a mysterious code name of Jesus Christ" (p. 107). Joseph de Prémare, however, though claiming to be a student of Bouvet, was not as obsessed with the prophecies of the *I-Ching* as the latter was when he sought the relics of primitive religious revelation in ancient Chinese texts. He preferred to study Chinese culture as an independent system, and is therefore called "the first to bring the ancient history of China out of the Judeo-centric Christian doctrine with a more rational attitude" (p. 109).

The study of the *I-Ching* by Bouvet and others had been promoted by Kang Xi himself. Fang Hao (1947) notes that, in 1710, the forty-ninth year of Kang Xi's reign, Fucquet "obeyed the imperial edict" (p. 90), and, in spite of his sickness, went to Beijing from Jiangxi to help Bouvet draft the *I-Ching*, so they could "present it for the emperor's review when he returned to Beijing" (p. 90). In the same year, Kang Xi repeatedly asked Bouvet about "the progress of interpreting the *I-Ching*" or "the progress of his studies of the *I-Ching*" (p. 90). In 1713, the fifty-second year of his reign, Kang Xi ordered Bouvet to independently study the *I-Ching*, "without having to recruit someone else, and without making a rush, and to report only upon completion" (p. 91). The Chinese emperor's interest in this matter further inspired the missionaries in China to study the *I-Ching*. It is said that the Vatican Library now contains fourteen research manuscripts of the *I-Ching* in Chinese by Westerners, some of which may have been written by missionaries in China during this period. Around the same time, various foreign language translations of the *I-Ching* began to arrive in Europe. Jean-Baptiste Régis translated the *I-Ching* into Latin under the title "The *I-Ching*, the Most Ancient Book of China."[5] Bouvet produced a version entitled "Manuscript of the Gist of the I-Ching." Claude de Visdelous's commentary on the *I-Ching* was appended to Antoine Gaubil's French translation of *Shang Shu* (*The Book of Documents*); and Gaubil himself mentioned in a letter in 1752 that the most important part of the existing translations of the *I-Ching* had not yet been sent to Europe, namely, Confucius' commentary on King Wen and his son Zhou Gongdan. His remark that "if no one has yet translated it, then I would like to work on it" (Quoted in Fang, 1947, p. 94) clearly refers to the translation of *Zhuan*, a part of the *I-Ching*.

In addition to the above translations of the *I-Ching*, paraphrases of its contents or individual points are often found in the various letters and writings of the missionaries. Besides the missionaries to China, those Europeans who had never been to China also introduced the *I-Ching* in their works, such as Du Halde's *Description de l'Empire de la Chine*. The *I-Ching* has been interpreted and elaborated throughout the Chinese dynasties, which has formed a long-established study, so Western missionaries did not pay attention only to the pre-Qin *I-Ching*, but also attached great importance to the different elucidations by later generations of scholars, especially the Confucians of the Song Dynasties. For example, Sun Zhang, in his *Xing Li Zhen Quan* ("A True Explanation of Reason") (1753), used the *I-Ching* of the pre-Qin Confucian scholars to attack the "primordial learning" of Shao Yong's *Huang Ji Jing Shi Shu* ("Book of Supreme World Ordering Principle") and Zhou Dunyi's *Taiji* Diagram, arguing that their interpretations of the *I-Ching* contradicted its original intent.

It can thus be seen that in the late seventeenth century and the first half of the eighteenth century, the *I-Ching* received unprecedented attention from Westerners through the medium of missionaries to China. This was especially attributable to the esteem and reference by the "Figurists." In the transmission of the *I-Ching* to the West, the most remarkable thing for our study is the correspondence between Bouvet

---

[5] The book is divided into three volumes. The first consists of eleven chapters discussing the authorship, value, and contents of the *I-Ching*, the hexagrams created by Fu Xi, and the value of the *Five Classics*, the second translations of the original text of the *I-Ching* and its commentaries, and the third commentaries on the *I-Ching*.

and Leibniz concerning the *I-Ching*, which is an important event in the history of cultural exchanges between China and the West.

The correspondence was carried on in roughly the eleven years from 1697 to 1707.[6] In a letter in 1698, Bouvet already mentioned the *I-Ching*, and believed that "the diagrams of Fu Hsi [Fu Xi] concentrate not only arithmetical and linguistic elements but also the natural principles of all sciences" (Mungello, 1977, p. 43). Thereafter, Leibniz sent Bouvet a list of binary arithmetic he had invented as a table of numbers from 0 to 32. In this arithmetic, there were only two signs, 0 and 1, with which all numbers could be written. "When I communicated this system to the Reverend Father Bouvet," Leibniz (1994, p. 133) said, "he recognized in it the characters of Fohi, for the numbers 0 and 1 correspond to them exactly if we put a broken line for 0 and unbroken line for the unity, 1." Therefore, on November 4, 1701, Bouvet sent Leibniz two diagrams—one was a circle consisting of sixty-four hexagrams, and the other was also a circle, but the sixty-four square hexagrams within was intentionally made to show the coincidence between the *I-Ching* hexagrams and Leibniz's binary arithmetic. Later, in their correspondence, the *I-Ching* was often used as the main reference for discussing Chinese philosophy.

The *I-Ching* diagrams provided by Bouvet, in fact, are the work of the Northern Song philosopher Shao Yong (1011–1077). According to the explanation of the formation of the Eight Diagrams in the *I-Ching*, Shao (2016) added Daoist thoughts and formulated a cosmic structure schema, namely "primordial Eight Diagrams," which are mainly about the orientation of the Eight Diagrams and the arrangement of the sixty-four hexagrams in order to speculate natural and human changes. It is said that this schema and its principle of "image number" had existed before there were heaven and earth, so its graphs are called "primordial diagrams" and its study "primordial science." The primordial diagrams were once named Fu Xi, and there were Fu Xi eight diagrams sequence, Fu Xi eight diagrams orientation, Fu Xi sixty-four hexagrams sequence and Fu Xi sixty-four hexagrams orientation. This creation made the *I-Ching* hexagrams systematic, and Zhu Xi recorded these four pictures in his *Original Meaning of Zhou Yi* in the Southern Song Dynasty, which was handed down to this day. Bouvet obviously had some knowledge of Shao Yong's above hexagrams.

Bouvet expressed mathematically the divination in Fu Xi Eight Diagrams Orientation (see Fig. 1).

The eight diagrams in Fig. 1 overlap in pairs and become sixty-four hexagrams, that is, the single trigrams become hexagrams. For example, the khien hexagrams change from trigrams in eight diagrams to hexagrams in sixty-four diagrams. These hexagrams were called by Bouvet as "hexagons" or "hexagrams," which have metaphysical function and represent a complete and harmonious celestial cycle, for the interpretation of the necessary principles of natural and universal transmission and

[6] Gorai Kinzo (1938, pp. 262–264) pays special attention to the correspondence between Bouvet and Leibniz when he studies Leibniz's new interpretation of the *I-Ching*, mentioning only the letters between them from 1697 to 1702. However, Mungello (1977, p. 40), an American scholar, says, "The Leibniz-Bouvet correspondence consists of at least fifteen letters dating from the year 1697 to 1707 or shortly thereafter."

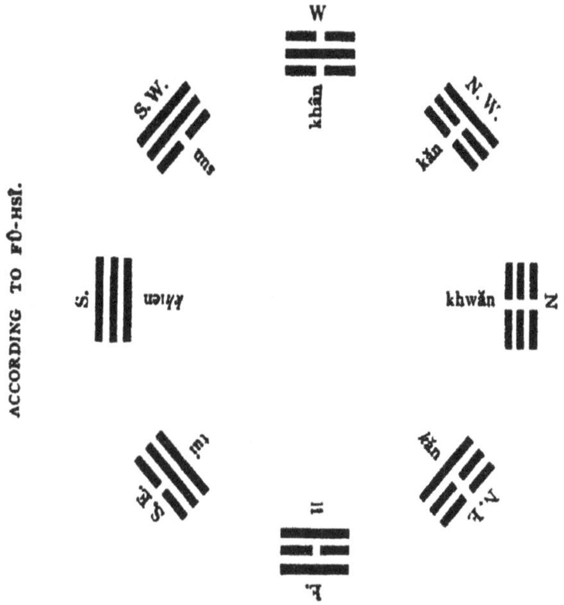

Fig. 1 The Fu Xi eight diagrams orientation (Quoted in Legge, 1963, p. 56)

destruction. He also contrasted the hexagons with the six days of creation, from which he explored the mysteries of Christianity (Roy, 1972, pp. 157, 159). Having been informed of Bouvet's ideas, Leibniz started to believe, too, that the hexagons of the eight diagrams could reveal the principles of natural theology and he thus further developed them.[7]

The prototype of the *I-Ching* hexagrams (see Fig. 2) given by Bouvet to Leibniz is also the orientation diagram of Fu Xi 64 hexagrams by Shao Yong (see Fig. 3). Fig. 2 follows a Chinese woodblock layout style, in which the Greek words were added by Bouvet, and the Arabic numerals from 0 to 63 marked beside the circular and square diagrams were calculated and added into the prototype by Leibniz according to the principle of the yin hexagram (–) for 0 and yang hexagram (–) for 1, as well as his binary principle. This figure is now kept in the Library of Hanover, Germany.

[7] In 1701–02, Leibniz replied to Bouvet in a letter, saying that the Eight Diagrams is composed of eight-line diagrams that Chinese regard as fundamental. Fu Xi used it to reveal the creation of the world: The universe comes from "0" and "1," which indicate the relations in the story of *Genesis.* "0" can be deemed as the emptiness created before heaven and earth, and in the following seven days, each represents the existence and creation. The first day "1" represents the existence of God, and the second day "2" the existence of heaven and earth created on the first day (in 000010, 0 represents the earth). The seventh day indicates the existence of all things, because it is the most complete day, or the so-called Sabbath, signifying the completion of the creation of everything. Thus "7" should be written as "111," which has nothing to do with "0" (Gorai, 1938, pp. 274–275). All this is obviously an extension of Bouvet's views.

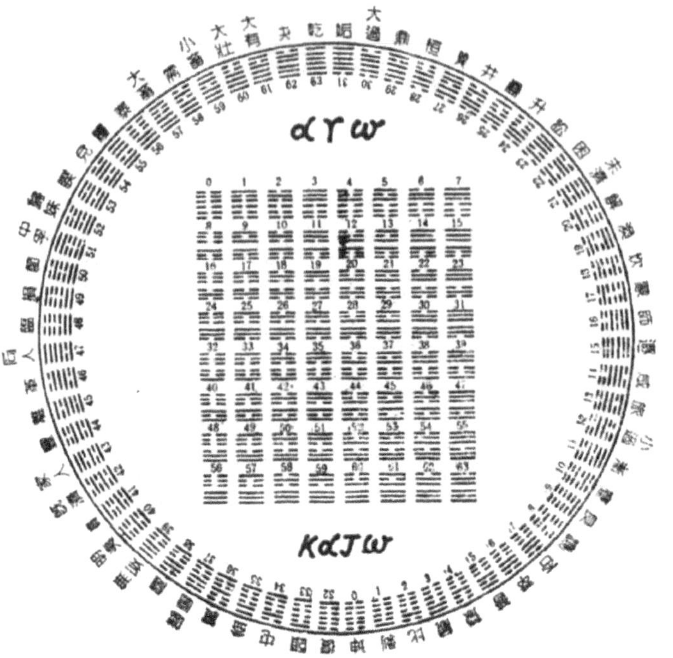

Fig. 2 The *I-Ching* hexagrams[8]

Leibniz (1994, p. 133) was very enthusiastic about the study of the "simplest" symbolic figures of the sixty-four hexagrams of the *I-Ching* sent by Bouvet: "Reverend Father Bouvet and I have discovered the meaning, apparently truest to the text, of the characters of Fohi, founder of Empire [...]. Several centuries after Fohi, the Emperor Ven Vam and his son Cheu Cum, and Confucius more than five centuries later, have all sought therein philosophical mysteries. [...] Actually, the 64 figures represent a Binary Arithmetic which apparently this great legislator [Fu Xi] possessed, and which I have rediscovered some thousands of years later." Evidently, Leibniz admitted that his thought was inspired by the *I-Ching* and admired Chinese philosophy as having a profound doctrinal basis. For this reason, when he sent the results of his research on binary arithmetic to the Academy of Paris in 1701, he included a copy of the 64 hexagrams of the *I-Ching* to explain this arithmetic. With Leibniz's prominent reputation and position in the European academic circles at that time, his high praise of the *I-Ching* naturally drew Westerners' attention to this ancient Chinese classic. Besides, that the members of the Physiocratic School and Linguet, their opponent, paralleled Quesnay's *Tableau* with the sixty-four hexagrams of the *I-Ching*, is exactly a reflection that the *I-Ching* had spread to Europe and had exerted considerable influence.

[8] This is the version Bouvet sent to Leibniz (Gorai, 1938, p. 265).

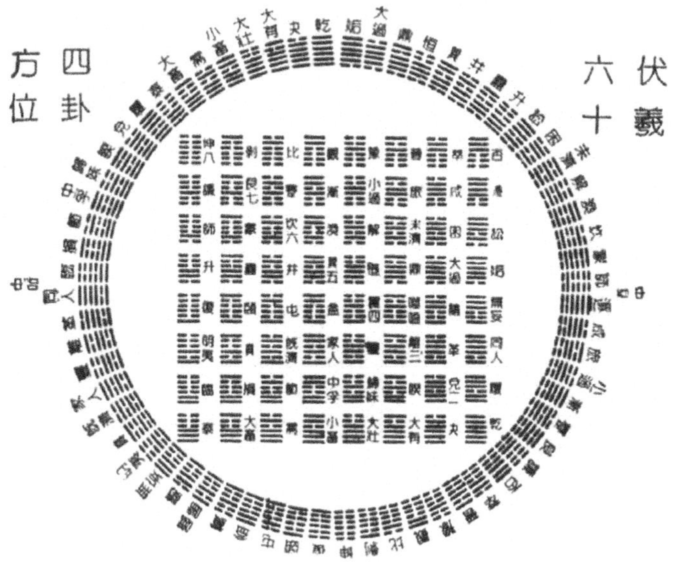

Fig. 3 The Fu Xi 64 hexagrams

The attitude of the Physiocrats towards the *I-Ching* is typically concentrated in Quesnay's exposition. When discussing the origin of the Chinese Empire, Quesnay (1946, p. 146) referred to the author of the *I-Ching*, Fu Xi (Fu Hsi), as the chosen leader of the third millennium B.C.: "[T]his ruler civilized the Chinese, and made a number of laws both wise and just. The annals not only depict this prince as a capable lawgiver, but also describe him as a profound mathematician, a creative genius to whom they owe many important inventions." When it came to the basic laws of China, he listed the *I-Ching*, or *The Book of Changes*, as the first of China's five "Sacred books or canons of the first order" by saying,

> This ancient book is mystical, and has greatly perplexed the wisdom of the Chinese, and particularly that of two emperors who undertook to throw light upon it through their commentaries, efforts which were without success. The obscurity of the commentaries only added to that of the text. Confucius cleared up the enigmatic lines of the *I Ching* and the works of the commentators; he recognized in it mysteries of great importance to the governing of states, and he drew from it excellent precepts on politics and ethics, which have been, since his time, the basis of Chinese learning. The scholars hold this book in the highest esteem, and Fu Hsi, whom they regard as the author, passes as the father of learning and of good government.
>
> (pp. 186–187)

Quesnay's commentary on the *I-Ching* and its legendary creator, Fu Xi, shows his respect for the works of the ancient Chinese sages. In particular, he attributed to Confucius the achievement of solving the riddle of the *I-Ching*, which even more reflects the admiration of this "Confucius of Europe" for his Chinese idol. The "enigmatic lines of the *I-Ching*" mentioned above obviously refer to the eight or sixty-four diagrams. According to Linguet's statement that the *Tableau Économique* came into being three hundred years later than the sixty-four hexagrams of the *I-Ching*, the hexagrams that Quesnay saw may be taken from a copy or annotated version of the *I-Ching* popular in the Ming Dynasty in China in the fifteenth century,[9] rather than from the original book. However, no matter which edition the hexagrams came from, the wide spread of the *I-Ching* and its hexagrams in Europe at that time was enough to arouse, and indeed aroused, Quesnay's keen interest in it. Therefore, it is by no means unreasonable to associate the *Tableau* invented by him with the sixty-four hexagrams in the *I-Ching*.

2. Elements of the *I-Ching*

The relationship between the *Tableau* and the sixty-four hexagrams of the *I-Ching*, according to the hints from the Physiocrats and their opponents, has been corroborated by the history of the spread of the *I-Ching* in Europe and by Quesnay's great admiration for the *I-Ching*. However, it is still not revealed what Quesnay had learned from the sixty-four hexagrams when he designed the *Tableau*.

Interestingly, the *Tableau* and the hexagrams in the *I-Ching* are mysterious things that are difficult to understand for the general Western scholars. As mentioned earlier, in the minds of Western missionaries in the seventeenth and eighteenth centuries, the *I-Ching* was synonymous with "mystery." Foucquet called it "a mysterious symbol," and Du Halde (Quoted in Wang, 1979, p. 111) said in his *Description de l'Empire de la Chine* that "this book is purely a riddle composed of lines." Influenced by these comments, Quesnay also thought that "this ancient book is mysterious," has "mysterious lines," or has "mysteries of great importance." Even in modern times, Needham (1966), a famous sinologist, still regards this work as "one of the greatest arcana of Chinese naturalistic philosophy" (p. 118), "one of the most remarkable works in all world literature" (p. 119), and "an elaborate system of symbols with their explanations-sixty-four patterns of long and short lines in all possible permutations and combinations" (pp. 118–119). This is the same case with the *Tableau*. Marx and Engels first compared the *Tableau* to the "riddle of the sphinx." Those who spoke of it later regarded it as a "vast mystery," saw it at first glance, because of its dazzlingly complex rows and columns, as a "mystic symbol" (Reichwein, 1925, p. 103), or lamented that "Quesnay's formulations of the *Tableau* were so condensed, disorderly, and enigmatic that nobody could really understand what he was getting at" (Meek, 1973, p. 118), so much so that "[n]o one can seriously claim that the Tableau Économique was free of obscurity" (Lekachman, 1959, pp. 83–84). "For the two centuries following the formulation of the first Tableau," Fox-Genovese (1976, p. 256) suggested, "an aura of mystery shrouded the true sequence of development." It is evident that people's impression of the *Tableau*, like that of the *I-Ching*, has accentuated its mysterious nature. What is left untouched, however, is whether there is

[9] The above-mentioned round and square 64 diagrams, given by Bouvet to Leibniz, were originally created by Shao Yong in his *Huang Ji Jing Shi Shu* in the eleventh century. The version that has been passed down to the present generation is the one annotated by Huang Ji. Huang lived in the late fifteenth century, 300 years earlier than the time when Quesnay created the Economic Table. It is yet to be clarified whether the 64 hexagrams mentioned by Linguet is this annotated version.

some common ground between these two mysterious works, or whether Quesnay, in conceiving his mysterious *Tableau*, learned anything from the mysterious hexagrams of the existing *I-Ching*. In our view, it is necessary to put forward at least the following points.

First, both Quesnay's original intention of creating the *Tableau* and his understanding of the *I-Ching* focused on the inner mechanism of state rule, which is the laws of the natural order.

The *I-Ching* interested Western missionaries because it was held to contain the secrets of so-called Christian doctrine. But from this "mystical" (Quesnay, 1946, p. 186) work with "enigmatic lines" (p. 187), Quesnay discovered, in the guise of Confucius, the "mysteries of great importance to the governing of states" (p. 187). This is in line with his own purpose in designing the *Tableau*, namely, to grasp "the whole essence of the economic government of agricultural states" (1962, p. 117). In explaining the *Tableau*, Quesnay stressed that it must always be remembered that prosperity is obtained if the administration of a country is well and honestly conducted. That is, any disruption of good governance is a political misfortune, and the difficulty in discovering a countermeasure to these various political misfortunes lies in not knowing the principle of governance (Mirabeau & Quesnay, 1764). This "principle" is the aforementioned "mysteries" or "essence." It can be seen that both Quesnay's original intention of creating the *Tableau* and his understanding of the *I-Ching* focused on the inner mechanism of state rule, showing a certain consistency in the guiding ideology of the two. Thus, Quesnay admired Confucius' derivation of "many outstanding political and ethical maxims" from the *I-Ching*, which is regarded as the origin of *The Analects*, and accompanied his *Tableau* with certain principles of economic management in the form of maxims, which is a practice that Zhu Qianzhi (2005b, p. 317) calls "borrowing from *The Analects of Confucius*."

Quesnay mentioned that the *I-Ching* contains implicitly "mysteries of great importance to the governing of states," but he did not specify what these "mysteries" are. It seems to us that these "mysteries" may be the laws of the natural order that he repeatedly emphasized in his *Tableau*, because the *I-Ching* is characterized by the importance it attaches to the laws of things.

According to the *I-Ching*, all changes of things are subject to a unified law, i.e., "all the movements under the sky are constantly subject to this one and the same rule" (Legge, 1963, p. 380). To grasp this law, it is necessary "to explore what is complex, search out what is hidden, to hook up what lies deep, and reach to what is distant" (p. 373). If we can do this, we will be able to control complexity with simplicity, and grasp the essence of the changes of all things: "With the attainment of such ease and such freedom from laborious effort, the mastery is got of all principles under the sky" (p. 349). The meaning of "the attainment of such ease and such freedom from laborious effort" is to focus on the relationship between laws and phenomena from the point of view of simplicity and complexity. Although the phenomena are complex, the laws are simple. As long as one grasps the law, one will not be confused by the complex and divergent phenomena: "(The diagrams) speak of the most complex phenomena under the sky, and yet there is nothing in them that need awaken dislike; the explanations of the lines speak of the subtlest movements under the sky, and yet there is nothing in them to produce confusion" (p. 361). One can thus grasp "all principles under the sky" that are characterized by "such ease and such freedom from laborious effort."

The specific expression of the above thought in the *I-Ching* might not be familiar to Quesnay, but the basic idea of attaching importance to exploring and mastering the laws of things had been repeatedly comprehended and interpreted by generations of Western scholars, and was obviously well known to a considerable number of Westerners who were concerned about Chinese culture. This can be seen from the general situation of the spread of the *I-Ching* in Europe at the time. We may well say that Quesnay understood the purport of the *I-Ching* to control complex phenomena with simple laws, and regarded it as a "mystery." Therefore, when he expressed the intention of the *Tableau*, he revealed the basic ideas which are very similar to the above viewpoints in the *I-Ching*. Quesnay (1962, p. 117) said,

> Thus the zigzag, if properly understood, cuts out a whole number of details, and brings before your eyes certain closely interwoven ideas which the intellect alone would have a great deal of difficulty in grasping, unravelling, and reconciling by the use of the method of discourse. Moreover these ideas themselves would be very elusive if they were not fixed securely in the imagination by the *Tableau*. Neither in themselves nor in their interrelationship will it now be possible for them to escape us; or at any rate it will be very easy to picture them as a whole in their order and interconnection at a single survey, so that we can contemplate them at our ease without losing anything from sight and without the mind having to worry about putting them in order.

Obviously, the purpose of Quesnay's *Tableau*, like that of the hexagrams in the *I-Ching*, is to control complexity with simplicity, and grasp the order of things, that is, the so-called "most permanent law" that runs through all parts of things and governs all of them, and then understand the intricate "panorama" of things through this law and corresponding relations. The commonality in this basic thinking between the *Tableau* and the *I-Ching* adds a corroborative argument to Clerc's elaboration above that the *Tableau* is the concretization and systematization of China's thought of natural order.

In addition, Quesnay placed particular emphasis on the fact that in depicting very intricate conceptions, it is obviously clearer and easier to rely on figures than on textual descriptions, so as to be able to conceive without any restraint. This view is very similar to that in the following statement in the *I-Ching*: "The written characters are not the full exponent of speech, and speech is not the full expression of ideas" (Legge, 1963, pp. 376–377). This statement, according to Xü Zhirui (1982, pp. 46–47), explains why the author of the *I-Ching* did not use words, but resorted to the form of hexagrams to express his complex ideas. The ancients realized that language, as a tool for expressing thoughts, has certain limitations, and sometimes it cannot fully express people's thought and artistic conception, so in the case that language can hardly be "the full exponent of speech," "[t]he sages made their emblematic symbols to set forth fully their ideas; appointed (all) the diagrams to show fully the truth and falsehood (of things)" (Legge, 1963, p. 377). That is, they expressed various complex thoughts with the help of hexagrams. It is still difficult to determine whether Quesnay's emphasis on describing complex ideas by relying on figures is inspired by similar thoughts in the *I-Ching* he admired. But it is noteworthy that his emphasis on figures in his creation of the *Tableau* is very similar to that embodied in the *I-Ching* diagrams, and that Quesnay was deeply inspired by such ideas when he created the *Tableau.*

Second, the *I-Ching* describes things by adopting a macro or overall analytical approach, and proposes in effect a systematic model for understanding the composition and development of the entire world, which is similar to Quesnay's *Tableau* in economics.

The *I-Ching* uses the eight diagrams of respectively Ch'ien, K'un, Chên, Sun, K'an, Li, Kên, and Tui, to symbolize eight natural phenomena of heaven, earth, thunder, wind, water, fire, mountain and marsh. Fung Yu-lan (1948, p. 141) compares the relationship between the eight to that between family members:

> In the trigrams, the undivided lines symbolize the *Yang* principle, and the divided lines the *Yin* principle. The trigrams *Ch'ien* and *K'un,* being made up entirely of undivided and divided lines respectively, are the symbols *par excellence* of the *Yang* and *Yin,* while the remaining six trigrams are supposedly produced through the intercourse of these primary two. Thus *Ch'ien* and *K'un* are father and mother, while the other trigrams are usually spoken of in the [*I-Ching*] as their "sons and daughters."

The origin of this generation of all things closely interconnected was later attributed to the interaction of the two forces of *Yin* and *Yang*.

The Chinese exegetists of the *I-Ching* throughout the ages have followed the *I-Ching*'s method of analyzing all things in the universe as a complete system from a macro or overall perspective, and created various diagrams and charts to vividly show the systematic model of the unified universe, in order to speculate on the changes in nature and society. The typical representative of this method of analysis and illustration is the orientation and sequence versions of the Eight or Sixty-four Diagrams by Shao Yong in the Northern Song Dynasty. Shao (2016) believed that the diagrams, though aided by no text or remarks, embody the principle of everything from heaven to earth, and that the *I-Ching* embodies *Taiji*, which unifies everything in heaven and earth. It can be seen that he took the macrocosm of "everything in heaven and earth" as the object of diagrammatic investigation. It was under the domination of this traditional idea, and with the purpose of schematically outlining a complete structure and evolution of the universe, that ancient Chinese scholars had been concentrating on the study of the *I-Ching* diagrams for a long time. In particular, the "Taiji Primordial Diagram" (see Fig. 4) thus worked out was widely circulated and had great influence. This diagram is intended to illustrate the significance and interconnections of the creation of the universe, the transformation of all things into living beings, and the way of human beings (Wu, 1982, pp. 13–20). Such a complex and profound meaning is represented by the whole diagram with only a few interconnected lines, and in the diagram, the schema is "reasonable in layout, distinct in hierarchy, and complete in system," which fully reflects the ancient Chinese macro-system concept and the ability to simplify the complex. As a characteristic feature of traditional Chinese culture, such diagrams were certain to have a unique influence on European thought as Chinese culture spread Westward.

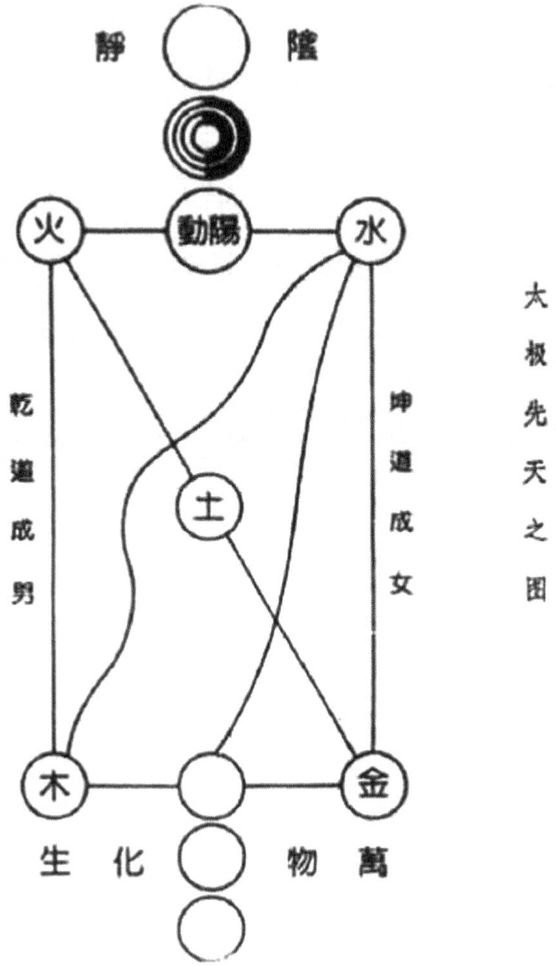

Fig. 4 The Taiji primordial diagram (Shanghai bookstore publishing house, 1988, Book 196)

The *I-Ching* and its exegetists' use of systemic concepts in pictorial form to analyze macro-objects as a whole has stirred up the interest of some modern Western scholars in a comparative study of China and the West from a different perspective. Reichwein (1925, p. 58 [Note]) claims that "we may mention in particular the fish-bladder ornament, which had so rich a development in the West, and the origin of which, whether as a form or as a symbol, goes back to the primeval Chinese symbolic figure of the *Tai Yi*, which is supposed to signify the mystic unity of Being and Not-Being." This indicates that the distinctive *I-Ching* schema has had a very peculiar influence in the Western world, which leads us to the concern about whether there are any similarities or parallels between the methods of analysis of the *I-Ching* and its diagrams, and those of Quesnay's *Tableau.*

In explaining his reasons for the *Tableau*, Quesnay stated that it was intended to capture the "whole picture" of the economic order and its relations with relevant things, and that the difficulty in understanding this *Tableau* lies in the fact that it relates to many things and requires that things be coordinated and mastered together (Mirabeau & Quesnay, 1764). This is clearly an overarching analytical view focusing on macro system. As a result, later scholars have summarized the economic doctrines of the Physiocratic School with particular emphasis on this methodological feature.

Spann (1930) emphasizes one of the contributions of the *Tableau* is that it is "based on the activities, not of economic individuals [...], but of economic subdivisions of society ('classes')" (p. 86), indicating that "the various branches of economic life are closely interrelated" (p. 86), so as to present "a vivid picture of economic life [...] and of its interlacement with the social process as a whole" (p. 87). Fox-Genovese (1976, p. 262) affirms that "Quesnay offers an analytical model for the description of the economic structure, performance, and strength of an imaginary state." Rubin (1979, p. 136) considers Quesnay's system to be "the first ingenious attempt to depict as a unified whole the entire *process of the reproduction, circulation, distribution, and consumption of a society's product*." Still some others specify that Quesnay drew on the relations between economic classes and the relationship between several aggregates to make a computational analysis of the overall economy, which is in fact the earliest overall analysis in the history of economics (Yu, 1986, p. 176). The application of the aggregate analysis method in economics falls under the category of macroeconomics. It is exactly a macro model that Quesnay's *Tableau* is to present. That is why Rima (2001, p. 386) claims, "Macroeconomic analysis [...] began with the Physiocrats. The *Tableau Economique* was concerned, not only with the allocation of resources, but also with the size of the net product and the requirements for its reproduction. [...], it is [...] to the Physiocrats that we are indebted for a fundamental concept of macroeconomic analysis." It can therefore be seen that in the history of Western economics, both the examination of macroeconomic phenomena and the conduct of aggregate analysis can be traced back to Quesnay's *Tableau*. This is indeed noteworthy!

It is also noteworthy that Quesnay is one of the originators of the use of diagrams to illustrate socio-economic activity. In the first section of this chapter, when describing the formation of the *Tableau Économique*, it is mentioned that there are two main types of the *Tableau*: the zigzag and the "Arithmetical Formula." In both types, the *Tableau* focuses on the exchange and circulation of the total product of society, and in both cases the movement of exchange and circulation begins with the acquisition of the total product at the end of the previous production year. However, the specific forms of exchange and circulation differ in these two different models of the *Tableau*. The zigzag, exemplified by the more mature version of the third edition (see Fig. 5), takes the form of curved connecting lines that represent the process of exchange and circulation of products between classes in a gradual, partial manner. The "Arithmetical Formula" (see Fig. 6), however, summarizes the entire, full-period circulation into five acts of exchange, and represents the process as a one-time aggregate proceeding (Chen, 1988a). Obviously, the second type is more capable of systematically capturing and presenting on a macro level the reproduction process of the entire national economy. It is on the basis of this "Arithmetical Formula" that Marx later claims that the *Tableau* uses a few thick lines to show the process of reproduction and circulation of social capital. The evolution of the *Tableau* from the complex model of the original zigzag, first to a summary model, and then to the basic model of the "Arithmetical Formula," is itself an indication of how Quesnay exhausted his efforts to vividly summarize his system of economic theory in a more concise and general diagram, the direct function of which is to elaborate on the reproduction process of the total capital of society by observing the exchange and circulation of wealth among the various social classes in the form of a total product. In this respect, Quesnay's deliberately expressing the whole of his system of doctrine in a simple *tableau* is strikingly similar to ancient Chinese scholars' devoted study of the *I-Ching* diagrams.

In particular, the various models of the *Tableau*, whatever their differences in content and form, all focus on pictorial representations of interconnected macroeconomic phenomena. Quesnay (1962, p. 117) himself stressed that it is difficult to grasp the intricate conception of economic phenomena by relying on textual descriptions alone: one may even forget it in the twinkling of an eye and not be able to keep it in one's mind for long; on the contrary, by relying on the *Tableau*, we can easily recall the whole picture. Accordingly, Du Pont regarded this *Tableau* as a surprising diagram that complements economic science (Quesnay, 1888). Modern scholars of economics are also extremely appreciative of the way the *Tableau* is presented. "The crowning achievement of [physiocracy]," Landreth (1976, p. 505) argues, "was Quesnay's table, which indicated, in very simple abstract form, the interdependence of various sectors of an economy." Schumpeter (1954a, p. 241) says that "the *tableau* method achieves a tremendous simplification. [...] A glance at the *tableau* suggests the idea of a Social Product or Total Output."

From the above analysis, it is clear that the overall analytical approach of the *Tableau*, which aims to grasp macro phenomena with a systemic concept, and its pictorial representation, are precisely the outstanding features of Chinese scholars who have studied the *I-Ching* throughout the ages. Besides, in the understanding of macro phenomena, according to the comparative study of ancient Chinese and Western thought, the Greek tradition focuses on what constitutes the world, i.e., the entities that make up the world, while the *I-Ching* in China has always put the question of how the world is created at the center of its thinking, focusing on the laws rather than such entities. For the author of the *I-Ching*, the entities that come out of the creation of the world are heaven and earth, so the combination of heaven and earth becomes a generic term for nature, which is viewed in its totality. The *I-Ching* is a direct approach to heaven and earth, exploring the laws by which they generate all things, rather than the constituents that make up heaven and earth as nature, as the Greek tradition does (Ren, 1983, pp. 618–619). In contrast, in terms of its basic ideas, Quesnay's *Tableau*, which focuses on the way of thinking and the overall analysis of economic phenomena from a macro perspective, is closer to the Chinese *I-Ching* than to the Western tradition of thought since ancient Greece.

Moreover, the schema of the *Tableau*, which once surprised Western economists, can be called an unprecedented pioneering work in the history of Western thought.

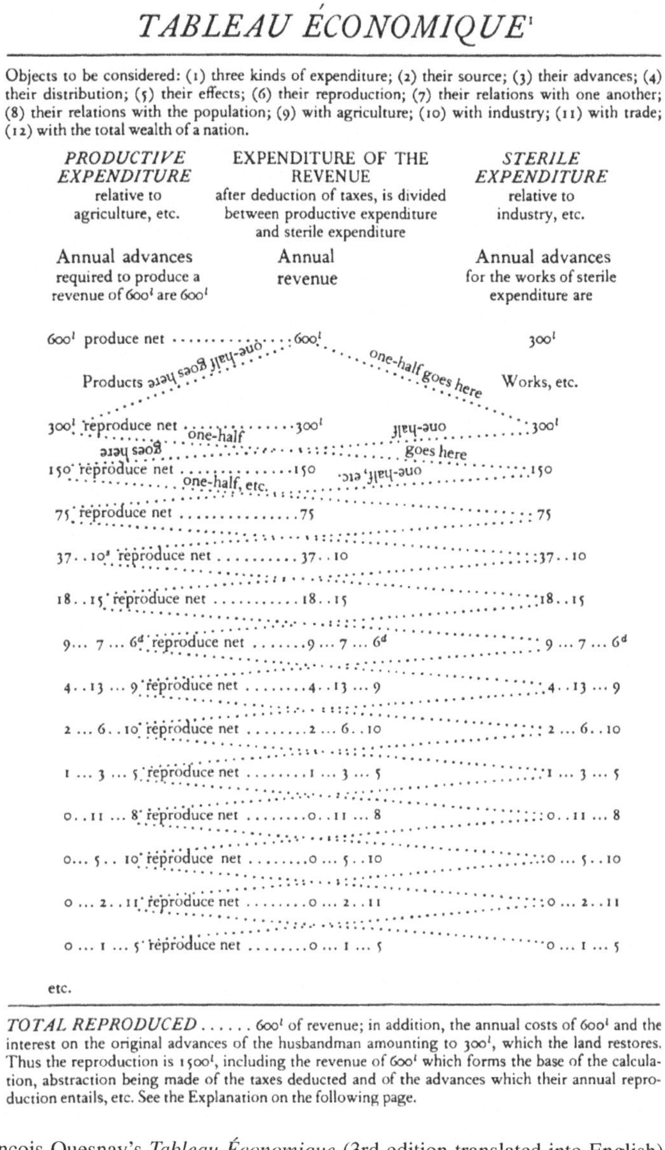

Fig. 5 François Quesnay's *Tableau Économique* (3rd edition translated into English) (Quesnay, 1972, p. xxxviii)[10]

However, in the various annotated editions of the *I-Ching*, this way of vividly expressing its profound implication is a good example to be followed by the *Tableau*. The aforementioned Primordial Taiji diagram is one of the prominent examples.

[10] In the *Tableau*, *Livre* (L), *sou* and *denier* are old French monetary units. One *livre* is equivalent to twenty *sous* and one sou twelve *denis*.

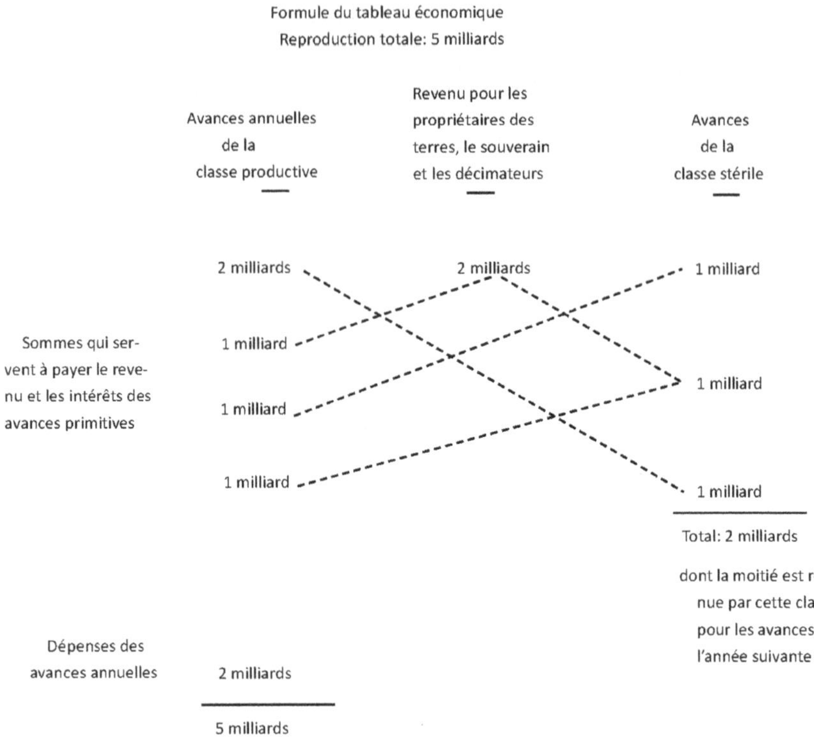

Fig. 6 *Tableau Économique* (Quoted in Du Pont, 1767)

Linguet, a contemporary of the Physiocrats, pointed out in particular that the sixty-four hexagrams in the *I-Ching* are linked by lines to show the change of every factor, which is comparable with the *Tableau*, implying that the illustrative method of the *Tableau* is modeled after the hexagrams in the *I-Ching* (Quoted in Higgs, 1897, pp. 149–150). A hundred years later, Marx (1992, p. 435) also praised Quesnay's *Tableau* for "show[ing] in a few broad lines" the reproduction and circulation of the total social capital. Of course, the schema of *Tableau* is far different from the hexagrams in the *I-Ching* in content and form, but both of them connect and explain the macro elements with a few lines. Such similarity in diagrammatic approach can hardly be explained by coincidence. This is why, in Quesnay's time, both his disciples and opponents associated the *Tableau* with the 64 hexagrams of the *I-Ching*, which reveals that the former was most likely to be directly inspired by the latter.

Third, the concept of equilibrium, as a theoretical premise of the *Tableau Économique*, can date back to the organic principle of the *I-Ching*.

In our analysis of the organic character of the Physiocratic concept of natural order, we have mentioned that Quesnay, in treating society as a living organism, advocated a physiological anatomical approach to the analysis of socio-economic processes, the purpose of which was precisely to explore and determine the equilibrium state of socio-economic functioning. That is why, in his view, the interrelated parts of the socio-economic whole tend to equilibrate in movement, and society is healthy only when it is in equilibrium. This is fully expressed in Quesnay's *Tableau*, which, including both the zigzag and the "Arithmetical Formula," embodies an exploration of the socio-economic process in equilibrium: how the economic sectors are mutually constrained and interdependent, and how the total product of society is distributed through circulation among the three classes so that its simple reproduction, i.e., reproduction on the original scale, proceeds. If these conditions are violated, the *Tableau*, in Mirabeau's words, "has lost its equilibrium" (Quoted in Meek, 1962, p. 287). Eltis (1975, pp. 196–197) points out, "The conditions for stationary state equilibrium are, as Quesnay and later Marx appreciated, the starting-point for an analysis of the conditions where growth will be achieved. Clearly there will be growth or decline in aggregate output if the equilibrium of the Tableau is disturbed. That is why the precise conditions in which the Tableau is in equilibrium are of such importance." Just as Rosenberg (1934–36) believes, the *Tableau* is intended to explicate the state of equilibrium.

Quesnay's *Tableau*, Fox-Genovese (1976) says, is "the first presentation of a circular-flow equilibrium in the history of economic thought" (pp. 50–51). Barna (1975) remarks, "It is well known that the *Tableau* describes stationary equilibrium in a closed system" (p. 486), and praises Quesnay's description of the circulation in a state of equilibrium that can sustain itself under certain assumptions as his "great achievement" (p. 496). Schumpeter (1954a) also gives high praise to the *Tableau*, regarding it as "the first method ever devised in order to convey an *explicit* conception of the nature of economic equilibrium" (p. 242).

At that time, how did this idea of equilibrium come into being? The *I-Ching*, which Quesnay valued, is a source that cannot be ignored. As already mentioned, Quesnay's idea of equilibrium can be directly deduced from the organic nature of his doctrine of natural order, which is considered to be independent of traditional European thought and to be derived from similar concepts in ancient China. One of the typical manifestations of this ancient Chinese concept is the doctrine of the *I-Ching*.

In the organic principle of the *I-Ching*, the idea of equilibrium has a quaint and primitive form. It regards nature and society as a whole, and starts from the premise of mutual constraint and interdependence among all things to investigate the creation of all things in the highest harmony, that is, in the state of "great harmony" (*taihe*). Cheng Yi explained this as follows: The way of heaven and earth, which is always lasting and unchanging, is to preserve and maintain harmony (Quoted in Chen & Zheng, 1989). This means that maintaining this supreme harmony is a necessary condition for things to always be cyclical and unceasing. This supreme harmony preceded Leibniz's so-called "first set of harmony," both belonging to the category of equilibrium.

The *I-Ching*'s idea of equilibrium has a strong traditional Chinese flavor. It takes the change of *yin* and *yang* as the general law that runs through the Dao of Heaven, of Earth and of Man, and treats equilibrium as a basic principle throughout the change. This equilibrium is evidenced in the law of *yin-yang* balance shown by Dong Guangbi's (1987, pp. 100–102) quantitative analysis of the *I-Ching* diagrams.

Furthermore, some scholars, on the basis of the frequent occurrence of *zhong* in the Chinese terms of *zhong-xing* ("middle line"), *zhong-dao* ("middle way"), *zhong-zheng* ("middle right"), *da-zhong* ("big middle"), *gang-zhong* ("strong middle") and *wei-zhong* ("in the middle") from the *I-Ching*, think that "*zhong* here embodies the sense of equilibrium, or more specifically, the meaning of static equilibrium," and thus argue that in the *I-Ching* can also be found the idea of dynamic equilibrium and even the market concept of "the equilibrium of supply and demand" (Hou, 1982, pp. 26–27). Though they use the concept of equilibrium in modern economic theory to explain the *I-Ching*, which is inevitably a little far-fetched, they do significantly uncover, at least in the basic sense, the similarity of the *I-Ching*'s early element of equilibrium to the modern principle of equilibrium.

The idea of equilibrium in the *I-Ching* is also reflected in other Confucian classics and, as it has been passed down through the ages, constitutes an important element of traditional Chinese thought. With the introduction into Europe of Chinese texts such as the *I-Ching*, this Chinese idea became better known to Westerners. Besides, in Quesnay's time, European societies still lacked an organic philosophical tradition,[11] and it seemed unlikely that the concept of general equilibrium in economics could have been independently developed only from the soil of Western thought. The founders of classical French political economy, including those before Quesnay, had paid attention to overall equilibrium, but it is difficult to explain the origin of their ideas from the European heritage system alone. We will devote a special discussion to this point below. Suffice it to say here that Quesnay, who is regarded by Western economists as the founder of equilibrium theory, was a great admirer of the *I-Ching*, an ancient Chinese book that is rich in equilibrium ideas. In the absence of such a tradition in Europe, the equilibrium model conceived by Quesnay in the *Tableau* can be seen as the result of his own creative thinking, but we cannot rule out the possibility that he was influenced by the principles and diagrams of the *I-Ching* introduced into Europe at that time. Up to now, no one has reached this conclusion among Western economists.[12] Far from a groundless argument, it is a logical inference from a comparative study of the cultural background of Chinese and Western sources of Quesnay's equilibrium ideas.

---

[11] Spann (1930) argues that, even though Quesnay's *Tableau* had "[given] an organic picture" (p. 86) of economic activities, later economists still stuck to a theory of the formal laws of value and price (pp. 109–113) and "no one seemed to be aware that an 'organic' system of economics had existed" (p. 11).

[12] Hou Jiajü (1982, p. 239) says, "Based on Confucianism, Quesnay's *Tableau Économique* is the origin of the general equilibrium theory. So, [...] it was distinctive ancient Chinese economy that bred the modern general equilibrium theory." Based on the analysis on ancient Chinese economic thought, Hou argues that China's economic thought has been taking the general equilibrium as the basis, and that incomes of different industries, under the state of general equilibrium, tended to be the same, as said by Sima Qian and Guanzi. However, Hou has never explained how ancient Chinese economic thought influenced Quesnay's *Tableau*.

The history of economic doctrines shows that the idea of equilibrium in Quesnay's *Tableau*, as well as the overall equilibrium concept of the pioneers of the Physiocratic School, did not attract enough attention for a long time afterwards. Not even the attention of Adam Smith, a famous economist who was very close to the Physiocrats. This indicates that Quesnay's concept of equilibrium was still rather alien to many Western economists at the time and for some time afterwards, and was not as easily understood and accepted by Western scholars as the product of the native-born European tradition of thought. It was not until Marx that the genius of Quesnay was fully recognized. Soon afterwards, in bourgeois economics, beginning with Lyon Walras, a growing interest was shown in Quesnay's idea of equilibrium, which formed the main source for the emergence and development of modern equilibrium theory.

Spengler (1968, p. 445) points out, "Walras developed a *tableau* he considered 'analogous' to Quesnay's. During the ensuing forty to fifty years much able scholarship was devoted to the physiocrats. With the emergence after 1930 of modern equilibrium and macroeconomic theory, together with national income accounting and input-output models, interest in relevant components of the physiocratic system increased, in Japan as well as in the West." Here, Walras is seen as the forerunner among bourgeois economists who rekindled interest in the study of the equilibrium ideas of Quesnay's *Tableau*. When discussing the four points of similarity between the *Tableau* and certain modern methods of analysis, Meek (1962, p. 292) first mentions the "parallel [...] between the *Tableau* and the Walrasian general equilibrium system."

For modern economists, Quesnay's *Tableau*, which emphasizes the interrelationship of all factors in the economic order and seeks to place them in a predictable input-output model, has influenced subsequent generations of economists (Spengler, 1968, pp. 443–446). Especially those scholars "of economic equilibrium and the stationary state have seen it (the *Tableau Économique*) as a major precursor of their own efforts" (Fox-Genovese, 1976, p. 246). Indeed, that Schumpeter "admit[s] François Quesnay into the Pantheon [is] presumably because his *Tableau Economique* was a precursor of general equilibrium" (Samuelson, 1982, p. 45). Phillips (1955, p. 144) claims, "The *Tableau Économique* marks the beginning of general equilibrium economic theories and well deserves mention in preface to Walras, Pareto, Cassel and Leontief."

In particular, Leontief (1951, p. 9) explicitly acknowledged the similarity between his and Quesnay's approach, claiming that it is best to regard his 1941 input-output table as an attempt to build up "a *Tableau Économique* of the United States." Since then, it has become a given in the history of Western economics that the Richter input-output table is the product of emulating Quesnay's *Tableau*. Samuelson (1982, p. 46) says,

> My old teacher Leontief (1941) had Quesnay very much in mind when he referred to his own endeavour to construct a statistical '*Tableau Economique* of the United States'. It is thus not surprising that members of Leontief's workshop [...] should have offered interpretations of the *Tableau* in terms of modern Leontief-Sraffa input-output systems.

Schumpeter (1954a) corroborates this line of argument by stating that Quesnay "did genuinely econometric work. This aspect [...] has acquired new actuality in our time through the great work of Leontief, which [...] revived the fundamental principle of the *tableau* method" (pp. 241–242). In addition, he proposes that "Quesnay identified general equilibrium, that is, equilibrium in the economy as a whole [...] with the equilibrium of social aggregates—exactly as do the modern Keynesians" (p. 243). Meek (1962, pp. 293–294) also believes that there are similarities between Quesnay's *Tableau* and the modern Keynesian approach, as well as modern dynamic methods of analysis. "Had economic analysis advanced to its present level of sophistication in Quesnay's time," Fox-Genovese (1976, p. 269) argues, "Quesnay would undoubtedly have delighted in expressing his insights in the equations of the Harrod-Domar model of dynamic equilibrium."

In short, the idea of equilibrium in Quesnay's *Tableau*, once rediscovered and revalued by future generations of scholars after a long period of negligence, has been a great inspiration to and has exerted an indelible influence on the evolution of Western economics. In this way, we can affirm that Quesnay's equilibrium ideas absorbed from ancient Chinese culture some elements such as those from the *I-Ching*, which means that the initial origin of modern equilibrium theory can be traced back to the ancient Chinese civilization through Quesnay along the line of inheritance first recognized by Quesnay and later acknowledged by other Western economists. Therefore, the theory of equilibrium, as one of the basic economic principles of modern Western countries, is by origin no longer a Western "patent," but a product of the combination of Eastern imports from China and Western concepts.

Above, we have discussed the connection or similarity between Quesnay's *Tableau* and the *I-Ching*, a Confucian classic, in terms of the principle of controlling complexity through simplicity in state rule, the concept of system, the method of macro or overall analysis, the diagrammatic representation, and the idea of equilibrium. This proves that Quesnay's disciples and contemporaries did not compare the *Tableau* with the *I-Ching* arbitrarily or in purely formal terms, but rather indicated that the *I-Ching* had a substantial influence on the formation of the *Tableau* in terms of a number of basic theoretical concepts and methods of analysis. In fact, the influence of the *I-Ching* on the *Tableau* is not limited to the above-mentioned aspects. Subsequent analyses will further supplement and explain the relationship between the two.

III. **The Chinese script**

The connection between the *Tableau Économique* and Chinese characters, strange to modern scholars, was obvious to the Physiocrats. The Abbé Baudeau, in the definition he gave to the Physiocrats in the April 1776 issue of the *Ephémérides*, stated, "In the *Tableau économique* they possess a formula with technical terms as precise as old Chinese characters" (Quoted in Gide & Rist, 1915, p. 3 [Note 1]). Later the French economists Gide and Rist (1915, p. 3 [Note 1]) argue accordingly that "this definition [...] shows us that the school possessed not a little of the dogmatism of the Chinese." The allure of Chinese characters to the Physiocrats lies in the fact that it is a kind of hieroglyph: in his letter to Mirabeau, Quesnay called the newly designed *Tableau* in *Philosophie Rurale* arithmetic "hieroglyphics" (Meek, 1962, p. 40), and "the critics of the nineteenth century have very often treated the zigzag lines of the

Tableau Économique as unintelligible hieroglyphs" (Lewiński, 1931, p. 51). In order to understand this connection, we need to first investigate what Westerners thought of Chinese characters at that time.

1. **Early Western views on Chinese characters**

In the seventeenth and eighteenth centuries, Chinese writing attracted much attention in Europe. Originally, Europeans generally believed that the original language of human beings should be Hebrew. However, from the seventeenth century onwards, with the introduction of Chinese writing to Europe by the Jesuits, many people began to hold that Chinese hieroglyphics seemed to be the most primitive form of human writing. But there were still various theories about the origin of Chinese writing at that time, which were only to prove that Chinese writing was not an independent creation of the Chinese, but was influenced by other nations, especially by the so-called new ancestors of mankind in the Bible. This was the prevailing view among Westerners at that time.

For the Jesuits in China at the time, the study of Chinese characters, just like that of the *I-Ching* and other ancient Chinese classics, was based on the belief that such characters contained a primitive religious revelation. Foucquet used the Chinese character for "zhou" to refer to the universe, from which he derived the meanings of the earliest world records and the treasure trove of universal lessons preserved in Noah's Ark after the flood. He thought that the character "ru" (Confucianism) comes from the combination of two other characters, respectively "ren" (man) and "xu" (need)—the latter refers to the ancient meaning of the character "xu" or the "xu" hexagram in the *I-Ching*—and interpreted "ru" as "a cloud falling from the sky," which "conforms to the biblical reference of God falling from the sky in a cloud." He also interpreted the Chinese character "qiu" (mound) as "the symbol of Adam and Eve" (Wang, 1979, p. 106). When "excavating" the Jewish knowledge preserved in China, Bouvet believed that Chinese characters "can express the mysterious meaning of things" (p. 138), and linked the structure of the Chinese characters to the 64 hexagrams of the *I-Ching*, pointing out that the hexagrams represent numbers, colors, and other meanings: "this ideogram can express any thought" (p. 139). Such arguments are a little obscure, some of which are purely for the purpose of defending religious doctrines, and their arbitrary nature can be found at a glance.

Still, these Jesuits' devoted search for the original religious revelation in the Chinese script helped reveal some typical features of the writing. Le Comte said, "The Chinese employ pictures to represent their writing, using natural images of objects on paper to express and communicate their thoughts" (pp. 137–138). In the same place, he added, "The Chinese use very simple images to create their writing, and they also invent many less natural characters to express meanings that pictures cannot express" (p. 138). This is the pictorial or ideographic feature of the Chinese script. Needham (1954) has mentioned that in the eighteenth century, the Europeans, though often poorly informed about Chinese civilization, often treated it as a model. One example of this is their attitude towards Chinese writing. This is because China uses pictographs that are very different from the alphabetic writing. As the recording tool of the oldest current language, this kind of writing has been used by many generations of Chinese. Its large number of users and its long history have been highly appreciated.

This feature led Westerners at the time to another one, namely, that the Chinese characters have nothing to do with pronunciation, and are more suitable for mathematics than Arabic. Needham (1954, pp. 32–33) gives a specific explanation for this:

> It is generally said that in Chinese the sound of a word as pronounced has no relation to the way in which it is written. This is true in the sense that the meaning of the written character is fixed and can be understood by speakers of different dialects who may pronounce it in mutually incomprehensible ways. It was this 'mathematical' quality in the language which impressed the early 14th-century Persians and which later attracted the attention of 18th-century European scholars [...], perhaps stimulating [...] the development of mathematical logic in Europe.

He specially adds that the Persians of the early fourteenth century were so impressed with "this 'mathematical' quality in the language" that they considered the Chinese ideographic language "as superior to alphabetic ones for science because the meaning of a character is independent of its pronunciation" (p. 218).

It was just because the Chinese script has these obvious characteristics that it aroused a kind of "utopian fantasy" in Europe at that time. People believed that the Chinese were speaking a rational language and writing in a real and universal script. Such "fantasy" reached the zenith in especially Leibniz's words and deeds.

Leibniz also doubted that Hebrew is the most primitive language of mankind, and believed that a primitive language should be related to the image of the thing itself. Starting from this, he showed great interest in Chinese hieroglyphics, saying that the Chinese, with their very different language and script, gave the Western world light, which is more necessary than the Greco-Roman knowledge that many Western scholars valued (Gorai, 1938, p. 275). He found that the study of the Chinese language is of infinite use. For example, there are only about 400 basic Chinese characters, and most of the other expressions are combinations of these basic ones, so he thought that this script is very useful for intellectual analysis. He devoted himself, in particular, to the exploration of the origin of Chinese writing, believing that it was a creation of Fu Xi based on a sophisticated theory, instead of a coincidence as in Egypt (Wang, 1979, p. 138). In his view, the true meaning of Xi's original creation of writing was little known among later generations, so they could only speculate, "[making] of these characters of Fohi (Fu-hsi) some kind of symbols and Hieroglyphs, as one customarily does when one has strayed from the true meaning" (Leibniz, 1994, p. 134). For this, Leibniz's explanation is: Fu Xi initially was to represent the number of sixty-four hexagrams and the stage of hexagrams, so with the most basic characters and strokes, his writing was formed. Later, due to the changes of the times, the characters and strokes changed frequently, which completely obscured the source of characters, as well as the origin of Fu Xi's divination. Therefore, Leibniz wanted very much to know the meaning of the *I-Ching*'s various hexagrams in the Chinese script (Gorai, 1938, p. 273).

Leibniz's attempts to look for the origin of Chinese characters in the *I-Ching*'s hexagrams were clearly influenced by the Jesuits in China. In his 1698 letter to

Leibniz, Bouvet suggested that Fu Xi's sixty-four hexagrams embody elements of mathematics and language. As a Chinese member of the Jesuit Society, and a prominent figure in the Ming Dynasty on a par with Xu Guangqi, Li Zhizao said, in his preface to the re-engraving of the book *The Real Records of the Lord of Heaven*, that "the *I-Ching* is the ancestor of writing." In his study of Fu Xi's *I-Ching* text, Leibniz (1994) did not aim for nothing, but hoped to invent a new kind of world language from it: This mysterious and implicit ideograph gave Westerners a way to hint at the truths about the most important scientific and natural philosophy of the Chinese, simplifying the path to revelation, and making all the novelties and differences acceptable because of Fu Xi, and this special language finally became used by the educated class of scholars, that is, it became the universal script. He suggested that Europe or France make use of this special language, with missionaries preaching the universal truth (Roy, 1972, pp. 49–50, 160).

Leibniz claimed that the sixty-four hexagrams of the *I-Ching* gives a major hint to the invention of the world alphabet, mainly because he discovered the principle of binary arithmetic from the alignment of the *I-Ching* hexagrams, which he considered to be "a new mathematical key" (Quoted in Reichwein, 1925, p. 82), a solution to the "incredible mystery" contained in the ancient script created by Fu Xi three thousand years ago. Thus, when he attempted to apply the Chinese script or the *I-Ching* system to the world script he always advocated, he first emphasized the mathematical qualities of the *I-Ching* script. He also cited Abdalla Beidavaeus, an Arab author, who "remarks that Fohi had found a *peculiare scribendi genus, Arithmeticam, contratus et Rationaria*, 'a peculiar manner of writing, of arithmetic, of contracts, and of accounts.' What he says confirms my explanation of the characters of this ancient philosopher-king whereby they are reduced to numbers" (Leibniz, 1994, p. 134). In fact, Bouvet, who corresponded frequently with Leibniz, stressed that the mystery of the *I-Ching* numbers comes from the mysterious revelation of the Creator, and strongly advocated that the mathematical principle of the alignment of the *I-Ching* hexagrams, which is equivalent to binary arithmetic, should be applied to the world script that he favored (Quoted in Rule, 1972, pp. 442–443).

All these remarks show that Leibniz used the mathematical principle in the *I-Ching*'s hexagrams as a fundamental link between the invention of the world script and ancient Chinese characters. In the 1920s, Masson-Oursel (Quoted in Needham, 1956, p. 326), a Western scholar, said, "[I]t (the *I Ching*) supposes a kind of translation of all natural phenomena into a mathematical language by means of a set of graphic symbols, germs of what Leibniz would have called a 'universal character'; thus constituting a dictionary permitting men to read Nature like an open book, whether with intellectual or practical aims in view." Leibniz claimed that the words derived from Fu Xi's text may be used as the beginning of an analytic conception, and of the rational calculations which he advocated (Gorai, 1938, p. 285), and that the world script (*Caractéristiques Universelles*) derived from the relationship between ideas and numbers in Fu Xi's text will have a much wider use. This is because the proof of numbers or algebra is the most definite, and may prove to be the most scientific, means to explain the abstract inevitable truth (p. 263), and this world script, characterized by the proof of numbers or algebra, is a philosophical symbol, and has incredible utility to explain the truth to the people who are separated by the language barrier, and live far away from each other (p. 263).

Leibniz's analysis and evaluation of Chinese characters, although based on his unique theory of universal writing, is representative of the European scholarship of that period. In addition, E. Fourmont, when compiling the first Chinese dictionary in 1722, commented that the Chinese had discovered philosophical and geometrical laws in the structure of hieroglyphs and that no natural science could show the kind of knowledge that the Chinese discoveries had shown. Such comment, along with Wolff's later use of the Chinese script as a clear proof of the high level of Chinese science, all corroborates the fact that Western scholars whole-heartedly appreciated Chinese characters at the time.

Two points can be summarized from the above Westerners' early discussions about the Chinese script. First, as a pictographic symbol, the script actually embodies far richer meanings than Western alphabetic writing. In other words, the Chinese pictographs have profound philosophical implications in their strokes. When some Western scholars were convinced that the *I-Ching*'s hexagrams are the rudiments of pictograms, they found the meaning of these characters is infinite and profound. Second, Chinese is a special language with mathematical characteristics. The reason for holding this view is either based on the fact that Chinese fonts, just like mathematical codes, have nothing to do with pronunciation and have their fixed meaning, or directly comes from deciphering the mathematical mystery contained in the eight diagrams or sixty-four hexagrams. This understanding of Chinese characters actually goes beyond mere linguistics. But in that period, such a wide range of traditional Chinese cultural content was precisely discovered in the process of Westerners' study of the Chinese script, which shows that Chinese characters had a great influence on European intellectuals at that time. As far as our research is concerned, the first point above mainly emphasizes the feature of Chinese characters to express various rich and complex meanings with their pictograms. When the origin of Chinese characters is traced back to the eight diagrams of the *I-Ching*, this feature can be regarded as the pictorial method of using simple hexagrams to express complex things. We will not describe it again, for we have already analyzed this point when we discussed the influence of the *I-Ching* on the *Tableau Économique*. Next, we will examine whether the second argument, that is, the so-called mathematical quality of Chinese characters, had any influence on Quesnay's creation of the *Tableau*.

2. **The mathematical quality of Chinese characters and the mathematical analysis of the *Tableau Économique***

In the era of the Physiocratic School, the study of Chinese characters was a hot topic, which naturally attracted Quesnay, an admirer of Chinese culture. Quesnay, like Leibniz, stood up for the independence of the Chinese script. He disagreed with the argument that the Chinese language was a combination of Egyptian and Phoenician on the grounds that ancient Chinese characters are similar to Egyptian hieroglyphs, thus deducing that the Chinese nation originated in Egypt. He retorted, "Even though the identification of the Chinese with the Egyptians may be established, why may one not suppose that the latter came from China, or, rather than that, that both the former and the latter had a common origin?" (Quesnay, 1946, p. 154) To take the Chinese script as originating from Egyptian or Phoenician is essentially to view it in terms of the origin of the Western script, and Quesnay's retort shows precisely his defense of the independence of the ancient Chinese civilization.

It has been pointed out above that many of Quesnay's contemporaries and those Westerners before him emphasized that Chinese hieroglyphics have mathematical meanings. In particular, Leibniz took the hexagrams in the *I-Ching* as the origin of Chinese writing, declaring that he had discovered in it the basic principle of binary arithmetic, which had been lost for two millennia. It seems that Quesnay echoed this argument, so he regarded Fu Xi, the legendary founder of the hexagrams, as "a man of mathematical skill." Quesnay himself did not discuss and explain the mathematical principle of Chinese characters and the hexagrams. But it is worth noting that his introduction of mathematical methods into the analysis of the *Tableau Économique* opened up a new path for the future study of economics.

Quesnay believed that his *Tableau* proves the law of net product expenditure as precisely as Newton has proved the existence of the earth's gravity. Mirabeau (Quoted in Eltis, 1975, p. 168) pointed out,

> The *Tableau Économique* is the first rule of arithmetic which has been invented to reduce elementary economic science to precise and exact calculations [...].
>
> Calculations are to economic science what bones are to the human body [...]. [E]conomic science is deepened and extended by examination and reasoning, but without calculations it will always be an inexact science, confused and everywhere open to error and prejudice.

Le Trosne (Quoted in Neill, 1949, p. 543), another Physiocrat, also explained the need to base economic science on "mathematical proof" by stating, "Economic science, operating on measurable objects, is susceptible of being an exact science, of being subject to calculus." Thus, both Quesnay and his followers regarded the precise calculation and test by mathematical or arithmetic methods as the remarkable feature of the so-called "new science of Physiocracy," that is, economic science.

Quesnay himself showed a great interest in mathematical calculations, especially after he stopped writing on economic problems in around 1768, and spent the rest of his life almost exclusively on the study of geometry. However, the mathematical methods he used in the analysis of the *Tableau* are not complicated and abstruse, but rather simple mathematical operations. And even these simple arithmetical formulas, in the opinion of modern economists, still contain a number of contradictions or confusions that are contrary to their presuppositions. The mathematical feature of the *Tableau*, therefore, is not so much that it is particularly brilliant in terms of the accuracy and precision of purely mathematical calculations; it is that it creatively proposes novel analytical methods for expressing complex economic theories in mathematical formulas, thus combining the verbal and mathematical formulation of theory and making it clear that economic science must have the same mathematical precision as the natural sciences.

Prior to Quesnay, William Petty (1623–1687) (1690, p. a4), an early English classical economist, once mentioned his intention to "express [himself] in Terms of Number, Weight, or Measure," and made extensive use of statistics to analyze economic phenomena and confirm the existence of objective laws of economic development. His *Political Arithmetick*, in particular, is hailed by posterity as the founding work of statistics, and he is regarded by modern econometricians as a pioneer of econometrics. In view of this, ordinary scholars, from the perspective of the evolution of Western economics, tend to regard the mathematical method adopted by Quesnay in his *Tableau* as a "development" of the method employed by Petty, implying the succession of the former to the latter. In fact, there is no direct inheritance between the two methods of mathematical analysis, and no credible information in this regard has so far been provided in the works on economic history. That is why Gide and Rist still claim that Quesnay is "the pioneer of the Mathematical school"[13] when it comes to his use of mathematical diagrams to illustrate the *Tableau*. Schumpeter (1954a), while affirming that "[t]he decisive impulse came from a small English group led and inspired by Sir William Petty" (p. 210) in establishing the spirit of mathematical analysis of economics, stresses that "the simplification of the analytic pattern achieved by the *tableau* method opens up great possibilities for numerical theory" (p. 241), arguing that "he (Quesnay) did genuinely econometric work" (p. 241). All these indicate that Quesnay's introduction of mathematical methods into economic analysis boasts originality and has not relied on Petty's viewpoint.

In this way, when we further investigate Quesnay's source of mathematical analysis in the *Tableau*, we find that at that time, in addition to the fundamental fact that the development of the natural sciences was bound to have an impact on the economic science, and thus on the way the *Tableau* was described, what is striking is that the continuing discussion of the mathematical quality of Chinese characters over a considerable period of time could also enlighten and motivate Quesnay in his studies of economic issues.

In terms of the so-called mathematical quality of the Chinese characters, Leibniz's view was probably the most influential at the time. Since he discovered the principle of binary arithmetic from the *I-Ching*'s hexagrams, Leibniz envisioned the development of a world script similar to mathematical language from the hexagrams. Its significance is twofold. First, it is the most scientific because it can explain the abstract inevitable truth with accurate mathematical proof. Second, it can break through the limitations of national languages in various places and create an unimpeded world language. Leibniz's understanding of Chinese characters, especially his belief that they are mathematically accurate to explain abstract truth, is no different from Quesnay's reason of emphasizing the importance of mathematical proof when he created the *Tableau*. And by likening the *Tableau* to Chinese hieroglyphics, the Physiocrats tacitly acknowledged the influence of the mathematical meaning in Chinese writing on the formulation of the *Tableau*. This influence of Chinese culture is even more evident when one considers the fact that Quesnay's mathematical system of

[13] Gide and Rist (1915, p. 19 [Note 2]) gives the following summary: "His (Quesnay's) explanation of the *Tableau* by means of mathematical tables gives him a claim to be considered a pioneer of the Mathematical school. Full justice has been done to him in this respect. An article by Bauer in the *Quarterly Journal of Economics*, 1890, recognises his claim, and there is another by Oncken in the *Economic Journal* for June 1896, entitled *The Physiocrats as Founders of the Mathematical School.*"

the *Tableau* drew on the pictorial representation of the *I-Ching*'s hexagrams. That is why Quesnay sometimes referred to his *Tableau* as the "hieroglyphics" of arithmetic (Meek, 1962, p. 40), and why the Abbé Baudeau said that in their *Tableau* they "possess a formula with technical terms as precise as old Chinese characters" (Quoted in Gide & Rist, 1915, p. 3 [Note 1]). According to Reichwein (1925, p. 109), a modern scholar, Quesnay's *Tableau* "was the ingenious translation into mathematics of a Chinese doctrine." This statement can serve as a conclusion to our discussion of the relationship between the *Tableau* and the Chinese script.

That the *Tableau* takes Chinese culture as one of its sources can at the same time be consolidated by the following two supplementary facts:

First, Quesnay's aphoristic inscription at the beginning of the *Tableau*—"Pauvres paysans, pauvre royaume! Pauvre royaume, pauvre roi!" (Quoted in Gide & Rist, 1915, p. 5)[14]—according to Hu Jichuang (1962, p. 512), is a virtual repetition of the famous Confucian saying in China: "If the people have plenty, their prince will not be left to want alone. If the people are in want, their prince cannot enjoy plenty alone" (Confucius, 1869, p. 195).

Second, the 50–50 split between Chinese landowners and those farmers who rented land, as was discussed by Quesnay (1946, p. 205),[15] is according to some Western scholars similar to the system of profit distribution embodied in the *Tableau* (Quoted in Ly, 1938). This rate was indeed very common in rural China at that time. According to Li Wenzhi (1957, pp. 71–72), the historical materials of the Qing Dynasty abound with such records as the following: *ge ban fen zu* ("half of the harvest was used to pay the rent"), *an ban fen cheng* ("the harvest is split in half between the landlord and the tenants"), and such other expressions that can be roughly paraphrased as "a landlord's land was divided among the tenants, and half of the total harvest was taken as rent at the end of the year." Coincident with this rent rate highly valued by Quesnay is the distribution of total annual income from agriculture, as is recorded in the "Arithmetical Formula" of the *Tableau* (Fig. 6): out of the five billion dollars' worth of total agricultural products created by the productive class in the past year, the shares of the productive class and the landowning class are two billions each in the value of total agricultural products in the *Tableau*, with the rest—one billion dollars' worth of original prepaid interest—used to compensate for the original prepaid depletion.

It should be noted here that although the prototype of the *Tableau* presupposes simple reproduction, Quesnay, in his description of the *Tableau*, suggested that if the consumption expenditure of the various classes of society on the products of agriculture and industry is greater or less than the ratio of the prototype, i.e. the so-called 50–50 ratio, then social reproduction will undergo a continuous expansion

[14] According to *History of Political Economy in Europe (1837–38)*, written by the French economist Jérôme-Adolphe Blanqui, this aphorism, which has never appeared in other editions of Quesnay's *Tableau Économique*, was originally written on the proofs of the *Tableau* printed in Versailles (Wu, 1989, p. 153 [Note 1]).

[15] Turgot's 11th question in his *Questions* goes as follows: "Is it common in China to have the land cultivated by tenants (*ouvriers*) who pay the landlord a certain portion of the harvest, like a half or a third?" (Quoted in Maverick, 1946, p. 50)

or contraction (Chen, 1988a). In this case, the 50–50 ratio is not an immutable norm. However, this situation does not affect our analysis above, because Quesnay actually shifted from an examination of simple reproduction to that of expanded or contracted reproduction, i.e., he based his analysis on the equilibrium state of simple reproduction. Since the analysis concerning the change in the scale of reproduction is based on that of simple reproduction, the 50–50 ratio of the prototype is the most basic equilibrium condition in Quesnay's *Tableau*, and all other analyses greater or less than this proportion are derived from this basic condition. Thus, it is an interesting question whether Quesnay's analysis of the *Tableau* beginning with the basic 50–50 consumption ratio drew any inspiration from the 50–50 split of the land rent ratio in Chinese agriculture. It is not known whether Western scholars have understood from this perspective the parallels between Quesnay's claim of a Chinese rent rate and the *Tableau*'s system of profit distribution. But in any case, this perspective adds a quite novel dimension to our understanding of the origins of the *Tableau* and its relationship with Chinese culture.

3 The Western Origin

It can be seen that when Western economists talk about the *Tableau*, they especially emphasize its circularity and the related significance in the history of economics. Schumpeter (1954b, p. 52) regards the *Tableau* as the first description of the circular flow of economic life. Fox-Genovese (1976, pp. 50–51) thinks that it is "the first presentation of a circular-flow equilibrium in the history of economic thought." Or as others say, the Physiocrats first tried to analyze the wealth in the economy in a systematic way (Bhatia, 1978, p. 57), and "the more important discovery [was made] by Quesnay that economic relations are resolvable into a circular flow" (Spengler, 1945, p. 347). Thus, Western economists' analysis of the sources of the *Tableau* mainly starts from its circularity.

Broadly speaking, there are two representative accounts about the Western sources of the *Tableau*. One is that it was inspired by the discovery of blood circulation in European physiology; the other is that it came from the French pioneers before the Physiocratic School. These two are discussed separately below.

I. The discovery of blood circulation

In 1628, the English physician William Harvey published his *Exercitatio Anatomica de Motu Cordis et Sanguinis in Animalibus* (*Anatomical Exercise on the Motion of the Heart and Blood in Animals*), which eventually established the doctrine of blood circulation. A century later, Quesnay also practiced medicine, serving for a long time as an attendant to noblemen and even to Louis XV. In his *Essai physique sur l'œconomie animale* (literally meaning "Physical Essay on Animal Economy") in 1736 (expanded in 1747), he studied Harvey's new inventions diligently, and used blood circulation as a metaphor in his later economic discourse.[16] Therefore, when analyzing the idea of circulation in the *Tableau Économique*, Western scholars naturally connect it with the physiological discovery of blood circulation.

Hector Denis (Quoted in Gide & Rist, 1915, p. 19 [Note 1]) has made a popular comment on the link between the two: "The discovery of the circulation of wealth in economic societies occupies in the history of the science the same position as is occupied by the discovery of the circulation of the blood in the history of biology." Accordingly, the French economists Gide and Rist (1915, p. 18) consider Quesnay to be "precisely the man to carry the biological idea over into the realm of sociology," or, as Othmar Spann (1930, p. 86) puts it, from Quesnay's *Tableau*, we find "the idea of a kind of circulation within society analogous to the circulation of the blood." This implies that the emergence of Quesnay's idea of circulation is inextricably linked to the discovery of blood circulation. Schumpeter (1954a, p. 240 [Note 9]), too, in his analysis of circular flow, which is a major part of Quesnay's achievement, proposes an "appealing" assumption that "this idea came independently to Quesnay, the physician, through analogy with the circulation of the blood in the human body." In a more explicit manner, Stollberg (1960) claims that Quesnay was inspired by the knowledge of human blood circulation and turned the product of the national economy around, attributing Quesnay's concept of circulation completely to the physiological discovery made a century ago.

There is indeed a similarity between the theory of blood circulation through the cardiovascular system of the body, and the idea of circulation as embodied by Quesnay in his *Tableau*. However, it must be pointed out that, if we look at the concept of circulation alone, we may find that, in the field of knowledge that Quesnay was familiar with or interested in, in addition to the possible inspiration from the European scientific community's knowledge of blood circulation, the Chinese cultural knowledge, which was imported into Europe in large quantities, also contain a rich content of the idea of circulation, and is a valuable resource for Quesnay to produce similar ideas.

Modern scholars have pointed out that the theory of cycles is directly related to the rotational patterns of celestial bodies. It is precisely in describing such celestial cycles that ancient Chinese culture has shown a profound and unique ability to understand and generalize, which has in turn led to the formation of China's traditional concept of circulation.

In Confucianism, the evolution of everything in the universe is considered to be a cyclical process, just like the movement of the seasons and the alternation of day and night in nature. This is reflected in the following statements in the *I-Ching*: "there is no state of peace that is not liable to be disturbed, and no departure (of evil men) so that they shall not return" (Legge, 1963, p. 81), and "[t]he subject of it [the Fû hexagram] … will return and repeat his (proper) course" (pp. 107–108). In the hexagrams in the *I-Ching*, celestial bodies' movement is described vividly and creatively. One of the basic points of this cosmology is its periodicity, that is, its cyclicism, which shows

[16] Turgot once also said that the circulation of wealth "constituted the very life of the body politic, just as the circulation of the blood did of the physical" (Quoted in Gide & Rist, 1915, p. 18).

a cyclical process of the growth and decline of *yin* and *yang*. Shao Yong (2016), a Neo-Confucianist in the Northern Song Dynasty, takes circulation and infinity as the important features of his innate map derived from the *I-Ching* hexagrams. Gorai Kinzo (1938, p. 26), a Japanese scholar, emphasizes the idea of circulation in the *I-Ching* by pointing out that the first specialty of the *I-Ching* is the sense of law, and that the changes in nature occur according to the law of circulation. As for Daoism (Taoism), Needham (1966, p. 98) says, "Nothing could be more striking than the appreciation of cyclical change, the cycle-mindedness, of the Taoists." At the same time, he quotes Granet's explanation that in Chinese thought, "[t]ime's typical virtue is to proceed by revolution" (Quoted in Needham, 1966, p. 98). It is interesting to note that the concept of circulation in ancient China, especially in the hexagrams of the *I-Ching*, is generally regarded as a closed system, that is, the evolution of everything in the universe is seen as a closed circular movement that keeps recurring. What's more, Barna (1975), a Western economist, believes that "Quesnay's *Tableau* describes stationary equilibrium in a closed system" (p. 486) and the "circulation in a state of equilibrium" (p. 496). For Quesnay, who was good at absorbing the essence of Chinese culture, it is obviously no coincidence that these two circulation systems are so consistent.

Another factor to be taken into account when discussing the origin of circulation in Quesnay's *Tableau* is that the ancient Chinese concept of circulation was used in the analysis of economic matters at a very early stage, and characterized by a very clear and complete economic cycle. A case in point is the doctrine of agricultural economic cycle, which had been spread for hundreds of years, from the fifth century B.C. to the second century A.D. Its influence continued to be felt for hundreds of years, in the Warring States Period and during Qin and Han Dynasties, and it was even mentioned by some people at the end of the Ming Dynasty (Hu, 1962, pp. 176–181, 278–280). This doctrine, with obvious irrationality, provides a precedent worldwide for analyzing the operation and causes of the agricultural production cycle. It is very similar to Quesnay's *Tableau* in analyzing the production cycle in ideal agricultural countries, focusing on the cycle in the economic field, acknowledging that there is some objective regularity in social and economic activities, and examining economic problems of the whole society rather than of individual phenomena.

Last but not least, even if it is true that the concept of blood circulation was a great inspiration to Quesnay in the creation of the *Tableau*, there are many examples in ancient Chinese culture that are similar to this concept. Harvey once said that the examples given by Aristotle of natural circular motion on an earth-wide scale inspired him to come up with the idea of the circular motion of blood (Mason, 1962, pp. 221–222). The ancient Chinese, in their experience of natural cycles, also developed early ideas about blood circulation in the human and animal bodies. As far as medicine is concerned, in *Huangdi Neijing* (*The Yellow Emperor's Classic of Internal Medicine*), which was written in as early as the Warring States period, there were records that the blood in the human body is "endlessly flowing and incessantly circulating" in the blood vessels, almost two thousand years before the discovery of blood circulation by the British scholar Harvey.[17] This concept of circulation was popular in almost every school of thought in ancient China, which is why a recent scholar has written an article entitled "The Concept of Circulation and Chinese Science" to elaborate on it. Furthermore, ancient Chinese scholars often used this doctrine of blood circulation as a metaphor for economic analysis. Yuan Mei (1716–1798), a Qing scholar who was roughly contemporary with Quesnay, when analyzing the importance of commercial circulation, said that money and grain in a country are like blood in the body, and that merchants in the country are like *qi* in the blood: one will get sick if *qi* does not exist for a day and blood does not flow for a day. In his view, the deliberate restraint of the activities of merchants is bound to cause "congestion" to circulation channels, just as the lack of blood and *qi* causes the human body to fall ill, which will result in the social disease of "surplus" or "shortage" of commodity distribution (Yuan, 1988). This doctrine of blood circulation for economic analysis is clearly closer to the idea of economic circulation in Quesnay's *Tableau* than the Western doctrine of blood circulation that adopts a purely physiological sense.

The various viewpoints on ancient Chinese doctrine of circulation listed above may not have been known to Quesnay, but the circulation thought embodied in these arguments, as a basic element of Chinese culture, was bound to flow into Europe with the spread of Chinese thought to the West, leaving a deep impression on Quesnay. Therefore, besides its Western origin, the circulation thought in Quesnay's *Tableau* very probably has some little-known close relationship with the traditional Chinese concept of circulation.

II. The French Pioneers of the *Tableau Économique*

Among the French pioneers of the Physiocratic School, Richard Cantillon is the first to be considered as having had a major influence on Quesnay's theory of the *Tableau*. It has been pointed out that Marx (1990) first noted Cantillon's general influence on Quesnay. That is, in a note to *Capital*, Marx mentions that Quesnay had "largely drawn" (p. 697 [Note 11]) from Cantillon's work. However, Marx did not explicitly address the scholarly relationship between Cantillon's work and Quesnay's *Tableau*, which began to attract increasing attention from Western economists only in the second half of the nineteenth century, when the English scholar Jevons highly praised the work of Cantillon.

Cantillon's masterpiece, *On the Nature of Commerce in General*, written between 1730 and 1734, was translated into French by the author himself and circulated widely among various industries, but it was not until after his death in 1755 that it was officially published. This work is considered to be most closely related to the theory of the *Tableau*, primarily in its analysis, in Chapters XII to XVI, of the

[17] Xiu Ruijuan (1987), a leading expert on microcirculation, also points out that China is a world leader in the theory of human microcirculation. She says that the clinical practice of microcirculation has been practiced in China since the fourth century BC, and that *Huangdi Neijing* (*The Yellow Emperor's Classic of Internal Medicine*), the earliest surviving medical text in China, contains a detailed account of the subject, more than 1300 years earlier than the earliest foreign record. This, according to her, shows that the study of microcirculation originated in China and that our ancestors were pioneers in this science.

incomes of the various classes of society, and of the way these incomes operate within society. The analysis covers the class divisions among landowners, farmers, and non-agricultural people, such as industrialists and merchants, the movement of expenditure and products of the whole society back and forth between these three classes, and the fact that the economic activity of a country depends on the mood of the monarch and the landed aristocracy—this mood in turn determines the manner in which the land is used—and the manner in which their needs for food are met (Cantillon, 2017).

The above views, according to Higgs's (1897, p. 37) analysis in 1896, are "the whole theory of the *Tableau Économique*," which was later accepted and further developed by Schumpeter. In his *History of Economic Analysis*, Schumpeter (1954a) says, "Cantillon was the first to make this circular flow concrete and explicit, to give us a bird's-eye view of economic life. In other words, he was the first to draw a *tableau économique*. And, barring differences that hardly affect essentials, this *tableau* is the same as Quesnay's, though Cantillon did not actually condense it into a table. Cantillon's priority is thus beyond question as regards the 'invention'" (p. 222). And all of Quesnay's *Tableau*, he emphasizes, "apart from the pictorial form, amounts to no more than a development in fuller detail of Cantillon's schema" (p. 240). Since then, Western economists, though seldom calling it "the Cantillon-Quesnay *tableau*" in the same way as Schumpeter, have often emphasized their intellectual connection. Meek (1973) argues that Cantillon's notion of a circular flow of income between different social groups "had a considerable influence on Quesnay" (p. 5), just like his first sketch of the *Tableau*, which had been put "in words rather than figures" (p. 5). Or, as Eltis (1975, p. 181) points out, Quesnay's circulation of the revenue in the *Tableau* "may have owed much to Cantillon's account of the role that rents play in the circulation of demand." Some scholars in China have also argued that Cantillon, in his aforementioned work, "made the first attempt to formulate a diagram of the circulation and reproduction of capital in agricultural countries" (Ji, 1963, p. 24).

From the above, it can be seen that Cantillon's description of the cyclic flow of income of various classes, although not graphically represented, is basically the same in content as Quesnay's well-known *Tableau*. Quesnay quoted Cantillon's work in his economic treatise, the French text of which was printed by Mirabeau, and Quesnay's followers also recognized Cantillon's description of the cyclical process, though only in words, as an important invention.

The affirmation that Cantillon's above discussion prepared for the first time in the European academic field the preceding intellectual materials for the emergence of Quesnay's *Tableau* means that the concept of circulation in the *Tableau*, in terms of its intellectual origin, is mainly traced back to Cantillon in the West. There is no way of knowing whether Cantillon's analysis absorbed the results of his predecessors. That Cantillon's circular view of the many stages through which the expenditure of agricultural income returns to its point of origin, Schumpeter (1954a, p. 222) says, is "something that is novel, something that is not explicitly present in the schemes of Cantillon's predecessors or contemporaries [...] or in fact in the schemes of most theorists of any time." This is nothing more than taking Cantillon as the first Western person to have explicitly presented the view of the economic cycle.

At the same time, Cantillon is seen, along with Quesnay, as having created a static analytical model of overall equilibrium for modern economics. General equilibrium analysis alone can be traced back further to Boisguillebert (1646–1714), who considered the entire national economy as a "complex" in which all things and commodities must be kept in constant equilibrium "as if it were a balance on a scale" in order to maintain a state of happiness. These unique descriptions of the equilibrium relations of the socio-economic whole may be useful for the later conceptions of Cantillon and Quesnay when they argued that all sectors and factors in the economic process are generally interdependent. It is no wonder that Schumpeter (p. 243) argues that the remarkable contribution of Cantillon and Quesnay's *Tableau* in this respect has to be "shared, to some extent, by Boisguillebert."

Both Cantillon and Boisguillebert are major pioneers of the Physiocratic School. In terms of the influence on Quesnay's *Tableau*, Cantillon's role is greater, but Boisguillebert's pioneering analysis of the overall economic equilibrium[18] cannot be ignored. The point is why, before Cantillon and Boisguillebert, there had been no similar concepts of economic cycles and overall equilibrium in the history of Western thought. They proposed these views in the seventeenth century, which was already the heyday of Chinese culture in Europe, especially in France. And Chinese culture has the ideas of circulation (including that of economic circulation) and overall equilibrium as two distinguishing features of its long tradition. Both authors are known to have been attentive to the news about China at that time and to have spoken highly of the Eastern Country. Cantillon (2017, p. 20), for example, once cited as an example China's effective rice cultivation and attributed the country's large population to its high productive level of its agriculture: "In the southern Provinces of China the Land yields Rice up to three crops in one year and a hundred times as much as is sown, owing to the great care which they have of Agriculture and the fertility of the soil which is never fallow. [...] it appears that one Acre will support there more than 10 Peasants. It is not surprising, therefore, that the population is prodigious in number." It is thus indeed thought-provoking in the history of economic thought that, although it is difficult, due to the lack of data, to infer any intrinsic connection between the economic thought of Cantillon and Boisguillebert and the transmission of Chinese culture to the West, the economic concepts pioneered by them in Western academic circles not only have no connection with traditional European thought, but

[18] Keynes (1964, p. 343 [Note 3]) thinks that, in the mid-eighteenth century, "Hume began the practice amongst economists of stressing the importance of the equilibrium position." Hu (1988, p. 563) points out that, in holding this view, "Keynes is either prejudiced on his part as a British economist or still ignorant of the long-standing existence of Boisguillebert's equilibrium analysis." In our analysis, Hume was precisely one of the early British economists who had the greatest admiration for Chinese culture and at the same time was very close to the key Physiocrats, such as Quesnay. Hume studied in France from 1734 to 1737, and then served as a secretary and counsellor at the British Embassy in France from 1763 to 1766. During this period of altogether six or seven years in France, he was at the heart and height of the Chinese vogue sweeping Europe. He was therefore the first economist to focus on "the equilibrium position." And since the sources of "the equilibrium position" might not be available in Britain, we cannot exclude the possibility that during his stay in France he might have drawn on traditional Chinese culture, which was popular at the time and rich in original equilibrium thought.

also appeared at the peak of the popularity of Chinese culture in continental Europe, which contained a large number of similar theoretical germs.

Of course, the influence that Cantillon had on Quesnay's *Tableau* should be evaluated objectively. Schumpeter explicitly affirms that Quesnay's *Tableau* is only a development of Cantillon's thought, but underneath this conclusion, Schumpeter adds a special note, claiming that the distribution of this "credit" between Cantillon and Quesnay is a "difficult" and "interesting" question, and frankly admits that he is reluctant to see Quesnay's contribution as a mere refinement of Cantillon's ideas by resorting to the bewilderingly attractive form of the *Tableau*. Schumpeter's inconsistency or hesitation on this issue is based on the realization that "[s]uch deep understanding and wholehearted absorption of another man's work is rare unless it is propelled by original perception of the same thing" (Schumpeter, 1954a, p. 240 [Note 9]). This means that Quesnay's idea of the *Tableau* is by no means a simple copy of Cantillon's concept, but is based on his deep understanding of the same economic phenomenon. Schumpeter's original intention in saying this is to assume that Quesnay, as a physician, having recognized blood circulation in the human body, could independently acquire the idea of circular flow in the economic sphere (p. 240). This assumption, in effect, suggests that Western economists believe that Quesnay's idea of circular flow, despite drawing on some of the ideas of the pioneers of the Physiocratic School, is still to a considerable extent his own original intellectual achievement. Schumpeter, as a Eurocentric theorist, limits his reasons for affirming the originality of Quesnay's achievement to the influence of the Western discovery of blood circulation, failing to see that Quesnay, as "the Confucius of Europe," may also have been inspired by the ancient Chinese idea of circulation, which, rich in implication, has passed down through the ages.

4 Comparative Analysis

In the history of economic thought, the origin of the *Tableau Économique*, which Quesnay himself avoided mentioning, wittingly or not, has been a mystery for more than two centuries. Shortly after the creation of the *Tableau*, the question of its intellectual antecedents had already been raised among the Physiocrats and their supporters and opponents. The explorations in this area have since been intermittent, which in general focus on no more than two aspects: (1) examining the relationship between traditional Chinese culture and the origins of the *Tableau* along the lines of the former's transmission to the West, and (2) searching for the forerunners of the theory of the *Tableau* by basing it on the European territory and within the vision of the Western academic heritage. These are behind the aforementioned two arguments for exploring the origin from China and from the West. Generally speaking, at the time when the *Tableau* was first popularized, its connection with the Chinese cultural tradition had been more often mentioned and remained so until the late nineteenth century. But from the end of the nineteenth century, especially since the publication of Schumpeter's thesis on the origin in the 1950s, the focus of research has shifted completely to the West's own inheritance. The argumentation for the influence of Chinese culture on the *Tableau* has been waning, until it is almost extinct among Western economists. Nevertheless, the two arguments, especially that for the Chinese origin, are to the mystery of the origin an important research clue worthy of deeper exploration.

The above early Western arguments about the Chinese origin of the *Tableau*, such as those on its connection with the Chinese principle of natural order, the Confucian classic *I-Ching* and even Chinese hieroglyphs, may seem absurd on the surface, but a close analysis reveals that the early Westerners who put forward these ideas were mainly followers of Quesnay and were not just paying lip service to such ideas. In the midst of the Chinese vogue at that time, based on their deeper knowledge of the Chinese culture introduced to Europe and their deeper understanding of the creative intention of their master, they were obviously more able than later Western scholars to appreciate the intrinsic connection between Chinese cultural tradition and the *Tableau*.

Take for example the Chinese term of "natural order." Although it does not appear in Chinese classics, similar or identical views abound in such works, and ancient Chinese scholars paid particular attention to the study of the laws of nature that govern human society rather than the external nature that has been emphasized in the traditional Western view of natural law. Therefore, Europeans in that period praised Chinese people for discovering the laws of social natural order, and Quesnay regarded China as an ideal country for observing such laws. His *Tableau* was used to envision and display graphically the socio-economic functioning of an ideal country under conditions of conformity with the natural order. That's why his contemporaries pointed out that by using the *Tableau* as a litmus test for social institutions, Quesnay was applying and developing China's "immutable insights" (Clerc, 1769, p. xiv) of the fundamental laws of the natural order, which was unparalleled in Europe. This statement reflects the profound understanding of Western scholars of that period about the relationship between the *Tableau* and Chinese culture.

Complicated as its relationship with the *Tableau*, the *I-Ching* itself is a bizarre classical text, with an integrated symbolic and conceptual system, rich in philosophy and rigorous mathematical logic, from which Western missionaries even "discovered" the secrets of the long-lost "original revelation" in the West. It is difficult to estimate the influence that such an ancient Eastern classic with a strong mystical flavor had on the Western academic circles after it was transmitted to Europe. However, one thing is certain: it had a very high status in the minds of Western scholars at that time. A testimony to this is the fact that Leibniz (1994) considered the hexagrams to be the most ancient monument in the science of the universe. Similar to Leibniz, Quesnay was one of the many admirers of the *I-Ching* in the West during that period.

Quesnay's (1946) veneration of the *I-Ching* lies above all in the fact that it reveals the "mysteries of great importance to the governing of states" (p. 187). Such "mysteries," according to Quesnay, probably lie in part in the *I-Ching*'s emphasis on controlling complexity with simplicity and on mastering the unified law of change in order to manage complex phenomena. The reason is that when he talks about the whole essence of the economic rule of an agricultural country in his *Tableau*, he is just saying that we should rely on this table to grasp the "most constant law" that runs through all parts of things and governs all of them, so as to understand the whole picture of the intricacies of things. The idea of "simplifying and controlling complexity" is based on the concept of a unified organism in which everything in the universe is interdependent and influences each other. The *I-Ching* is also a representative work of traditional Chinese organic philosophy. According to this organic viewpoint, the *I-Ching* and its researchers in previous dynasties have always been accustomed to viewing the entire universe from a macroscopic point of view, proposing various system models in order to understand the "principle of the universe," which usually adopts a general analytical method that is not based on the isolated study of individual things. The organic theory of the *I-Ching* not only regards nature and society as an interconnected and mutually constrained whole, but also emphasizes the need to maintain *Taihe* (harmony and coordination among all things), that is, the highest state of harmony, which is manifested in the mathematical law of conservation and balance of *yin* and *yang* in the changes of the hexagrams. These concepts, together with *zhong-xing* ("middle line") and *zhong-dao* ("middle way") mentioned many times in the *I-Ching*, constitute a unique and prominent ancient Chinese equilibrium system of thought. Indeed, those important contributions in Quesnay's *Tableau*, such as macro or general method of analysis, system concept, equilibrium theory, and description of the whole organic system of economic life, that are to be praised by future generations of economists, can easily find their similar elements in the *I-Ching*, which he regarded as sacred.

By pointing out that the *I-Ching* already contains the prototypes of some important principles and methods in the *Tableau*, we actually mean that Quesnay may in the process of creating the *Tableau* have directly absorbed or been influenced by these precursor elements from the *I-Ching*, which he was familiar with. At the same time, in the ancient Western cultural system, there is no tradition of organism, and economic views since ancient Greece and Rome are mostly concerned with individual economic problems, instead of socio-economic problems as a whole, especially those that deal with the issue of overall equilibrium. It is thus all the more likely that Quesnay drew his inspiration from ancient Chinese texts that have this organicist tradition and focus on a similar overall equilibrium analysis. In addition, the linear descriptions of the *I-Ching*'s hexagrams obviously had a certain inspirational effect on Quesnay's initiative to describe socio-economic activities in the form of diagrams, a fact acknowledged by both his followers and his opponents at that time.

That the mathematical quality of Chinese characters was used as a metaphor for the precision of the *Tableau* is a typical reflection of the admiration that European scholars had for the Chinese culture transmitted to the West during that period. Quesnay's followers, who made this metaphorical claim, understood the Chinese hieroglyphic script, like many others at the time, as a unique system of writing boasting many embryonic scientific functions, of which precision is particularly similar to that of the mathematical proof that is actually the origin of the mathematical analysis of the *Tableau*. The possible influence in terms of the common ground of mathematical precision, as is embodied in the metaphor, may not seem worth paying attention to now, but is definitely reasonable when seen against the special background of the cultural exchanges between China and the West at that time.

The above arguments that emerged in the era of the Physiocratic School, each one linking the *Tableau* to Chinese culture, are in themselves very thought-provoking. This link, whatever its specific content, is enough to prove that the transmission of Chinese culture to the West had an undeniable influence on the creation of the *Tableau*. With the passage of time, Westerners gradually lost sight of the special mark left on the creation by this period of cultural interaction between China and the West. As a result, their search for the origins of the *Tableau* has never gone beyond the traditional vision of the West.

Admittedly, as a theoretical product of a specific historical situation, the birth of the *Tableau* depended above all on the socio-economic realities of France in the mid-eighteenth century, followed by the rise of European Enlightenment, the characteristics of political domination, the prevalence of various economic theories, especially anti-mercantilism, and even the development of natural sciences. "The *Tableau*," Leontief (Quoted in Meek, 1962, pp. 295–296) points out, "is far from being the ideal and airy thing which it is sometimes made out to be: on the contrary, it is one of the most striking examples in the whole history of economic thought of the achievement of a harmonious unity between abstract theory and concrete investigation." Fox-Genovese (1976, p. 252) also argues, "The Tableau économique represents a revolutionary breakthrough in economic analysis and reflects the historical reality of its conception." These observations are valid in their own way. But they cannot lead to the conclusion that the sources of ideas for Quesnay's *Tableau* are restricted to Europe. He was equally able to draw on all the foreign ideas he encountered. In fact, the Chinese culture, which was constantly imported into Europe, was an important source filling him with admiration. This applies not only to his *Tableau*, but also to his other important economic theories.

The Western origin of the *Tableau*, since it was put forward by Western economists in the late nineteenth century, has become the dominant viewpoint in the history of economic theory. However, in our view, the underlying arguments are highly debatable. For example, the statement that the concept of circulation in the *Tableau* was inspired by the phenomenon of blood circulation in the human body. Regardless of whether this physiological discovery made a hundred years ago "had lost nothing of its freshness," as Schumpeter (1954a, p. 240 [Note 9]) says, by the time of Quesnay, the basic spirit of this statement is nothing more than to show that Quesnay realized the circulation principle in social and economic activities from the physiological phenomenon of blood circulation. However, many examples can prove that the concept of circulation is also a basic category of traditional Chinese culture, and that the importance of this ancient Chinese concept of circulation in people's thinking, its long history, its clear way of expression, and its wide use, including its direct application to the economic analysis of the abstract idea of circulation and the metaphors of blood circulation and vital energy, are all beyond the reach of the traditional Western concept of circulation. Since Chinese culture is so rich in ideas of circulation, Quesnay's circular ideas and their application in the field of economic analysis may well have been nourished by the Chinese culture that he absorbed.

The earliest and most important explorations of some of the principles of the *Tableau*, from a European point of view, generally go back to the contributions by the pioneers of the Physiocratic School, such as Cantillon's analysis of the cyclical process of social income and Boisguillebert's study of overall equilibrium. However, two points must be put forward. First, it is possible that Quesnay could have absorbed other ideas independently of Cantillon and Boisguillebert. There is a certain inheritance in the relationship between Quesnay's *Tableau* and some theoretical viewpoints of the pioneers of Physiocracy, but Quesnay's originality is obviously different from or superior to that of his forerunners. Even Schumpeter, who pioneered the concept of "Cantillon-Quesnay *Tableau*," is hesitant about evaluating Cantillon's contribution. Second, the simultaneous ups and downs of the *Tableau* and the Chinese culture imported into Europe at the time seem to provide some evidence for the *Tableau*'s inheritance of both the French precursors' thought and Chinese culture. It is true that Cantillon's and Boisguillebert's economic discourses, though predating Quesnay's *Tableau*, belong to the seventeenth and eighteenth centuries and were inevitably influenced by the Westward transmission of Chinese culture. But under such historical conditions, especially in the absence of similar sources of thought in European antiquity, it is difficult to say that the two scholars' originality is in any way unrelated to the importation of Chinese culture. Moreover, as an important contribution to economic theory in this historical period, the *Tableau*, which embodies the thoughts and achievements of Cantillon and Boisguillebert, coincided with the influence of Chinese culture that swept through Europe. Since then, as Chinese traditional culture lost power in Europe, the *Tableau* had been put in limbo and remained unknown for 100 years, and it was not recognized again until the middle of the nineteenth century. Such historical phenomenon points to the influence of Chinese culture, along with the European own tradition, on the creation of the *Tableau*.

From the above, it can be seen that some unique theoretical viewpoints in the *Tableau* have their preliminary presence in ancient China and the West, while others are hard to see in ancient West, but are richly documented in ancient China. In the Western history of economic thought alone, some of the precursor ideas in the *Tableau* were not clearly discussed until the seventeenth century by Boisguillebert and Cantillon. However, both scholars lived at a time of great cultural exchanges between China and the West, and it was difficult for their ideas not to be greatly influenced by ancient Chinese culture. Besides, in creating the *Tableau*, Quesnay, as "the Confucius of Europe," though having necessarily retained certain elements of the Western tradition, must have turned to the East in forming some of his main ideas.

The "rediscovery" of the *Tableau* has brought it great honor: Fox-Genovese (1976, p. 252) hails it as a "revolutionary breakthrough in economic analysis," and Marx (1969, p. 344) even praises it as "the most brilliant [conception] for which political economy had up to then been responsible." According to the above analysis, the "most brilliant" or "revolutionary breakthrough" of the *Tableau* lies not simply in following the traditional Western ideas, but more importantly, in absorbing the beneficial elements of Chinese culture that were foreign to Europe at that time, thus creating a new blend of Chinese and Western cultures. It can be said that traditional

Chinese culture includes almost all the germ of some of the most original and important ideas and methods in the *Tableau*, such as natural laws, the principle of keeping complexity under the control of simplicity, the macro or general concept, the system idea, the theory of overall equilibrium, the concept of circular flow, and the methods of mathematical analysis and graphical display. Reichwein (1925, p. 104) argues,

> If we take the trouble to separate, in the work of Quesnay, that which is really personal to him, we find that it is principally the method employed in building up all the material of his knowledge into a mathematically clear system. As one of his pupils said: "Method was the speciality of his genius [...]."
>
> Everything except his method Quesnay owes to the models he had before him; to Chinese tradition in particular he is indebted for certain basic ideas.

In our opinion, however, even the method used by Quesnay in the analysis of the *Tableau*, as described above, can be found in Chinese traditional culture.

In short, it is by no means accidental that the transmission of Chinese culture to the West aroused the concern of Europeans about the origin of the *Tableau* in eighteenth-century Europe. This means that ancient Chinese culture did have an influence on the *Tableau*, which, far from remaining at a superficial level of contact, has penetrated deeply into the theoretical system of the *Tableau*, and formed an important part of its source. It is only for this reason that Oncken regards Quesnay's great achievement in creating the *Tableau* as the completion of Confucius' legacy (Zhu, 2005b, p. 317). This is an overstatement, but it reflects the close connection between the *Tableau* and Chinese culture, because, for Quesnay, Confucius is not just a "feudal signboard" (Marx, 1992, p. 436), as some people say, but a symbol of Chinese traditional culture. It is in the name of inheriting Confucius' legacy that Quesnay made use of the treasures of Chinese culture by creating the *Tableau*. In this way, the *Tableau*, which was nourished by both Chinese and Western cultures, still retains its fresh vitality in the development of economics, and "it is not only economic antiquarians who can benefit from its study" (Meek, 1962, p. 296).

Chapter 6
Laissez Faire

The *laissez-faire* doctrine of the Physiocratic School has been an important topic in the history of economic theory. However, those who deal with it in economic writings in China and abroad generally place it in the development of Western economic thought, seldom considering the factors outside the West. In this chapter, we will systematically examine the Physiocratic concept of *laissez faire*, in terms of its Western origin, its main meanings, and its compatibility with the ancient Chinese thought of *wu wei* (inaction). In particular, we will explore the unique way in which the Physiocratic theory of *laissez faire* was influenced, in the light of its basic feature, by ancient Chinese thought.

1 *Laissez Faire*: Concept and Theory

Here, we first examine the wording and definition of the *laissez-faire* concept, then discuss the basic feature of *laissez faire* as a Physiocratic theory, while comparing it with the ancient Chinese ideas imported into Europe at that time, to verify whether the origin of this theory is exclusive to the traditional Western thought.

I. **The concept: wording and definition**

Below, we first give an overview of some popular claims about the origin of the Physiocratic concept of *laissez faire*, and then analyze its main meanings.

1. **Wording**

Disputes arise as to who first gave the wording of *laissez faire*, originally a French expression. Broadly speaking, the following accounts are popular.

One is that some Physiocrats, such as Mirabeau, Du Pont, and Mercier de la Rivière, attributed it to Gournay (1712–1759). The fact that Du Pont listed Gournay and Quesnay as the founders of the Physiocratic School, and that two of Gournay's

M. Tan, *The Chinese Origin of Physiocracy*,
https://doi.org/10.1007/978-981-97-9703-5_6

famous followers, Turgot and Cantillon, were closely associated with the Physiocrats, strengthens the idea that the principle of *laissez faire* was first articulated by Gournay and then accepted by both the Physiocratic School and the School of Gournay.[1] Those who disagree with this believe that Gournay's contribution lies in nothing but his effort "to have popularised" (Higgs, 1897, p. 67) the famous maxim of *laissez faire*. After his appointment as intendant of commerce in 1751, Gournay adopted a series of measures aimed at opposing the state's rule of handicraft workshops and its exclusion of commerce, which reflected the spirit of the *laissez-faire* policy. That's why some scholars say that his "official position gave wider political significance to the policy" (Handman, 1931, p. 3), or that he was the first to put into practice the formula of *laissez faire* (Volgin, 1983, p. 83). In other words, Gournay was the popularizer and practitioner of the *laissez-faire* principle, not its first advocator.

Another account is found in Turgot's *Éloge de Gournay*, in which reference is made to Le Gendre, a merchant of Colbert's time. It is said that in 1680, when Colbert, then Louis XIV's Minister of Finance, consulted a meeting of French businessmen on what the State could do to help them, Le Gendre replied sharply, "*Laissez-nous faire*." The reply differed only slightly from the term "Laissez faire," which was to become fashionable, with the deletion of the word "we" (nous). Will and Ariel Durant (1963, p. 25) also state, "'Liberty,' he (Colbert) (or one of his critics) said, 'is the soul of commerce. We must let men choose the most convenient ways' (*Il faut laissez faire les hommes*); here was a phrase destined to make history." Heckscher (1936, p. 53) points out that "the expression, *la liberté est l'âme du commerce*, occurs hundreds of times in the correspondence of Colbert," and on this basis, finds it certain that even this famous mercantilist believed in commercial freedom in principle. Higgs (1897, p. 67 [Note 2]) notes, "The erudite professor of history, Lord Acton, in his introductory lecture at the University of Cambridge, refers to 'the economic precept *Laissez-faire*, which the eighteenth century derived from Colbert'." This view has been refuted by some people. But in any case, the idea that the term *laissez faire* arose in Colbert's time is accepted by a considerable number of economists.

Still another account is given by scholars represented by Oncken. In his *Die Maxime Laissez Faire et Laissez Passer*, Oncken suggests that the origin of this principle should be attributed to the Marquis d'Argenson (1694–1757), a pioneer of the Physiocratic School, who used the expression in his Memoirs of 1736. The Marquis, according to Rubin (1979), advocated at the time that "Do not interfere" should be regarded as the motto of every public authority (p. 101). The statement "Do not interfere" here is said to be the original *laissez faire* in French. Rubin claims that it is in the writings of the Marquis d'Argenson that we first meet with that famous formula of the free traders, '*laissez faire*'" (p. 101), that is, the Marquis is in fact the first to coin the famous expression *laissez faire* (p. 29). Rozenberg (1934–1936) argues that the Marquis made *laissez faire* his creed unconditionally, unreservedly

[1] Different from, but parallel to and almost simultaneous with, the Physiocratic School, a group of economists revolving around Gournay emerged in France, who "were primarily interested in practical matters, and left behind no works of theoretical value" (Rubin, 1979, p. 102).

and unequivocally. Also, it is affirmed in the entry "LAISSEZ-FAIRE" of *The Encyclopedia Americana* that "[i]t was the Marquis d'Arguesau [d'Argenson] who first [...] made the phrase 'laissez faire' a postulate for political argument. 'Laissez-faire, he declared, as early as 1735, should be the fundamental rule of government [...]. 'To govern better,' he said, 'it is necessary to govern less,' a pronouncement which was to become the palladium of liberty [...] with individualists everywhere for a century and a half to come" (Pfeil, 1957, p. 655).[2] Oncken mentioned that, although Boisguillebert did not say anything like *laissez faire*, such words were already on his lips (Rozenberg, 1934–1936): Boisguillebert said, for example, that "[n]ature must be allowed to operate" (Quoted in Anikin, 1979, p. 91), and that "[i]t is [...] simply a question of letting people alone" (Quoted in Gide & Rist, 1915, p. 33 [Note 3]). The idea of *laissez faire* was thus clearly expressed.[3]

On the basis of these various statements, Higgs (1897, p. 67) makes the following summary: "[T]he expression *Laissez-faire* is really due to Le Gendre [...]. Boisguillebert and D'Argenson had used it also before Gournay, who may, however, be said to have made it classical in its later form. His personal influence stimulated many persons."[4]

The above discussion of the phrasing of *laissez faire* comes mainly from French intellectual circles. In English-speaking countries, it has been argued that the concept emerged early, especially in England—to a lesser extent, in France, thanks to the effort of prominent figures such as Sir Josiah Child (1630–1699), a wealthy English businessman (Rima, 2001, p. 45).[5] This view may be based on the fact that Gournay once translated and introduced the works of some British mercantilists, including Child, to the Physiocratic School. In fact, France had already seen in Colbert's time the formation of the concept of *laissez faire*, and did not have to rely on the roughly contemporaneous and somewhat later English Child and others, whose views, according to Schumpeter's (1954, p. 363 [Note 1]) assessment, "have no place in a history of scientific economics." Thus, it has been pointed out that the earlier history of the doctrine is obscure in the English-speaking world (Rima, 2001, pp. 45–46). The first use of *laissez faire* in English is said to have been expounded by the eminent American Franklin in 1774 in his elaboration on the principles of trade, where he quoted the aforementioned conversation between Colbert and Le Gendre, but did not provide any further explanation for the implications of the term. Moreover, the American statesman Jefferson's widespread assertion "that government is best which

[2] *Laissez faire* in French also means "do not govern too rigidly."

[3] Kingsley Martin (1963, p. 60) also claims, "The Liberal theory of the harmony of natural interests, with its logical deduction of *laissez-faire*, is implicit in his (Boisguillebert's) writing. [...] Boisguillebert was the first economist to hold the optimistic view that the interests of man and Nature are identical."

[4] Professor Chen Daisun (1988b, p. 1394), a Chinese scholar, also points out that the code of "laissez-faire" may be traced back to the French merchant Le Gendre, a contemporary of J. B. Colbert, and was aphorized by Gournay.

[5] In this book, Rima (2001, p. 45) also lists both the Netherlands and France as the countries with an early tendency towards *laissez faire*, and argues that Italy and Germany deserve no credit for this.

governs least" is seen as a continuation of the political maxim of the French Marquis d'Argenson. These statements clearly reflect the spread and influence of the concept of *laissez faire* in English-speaking countries after it took form.

Therefore, it is certain that the term of *laissez faire*, whoever its originators may be, is a product of the period from the late seventeenth to the early eighteenth century, and that it owes much to the French intellectual community.

In the history of economic theory, *laissez faire* had been a mundane expression that became important only when it began to be used as a slogan by a famous school of thought. That is to say, only after the systematic argumentation and fanfare of the Physiocrats did *laissez faire* become a complete and full-fledged ideological principle and economic policy that distinctly embodied economic liberalism, turned into a battle slogan marking the new era, and was to have a profound influence on the economic theory and practice of future generations. It is generally believed that for more than a century, that is, from the time of the Physiocrats to the 1930s, the *laissez-faire* theorists prevailed all the time, although there emerged some schools of thought that advocated state intervention. During this period, most capitalist countries adopted a *laissez-faire* economic system.

Within the Physiocratic School, the maxim of *laissez faire*, according to Oncken's study, was used only once by Quesnay in an indirect way. It was Quesnay's disciples who gave the maxim a broader and purer character, and made it more and more frequently repeated. That, however, does not prevent us from regarding *laissez faire* as an important marker of the entire Physiocratic system and the economic policy represented by Quesnay. This is one of the issues that needs to be clarified before we compare the *laissez-faire* principle of the School with ancient Chinese thought.

2. Definition

Laissez faire[6] is equivalent to several other expressions in French, such as *laissez passer*,[7] *laissez aller* and *le monde va de lui-même*.[8] It is frequently cited, together with *laissez passer*, by the economists of various countries. It is noted that after *laissez faire* was created, *laissez passer* might be added by Gournay. The two, according to Oncken, have different emphases: the former on freedom of production and the latter on freedom of trade. Similarly, A. Marshall (Quoted in Samuels, 1962, p. 157) may have on the basis of this interpreted them as "let people make whatever they like and move wherever they like." In a slightly different way, Haney (1911, p. 140) states that *laissez faire* means to "let things alone," and *laissez passer* to "let them take their course." But whatever the different interpretations, the common point of all these French expressions is obviously the spirit of economic liberalism. *Laissez faire*, in particular, has now become a common economic term in the history of economic doctrine and typically embodies the specific meaning of economic liberalism.

[6] This term has many English variations, such as "leave it alone," "freedom to do," and "freedom to make."

[7] The English equivalent is "let go" or "freedom to pass."

[8] Its English translation is "the world goes on of itself."

It was from the natural order that the Physiocrats derived economic liberalism. The French dauphin once inquired of Quesnay how to govern:

> "What then," asked the Dauphin, "would you do if you were king?"
>
> "Nothing."
>
> "Then who would govern?"
>
> [A]nd the laconic answer was,
>
> "The law."
>
> (Quoted in Higgs, 1897, p. 45)

What Quesnay referred to here is the law of natural order. This is a clear indication of how the Physiocrats understood the relationship between *laissez faire* and the natural order. That is why *laissez faire* is said to have originated from natural law, and become a necessary trend in the philosophy of natural order.

For the Physiocrats, the essence of natural order is the unity of individual and public interest, which can only be realized within a free and unfettered system. Quesnay believed that "*the perfection of economic conduct consists in obtaining the greatest possible increase in enjoyments through the greatest possible reduction in expense*" (Quesnay, 1962, p. 211), and that "[w]hen every one does this the natural order, instead of being endangered, will be all the better assured" (Quoted in Gide & Rist, 1915, p. 11), thus refuting the view that "individual interest is in contradiction with general interest" (Quoted in Quesnay, 1962, p. 211). In the same vein, Quesnay's disciple Mercier de la Rivière argued, "The movements of society are spontaneous and not artificial, and the desire for joy which manifests itself in all its activities unwittingly drives it towards the realisation of the ideal type of State" (Quoted in Gide & Rist, 1915, p. 11). That is why Quesnay (1888) said that only freedom and private interests can make the state thrive. Revealed is thus the true meaning of *laissez faire*.

The manifestation of *laissez faire* in the economic policy of the Physiocrats is their advocacy of free trade. They argued for the abolition of all restrictions on the domestic circulation of commodities between provinces and between regions within each province, and allowed the free export of agricultural products, especially grain, to other countries, and the free import of industrial goods from foreign countries. For them, only free competition is compatible with the natural order, and all artificial monopolies, restrictions and interventions are contrary to it. Thus, despite the fact that their pioneers had been in favor of free trade and "their attitude towards it (commerce) was one of disdainful *laissez-faire*" (Gide & Rist, 1915, p. 29), they were still "to be regarded as the founders of Free Trade" (p. 29) and "the 'first school of free trade'" (Bloomfield, 1938, p. 731), and Quesnay was to be seen as the "basic source" of Smith's free economic ideas that had given much stimulus to British free trade policy (Feng, 1979, p. 41).

Laissez faire is synonymous with rejection of government interference. According to the Physiocrats, since the natural order is the best and the most reasonable, everything should be left to run its own course without government interference. "Remove all useless, unjust, contradictory, and absurd laws," Baudeau (Quoted in Gide & Rist,

1915, p. 33 [Note 3]) said, "and there will not be much legislative machinery left after that." The purpose is to reduce government legislative activity to a minimum.

In short, the main meanings of *laissez faire* as a slogan of the Physiocratic School include: economic life is regulated by the laws of nature and should be kept away from state interference; inversely, the state should pursue a liberal economic policy that allows the members of society to maximize the public interests in the pursuit of their individual interests. This definition may well serve as the basis for our comparative study of the Physiocratic theory of *laissez faire* and the ancient Chinese doctrine of *wu wei* (inaction).

II. **The theory: enlightened despotism as the basic feature**

Many scholars, in studying the Physiocratic theory of *laissez faire*, have noted that the School also fervently advocated "enlightened despotism" or "legal despotism." This seems to be a contradiction, for those arguing for *laissez faire* seek to exclude the interference of the State, whereas those for enlightened despotism uphold the monarchical system of the State. Various viewpoints have been expressed on this.

One view, such as that of Gide and Rist, is to understand this peculiarity of Physiocracy in a positive light, and to see no contradiction in their quest for "the minimum of legislation with a maximum of authority" (Gide & Rist, 1915, p. 34). Marshall (Quoted in Samuels, 1962, p. 157) argues, "*Laissez faire* did not imply that Government should abstain inertly from constructive work: it meant simply that anyone who thought that he could make anything with advantage, whether on old lines or by a new method, should be at liberty to do so." The implication is that government involvement in economic activity is a proper part of *laissez faire*.

Another view is put forward by Schumpeter (1954a, p. 230), which goes as follows:

> [I]t is necessary [...] to distinguish doctrinal frills from underlying common sense. Thus, Quesnay taught laissez-faire [...] as [an] absolute norm of political wisdom. But [this imperative] must be viewed in the light of the physiocrats' hostility to all kinds of privileges and to a great many things that seemed to them to be abuses, monopoly positions among others. Since these could not have been abolished without a good deal of governmental 'interference,' Quesnay urged upon government what really was an activist policy, and not at all one of doing nothing. Moreover, in spite of his wholesale condemnation of government regulation or control, it is relevant to observe that what he actually faced were regulations that were inherited from the past and no longer fitted current conditions: the absolute norm of laissez-faire acquires in such a case a relative significance that differs greatly from what its absolutism suggests.

In much the same vein, Samuels (1962, p. 158) points out,

> *Laissez faire, laissez passer* thus had an important role in the Physiocratic theory of economic policy [...]. But *laissez faire, laissez passer* is not the sum total of the Physiocratic theory of economic policy; for clearly the Physiocratic concept of the role of government in the economy was not one of sitting back and relaxing and letting the world and the economy go by on its own. Individuals [...] were still to operate within the social controls [...]. [...] [G]overnment had a more thorough and activist role, being given specific positive tasks and ends."

Thus, he argues that "laissez faire is an inadequate characterization of the Physiocratic theory of economic policy" (p. 145), for it "has a place only within the broader dimensions of the Physiocratic theory of economic policy" (p. 145). D. H. MacGregor (Quoted in Samuels, 1962, p. 145), a writer, is said to have remarked, "Laissez faire was a leaf out of their book, but not enough to be the title of what they had to say." These views are not without pertinence in their regarding as a "supposed paradox" (Samuels, 1962, p. 160) the two coexisting views of economic freedom and political absolutism, and in their seeking to give a rational explanation through analysis.

The third view is that there is indeed a contradiction between *laissez faire* and authoritarian monarchy of the Physiocratic School, of which the Physiocrats were "apparently unaware." Their conception of government was diametrically opposed to the liberal model, and in particular their choice of the term "despotism" aroused indignation. This may be illustrated by the fact that Rousseau (1997, pp. 268–271) had resentfully denounced the Physiocrats as flattering the king by advocating "legitimate despotism" and declared that he would no longer accept the publications presented by the Physiocratic School. "[T]hey (the Physiocrats)," Gordon (1968, p. 546) points out, "did not in fact hold as a principle that the state should never interfere in economic matters, so they ought not to be characterized as espousing a laissez-faire doctrine."

As a matter of fact, advocating enlightened despotism is one of the basic features of the Physiocratic theory of *laissez faire*, and it is precisely this feature that clearly reflects the profound influence of ancient Chinese thought and system on the Physiocratic School. Therefore, a correct understanding of the significance and role of enlightened despotism in the Physiocrats' theory of *laissez faire* is an important part of an appropriate evaluation of the influence that ancient Chinese culture had on their creation of this theory.

Quesnay and Mirabeau co-authored an unpublished draft of the *Treatise on Monarchy* as early as 1758. That was to provide a systematic historical and theoretical analysis of the monarchy in order to discover what was wrong with it. After eight or nine years, Quesnay outlined "legal despotism" in his *Despotism in China*, and soon directed Mercier de la Rivière to elaborate on it in his *The natural and essential order of political societies* (1767).[9] Legitimate despotism is generally regarded as the pivot upon which the entire political doctrine of the Physiocrats rests. Their economics cannot be understood apart from their political theory, especially the doctrine of "enlightened" or "legal" despotism, because, just as Fox-Genovese (1976, p. 46) puts it, "[t]he physiocrats saw both political and economic theory as integral parts of a single science grounded in private property."

[9] Auguste Oncken (Quoted in Maverick, 1946, p. 137), when publishing a collection of Quesnay's works in 1887, added a note to his inclusion of *Le despotisme de la Chine*, which reads: "This [work] may be considered in a sense to be the forerunner of Mercier de la Riviere's work, *The natural and essential order of political societies*. ... Generally speaking, the essay did not attract much attention, nor does it rank among the best works of the author. However, for the history of the physiocratic system, it is noteworthy, for it shows that Quesnay's political opinions took their final form later than his economic opinions. It may be noted that the Maxims, which were incorporated later in the *Maximes generales* (...), are composed in a political vein."

Quesnay's (1962, p. 231) first of his thirty "General Maxims" reads: "*That there should be a single sovereign authority, standing above all the individuals in the society and all the unjust undertakings of private interests.*" The "sovereign authority" here is different from the democratic self-government of the Hellenic Republic or the parliamentary politics of England. The Physiocrats clearly expressed their abhorrence of democratic elections and aristocracy.[10] Quesnay (1946, p. 268) argued, "The authority must be unique ... and be united under a head who alone holds executive power." It is evident that the Physiocrats' ideal is absolute monarchy, for Du Pont claimed, "Only in the case of hereditary monarchy can all interests, both personal and individual, present and future, be clearly linked with those of the nation" (Quoted in Gide & Rist, 1915, p. 34 [Note 2]). But how can these diverse interests be combined, or what is the common basis for the realization of these interests? Pursuing this line of thought, we will find that the Physiocrats had a very unique understanding of despotism, which has the same origin as the theory of *laissez faire* does.

For the Physiocrats, despotism is the product of freedom, not slavery, and is not subordinated to the individual will of the monarch, but only reflects the rule of the natural order. In other words, the monarch, as the embodiment of despotism, is an instrument for conveying the laws of the natural order. He is like the conductor of an orchestra, to whom every musician must obey his gestures and follow his directions, never allowing any deviation or error. This despotism of the conductor is based on his absolute obedience to the score, and there is no tyranny. By the same token, "Euclid is a veritable despot, and the geometrical truths that he enunciates are really despotic laws" (p. 35 [Note 3]). Mercier de la Rivière's conclusion is as follows: "The personal despotism will only be the legal despotism of an obvious and essential order. In legal despotism the obviousness of a law demands obedience before the monarch enjoins it" (p. 35 [Note 3]). Thus, the "personal" nature of the despotism lies in the fact that the monarch alone gives the orders, while its "legal" nature lies in the fact that the monarch himself must first obey the laws of the natural order.

The natural order, for the Physiocrats, means that an ideal system has to be discovered by men of genius, and can be realized only under enlightened despotism. Quesnay (1962, p. 231) repeatedly spoke of an "enlightened" or "wise" government, but what makes a dictatorship "enlightened" is also, above all, that it must make it clear that "*the nation should be given instruction in the general laws of the natural order, which constitute the form of government which is self-evidently the most perfect,*" that "those who are destined for administrative positions should be obliged

[10] Quesnay (1946, p. 267), when discussing the diversity of the governments, says, "This authority must not be aristocratic or turned over to the great land-owners, for they may, by confederation, form a power superior to the laws, and reduce the nation to slavery, and may cause havoc, disorders, injustices, the most atrocious acts of violence, and the most unbridled anarchy, by their ambitious and tyrannical dissensions. [...] This authority must not be democratic, because the ignorance and prejudices that are dominant among the common people, the unbridled passions and transitory furies to which the latter are susceptible, would expose the state to uproars, revolts, and horrible disasters." Baudeau (Quoted in Gide & Rist, 1915, p. 34 [Note 2]) also expressly disapproved of the democratic self-government in ancient Greece when he argued, "The Greek republics never became acquainted with the laws of the order." And Du Pont (p. 34 [Note 2]) held a similar view by stating, "The sovereignty of the natural order is neither elective nor aristocratic."

to make a study of the natural order which is most advantageous to men combined together in society, [...] [and] that the practical knowledge and insight which the nation acquires through experience and reflection should be brought together in the general science of government, so that the sovereign authority [...] should institute the best laws and cause them to be scrupulously observed, in order to provide for the security of all and to attain to the greatest degree of prosperity possible for the society" (p. 231). Quesnay also called this regime a "protective regime" to support the observance of these natural and fundamental laws of the body politic, i.e., the administration of the state by means of decisive and immutable positive laws that are compatible with the natural law. In his view, only by knowing the highest law of natural order can we always maintain the stability and prosperity of the empire, which is why the natural order is the order most beneficial to the monarch, and "what is really the most advantageous to the sovereign is the most advantageous to his subjects" (p. 54). In short, only "a nation [...] informed of the intentions and the irrevocable laws of the all-powerful, and guided by the light of conscience" (Quesnay, 1946, p. 280), can have the enlightened despotic regime of the Physiocratic ideal, and only a ruler who is aware that his "authority is instituted in order to make these laws known and observed" (p. 280) can be the enlightened despotic monarch of such a regime.

Enlightened despotism has as its object the observance of the laws of the natural order, so legislation, if in accordance with nature, is unnecessary, and if against nature, is sure to fail, for nature is the strongest in the long run. The Physiocrat Du Pont argued, "As kings and governors you will find how easy it is to exercise your sacred functions, which simply consist in not interfering with the good that is already being done, and in punishing those few persons who occasionally attack private property" (Quoted in Gide & Rist, 1915, p. 37). In other words, according to the norms of the natural order, the function of the despotic monarch is not to interfere in economic life, except to protect the right to private property. Another important duty of the despotic monarch is to instill the concept of natural order in the consciousness of the people: "Universal education," said Baudeau, "is the first and only social tie" (p. 37). At the same time, popular education and educated public opinion were also seen as effective guarantees against the degeneration of despotic monarchy into arbitrary tyranny. Quesnay opposed ruling the state with guns and halberds and proposed instead following public opinion. What is meant here is that it is the enlightened public opinion that guides the rule of the state.

This shows that what the Physiocrats called despotism, like their concept of *laissez faire*, is based on the doctrine of natural order. On the one hand, when the various economic and political systems, decrees and regulations of the authoritarian State, i.e. "the man-made order" or "the positive order," are adapted to the requirements of the natural order, the society is in a healthy state, which means that the *laissez faire* of social and economic activities prevails, and that human beings enjoy the greatest happiness. In this ideal state, according to the Physiocrats, the national territory will still need a sovereign whose duty is to maintain social order and encourage social education and, just as natural scientists such as Newton discovered the great laws of harmonious order that govern the physical world, to discover similar laws that do govern the moral order of the human social world (Higgs, 1897, pp. 69–70).

On the other hand, if the positive order violates the natural order, a society will fall into a state of disease. This is where a strong "enlightened monarch" needs to appear, to diagnose and treat diseases, so as to make the society return to the natural order. Even in this case, the purpose of the intervention of the enlightened sovereign, according to the principles of Physiocracy, is simply to remove all man-made obstacles so that socio-economic life can develop on its own in accordance with the basic laws of the natural order. This is undoubtedly to create the conditions for the principle of *laissez faire* to be put into practice. Thus it has been said that the Physiocratic principle of *laissez faire* not only preserves the full political power of the monarch, but also adapts his activities strictly to the natural order that governs things. Obviously, the *laissez faire* and enlightened despotism of the Physiocrats are united on the theoretical fulcrum of the natural order, which constitutes a distinctive feature of Physiocracy.

That the Physiocrats integrated enlightened despotism into *laissez-faire* thought was the product of the specific historical conditions. In the first half of the eighteenth century, the ideas of "enlightened monarchy" and "enlightened despotism" in France were widely spread. This trend demanded the implementation of progressive reforms and opposed the usurpation and privilege of feudal aristocrats. The "enlightened" or "legitimate" absolutism of the Physiocrats was no exception. Many scholars, when discussing the reasons for the formation of this characteristic of the Physiocrats, are accustomed to looking for its roots in the Western tradition, presuming that the French despotism of the eighteenth century can be traced back to the Middle Ages. But other scholars, in the course of their research, have found that there is something unique about this thought of the Physiocrats that differs from the Western tradition. Fox-Genovese (1976, p. 22) notes, in the discussion of monarchy, that "only Quesnay's economic analysis radically differentiated their (Quesnay's and Mirabeau's) thought from that of their contemporaries and predecessors." Reichwein (1925, p. 101) also states, "Quesnay's theory is the 'enlightened' justification of political absolutism. That feature of it which forms a new departure in European thought, and is, therefore, presumably original, is the character of the justification, the fact that it is based on economic considerations." These fundamental differences from the Western tradition, which are "creative" or "alternative," are what we need to pay special attention to when we study the connection between the *laissez-faire* thinking of the Physiocrats and ancient Chinese culture.

2 *Wu Wei Er Zhi*: The Precursor

In the history of world economic thought, economic liberalism is an important principle that has attracted widespread attention. In the West, it was first embodied in *laissez faire*, a slogan openly and explicitly put forward by the Physiocratic School, while in ancient China, this idea had a much longer tradition and can be summarized as *wu wei er zhi*, the motto of governance. A comparison of this traditional Chinese thought with the Physiocratic theory of *laissez faire* reveals that the two are surprisingly consistent in their basic meanings, which fits in with the historical background of the cultural exchange between China and the West at that time.

I. **Ancient Chinese tradition of liberal economic thinking**

In China, as early as the pre-Qin era, some relatively mature views of free economy were developed and widely disseminated. Among them, the most representative and the most influential to future generations are the Confucian and Daoist doctrines of *wu wei* (inaction).

The Confucian thought of *wu wei* is already crudely formulated in the *I-Ching*: "In (all these operations forming) the Yî, there is no thought and no action. It is still and without movement; but, when acted on, it penetrates forthwith to all phenomena and events under the sky" (Legge, 1963, p. 370). Here, "no action" (*wu wei*) includes the implication of a primitive free economy. It is expressed more explicitly in what Confucius (1869) taught his disciples: "*[T]he person in authority* makes more beneficial to the people the things from which they naturally derive benefit" (p. 262). The "benefit" here depends on natural forces in the sense of material production. He also said, "Does Heaven speak? The four seasons pursue their courses, and all things are *continually* being produced, *but* does Heaven say anything?" (p. 244) "Heaven" represents all natural forces and is the origin of all things. Such natural forces are beyond the control of people and operate independently, so "the things from which they [the people] naturally derive benefit" can only be guided by the trend without interference. This means that government activities ought to be reduced to a minimum. That's why he said, "May not Shun be instanced as having governed efficiently without exertion? What did he do? He did nothing but gravely and reverently occupy his imperial seat" (p. 222). This is a clear indication of the ruler's belief in *wu wei er zhi*. In this regard, Mencius (1875) used the story of a stupid person's assisting the corn to grow long by pulling it out, to argue that government interference is not only of no benefit, but also harmful (p. 166). "If those wise men [administrators] would act as Yu did when he conveyed away the waters," he said, "there would be nothing to dislike in their wisdom. The way in which Yu conveyed away the waters was by doing that which gave him no trouble. If your wise men would also do that which gave them no trouble, their wisdom would also be great" (p. 264). The so-called "doing that which gave him no trouble" (*wu shi*) is Confucius' expression of *wu wei er zhi*. Their conclusions on governance are based on the understanding that there is an inherent regularity in the operation of all things in heaven and earth. Mencius said, "There is heaven so high; there are the stars and zodiacal spaces so distant. If we have investigated their phenomena, we may, while sitting [in our places], ascertain the solstices for a thousand years [past]" (p. 264). Here, what is sought for is annotated by later scholars as "the principle of the world," which is the natural law that the administrators must follow to avoid intervention, that is, they can "sit" and "ascertain the solstices" for their own good.

The pre-Qin Confucianists generally believed in the following from *The Doctrine of the Mean*: "Such being its nature, without any display, it becomes manifested;

without any movement, it produces changes; and without any effort, it accomplishes its ends. The way of Heaven and Earth may be completely declared in one sentence" (Confucius, 1869, p. 310). Even Xunzi, who advocated "regulating what Heaven has mandated and using it" (Xunzi, 1994, p. 21), said that, once the ruler of a country understands the objective laws of the outside world and formulates and follows the appropriate state laws and regulations, "what further exertion must he make? He has only to let the lower and upper garments hang down and the world will be settled" (1990, p. 164). The pre-Qin Confucianists, in their adherence to the *wu-wei* doctrine, advocated following nature, which is not only the nature of heaven and earth, but especially that of human nature. Mencius (1875, p. 263) said, "All who speak of the natures [of things], have in fact only their phenomena [to reason from], and the value of a phenomenon is in its being natural." The word "value" is interpreted by Zhu Xi (2016) as *shun*, which means to follow the requirement of nature instead of one's pretension. It follows that human nature is in accordance with nature, and to follow human nature is to follow nature. Thus, the ancient Confucianists preached that "they derived rules (for their courses of labour) from the heavens" (Legge, 1885, p. 425), highlighting the doctrine that "Heaven hears and sees as our people hear and see; Heaven brightly approves and displays its terrors as our people brightly approve and would awe" (1879, p. 56), or "Heaven sees as my people see, Heaven hears as my people hear" (Mencius, 1875, p. 281), which means that the will of the people mirrors that of heaven, and cannot be defied. In the view of Confucius and Mencius, in order to follow the natural course of human nature, the ruler must treat the cultivation of the individual's character as the foundation of state governance, for "[t]he root of the kingdom is in the State; the root of the State is in the clan; the root of the clan is in the person" (p. 237). At the same time, according to Confucius' and Mencius' doctrines of "benevolent governance," rulers must abide by moral and ethical norms and implement "benevolent governance," so as to moralize people and win their hearts.

The economic liberalism of pre-Qin Confucianists is closely related to their moral concepts. Confucius believed that the reason why Shun was able to "rule by doing nothing" was precisely because he was the one who "respected his own virtue." By extension, Confucius' (1869, p. 121) basic principle of government was formed: "He who exercises government by means of his virtue, may be compared to the north polar star, which keeps its place and all the stars turn towards it." An authoritative interpretation of this remark by later Confucianists is that "the virtuous do nothing, as if the North Star stays still, with many other stars revolving around it," linking "virtue" directly with *wu wei*. That's why Liu Baonan (1990) argues that "virtue" originally refers to unspeakable transformation and natural governance, with *wu wei* acting as the rule, and Zhang Boxing (1994) claims that *wu wei* is natural, having nothing to do with man. This means, according to Zhu Xi (2016), that if the sage is virtuous, his people will follow suit, not waiting for any action from the ruler. It is worth noting that Confucius (1869, p. 167) seldom spoke of "profitableness." Mencius (1875, p. 124), too, argued, "Why must your Majesty use that word 'profit'? What I am likewise provided with are [counsels to] benevolence and righteousness; and these are my only topics." This argument, as a view of wealth and profit conforming to moral and ethical norms, was not only the dominant economic thought in feudal times, but also an important basis for the long-standing and deep-rooted concept of "ruling by doing nothing" in ancient China. In other words, the ancient Chinese idea of free economy can easily find its theoretical basis in the pre-Qin Confucian concepts of righteousness and profit. It was from the moral code of Chinese Confucianism that the Physiocrats later found the ideal model for implementing their slogan of *laissez faire*.

Another prominent representative of the idea of *wu wei er zhi* in the pre-Qin era is the Daoist school. In *Lao Zi* (*Tao Tê Ching*) and *Zhuang Zi*, the Daoist scriptures, there are many references to the maxim that a ruler should "do nothing." The Daoists believed that the source of all things in the universe is "Dao" (Lao Zi , 1994, p. 195), which is *wu wei* and "nature," and that human beings, to emulate "Dao," should also focus on *wu wei* (pp. 137, 145). In essence, they recognized the objective regularity of the changes of all things, and applied this regularity to their observation of social phenomena, so that people's actions, especially the words and deeds of rulers, must conform to the laws of nature, and they must not act arbitrarily, but do everything in accordance with the principle: "This he does; but dare not act" (p. 222). As all things are changing, the so-called inaction of people following nature is in fact action. That is why Lao Zi (p. 188) said,

> Tao never does;
> Yet through it all things are done.
> If the barons and kings would but possess themselves of it,
> The ten thousand creatures would at once be transformed.

This concept of inaction, from its emphasis on compliance with nature, requires people to act according to the following:

> The more prohibitions there are, the more ritual avoidances,
> The poorer the people will be.
> [...]
> So long as I act only by inactivity the people will of themselves become prosperous.
> (p. 211)
> Without law or compulsion, men would dwell in harmony.
> (p. 183)
> Doing-nothing, they could use the whole world in their service and might have done more [...].
> (Zhuang Zi, 1891, p. 333)

What is advocated above is as much economic liberalism as the pre-Qin Confucian doctrine of *wu wei*. In addition, the Lao Zi-Zhuang Zi School, which created the doctrine of "Heaven's Way and Nature," opposed all kinds of oppressive laws, wars of annexation, and heavy tax burdens, and demanded that the state pursue a policy of non-interference in social and economic activities. Therefore, the Daoist (Taoist) idea of *wu wei* became one of the strong bases for the advocacy of economic liberalism throughout the dynasties, and was absorbed by the Confucianists of later times to varying degrees.

It is true that a careful examination may reveal that the pre-Qin Confucianism and Daoism are different in the meaning of *wu wei*. The Confucianists emphasized their idea of "virtue," while the Daoists advocated their perspective of "Dao." The latter focus on acting in accordance with the laws of nature, regarding "ruling" as secondary, while the former adhere to the principle of "ruling" as their purpose. However, their unanimity in the basic meaning of adapting to the changes of nature has constituted a major feature of traditional Chinese culture.

In addition to Confucianists and Daoists, there were many other philosophers of the pre-Qin period who discussed *wu wei* or similar ideas. In the late Warring States period, it was proclaimed in the masterpiece *Lüshi Chunqiu* (*Lü's Spring and Autumn Annals*) that "[a] man who has attained the Dao, [...] takes Heaven as his model" (Lü, 2000, p. 348); and that "[h]e is able to hold fast to doing nothing; therefore he is able to employ the actions of the many. Understanding nothing, being able at nothing, and doing nothing are principles to which a lord holds firm" (p. 632). What is argued here is similar to the Daoist idea of the concept. Besides, among the early legalists, Deng Xi had the doctrine of *wu wei*, and Shen Dao (2002, p. 1) believed that so long as the people enjoyed peace for themselves, the Sage of heaven and earth can have nothing to do. The so-called "nothing" is an alternative form of the Daoist sense of *wu wei*. Later, Han Fei Zi (1939), that is, Han Fei Tzŭ, the master of Legalism, also advocated that "the intelligent ruler does nothing" (p. 32) and that "[s]uperior virtue is non-assertion and without pretension" (p. 171). "To avoid action," Guanzi (2001) declared, "is [the way of] the emperor. To act, but without any deliberate purpose, is [the way of] the king" (p. 116). Here, the philosophical basis is the same as the popular concept of Heaven at that time: "Those who accord with Heaven will retain their achievements" (p. 85). That is, Dao is regarded as natural law and the Way of Heaven must be obeyed.

In the early Western Han Dynasty, the pre-Qin thought of *wu wei er zhi* was embodied in the economic policy of "lessening the control over the people." Under the guidance of the principle that "the way to govern was through purity and stillness, so the people of themselves would find peace" (Sima, 1971, p. 422), those in charge made remarkable achievements in that they "governed with purity and stillness, [a]nd the people were at peace" (p. 425). At the same time, the idea of *wu wei* was further developed and elaborated. Lu Jia (1935), a Confucian advocate of supplementing Confucianism with the teachings by the Yellow Emperor and Laozi, argued that there is nothing more important in Dao than *wu wei* and that *wu wei* is thus nothing and everything. He highly praised the rule of Yao and Shun, stating that, if there is no intention to govern the country, and if there is no disturbance to the people, then the country will be ruled all by itself. He accused the Qin Dynasty of taking violent measures counterproductively, claiming that the more annoying its ruling was, the more chaotic the country was; that the more noxious its laws became, the more rampant villains were; that the more numerous soldiers and horses were, the more numerous enemies were. He painted an ideal picture of a sage's rule: Nothing happens, as if there is no noise in the street, no officials in the government, no people in the villages, no quarreling in the neighborhood, no people, old or young, worrying in the courtyards, no gossip exchanged by the near or spread by the far, no nights packed with soldiers hurrying on the post roads, levies issued in the countryside, dogs barking, or fowls crowing, but only the aged dining in peace in the halls, and the stalwart men ploughing in the fields. What a wonderful scene under *wu wei er zhi* ("ruling by doing nothing")!

Later on, Liu An (2010), the king of Huainan, presided over the compilation of *The Huainanzi*, which repeatedly demonstrates the principle of "doing nothing and everything." Focusing on the Dao of Nature and Heaven, he argued, "It [The Way] covers Heaven and upholds Earth. [...] So high, it cannot be reached. So deep, it cannot be fathomed" (p. 48). He also said, "[T]hose who break through to the Way return to clarity and tranquillity. Those who look deeply into things end up not acting on them" (p. 57). The opposite is also true: "They [Fuxi and Nüwa] acted non-actively and were united with the Way. They spoke non-actively and were suffused by its Potency" (p. 50). In his view, all things in the universe are derived from *Dao*, and the principle of *wu wei* is in accordance with *Dao*, which means that "nothing is non-action." He said,

> In stillness they take no deliberate action, yet there is nothing left undone.
> In tranquillity they do not try to govern, but nothing is left ungoverned.
> What we call "no deliberate action" is to not anticipate the activity of things.
> What we call "nothing left undone" means to adapt to what things have [already] done.
> What we call "to not govern" means to not change how things are naturally so.
> What we call "nothing left ungoverned" means to adapt to how things are mutually so.
> (p. 44)

Here, "what things have [already] done" or "how things are mutually so" emphasize the observance of the natural laws of things, which is the so-called *Dao*. In other words, "if things first have what is natural to them, afterward human affairs can be governed" (p. 803), which means that the governance of human affairs must be kept in accordance with the laws of nature. This seems to be inaction, but it means actually that "the best words reject words [altogether], and the best acts are devoid of action" (p. 441). In the same way, Liu An's view of *wu wei* discards the negative attitude of the pre-Qin Daoists who demanded a return to the original state of nature, and embodies a positive spirit of basing political rule on the laws of nature. This is why he said that "non-action is the Ancestor of the Way. Attaining the Ancestor of the Way, one responds to things without limit" (p. 304). Conversely, "[i]f you are unable to act without purpose, you will be unable to have anything purposeful" (p. 627). These arguments mark a new peak in the ancient Chinese thought of *wu wei er zhi*, both in theory and practice.

Since then, with the consolidation of the feudal hierarchical order, interventionism had been widely on the rise. However, even in "the transformation of Western Han Dynasty's economic thought from 'inaction' to 'action'" (Zhao, 1986, p. 227), some famous figures still insisted on economic liberalism. A typical example is Sima Qian (1993), who argued in *Shi Ji 129: The Biographies of the Money-Makers*,

"[T]he highest type of ruler accepts the nature of the people, the next best leads the people to what is beneficial, the next gives them moral instruction, the next forces them to be orderly, and the very worst kind enters into competition with them" (p. 434). What he meant is that socio-economic activity is an objective process that does not depend on people's will, so it is best for the state to adhere to the following order of priorities: firstly, to let socio-economic activity develop naturally without interfering; secondly, to guide it according to objective needs; thirdly, to teach and prevent certain behaviors that are detrimental to the economy of the society; fourthly, to organize and standardize economic activities that are spontaneous and incongruous; and fifthly, also the worst, to let the government compete against the people for profits in its own economic undertakings. In his view, all aspects and regions of social production spontaneously divide labor and cooperate to meet each other's needs, and all people engaged in agriculture, industry and commerce go out to engage in production and circulation activities, requiring no interference of "government directives, mobilizations of labour, or periodic assemblies" (p. 434). These views are typical of free economic thinking.

In the debate on salt and iron in Sima Qian's time, scholars with free economic thinking strongly opposed the government's economic intervention, arguing that it was against the law of nature: "Follow the principles of Heaven and utilize the wealth of the Earth, and you will accomplish deeds without laborious effort" (Huan, 1931, p. 77), and "the people each get their own convenience and the ruler has nothing to do" (2016, Chapter. XXXVI). This led to a head-on clash between the view of free economy and interventionism, which had already existed in the pre-Qin era. This struggle manifested itself in almost all the economic issues throughout the feudal landlord economy, especially in its early stages. It showed that the feudal economy required a more fixed hierarchical order so that social life could be conducted according to certain traditional regulations, which was the objective basis for the emergence of the so-called economic "interventionism." But the feudal economy was decentralized, small, household and self-sufficient, and too much interference is very likely to provoke its free-economy requirements (Hu, 1963, p. 499). In general, many ancient Chinese thinkers inclined to a policy of free economy under enlightened despotism, which is typically embodied in the following remark: "So long as I work after sunrise and rest after sunset, digging wells for water, and ploughing the fields for food, the power of the emperor means nothing to me" (Huangfu, 2010). This is unique to China but not to the West.

It must be pointed out that after the Tang and Song Dynasties, with the slow development of the feudal economy, the idea of *wu wei* made some progress, as can be seen in the following three aspects.

Firstly, as the commercial capital infiltrating into the feudal economy was strengthened, state monopoly and economic interference were weakened, thus highlighting the influence and guiding effect of *wu wei* on social and economic activities. As a socio-economic factor, this first point is just briefly mentioned here. The other two, however, are grounded in the history of economic thought and deserve an analysis below.

Secondly, the Confucian and Daoist doctrines of *wu wei*, in their evolution, were united, mainly because Confucian scholars critically absorbed the Daoist *wu-wei* thought. Zhu Xi (1992), a scholar of the Southern Song Dynasty, believed that Confucius' (1869, p. 121) maxim of "exercis[ing] government by means of [...] virtue" means that virtue training for oneself naturally makes others follow suit, and argued that if the monarch possesses the virtue training for himself, practices it before the people, and uses his own virtue to educate and inspire the people, he does not wait for his people's subjection and the world turns to him as the stars revolve around the North Pole. He claimed that the emperor, if doing politics by virtue, needs to do nothing else and the world will still turn to him, and specially added that a sage, like Shun, is not a man who does nothing, but does many things. The criterion of *wu wei* (inaction), in his view, is "just not to cause trouble and disturb the people," but to act "according to one's own duty." This is completely consistent with the basic meaning of the statement that "the holy one does virtue above, and the people turn to him willingly. This subordination entails no coercion at all." According to this, someone asked him whether Confucius' thought of "exercis[ing] government by means of [...] virtue" and "Lao Zi's idea of inaction" are similar. Zhu Xi replied, "Lao Zi's so-called inaction means doing nothing at all, while the so-called *wu wei* of Confucius means not doing nothing at all, but just the same as Shun, who did nothing but gravely and reverently occupy his imperial seat."[11] Zhu Xi's criticism of Lao Zi's doctrine of *wu wei* as a complete lack of action is not entirely accurate. The reason is that when he repeatedly emphasized that the so-called *wu wei* of the "sages" is to do something, he instead accepted Lao Zi's (1994, p. 188) argument that "Tao never does; [y]et through it all things are done." Therefore, both the understanding of Confucius' thought by analogy with Lao Zi's inaction theory in the Song Dynasties, and Zhu Xi's absorption of the core of Lao Zi's thought under the banner of criticizing his doctrine of inaction, show the unity of Confucianism and Daoism in the theory of inaction, which is consistent with the development trend of "integrating Daoism into Confucianism" in the Song Dynasties. This unity undoubtedly strengthened the traditional position of the *wu-wei* doctrine in ancient Chinese economic thought.

Thirdly, the mutual penetration between the *wu-wei* doctrine and the concept of private property was becoming more and more obvious. Li Zhi (1961), a scholar of the Ming Dynasty, firmly believed that the highest Daoism has no action, the highest governance no sound, and the highest education no words. In his view, people and objects in the world are numerous, and any desire to make them organized is beyond nature, not to mention the intervention of the ruler. So it is better, and much easier, to let people follow their own preferences, each relying on his own strengths, and have the freedom to choose. That is why the sage is above all, and all things have a reason to be as they are. In line with this concept of *wu wei*, Li Zhi (1974) openly praised private ownership and private accumulation as the natural principle, which must be followed, and regarded as useless and insufficient all the theories that deny private ownership. In this way, the new spirit of the times defending private ownership was

[11] The quotations of Zhu Xi in this paragraph, unless otherwise stated, are from Li Jingde's (1986) *Dialogues Between Zhu Xi and his Disciples* (Vol. 23).

injected into the traditional thought of *wu wei*. Gu Yanwu (1924, p. 10), a scholar from the Ming and Qing Dynasties, also proposed that "an individual's concern for his own interest always comes before his desire to work for the Son of Heaven or for the people," and that "the sage uses the world's selfishness to make his selflessness, so that the world is well governed." In other words, the selfishness of the individual is sufficient to make public the sage who governs the world, which means that the ruler has to use it for that purpose and does not have to interfere with private economy. By the same logic, Huang Zongxi (1993) protested against any taxation of private land as unkind to the people, regarding those who taxed private property not as sovereign fathers. In the early Qing Dynasty, Tang Zhen (1955) also favored the principle of inviolability of private wealth, believing that the sages have no art of generating wealth, but if they follow the natural course by not disturbing the people, wealth will be inexhaustible. It can be seen that the above scholars all argued for private ownership in their advocacy of *wu wei er zhi*, as opposed to feudal economic interference.

In short, the thought of free economy in ancient China, as is represented by *wu wei er zhi*, had originated very early before it spread widely when its different schools emerged. Its meaning became richer and richer, with the changes of social economy. Since the pre-Qin period, it had been competing with interventionism and had become a basic economic idea that ran through the whole feudal economy. Its position underwent some changes in various historical periods in ancient China, which corresponded to the strengthening or weakening of the economic interventionist forces. Many ancient Chinese thinkers, however, though emphasizing either interventionism or economic liberalism, tended to mix the two, rather than absolutely insist on either one. In general, economic liberalism was always regarded as a product of conforming to nature and an ideal state that people strived for, and state intervention was generally regarded as unavoidable in theory and was in practice often used as an expedient measure to deal with social and economic difficulties or national financial crisis. As a result, the free-economy thinking was able to flourish in ancient China and had considerable influence. This was not the case in the West.

II. **Origin of the physiocratic theory of *laissez faire***

From the above analysis, we can see that the Physiocratic theory of *laissez faire* can be traced back, in almost all its important meanings, as are summarized below, to the ancient Chinese thought of *wu wei er zhi*.

Firstly, the Physiocrats derived the *laissez-faire* principle from the natural order, the focus of which is nothing but the ancient Chinese confirmation to nature. The Chinese thought of *wu wei er zhi*, governed by Heaven's Way, advocates "mak[ing] more beneficial to the people the things from which they naturally derive benefit" (Confucius, 1869, p. 262). Here, "Heaven's Way" emphasizes "the way of the highest heaven" or "deriv[ing] rules [...] from the heavens" (Legge, 1885, p. 425), which means that all human actions must conform to nature. The Physiocrats were obviously familiar with this traditional Chinese thought. Quesnay learned from Silhouette's writings[12] that the works by Confucius "[are] useful for the study of the natural law [and] make us see that nature by herself is able to work things out, if we will but listen to her counsels" (Maverick, 1946, p. 28). Silhouette in turn, Maverick (pp. 27–28) points out, took this idea from the *Confucius Sinarum philosophus* (1687), which led him to think that the Chinese thought of *wu wei er zhi* could be used to enrich the study of natural law in the West. Very likely was thus the influence relayed to the formation of Quesnay's *laissez-faire* thinking.

Secondly, the Physiocrats' naturalistic concept of individual self-interest is reflected in the ancient Chinese idea of *wu wei er zhi*. The former is a subtheme of the Physiocratic principle of *laissez faire* that seeks to "achieve maximum enjoyment with minimum expenditure" and to maximize social benefits through individual profit-making activities. And the latter emerged frequently in China's history, first in the form of self interest in the pre-Qin period, and later in the Ming and Qing Dynasties as Gu Yanwu's (1924, p. 10) advocacy that "the sage uses the world's selfishness to make his selflessness, so that the world is well governed." Both *laissez faire* and *wu wei er zhi* embody, therefore, the concept of private ownership.

Thirdly, the principle of "free passage" upheld by the Physiocrats in their trade policy is no different from the pre-Qin Confucians' maxim of levying no taxes at the passes and in the markets (Mencius, 1875, pp. 147–148). If we make a further investigation, we may find that the phrase "free passage," which was specially used in trade when the slogan of *laissez faire* became popular in the early eighteenth century, may be inspired by China's traditional view in favor of free trade.

Fourthly, *laissez faire* is in terms of its wording compatible with *wu wei er zhi*. Synonymous with opposition to government interference, *laissez faire* is no different from the ancient Chinese maxim that the monarch "rules by doing nothing," and "has only to let the lower and upper garments hang down and the world will be settled" (Xunzi, 1990, p. 164), or that "the highest type of ruler accepts the nature of the people" (Sima, 1993, p. 434). Even the word "Nothing," used by Quesnay in reply to the French dauphin's question about how to rule, can be directly translated into Chinese as *wu wei* (inaction) or *wu shi* (nothing).

Fifthly, the Physiocrat's indoctrination of the natural order is equivalent to ancient Chinese sages' advocacy of educating the people by moral ethics. In the Physiocrats' ideal state of *laissez faire*, that the government's duty is mainly to recognize and abide by the law of natural order, and to make people understand this law and adapt to it through indoctrination, is a replica of the pre-Qin Confucian thought of "exercis[ing] government by means of [...] virtue" (Confucius, 1869, p. 121), or its interpretation that "the virtuous do nothing" but educate and influence Chinese people by moral ethics.

Indeed, in many important meanings, Physiocracy is so similar to Chinese Confucianism that it is no wonder that some modern scholars, when analyzing the origin of the Physiocratic theory of *laissez faire*, have linked the theory to the ancient Chinese

[12] One work, according to Maverick, is the *Idée générale du gouvernement et de la morale des Chinois* (1729). In 1759, Silhouette was made Controller-General of France, and drew the attention of the Physiocrats for his determined attempt to push forward reforms (Maverick, 1946, p. 27).

idea of *wu wei*. The British scholar Hudson (1931, p. 322) points out that, according to Quesnay, "[w]hen the king has reformed legislation he should then 'do nothing, but let the laws rule'; this is the *wu wei* of the Chinese ideal monarch." The Japanese scholar Takimoto Seiichi (1931) puts it more clearly, arguing that the *laissez-faire* approach of the Physiocrats is exactly the same as the ancient Chinese doctrine of *wu wei* (p. 25), and that even the instances of incompleteness, or rather the literal contradictions, of Quesnay's theory of *laissez faire* are almost identical to those of *wu wei* (p. 26). Many Chinese scholars also support this argument, such as Hou Jiajü (1982, pp. 10–11), who believes that "Chinese Confucian economic thought has inspired Western liberal economic theories."

However, Quesnay favored Confucianism only, not Daoism. He described the Lao Zi School as an "intruding religion" that exploited people's ignorance to spread superstition and idolatry, and believed that its continued development in China was due to the Chinese government's tolerant attitude (Quesnay, 1946, pp. 254–255). He did not understand the difference between Daoism and the Daoist religion, nor did he realize that some positive or beneficial elements of Daoism were either shared by Confucianism or absorbed by Confucian scholars. A typical example is the idea of *wu wei er zhi*. If it is "the great *wu wei* doctrine of the Taoists" (Needham, 2004, p. 92) to let things develop naturally, to let nature follow its normal course, to follow the reasoning of things, to make the best of them, and to know how not to interfere, Confucians, especially scholars of Song Confucianism, when discussing the dominant principles in the social, political and economic spheres, have obviously absorbed and made full use of this Daoist *wu-wei* doctrine that "refrain[s] from activity contrary to Nature" (1956, p. 68). The Physiocrats could thus also, though unwittingly, obtain the rich nourishment in the Daoists' inaction theory from the similar ideas of Confucianism. That "the Confucian school [...] was only interested in social justice" (1946, p. 247) instead of nature is precisely the reason why the Physiocrats especially appreciated Confucianism when they were troubled by the same social problems. On the one hand, Quesnay's rejection of the Daoist doctrine of *wu wei* shows that, at a time when Daoism was still far less popular than Confucianism on the European continent, it was impossible for him to understand the similarities between Daoist and Confucian *wu-wei* doctrines, and to learn about later scholars' integrating Daoism into Confucianism in their views on *wu wei*. On the other hand, the rejection shows that the Confucian doctrine of *wu wei* takes "governance" as its purpose, especially stressing "ruling by virtue," which is not as passive as the Daoist counterpart, and was obviously more enlightening for Quesnay when he was actively seeking a new economic principle to replace the mercantilist policy of state intervention in economic activities, which he strongly opposed.

It can be seen from the above that the *laissez-faire* principle of the Physiocratic School is in fact mainly an alternative form of Chinese Confucian idea of *wu wei*. In this regard, Needham's (2004) analysis is noteworthy: "Even when the old 'Asiatic' society had given place to 'bureaucratic feudalism' such conceptions (as *wu wei*) remained very much alive in Chinese political practice and government administration that had been inherited from ancient Asian society" (p. 16), but this principle of *wu wei* "was not congruent with characteristically occidental 'interventionism', so natural to a people of shepherds and sea-farers [, and] was not capable of allowing the mercantile mentality a leading place in the civilization" (p. 17).[13] This analysis of the principle of *wu wei* that was dominant in ancient China is the conclusion reached by Western scholars after a comparative study of the ruling styles of Chinese and Western antiquity. From a Western point of view, the adherence to *wu wei* in ancient China is like that to interference in ancient West, each forming a typical feature of its respective traditional culture. That is why Needham feels strongly that the Chinese principle of *wu wei* is so incompatible with the typical Western "interventionism." Some of his specific arguments may not be appropriate, but his comparative analysis of the socio-political and economic foundations of Chinese and Western societies and traditional thought provides us with insights into the intrinsic connection between Quesnay's *laissez-faire* theory and the ancient Chinese view of *wu wei er zhi*. In particular, his analysis demonstrates the lack of a typical Western tradition of *laissez faire*, which should be taken more seriously. This is a far better approach than that of those who seek the roots of Quesnay's advocacy of free trade only in his personal medical practice, especially in his preference for a natural approach to medicine (Fox-Genovese, 1976, p. 94; Anikin, 1979, p. 155).

In the following, we will examine in detail the Physiocrats' digestion of the research materials from Chinese culture, while elaborating on China's enlightened despotism, especially its key features known in eighteenth-century Europe and its being treated as the ideal that led to the creation of the Physiocratic theory of *laissez faire*.

3 China's Enlightened Despotism: The Ideal

The compatibility between the Physiocrats' *laissez-faire* principle and the Chinese idea of *wu wei er zhi* ("ruling by doing nothing") shows that the Physiocrats had a deep understanding of Chinese cultural tradition. They attached importance to this Chinese idea not only because they were influenced by the Confucianism introduced into Europe at that time, but more importantly, because, when they sought theoretical weapons against mercantilist policies, they found a model of creating and observing the *laissez-faire* principle from the so-called "enlightened" Chinese despotic system that embraced *wu wei er zhi*.

I. **Key features known in Europe**

In the seventeenth and eighteenth centuries, there were numerous introductions, reports, and commentaries by Western authors on the Chinese political system. These circulating written works outline a so-called perfect enlightened system, of which at least the following characteristics can be summarized.

---

[13] Max Weber (2005, p. xxxvi) also says to the effect that the idea of *laissez faire* has always been prevalent in China.

First, a political system based on a father-son relationship. A basic view of the Chinese government by the Western missionaries is that it was "an extension of the family system and filial piety" (Wang, 1979, p. 157). "The Chinese government," as is recorded in Du Halde's *Description de l'Empire de la Chine*, "was based entirely on a father-son relationship, with the emperor acting as the father of all the people and the chief official as the father of a province, of a town and even of a village. The people had a heartfelt obedience to the officials, who thus assisted the emperor in maintaining the stability of the whole country" (p. 157). This way of ruling was cited as an example by all European personalities of that period. Silhouette stated that "the government of a state is like the government of a family, that the emperor is the father of his country, and the mandarin is the father of his province" (Maverick, 1946, p. 29). Voltaire even bluntly claimed that "the organization of [the Chinese] empire is in truth the best that the world has ever seen, and moreover the only one founded on paternal authority" (Quoted in Reichwein, 1925, p. 89). W. Temple, an Englishman of the seventeenth century, argued, in accordance with the Chinese political system, that the way to rule a family is the way to rule a country, and that the government rules people, rather than merely relies on laws (Fan, 1943a, p. 6). In an October 1711 issue of *The Spectator*, J. Addison cited Le Comte's example of Chinese filial piety to illustrate that the obedience of children to their parents was the basis of all politics, and one's obedience to those at the top depended on one's obedience to one's parents (1943b, p. 112). All of these used the so-called "argument from the Chinese" as the criterion to judge the merits and demerits of a political system. This is why some modern Western scholars have argued that the British government was in many ways modeled on China, because they believed that the Chinese regime was full of father-son tolerance and understanding.[14] The German philosopher Wolff was also a devout admirer of the Confucian view of the patriarchal state. He repeatedly emphasized in his *Politics* that the relationship between rulers and subjects is like that between a father and his son, and spoke highly of the reported Chinese relationship between rulers and subjects modeled on that between a father and his son, and the Chinese practice of establishing this relationship as the cornerstone of the state (Zempliner, 1962).

Second, moral politics. The patriarchal basis of state rule as described above was maintained in ancient China in accordance with the moral and ethical codes of Confucianism. The Chinese philosophers, according to Du Halde's introduction, grouped all morals into five ethics, and demanded respect for parents and teachers, and obedience to the emperor from all classes of Chinese, which served as the social and moral bases for the Chinese, so that China was well governed (Wang, 1979, p. 158). Le Comte said that no other ancient conceptions of government could help build a monarchy as complete as that of China (Gorai, 1938, p. 166). The Englishman Temple (1770, p. 323), in his *Of Heroic Virtue*, thought highly of Confucius' doctrine:

> The sum of his writings seem to be a body or digestion of ethics, that is, of all moral virtues, either personal, œconomical, civil, or political, and framed for the institution and conduct

[14] In a work published in Paris in 1981, the author discusses the influence of the Jesuits in China on Quesnay (Geng, 1987, p. 23).

> of men's lives, their families, and their governments, but chiefly of the last: the bent of his thoughts and reasonings running up and down this scale, that no people can be happy but under good governments, and no governments happy but over good men; and that for the felicity of mankind, all men in a nation, from the prince to the meanest peasant, should endeavour to be good, and wise, and virtuous, as far as his own thoughts, the precepts of others, or the laws of his country can instruct him.

Silhouette also mentioned that "Confucius derived the natural law and the five relationships from the implanting in men's breasts of universal love, [and made] an elaborate application of the golden rule" (Quoted in Maverick, 1946, p. 32). This means that Confucian ethical doctrine based on the patriarchal relationship between rulers and subjects arises from the natural law or heavenly law and is therefore eternal and unchangeable. In this regard, Wolff's analysis is that people's inherent ethical obligations require them to support an order of various social relations, and that any threat to this social relationship will lead to an incoherence of the laws of the world (Zempliner, 1962). What he emphasized is the reason for the model of ancient China in his time in terms of moral doctrines and state system.

These descriptions of China's moral politics had great repercussions among some Enlightenment thinkers. Holbach is a typical example. He said that China was the only country known in the world that combined the fundamental law of politics with morality and made morality the only religion of the people, stressing that European governments must follow China's example (Quoted in Wang, 1981, p. 131). This view had a profound influence on the Europeans, and later even Hegel (1899b), who, though disdaining Confucius' moral philosophy (p. 136), pointed out that Confucius' morality was "just like moral laws" (p. 71), and that the Chinese state system, which was based on the moral union of family relations, was already quite strong at that time because of the absolute binding force of family obligations (pp. 120–121). He claimed admiringly, "The Chinese State (that is, the decadent Qing Dynasty) has consequently been often set up as an Ideal which may serve even us for a model" (p. 124).

Third, a system of restraint and supervision that prevented the monarch from arrogating power. One view is represented by Bouvet (1699), a missionary to China, who said in his introduction of the Eastern country to the Europeans that China was an authentic monarchical dictatorship, that its emperor enjoyed supreme power, and that its political system itself was perfect. The so-called "perfect" system here was held by those missionaries to include a set of supervisory checks on the despotic monarch, an example of which is that ancient Chinese were held to believe that the great fundamental law of the natural order had control over the despotic monarch. Le Comte (Quoted in Maverick, 1938, p. 65) reported,

> An unbounded Authority which the Laws give the Emperor, and a necessity which the same Laws lay upon him to use that Authority with moderation and discretion, are the two Props which have for so many Ages supported this great Fabrick of the Chinese Monarchy. … Interest [is] a motive to the Emperor […] to adhere to the Laws. They are so wholly made for his advantage, that he cannot violate them without doing some prejudice to his own Authority.

This is to emphasize the constraining effect of the laws of natural order on the despotic monarch. Another view is that the absolute imperial power in China was not tyrannical because the political principles practiced in the country required the people to be filial to the emperor and their fathers, and in the same way the emperor was obliged to rule as moderately as the father did. This, in turn, relates to the so-called popular Chinese belief that the emperor should devote his energies to the interests of the state. If he deviated from this way of behavior, he would suffer public contempt and feared a popular uprising. This actually treated the ancient Chinese "people-oriented" thought as another important factor that limited the emperor's power.

The above two views, in Silhouette's case, were combined to explain why the Chinese despotic emperor had not abused his reputation and power for so long. He mentioned that "the emperors provided at their gates, tablets upon which the people might offer complaints and suggestions. This purpose was also carefully kept in mind on the emperor's tours of the country" (Quoted in Maverick, 1946, p. 30). Later on, J. F. Melon, too, "approved of the Chinese procedure of inviting comments and criticisms on government and administration from all citizens" (pp. 33–34). However, with regard to these specific supervisory measures, it was the system of admonition in ancient China that attracted the most admiration and interest in the West. Voltaire concluded from this system that China's despotism was different from those despotic systems where "the monarch does not obey the law and arbitrarily deprives the people of their lives and property" (Quoted in Zhu, 2005b, p. 293), and lamented that "human wisdom could not devise a better political organization than Chinese politics" (p. 358). In 1738, in an article on China published in London in the *Gentleman's Magazine*, the author was surprised by the system of Chinese imperial historians that Du Halde introduced. It was a time when R. Walpole, a Whig, was in power, and when some political commentators often ridiculed the imperial government with "the argument from the Chinese," and even suggested that Britain should follow the example of China to adopt the imperial system of history and establish an admonition system (Fan, 1931, pp. 389–395).

Fourth, scholars' rule. As early as the sixteenth century, an anonymous European writer, who was said to have lived in China for six years, commented on the Chinese political system: Chinese officials were "chosen for their learning and great prudence, without regard to anything else, and if the sons are as able as their fathers they succeed them in their offices; otherwise they are not admitted by the king into his service" (Hudson, 1931, p. 243). Feynes, a French traveler, the author of *Voyage fait par terre depuis Paris jusques à la Chine* (1636), praised China as having a "politics of the philosophers" (Quoted in Zhu, 2005b, p. 77), where scholars participated in the ruling. The selection method was that scholars discussed problems in court, and then those who gave the best answers were granted the official positions. "Instead of arbitrary politics," Feynes concluded, "the ideal of scholars' rule would be the better way to describe China's government. The Chinese universities are entitled to unparalleled honor in the world, because young men compete for admission to the universities to discuss the laws of the country and the lives of the people, with which they should be familiar in their future careers" (p. 77).

These views were later confirmed or supplemented in the writings by the Jesuits sent to China. Le Comte mentioned in a letter entitled "On the policy and government of the Chinese," "Nobility is never hereditary, [except] the family of Confucius, ... When a viceroy or governor of a province is dead, his children, as well as others, have their fortunes to make, and if they inherit not their father's virtue and ingenuity, his name which they bear, be it never so famous, gives them no quality at all" (Hudson, 1931, p. 313). Bouvet (1699) also said that since ancient times in China, learning had been the criterion for the appointment of officials; that a studious and diligent academic attitude was regarded as the criterion of political excellence and good statesmanship; that people regarded morality and philosophy as the main learning; and that it was because people had acquired this knowledge comprehensively that they formed the basis of good government. During that period, Westerners held in high esteem the prevailing Chinese "politics of the philosophers" and the series of measures taken to ensure that scholars of both virtue and talent ruled, such as the system of selection and examination, which, along with the aforementioned system of admonition, called for their emulation. For example, *The Bee*, launched in 1730, called on the British government to adopt these Chinese systems to rectify the bureaucracy.

Fifth, the enlightened image and exemplary role of the despotic monarch. Westerners first learned about some principles from Confucian writings in terms of the image and role of the Chinese emperor. Bernier, a famous student of the Near East, produced a manuscript on China, of which only the introduction was published in 1688. After examining the manuscript, Pinot (Quoted in Maverick, 1946, pp. 16–17) said,

> It bears the subtitle "The science of princes"; Bernier explained that his choice of this subtitle was in recognition of the splendid guidance offered by Confucius. Confucius counseled princes to enter into the details of administration, to listen to complaints and remonstrances, to suggestions and advice; he told the princes that they should have no other concern than the welfare of their subjects. Bernier asserted that China offered a model [...] of a humane and enlightened despotism, where the authority of the sovereign was not exercised by force, but by persuasion, by love, and by the knowledge that his subjects kept their eyes upon his person, and emulated his conduct.
>
> "This type of limiting the arbitrary power of the ruler by 'gentling' him," Maverick (1946, p. 17) concludes, "is easily distinguished from the proposals of the European constitutionalists who would impose *legal* limitations upon the powers of the prince."

At that time, the idea of enlightened despotism was widely spread in European countries, and the Chinese emperor was always seen as the ideal symbol of an enlightened and authoritarian monarch. In particular, some of the French Jesuits who had been to China portrayed in detail their impressions from their direct contacts with the Chinese emperors, especially the Kang Xi Emperor, which made even stronger the belief in honoring the Chinese emperor as an enlightened monarch in the minds of many Westerners.

The Jesuit Gerbillon (1735) had been in contact with the Emperor in 1689 when he served as a Qing court interpreter in the negotiation of the Sino-Russian Treaty of Nebuchu. He described the emperor as a thrifty enlightened ruler who never hesitated to spend money, and never complained of excessive spending, on the state, or to set up businesses for the benefit of the state, but was ready to cut taxes for the needy in years of famine.

Bouvet was a long-time lecturer of Western mathematics, astronomy and other natural sciences in the Chinese imperial court, and was a great favorite of Kang Xi. When he returned to France in 1697, Bouvet (1699) presented a memorial to Louis XIV to introduce Kang Xi: he praised the emperor in every possible way, admiring him for his great gifts, his erudition, his superior intellect, his discernment; his strength and perseverance in dealing with complicated matters, his strong will to formulate, direct, and realize grand plans; his fairness, his justice, his advocacy of virtue, his love for his subjects; his obedience to the truth; and his self-denial that absolutely suppressed lust. He said something to the effect that such noble virtues were too numerous to list, and that Emperor Kang Xi possessed all the virtues of the world, and was one of the most perfect and wise monarchs who had ruled the world since ancient times. In order to dispel the doubts of Western readers about the above accounts, Bouvet published the "postscript" of the memorial, repeatedly declaring that his description of the Kang Xi Emperor was a fact that he saw with his own eyes, and an introduction of extremely accurate knowledge, and its content was a truth that is hard to deny word for word, so it rightly deserved the full trust of its readers. These compliments were indeed the highest possible. For Bouvet, they were to gain the favor of Emperor Kang Xi, the "first monarch of the East," but for Westerners who advocated enlightened monarchy at the turn from the seventeenth to the eighteenth century, they exerted an extraordinary influence and power.

Leibniz (1994) advocated enlightened despotism, using Emperor Kang Xi as a yardstick for an enlightened monarch: he argued that Chinese monarchs, because of their own greatness, were worshipped like gods, though they were men and that the present Emperor Kang Xi of China was an unprecedented monarch, with great wisdom because he had both Chinese and Western knowledge. Such quasi-religious tributes were clearly due to the influence of Bouvet, whose biography of Kang Xi, written in French, was translated into Latin by Leibniz and reprinted in 1699.

In addition, the ideal of enlightened and despotic monarchs, described by Wolff, completely followed the example of Chinese rulers (Zempliner, 1962); and Poivre called on Europeans to go to Beijing to pay homage to the Chinese emperor as "the mightiest of mortals" (Hudson, 1931, p. 318) and "the true and perfect image of Heaven" (p. 318).

All these show that many Westerners at that time were convinced of and aspired to the enlightened image of the Chinese emperor, even with a degree of fanaticism that is unimaginable in modern times.

The above key features of China's enlightened despotism that were widely reported in Europe, in the opinion of many Western scholars, dictated that the despotic monarch could only rule calmly and let things develop naturally, and that he was not allowed to interfere at will. In other words, the system of enlightened despotism not only did not contradict the policy of *laissez faire*, but was precisely the basis and conditions that ensured the implementation of this policy; even this policy itself was conceived, formed and developed in the soil of the enlightened despotism. In this respect, a passage in Silhouette's (Quoted in Maverick, 1946, pp. 29–30) introduction to Chinese political rule is quite representative.

> An early emperor, Shun, of heroic accomplishments, was said to govern by his repose. He looked serenely toward the south, and let affairs follow their course.
>
> The good man or sage does not exhibit directly his virtues or powers, but, like the soil, he makes his qualities known by his accomplishments. His actions are quiet and straightforward, and his movements are as uniform and tranquil as those of the stars. He appears to do nothing, but in reality, does much; he is active in his very inaction. *Que ce silence est éloquent!*

Obviously, in this Western formulation of China's enlightened despotism, it is the ancient Chinese idea of *wu wei er zhi* that is revealed.

The enthusiasm of many Europeans to understand and preach the Chinese despotism during that period was a response not only to the trend towards enlightened despotism in Europe at the time, but also to the numerous reports on China by Jesuits and travelers to China since the sixteenth century, which gave the Western world a desirable picture of an East with an ideal model of enlightened despotism. This praise of the despotic monarchy of ancient China, came either from the Jesuits' or travelers' own experience, or from the deep impressions they gained from contact with Chinese scholars or the study of ancient Chinese texts, especially from the prosperity and power of the Chinese Empire, which remained among the foremost in the world until the eighteenth century. However, due to the limitations of historical conditions, they could not have seen the unfavorable factors that hindered the socio-economic development of the Chinese feudal system, and certainly could not foresee that these unfavorable factors would make the Chinese Empire lag behind the Western countries, so their glorification of the ancient Chinese despotic system was inevitably tinged with exaggeration. This is what we must be aware of when we analyze the perceptions of enlightened despotism in Western public opinion at that time. However, in the process of promoting China's enlightened despotism, Westerners explored in depth those features of the system which, in their opinion, were worthy of emulation by Western countries, such as the basis of paternity in the political system, moral politics, a supervisory system to keep the monarch in check, scholarly rule, and the exemplary role of the enlightened despot, and attributed these enlightened features of China's despots to their adapting to the changes of nature and pursuing the policy of *wu wei er zhi*. Regardless of whether these characteristics, as generalized or summed up by Westerners, are correct or not in themselves, they are in fact of great importance to the Physiocratic School in exploring the root causes and inner laws of the Chinese Empire's long history and prosperity, and in promoting the *laissez-faire* principle in economic policy.

II. **The ideal of the physiocrats**

The argument of Westerners at that time that the Chinese ruling system was an enlightened despotism was almost entirely accepted by the Physiocratic School. In the writings of Quesnay and other Physiocrats, a wealth of materials about China have been collected and referenced, and their yearning for the ideal enlightened despotism is evident everywhere. A typical example is Quesnay's *Despotism in China*.

In this work, Quesnay (1946) described China's enlightened despotism with great reverence: "[T]he constitution of the government of China [was] based upon natural law in such an irrefragable and so emphatic a manner that it deter[red] the sovereign from doing evil and assure[d] him in his legitimate administration, supreme power in doing good; so that this authority [was] a beatitude for the ruler and an idolized rule for the subjects" (p. 225); the Chinese emperor was the Son of God and "the principal heir to his (the Shang-ti's) grandeur on earth" (p. 180), and was therefore virtuous, penitent, and fatherly for his subjects; "the Chinese constitution [was] founded upon wise and irrevocable laws which the emperor enforce[d] and which he carefully observe[d] himself" (pp. 141–142), and those who attempted to abolish the laws in favor of tyranny were overcome by them and inevitably dethroned by the people (p. 245); the ethical precepts were the foundation of the religion, law and education of the empire, and the sacred and stable relations between the monarch and the people were established on the basis of strict ethical precepts (p. 157); "[t]he custom of remonstrating with the emperor [had] been encouraged" (p. 214), so as to impose a restraint on the absolute power of the monarch, and "[t]here [was] perhaps no other country in which remonstrances [might] be made to the sovereign with more freedom than in China" (p. 216), which was the most praiseworthy feature of the Chinese system of remonstration at all levels; "the most illustrious family in China, and the only one in which nobility [might] be transmitted by heredity, [was] that of the philosopher, Confucius" (p. 174); Chinese officials were selected by merit and capacity through the imperial examination system (p. 172) and were very learned, their sole function being to protect and educate the people (p. 237); Emperor Kang Xi promulgated sixteen educational maxims on instructing the people to respect the basic laws of nature (pp. 196–200), made frequent visits to various places, did justice to an elderly victim, and punished tyrannical officials, etc. (pp. 252–253).

The great exaggeration of the superiority of the Chinese despotic system by Western public opinion aroused in France the disgust and criticism of Enlightenment scholars like Montesquieu. For this reason, Quesnay again devoted a considerable part of this book to analyzing and refuting Montesquieu's criticism. Since these debates fully reflect Quesnay's understanding and glorification of China's despotic system, it is appropriate to present them in detail here.

Quesnay focused on Montesquieu's views on the Chinese despotism in Sect. 1 of Chap. 3, and Sect. 1 of Chap. 7, the former for mainly citing Montesquieu's views as proof that China had a good legal system, and the latter for refuting one by one Montesquieu's criticisms of China's despotic regime.

Within the Sect. 1 of Chap. 3 (pp. 212–213), Quesnay, on the basis of the reports of the missionaries to China, and with reference to Montesquieu's statement that Confucius had lumped together "religion, laws, customs, and manners" as morality, and the rites that "formed the general spirit of the nation," argued that in China, religion, politics and laws were inseparable, and were all absolutely governed by the laws of nature, the exhaustive study of which was the main object of the sovereign and of the scholars entrusted with the specific administration. In his view, "everything is permanent in the government of that empire, like the immutable general and fundamental law upon which it is established, firmly and with enlightenment." He thus generalized the concept of "natural law" from the way China was governed.

In the Sect. 1 of Chap. 7 (pp. 239–254), Quesnay argued that the despotism or absolute power of the Chinese monarchy had been exaggerated, or at least examined with "considerable antipathy," by some Western political thinkers, among them Montesquieu. For Quesnay, Montesquieu's "many conjectures" about the rule in China were nothing but "so many specious sophistries against that government," and it was necessary to "expose" them.

The objections of Montesquieu quoted by Quesnay can be roughly summarized as follows:

First, the missionaries praised the principles of Chinese government as a mixture of fear, honor and virtue, but China was in fact a country where the people could "be made to do nothing without beatings" and where there was no honor. Second, Western businessmen in China never mentioned this kind of moral character that missionaries talked about. Third, the missionaries described in their letters the Chinese emperor's punishment of several princes for their conversion to Christianity, as well as China's "affronts to human nature done as a matter of rule." Fourth, the missionaries who had first been to China were "deceived by an appearance of order," and because the priests were ruled by the Pope's personal will, they pinned their success in preaching to the Eastern countries on persuading the monarchs that "they can do everything." Fifth, China's population was so large that, if the people's livelihood was not secured, there would be sudden disturbances and the "bad government there [would be] immediately punished." Sixth, a bad reign meant less happiness in the next life, less power and less richness in this one for the Western monarch, but the loss of "his empire and his life" for the Chinese emperor. Seventh, China, because of its increasing population, required the utmost attention and care from the government to enable every man to work, and to make the land productive enough to sustain the people. Eighth, in China there had been an attempt to make law and despotism go hand in hand, which, instead of putting chains on Chinese despotism, only armed it with its own chains, and made it grow more violent (Montesquieu, 1989, pp. 126–128).

The above objections were refuted by Quesnay (1946, pp. 239–254) one by one in his strong defense of the Chinese despotism, which goes as follows:

First, the fact that Montesquieu did not say a word about China's use of so many methods to inspire "emulation and honor" was "a very evident proof of his exaggeration and of his emphatic intention to represent the Chinese to us as servile men and slaves under a tyrannical authority." The bastinado in China was a punishment for criminals, just as in any other country there was a penal system, and no other country in the world strived to inspire honorable conduct as China did.

Second, it was unjust to adopt the comments of the European foreign-trade merchants to China on the virtue of the Chinese, as these merchants, unlike the missionaries, did not "represent the husbandmen and the rest of the inhabitants." The merchants did not penetrate far into the interior of the country, so that their statements should not be the basis for judging the Chinese political system. But the missionaries had been living in China for a long time and had travelled extensively, so that it would be more reliable to quote their reports.

Third, it was highly inappropriate to use as an example of China's frequent atrocities the emperor's punishment of the princes, who "had embraced Christianity." There were instances in all kingdoms of the world of large numbers of martyrs being punished for religious reasons, which was fully sanctioned by their laws. Besides, the above-mentioned incident was said to have been the result of the Princes' conspiracy, and to have been "merely a case of politics," so that it "really has nothing to do with despotism in China, not even with the intolerance of the government of that Empire, where cruelties for religious causes have hardly ever been practiced." The Chinese emperor was actually "recognized as one of the good [emperors] who has reigned there."

Fourth, China's orderliness described by the first missionaries to China was true and reliable. If the missionaries had been deceived by the orderly appearance of the country, why were their descriptions, which they themselves did not later deny, not contradicted by the reports of other missionaries who went to the country in succession? Moreover, it sounded "very ingenious to find that the missionaries think of the despotism of the sovereigns of Asia as being favorable to the success of their missions." But in fact the Chinese emperor was bound by law, so that "the will of one man is therefore not sufficiently decisive in China to have facilitated the success of the missionaries, nor to have induced them to build their entire hope upon this despotism."

Fifth, Montesquieu's reasoning that China's large population might give rise to sudden disturbances implied a "contradiction," because "[a] prodigious people and a bad government cannot be found together in any kingdom in the world." "A large population can accumulate only under a good government," Quesnay argued, "for bad governments destroy wealth and men. A little attention bestowed upon this prodigious population suffices to disperse all the clouds under which one would wish to place the government of China."

Sixth, it was still uncertain whether human laws were "more powerful and more compatible with the permanent solidity of a good government." If Montesquieu had been "more enlightened about religion" than the Chinese emperors, he should have "recognize[d] the dogmas of the [Chinese] natural law and [their] belief in a future life." But he was concerned with "the spirit of human laws, established [...] for the security of nations against irregularities of governments, and against abuses of power by the sovereigns whose activities must be moderated by counterbalances to keep them in order."

Seventh, Montesquieu "[took] the effect for the cause" in his observation that China's large population forced its despotic government to consider the livelihood of the people. He failed to understand that "this prodigious number of people can be only a result of good government in the empire," and that "in fact these good laws so frequently spoken of have been established there since time immemorial."

Eighth, Montesquieu's view was confusing that China was a country where the law, because of its being joined to despotism, lost its effectiveness and made the despotism more violent. "Good laws," Quesnay argued, "make a good government; without observance of the laws, the government would have no reality. The harsh despot, strengthened by laws, will rigorously enforce them, and good order will prevail in his state." Montesquieu was contradictory in speaking of the Chinese government, "which is the oldest, largest, most humane and most flourishing which has ever existed in the world." He thought that the Chinese government "caused so much disturbance [...] because it [was] ruled by a despot." That is, he "always [saw] in despotism an arbitrary and tyrannical government."

The above refutation was made in a rather absolute manner. The Chinese despotism, rejected by Montesquieu, was portrayed in Quesnay's hands as the perfect form of rule. Using the same Chinese sources, the two came to diametrically opposed conclusions. In this controversy, Quesnay presented himself as the promoter and defender of the Chinese despotism, which is why Maverick (1946) regarded Quesnay's above book on China as "the apex of the movement of admiration for China" (p. 111).

Quesnay's glorification of the Chinese despotism was an attempt to generalize and summarize, from the wealth of Chinese sources, an ideal political system equally suitable for European countries, especially France. This is his purpose in Chap. 8 of his book, which undertakes a "comparison of Chinese laws with the natural principles underlying prosperous governments." This chapter is widely regarded as the most important in the book. It summarizes the contents of all the preceding chapters and, in the words of the Abbé Baudeau, a disciple of Quesnay, focuses on "a parallel between the natural basis for the proper government of nations, and the principles of government as that science is taught and practiced in China" (p. 138). That's why Neill (1949, p. 547), a modern Western economist, claims that "in the eighth chapter of his *Despotisme de la Chine*, [...] he [Quesnay] tries to give a 'systematic digest of the Chinese doctrine.'"

Although many modern scholars are unconvinced or doubtful that ancient Chinese culture had a profound influence on the economic doctrines of the Physiocratic School, they are generally positive about the historical fact that China's despotic system had inspired and enriched the Physiocratic thought of enlightened despotism. Maverick (1946, p. 128), as one of the most active in fully affirming this fact, points out,

> In the eighth and final chapter, Quesnay undertook to apply the lessons of China to the desperate problems of France, and to formulate general principles of government. His ideal was an enlightened despotism, under which the "positive" laws (the statutes) would be designed primarily to give effect to the natural laws, that sublime set of principles.

In another place, Maverick (1946, p. 131) mentions again the ideal Chinese monarch in Quesnay's mind,

> An absolute monarch it [the Chinese government] had, but one who governed according to the Natural Law, who was himself subject to that law, and whose false steps from the proper path were promptly pointed out to him by faithful mandarins, with the result that he then corrected his practices. This was "enlightened" despotism.

Hudson (1931, pp. 317–318) cites all the proponents of "enlightened despotism" as a school of thought in eighteenth-century France, saying that they

> found their exemplar and vindication in China. The reason for their cult of China is really very simple. They appealed to Asia because there was nothing in the past of Europe on which they could take their stand. [...] But in the Far East was an empire as old as Rome, yet alive in the present, as populous as the whole of Europe, free from privileges of caste nobility and Church, ruled by heaven-bestowed royalty through a bureaucracy of scholar-officials. Here was the model for the neo-monarchists, and an example to quote.

On this basis, he judges that the Physiocratic ideal of enlightened despotism "had obvious reference to the Chinese model which they had always in view" (p. 325).

Reichwein (1925, p. 88), for his part, emphasizes,

> Of particular importance were the details given by the Jesuit Fathers concerning practical political matters in the Chinese Empire. On the one hand they helped forward the advocacy of enlightened despotism by philosophy, while on the other they gave a backbone to the physiocratic movement – that movement which [...] attempted to bolster up once more – this time from the economic side – the Absolutism of the seventeenth century.

He also affirms, "[T]hat which excited the admiration of Voltaire and all his contemporaries, including Quesnay, who took '*despotisme éclairé*' for their political ideal, was the fact that in China this form of government had maintained for centuries the 'peace and happiness' of the inhabitants" (p. 106).

Gorai Kinzo (1938, p. 109) even asserts that the so-called enlightened despotism of European thinkers, including that of Quesnay, is part of the core of Chinese Confucianism: These thinkers all thought highly of Eastern thought, and at the same time took China as the ideal country for the realization of their doctrines. Even a natural scientist like Joseph Needham (2004, p. 15) says, "The term 'oriental despotism' recalls of course the speculations of the Physiocrats in 18th-century France, who were deeply influenced by what was then known of the Chinese economic and social structure. For them, of course, it was an enlightened despotism, which they much admired."

In the meantime, there are a number of other Western scholars who, although not as determined and certain as the above-mentioned scholars, reveal, in various ways and to varying degrees, the connection between the enlightened despotism of the Physiocratic School and the Chinese despotic system. Gide and Rist (1915, p. 36) claim, "The sovereign who best represents the Physiocratic ideal is perhaps the Emperor of China." M. Einaudi (1938, p. 66) argues that "Quesnay limited himself to a generic discussion, repeatedly pointing, however, to the supremacy which the courts enjoyed in the ideal state, China." Mably (Quoted in Higgs, 1897, pp. 108–109) is quoted to have said that, in the eyes of the Physiocrats, the "magistrates are to be perfectly wise, but such men are rare out of China, where the *Économistes* think nature has been pleased to mould a nation of sages. The magistrates are a check upon the imperfections of the Despot." According to Martin (1963), "[t]he Chinese, the Physiocrats believed, had so far been alone in appreciating th[e] truth" (p. 230) that whether a country's rule is good or not is completely determined by observing or violating the laws of nature.

The Physiocrats wrote books to publicize China's enlightened despotism, which not only supported their political ideals, but also had a significant influence on the economic theories that made up their system. "Just as Confucius attributed his own wisdom 'to the great legislators Yao and Xun'," Fox-Genovese (1976, p. 75) points out, "so would Quesnay place his maxims in the mouth of the great Sully." This statement is rather obscure. In fact, Quesnay himself had clearly deduced his economic principles from the Chinese political system. He saw as an important sign of China's enlightened despotism the Chinese despotic monarchs' obedience to the dictates of the laws of nature and the appointment of philosophical officials with a high degree of moral cultivation to rule in "silence." The so-called "silent rule" here is consistent with the *laissez-faire* principle that the Physiocratic School strongly advocated. Quesnay (1946, p. 228) described the "silent rule" of China as follows:

> It may be difficult to believe that the emperor of China has time personally to look into the affairs of such a vast empire and to receive the homage of that host of mandarins he appoints to vacant positions, or that seek to obtain appointments; but such marvellous order is kept there, and the laws have so well provided for all difficulties, that two hours a day suffice for all his duties.

It can be seen that Quesnay had a deep understanding of the *wu-wei-er-zhi* approach under China's enlightened despotic system, so that he was able to depart from the European intellectual tradition, to take up the banner of *laissez faire* and to push it to a new stage of development. As the physician of a French despotic monarch, he not only put forward his *laissez-faire* theory, which was deeply influenced by the traditional Chinese thought of *wu wei er zhi*, but also by adopting the *laissez-faire* attitude under the enlightened despotism in ancient China, and digging into this economic phenomenon unique to China but unprecedented in the West, established his special harmonious unity of *laissez faire* and enlightened despotism.

Of course, the Chinese despotic system need not be a progressive idea in theory, nor a good system in practice. It is Quesnay's personal prejudice to preach great things about the Chinese despotism. But this can be used as the very basis to prove the Chinese origin of his thought. In other words, his *laissez-faire* theory, in addition to the objective political and economic conditions in France, has elements from China. It must be emphasized that *laissez faire* and despotic monarchy, whether or not they are correct in themselves, are the crucial evidence of Quesnay's acceptance of Chinese thought. This is because they have been part of the traditional view in China for thousands of years, whereas the liberal ideas of the West, especially after the Renaissance, have always been opposed to despotism. Therefore, Quesnay's insistence on *laissez faire* under an enlightened despotism is Chinese in its origin.

Chapter 7
Agricultural Primacy

So far as the importance attached to agriculture is concerned, Physiocracy in eighteenth-century France and traditional Chinese thought are indeed very similar. This similarity is often the starting point of many modern scholars' discussion and research of the influence of Chinese culture on the Physiocrats. The two systems of agricultural primacy, however, are also different, each representing a variety of production relations and social classes, which is a result of various historical conditions. What is then the specific role China's ancient agricultural thought played in the formation of the relevant Physiocratic doctrines, at a time when the Chinese vogue swept through Europe? This question is to be answered below from three perspectives: (1) the Physiocrats' emphasis on agriculture, (2) their concept of net product, and (3) their attitudes towards industry and commerce as are related to agriculture.

1 The Influence from China's Traditional Agricultural Emphasis

The so-called "Physiocratic School" and "Physiocracy," according to their Chinese translations, seem to be mainly characterized by the primary emphasis on agriculture. It should be pointed out, however, that the Physiocratic School created by François Quesnay and its theoretical system have always been dominated by the natural order. In this sense, what Quesnay saw in China's agriculturally-oriented thoughts and policies is not only specific perspectives and practices, but more importantly, adherence to the natural order.

I. **The agricultural primacy and the natural order**

It has been discussed above that Physiocracy, originally referring to "natural domination," does not merely—as Adam Smith summarized—argue for an emphasis on agriculture. Then, how did the Physiocratic school associate "the natural domination,"

M. Tan, *The Chinese Origin of Physiocracy*,
https://doi.org/10.1007/978-981-97-9703-5_7

that is, the natural order, with the primacy of agriculture? In this regard, two points must be made at this step. Firstly, according to the traditional Western concept of natural laws, conforming to nature does not necessarily equate to emphasizing agriculture. In the Middle Ages and before, the notion of conforming to nature did not have to include agriculture. Aristotle, for example, referred to all natural needs when talking about the conformation, and in the Middle Ages, the notion was applied to the discussion of price. Secondly, in the West, the importance of agriculture, though touched upon in the past, had not led to a specialized system of the Physiocratic doctrine. Eventually, it was on exactly the basis of the natural order that Quesnay established his Physiocratic system.

Starting from the natural order, Quesnay (1946) argued that agriculture is the economic field that best reflects nature's dominance. To show that the primitive and simple ruling work in agriculture is subordinate to the "fundamental truth" of natural laws (pp. 282–287), he assumed, in an abstract analysis, "the state of agriculture in its simplest form:" "This colony [in its primitive state] [...] must cultivate to subsist, [and] here finds itself subject to the laws that nature lays down, for the success of its labor and for the security of its establishment" (pp. 285–286). Such rules are "the natural, primitive laws" (p. 286). This primitive agricultural society does not refer to the social state "surrendered to the barbarity of usurpers, who are but illegitimate sovereigns" (p. 287); and the "natural and voluntary development" (p. 287) of this society, "dictated by the natural and constitutive order of agricultural nations" (p. 287), in Quesnay's view, applies to all countries and all ages. "All of these rules," he claims, "[...] are the best possible rules for the interest of the individuals separately, and for the general good of society" (p. 287).

It is precisely because Quesnay believed that agriculture and the natural order have the above-mentioned close relationship, that is, only in the agricultural field is the natural order fully reflected, that some people regard his sense of agriculture as the basis of the natural order. That Takimoto Seiichi questions whether it was the study of agriculture that led Quesnay to the concept of natural law, or it was the concept of natural law that aroused Quesnay's interest in the study of agronomy, is simply a testament to the fact that, in Quesnay's economics, agriculture and the natural law are most closely related with each other. That is why Quesnay, as a scholar paying the most attention to the natural law, held that agronomy is the most important learning in the world and that agriculture is the most important profession in society (Takimoto, 1931, p. 28).

It is inevitable, when discussing Quesnay's thoughts on agriculture, to cite his theory of natural order, but his agricultural primacy has independent significance and is an important aspect of his economic thought. The connection that we investigate here, between Quesnay's theory of emphasizing agriculture and the central idea of ancient Chinese agricultural system, is exactly this thought of agricultural primacy, which is based on the natural order and has the status of being an independent economic theory.

II. The thought of Chinese agricultural primacy in the west

In what the Physiocrats were eager to learn about the Chinese Empire in the East, the idea of agricultural primacy was especially treasured, which was prevalent in a large number of reports on Chinese culture in the seventeenth and eighteenth centuries.

As early as 1675, before the French replaced the Spanish and the Portuguese in playing a most active role in missionary activities in China, a Dominican missionary published *An Account of the Empire of China, Historical, Political, Moral, and Religious.*[1] This book cites some Chinese people as follows:

> The Chineses say, that the Emperor's principal Care ought to be for the Husband-men, and to allow them as large Privileges as may be, because all the Empire subsists by their Labour and Industry. [...] we should [admire the Chinese and] follow their example.
>
> (Quoted in Maverick, 1946, pp. 14-15)

From the onset of the eighteenth century, the writings that preached the idea of China's emphasis on agriculture were increasing and spreading throughout Europe. In France, the most prestigious was the work by Jean-Baptiste Du Halde, who discussed in detail Chinese agriculture and the respect it received:

> Despite the differences in soil and climate, [...] such was the industry of the husbandmen that there was no province that was not very fertile, and scarcely any but that supported an inconceivably large population ... [because] [a]griculture was highly esteemed, and the husbandmen, whose profession was considered to be the most necessary to the state, there held a considerable rank; they were given great privileges and were preferred to merchants and to artisans ... That which stimulated to such care, those who cultivated the soil, was not merely their own interest, but was even more the respect that had been shown to agriculture since the birth of the empire.
>
> (p. 23)

Among those relevant books in England stood out the anonymous work of 1762, *A Voyage to the East Indies in 1747 and 1748*, which reads:

> "In China, ... the people are so industrious, and such lovers of agriculture, that there is scarce an inch of uncultivated ground to be seen."
>
> There is an abundance of fish; there are many navigable rivers, and canals in good condition. "The roads are generally broad and kept in good repair."
>
> ...
>
> "Agriculture is of such esteem in this empire, that some of the Emperors have thought it not unworthy of their royal care to promote it, and even to teach it to their subjects."
>
> (pp. 38-39)

For the above, the author cited an emperor as an example:

> "The Emperor called Wen Ti held the plough himself, and his Empress assisted in planting mulberry-trees, and kept a house for silk-worms in the palace, in order to set a good example to their subjects. All the clothes the Emperor wore were of the Empress's own making; and a feast was at that time instituted, to the honour of agriculture, which is held annually [...]."
>
> (p. 39)

---

[1] The author of this book, originally in Spanish, is Domingo Fernandez Navarrete, who published the English version of the work in London in 1681 or 1684.

Even Swedish writings were not lacking in the thoughts of China's emphasis on agriculture. For example, in the two books on China published in Swedish in 1757–1758, it was noted that Chinese people's.

> "[h]usbandry is admired for the perfection it has risen to." [...] Husbandry, especially agriculture and gardening, are in a most flourishing state. [...] Emperor Wen Ti in 179 B. C. established the imperial precedent which has since been followed of the ceremonial spring ploughing. "The Emperor Cang-ti (K'ang Hsi ...) particularly favoured countrymen," and showed honours to those who excelled. ... "The pitch to which agriculture, and especially the culture of rice, has been carried in China, is the principal foundation of the happiness of this country."
>
> (p. 38)

Such arguments were very common in the various China-introducing works that flooded into Europe at the time.

In addition to the direct influence from the writings of predecessors such as Du Halde, the Physiocrats benefitted greatly in their understanding and reception of China's agricultural concepts and systems from their contemporaries' heated discussions of Chinese people's emphasis on agriculture. A case in point is Étienne de Silhouette, who once drew close attention from Quesnay and others. Silhouette talked about the Chinese government's care for agriculture, exemplified in the ceremonial ploughing in particular:

> Agriculture is a principal concern of the government. In the spring, the emperor himself ceremoniously plows a number of furrows, to stimulate the husbandmen to the cultivation of their farms. Later, the produce from the field he has worked is sacrificed to heaven. The mandarins of the cities also engage in ceremonious plowing. A mandarin who is properly aware of the great importance of agriculture, visits all the fields in the spring; he honors the careful farmer and punishes him who is guilty of neglect; he helps those who are not able to cultivate their land. If the farmer cannot afford a bullock to cultivate his field or lacks grain for seed, the mandarin advances to him the necessary money or furnishes the seed. In the autumn, when the harvest is in, he contents himself with receiving back the advance without interest.
>
> (p. 31)

Silhouette also sketched out China's excellent canal system, which was used for irrigation, for transport, and for flood-prevention (p. 31).

Another example is Pierre Poivre, who kept close contact with Anne Robert Jacques Turgot, and delivered two addresses on agriculture, which were widely admired, especially by the Physiocrats. One of the main themes of these speeches is that agronomy in every climatic condition is a universal human skill, but is not equally thriving in every place. In his view, agriculture can only develop well in a wise country where the people fully understand the necessity to respect and encourage agriculture, and China was such a wise country that had long adhered to this principle. He said,

> Agriculture flourishes in China more than in any other country in the world; yet it is not to any process peculiar to their labour, it is not to the form of their plough, or their method of sowing, that this happy state, and the plenty consequent on it, is to be attributed; it must chiefly be derived from their mode of government, the immovable foundations of which

> have been laid deep, by the hand of reason alone, coeval almost with the beginning of time, and from their laws, dictated by nature to the first of the human race, and sacredly preserved from generation to generation, engraved in the united hearts of a great people, not in obscure codes, devised by chicanery and deceit.
>
> The whole attention, in general, of the Chinese government is directed towards agriculture. (pp. 43–44)

These remarks were very prominent and typical at the time, which is why Zhu Qianzhi (2005b, p. 307) is convinced that Poivre "undoubtedly passed directly to the Physiocrats the influence of China's agricultural primacy he had received."

In particular, Voltaire, an advocate for Sinification, argued that China was unparalleled in the world in their emphasis on agriculture, and called on European ministers to read stories from the Jesuits about Chinese emperors' respect for agriculture and their ceremonial ploughing during the harvest period. He couldn't help claiming, "What should our European rulers do by learning such examples [of the Chinese emperors]? Blush! Admire them! Especially imitate them!" (Voltaire, 1829, p. 135) Baron d'Holbach, according to Gorai Kinzo (1938, p. 360), said that the great Chinese emperors took part in cultivation, to make the subjects understand the usefulness and necessity of labor, rather than regard it as shameful. Even Montesquieu (1989, p. 237), who lashed out at the despotic regime of China at that time, acknowledged that China's ideas and policies on agriculture were quite desirable. He said,

> [T]he emperor performs [the ploughing ceremony] every year to open the cultivation of the fields. By this public and solemn act one has wanted to rouse the peoples to their plowing (p. 237).
>
> [E]ach year the emperor is informed of the plowman who has most distinguished himself in his profession; he [referring to the emperor] makes him a mandarin of the eighth order (p. 238).
>
> The monarchs of Asia make edicts about almost nothing except the exempting each year of some province in their empire; such manifestations of their will are kindnesses. But in Europe, the edicts of the princes cause grief even before they are seen because they always speak of their needs and never of ours (p. 223).
>
> The maxim of the great eastern empires, that taxes should be returned to provinces that have suffered, could well be brought to monarchical states (p. 225).
>
> This is the spirit of the fine ordinances of the Chinese emperors. "Our ancestors," says an emperor of the T'ang family, "took it as a maxim that if there were a man who did not plow the fields, a woman who did not spin, someone in the empire would suffer from cold or hunger [...]" (p. 102).

We can thus conclude that in the era of the Physiocrats, the influence of China's concept of agriculture on European people was deep, extensive and long-lasting.

III. **The physiocrats' praise of China's agricultural primacy**

A large number of reports on China's agriculture, which were sent back by missionaries in China, and were widely disseminated in Europe, greatly edified the Physiocrats on agricultural primacy. Maverick (1938, p. 60) points out,

> Quesnay and his associates concluded from the reports that in China agriculture was held in great esteem and was given governmental assistance; that the natural order prevailed in simple perfection with a minimum of interference by man-made statutes; and that the intellectual mandarins were given such power that it might be said that China exemplified the dream of Plato as the country where philosophers were kings.

This is an appropriate comment. Needham (1956, pp. 68–74), when analyzing the concept of *wu wei*, says something to the effect that, in an agricultural society dominated by farming, it is often the less a man intervenes, the better the crops grow; and so long as he does not touch them before harvesting, they follow their way, and finally make him profit. The concept of *wu wei* ("refraining from activity contrary to Nature") is thus deeply in line with the life of farmers. What Needham means is that China's concept of *wu wei* reflects the inevitable requirement of agricultural production in accordance with natural laws, and that *wu wei* and the emphasis on agriculture complement each other. It was exactly in this sense that the Physiocrats showed immense enthusiasm for China's agricultural thought.

The purpose for the Physiocrats' praise of China's agricultural thought was to change the then prevalent situation in France. Quesnay (1946, pp. 205–206) claimed,

> There is a certain kingdom in Europe [referring to France] that has not yet felt the importance of agriculture or of the wealth that must be advanced to prepare the soil for cultivation [...]; in that country farmers are regarded as simple peasants or laborers, and their rank is fixed below that of the common people of the cities. [...]
>
> In China, on the contrary, agriculture has always been held in veneration, and those who profess it have always merited the special attention of the emperors. [...]

Quesnay's understanding of Chinese agriculture was mostly based on the writings of the above-mentioned previous generations and his contemporaries. When discussing China's "fundamental laws" in *Despotism in China*, Quesnay (pp. 204–205) devoted a section to "Agriculture" and focused on the information he had in this area:

> The humbler classes in China live almost entirely upon grain, herbs, and vegetables, and nowhere in the world are kitchen gardens more common or better cultivated. There are no uncultivated lands near the cities; [...] they would be afraid to leave the slightest piece of land unused.
>
> In the southern provinces, as the land is not level, the hills, even the mountains, are cultivated from base to summit. There is nothing more slightly than a long series of hills each surrounded as though crowned, by a hundred terraces that rise above one another, following the contours; it is with surprise that one sees mountains, which elsewhere would scarcely produce brambles or thickets, here become smiling pictures of fertility.
>
> The soil commonly yields three crops a year [...]. The Chinese spare no pains in collecting all kinds of sweepings suitable for fertilizing their lands, and this contributes greatly to maintaining cleanliness in the cities.
>
> All the grains that we are familiar with in Europe such as wheat, rice, oats, and millet, as well as peas and beans, grow well in China.[2]

[2] When discussing "classes of citizens" in the fourth section of the first chapter in the same book, Quesnay also mentioned that "there is not an inch of cultivable land unused in the empire."

He also said that "[nature] seems to have assembled in that country alone, almost all the products which one may find scattered about the rest of the world" (p, 144). Since China enjoys such "liberality of nature" (p, 144), together with such a "laborious," "sober" and "industrious" people, "no one can deny that [in every period of human history,] this state is the most beautiful in the world, the most densely populated, and the most flourishing kingdom known" (pp. 164–165, 170).

According to Quesnay, the management of agriculture is like a model for the rule of a whole country. Not only the farmers must obey the natural order, focusing only on the actual laws and the conditions that such laws prescribe to them, but the authorities must also abide by these rules and conditions in their administrative work. When investigating China's agricultural affairs, Quesnay paid particular attention to and sang high praise of the emperors' active support for agriculture. He quoted Chinese historians on the issue: as early as the Shen Nong era, the emperor "taught his subjects how to sow grain, how to extract salt from sea water, and nourishing juices from various plants" (pp. 146–147). Emperor Yao, instead of allowing his son to succeed him, passed his throne to Shun, a young farmer who was highly praised for his intelligence and honesty. The reign of Shun was as glorious as that of his predecessor. One of his principal objectives was the promotion of agriculture. He "expressly prohibit[ed] provincial governors from diverting farmers from their agricultural pursuits to forced labor." Shun gave his throne to Yu, and the latter, "by the invention of canals, found a means of causing the waters that covered a part of the empire to flow into the sea, and he employed canals to make the soil fertile by irrigation." Because of Yu's succession to the throne, agriculture "came to flourish so splendidly." The relevant laws established by Yao, Shun and some others during their reigns for the prosperity of agriculture were lauded by Quesnay as "the monuments that they left of their science, and their wisdom" (pp. 155, 158–160, 206–207).

These "monuments," according to Quesnay, continued to be inherited and carried forward by Qing emperors. He quoted verbatim the sixteen articles of *Sheng Yü Guang Xun* (*The Sacred Edict of Emperor Kang Xi*), promulgated by Emperor Kang Xi and elaborated by Emperor Yong Zheng. These maxims, according to Oncken, had a bearing on the development of Quesnay's maxims of government, and of his political thinking in general. The fourth article of the Edict emphasizes the need to "put high esteem on the occupations of husbandry and of those who cultivate the mulberry tree, so that there will be no lack of grain for food or of clothes to wear" (p. 197). He also praised Yong Zheng, Emperor Kang Xi's successor, who

> ordered the governors of all the cities to find out every year in their respective districts which farmer was the most distinguished in application to the cultivation of the soil, and in reputation for integrity, and for wise and intelligent management. This estimable farmer is elevated to the degree of mandarin of the eighth order, and he enjoys nobility and all the prerogatives attached to the rank of mandarin.
>
> (p. 206)

What was particularly interesting to Quesnay, among these specific agricultural measures, was the legendary Chinese ceremonies held every spring. In his *Despotism in China*, he detailed the entire process of holding such a ritual in rural China.[3] In the view of the Physiocrats, the Chinese emperors' personally ploughing the soil was no less than a prominent sign that they respected agriculture. Thus on the first page of Chapter One of Marquis de Mirabeau's *Philosophie Rurale* (fourth edition), written under the guidance of Quesnay, a decorative pattern showing the Chinese emperor in the ranks of land cultivators was specially designed to express the Physiocrats' emphasis on agriculture. When analyzing the Physiocrats' treating the emperor of China as their ideal, Gide and Rist (1915, p. 36) claim, "As the Son of Heaven he [referring to the Chinese emperor] represents the 'natural order', which is also the 'divine order.' As an agricultural monarch he solemnly puts his hand to the plough once a year. His people really govern themselves; that is, he rules them according to custom and the practice of sacred rites."This Physiocratic promotion of ancient China reached a high pitch when the Physiocrats succeeded in persuading Louis XV and his son to solemnly follow—in consecutive reigns—the example of the Chinese emperors' ceremonial ploughing.

In short, the Physiocrats' praise and advocacy—Quesnay's in particular—of imitating China's agricultural primacy, show that, what they gained from Chinese traditional economic thinking was not simply its general influences, but its deep infiltration into their doctrines.

2 The Theory of Net Product

The extent of the deep influence of China's agricultural thought on Physiocracy depends on the possibility of the former giving birth to the latter. The theory of net product is commonly recognized by modern economists as the core and cornerstone of Physiocracy, as well as its economic program. Or as one academic has put it, the key economic assumptions that play a very important role in the theory and policy of the Physiocrats are built on the root of net product. At the same time, this theory, with a rich perspective on future development, was seen as a challenge to various economic schools of thought at the time, especially to mercantilism. More importantly, it was by way of the theory of net product that the Physiocrats shifted their research focus from circulation to production. This shift is of great significance in economics, as is shown in Marx's (1991, p. 455) incisive summary: "The genuine

[3] François Quesnay (1946, p. 207) described this process in Sect. 8, Chap. 2 of *Despotism in China*: "There is a spring festival for the country people; it consists of taking out into the fields a great cow of baked clay, whose horns have been gilded. This figure is so immense that forty men can hardly carry it; it is followed closely by a young child with one foot bare and the other shod, who strikes it with a stick as if to drive it forward; this child is the symbol of diligence and labor. A multitude of farmers, with all the tools of their profession, surround the figure, and the procession is closed by a troup[e] of masquers. All of this multitude repair to the governor's palace or that of the mandarin of the place. There the cow is broken and from its belly are taken a number of small clay cows with which it had been filled (a symbol of fecundity), and they are distributed to the onlookers. The mandarin delivers a speech in praise of agriculture, and this terminates the ceremony."

science of modern economics begins only when theoretical discussion moves from the circulation process to the production process." Therefore, studying the relationship between China's thought on agricultural primacy and the theory of net product has a very important reference value for discovering and understanding the pioneering material of this economic theory.

I. The physiocrats' theory of net product

In 1757, Quesnay began to use the term "net product" in the article "Grains" that he wrote for the seventh volume of *l'Encyclopédie*, to show that land and agricultural production are the most abundant source of wealth and the main support for the population. In his following series of writings, he repeatedly emphasized the same theme that net product is "the earth's bounty" (Quesnay, 1962, p. 115), that "*the sovereign and the nation should never lose sight of the fact that the land is the unique source of wealth, and that it is agriculture which causes wealth to increase*" (p. 232), and that "it is the land and the advances of the entrepreneurs of cultivation which are the unique source of the revenue of agricultural nations" (p. 238). Thus emerged the unique theory of net product.

Quesnay's doctrine of net product was further explained and elaborated by other Physiocrats. Mirabeau (Quoted in Lewiński, 1931, p. 55) claimed, "A society without a net produce 'does not possess conditions of security, freedom, and well-being.'" Pierre Samuel Du Pont (Quoted in Gide & Rist, 1915, p. 12 [Note 1]) said, "The prosperity of mankind is bound up with a maximum net product." And Le Trosne (p. 12 [Note 2]) repeatedly emphasized the following: "Labour applied anywhere except to land is absolutely sterile, for man is not a creator. [...] This physical truth that the earth is the source of all commodities is so very evident that none of us can doubt it." Even at the memorial service of Quesnay, a disciple, when delivering a speech to recall the great achievements of this "veritable benefactor of humanity" (Quoted in Higgs, 1897, p. 49), declared, "Religion was a solace and a ruling power only to a few elevated souls. The terrestrial guide of conduct based upon the *produit net* appealed to the reason and intelligence of every man, persuading him by the enlightened pursuit of self-interest to promote the welfare of mankind at large" (p. 50).

Turgot, though having never become a member of the Physiocratic group, fully agreed with Quesnay's doctrine of "net product." As one of the most incisive expounders of this doctrine, he reiterated the same line of argument that "[t]he husbandman is the first mover in the circulation of labour" (Turgot, 1898, p. 7), that his labor "retains ... primacy [and] ... pre-eminence"(p. 7) and "is one of physical necessity" (p. 7), that only a farmer's work can produce something beyond the wages of labor, that the farmer "is the sole source of all wealth" (p. 8), that the "residual product" of this labor is "a *gift of nature*" (p. 44),[4] that "[i]t is the earth

[4] Some people think that there is a difference between Quesnay and Turgot in understanding the nature of net product: Quesnay regards net product as compensation for land prepayment, while Turgot believes that net income is purely "a gift of nature" (Turgot, 1898, p. 44). In fact, from the point of view of surplus-value, the part of the income that exceeds the agricultural labor expenditure

which is always the first and only source of all wealth" (p. 46), and that "[t]here exists no truly disposable revenue in a State except the net produce of lands" (p. 95).

In summary, the Physiocrats' theory of net product is based on agriculture as the only production sector that creates wealth. They argue that only agriculture can increase the amount of material wealth sufficiently enough to produce "net product," that is, agricultural products after the deduction of production costs. Industry and commerce are "not productive," dealing only with the circulation of wealth or the processing of raw materials produced by agriculture, without increasing the amount of material wealth. The source of "net product" is not circulation but production, which can only be explained by the difference of the value of use between the input and output of the production process, and this difference, as "purely a gift from nature," can only be explained by the land participating in agricultural production.

This theory of net product, however, is criticized by some modern scholars. Rubin (1979, p. 124) labels it as the "theory of *the exclusive productivity of agriculture*" to show its one-sidedness. Gide and Rist (1915, p. 12) think that the Physiocratic argument for "the predominant position which land occupied as an agent of production [is] the most erroneous and at the same time the most characteristic doctrine in the whole Physiocratic system." And Jan Stanisław Lewiński (1931, p. 62) gives the following criticism: "This theory is quite wrong, because it mixes up the existence of material *net produce* with the formation of *net revenue*." That is to say, the theory confuses value with use value. But in any case, it was the Physiocrats who, though under the prevailing influence of mercantilism, first proposed the important principle that "net product," that is, surplus-value, is not created in the sphere of circulation but in that of production. In evaluating this principle, Marx (1969, p. 45) points out, "The Physiocrats transferred the inquiry into the origin of surplus-value from the sphere of circulation into the sphere of direct production, and thereby laid the foundation for the analysis of capitalist production." Below we take this important principle as our guidance to study the influence of ancient Chinese agricultural thought on the Physiocrats' theory of net product.

II. The influence from China's agricultural primacy

In ancient China, there was no clear concept of "net product." Yet extensive historical elaborations on the importance of agriculture, especially on the nature of agricultural production, were enough to become the precursor of some theoretical bases for the establishment of the theory of net product. The pre-Qin era already witnessed a relatively broad understanding of agriculture. Agriculture was at the time summarized, with a certain degree of abstraction, to cover *nong* (farming), *pu* (gardening), *mu* (animal husbandry), *heng* (measurement), and *yü* (knowledge about mountains, lakes, birds and beasts). The ancients, however, often linked *nong* (farming) with *gu* (grains), that is, grain production. Just as what is noted in *Zhong Zai*, a section in *Zhou Li* (*Rites of Zhou*), "The first is agriculture [farming], which produces the nine grains

---

used to compensate for the prepayment of land is, in the view of Quesnay, ultimately derived from the "bounty of land" as a natural gift. Just as Marx's analysis reveals, for the entire Physiocratic School, "[t]he surplus-value appears therefore as a *gift of nature*" (Marx, 1969, p. 51).

in various geographical areas" (Yang, 2004, p. 21). In the Han Dynasty, the thought of agricultural primacy was reduced to the concept of *gui su* (putting emphasis on the growth of millet): "The millet is of great use to the king and is the focus of the State administration" (Quoted in Huang, 1991, p. 92). This narrow sense of agriculture was consistently the dominant agricultural concept in ancient China. Quite interestingly, Quesnay's initial research on economic issues began with an examination of the production of cereals. In "Fermiers," his first economic article, Quesnay made a comparison between the two types of farming, large- and small-scale, in grain production, reaching the conclusion that only the former can still have the surplus to contribute to the national wealth after compensating for its costs. And his second economic work "Grains" employs the concept of "net product" to prove that the agricultural production of grain is "the source of the state's revenue" (Quesnay, 1962, p. 76) and the basis of all wealth (1888). Oncken thought that Quesnay's turn to economic studies was abrupt, but it is worth noting that such a turn, though it is difficult to say whether Quesnay was inspired by the traditional Chinese agricultural concept, was nevertheless attributable to his initial interest in the issue of grain, which is quite similar to the tradition of emphasizing grain production in ancient China.

At a very early time, ancient Chinese people had defined agriculture as *sheng jiu gu* (literally, "producing nine grains") (Xu & Chang, 2014, p. 33) or *zhang di cai* (literally, "growing land wealth") (Ibid., p. 860), which means "producing wealth," to set agriculture apart from the work of manufacturers' making products and merchants' circulating products (Ibid., p. 33). A large number of ancient Chinese scholars then regarded strengthening agricultural production as the base on which the country and the people could be enriched, as can be evidenced, for example, in the following quotations:

(1) "[F]armers' losses lead to the country's poverty" (Quoted in Huang, 1991, p. 72).

(2) "Public storehouses and granaries are full because of the people's devotion to the primary duties of tilling and farming" (Han Fei Tzŭ, 1959, p. 232).

(3) "There is [...] no other means of enriching the realm apart from applying oneself to the development of agriculture, the fundamental industry" (Huan, 1931, p. 87).

(4) "[C]ultivating the fundamental, the people were prosperous" (Huan, 1934, Chap. XVIII).

(5) To obtain wealth by emphasizing farming, forestry and animal husbandry is in conformity with the principle that "the best kind of wealth is that which is based upon agriculture" (Sima, 1993, p. 449).

Here, whether agriculture is undermined or strengthened is used as the main indicator of poverty or prosperity in the country, which actually implies that agriculture can provide surplus products to make the country rich. "Surplus" has actually been the basic feature of the theory of net product.

The ancient Chinese made a fairly thorough analysis of the importance of agriculture. A typical example is, as is recorded in the section of *Zhou Yu I* of *Guo Yu*, the admonishment that Duke Wen of Guo made to King Xuan of Zhou about the latter's failure to conduct the "ceremonial ploughing" upon his enthronement in the Western Zhou Dynasty: "Agriculture is a critical issue to the people, in which are guaranteed the sacrifices to God, the reproduction of the people, the supply of things, the harmony between neighbors, the abundance of finance, and the prosperity of the country" (Xü, 2002, pp. 15–16). That is to say, as a "critical issue to the people," agriculture serves as the basis or condition for the above six aspects. This shows that the ancient thinkers deemed agriculture as the sole source of wealth production, and that they understood the nature of wealth mainly in terms of use value. These two points are also the basic arguments of Quesnay's Physiocracy. In his summary of China's traditional thought of agricultural primacy, Quesnay (1946, p. 285) argued that "it is agriculture that is the source of the wealth that satisfies the needs of men and supports the armies necessary for their security." This statement conforms to the arguments for constructing "a rich country with a strong army" in China's pre-Qin period, especially to Shang Yang's strategy of "linking farming and war closely together."

The above-mentioned views about the ancient Chinese primacy of agriculture had been passed down from generation to generation before Quesnay's time, and were bound to, with the spread of Chinese culture to the West, reach European intellectuals, Quesnay in particular. We may again turn to the pre-Qin Confucianism most revered by Quesnay. It is self-evident that Confucius (1869, p. 193) paid special attention to agriculture, the most representative of which can be found in his answer to Zi Gong's question about government: "*The requisites of government* are that there be sufficiency of food, sufficiency of military equipment, and the confidence of the people in their ruler." "[S]ufficiency of food" is listed as the priority for government. Yet, Confucius' economic thoughts are relatively simple, consisting of only some general principles. Of the early Confucian scholars, no one more than Mencius paid attention to economic problems. Western missionaries' promotion of Mencius had not been as much as that of Confucius. But since the mid-seventeenth century, there came to be some texts introducing Mencius and his doctrines. In the early eighteenth century, there even appeared a Latin translation of *Mencius*.[5] The most important influence on Quesnay in this aspect, however, came from Du Halde's *Description de l'Empire de la Chine*, which contains a broad and detailed summary of Mencius' doctrines. Quesnay repeatedly mentioned this book in his writings, and often cited and even copied it paragraph by paragraph. Of course, he was already familiar with the introduction of Mencius in the book. In addition, many other books devoted to a general introduction of China also convey some of Mencius' doctrines. Or as Maverick says, even if these general introductions do not directly mention Mencius, their description of ancient China's cultural and moral atmosphere

[5] In 1658, the Italian Jesuit Martin Martini published in Munich his Latin version of China's ancient history, *Sinicae Historiae Decas Prima*, in which Martini devoted a dozen pages to the introduction of Mencius and his doctrines. This book was translated into French in Paris in 1692. These introductions about Mencius' doctrines were also quoted by a Dominican missionary in his book of 1675. The full text of the book *Mencius* made its first appearance in Latin in the collection of Father Noël's works in 1711.

is deeply influenced by Mencius.[6] Since Quesnay paid great attention to such works, his theory of net product is inextricably linked with Mencius' economic thoughts.

In his discussion of the way of politics with rulers, Mencius (1875) always placed his final focus on agricultural production whenever economic issues were involved. He not only stressed that agricultural production must comply with "the seasons of husbandry" (p. 127), so that cereals, fish, forests and other agricultural products will be "more than can be eaten" (p. 127) or "more than can be used" (p. 127), but also paid special attention to the problem of surplus products in agricultural production. He said,

> If you do not have an intercommunication of the productions of labour and an interchange of [men's] services, so that [one from his] overplus may supply the deficiency of another, then husbandmen will have a superfluity of grain, and women a superfluity of cloth. If you have such an interchange, then cabinet-makers, builders, wheel-wrights, and carriage-builders may all get their food from you.
>
> (p. 220)

Here Mencius pointed out, in a discussion about the necessity for the division of labor, that if there are no exchanges of products and services, the grain produced by the farmers and the cloth woven by the family women who operate agricultural and sideline businesses will not be sold except for their own consumption, forming "a superfluity of grain" (*yü su*) and "a superfluity of cloth" (*yü bu*). What is conveyed is a clear concept of surplus agricultural products. According to Mencius, other handicraft workers, such as carpenters and car mechanics, "all get their food," a kind of living expenses, through exchanges with farmers, that is, such exchanges are based on the remaining products in agricultural production.

Furthermore, Mencius, in his frequent discussions of ideal small land management, actually described the surplus production under the then agricultural conditions: five acres of mulberry-trees planted about the homesteads can provide adequate silk for persons of fifty years to wear, and the livestock kept by one household can provide enough flesh for persons of seventy years to eat. The so-called fifty- or seventy-year-old persons refer in a general way to those who do not participate in an agricultural production activity or have lost their ability to work. Agricultural production can enable these people to wear silk and to eat meat, which means that there is a surplus of production. Mencius made a general statement by saying, "Let there not be taken away the time that is proper for the cultivation of the field-allotment of a hundred acres, and the family of several mouths will not suffer from hunger" (p. 128). If we take into account the agricultural productivity standards provided by

---

[6] Maverick (1946) said that it was on "reading the ancient Chinese philosopher Mencius" (p. 111) that he "realized how strongly Mencius' writings resemble those of the Physiocrats of eighteenth century France" (p. 111), so he was "resolved to search out the channels by which the Chinese had influenced the French men. The study has taken [him] to libraries in France, England, and America, and has enabled [him] to appreciate the influence of this great man [referring to Mencius] and of the Chinese culture in general, upon the Physiocrats, and upon a number of other European thinkers as well" (p. 111). In the meantime, this study has drawn his attention to other fields on the basis of his primary interest in China's influence on Europe's economic and political thinking.

Mencius, we may then see that the surplus production at that time varied with the level of productivity, as is reflected in the following observation:

> As to those who tilled the fields, each head of a family received a hundred mow. When these were manured, the [best] husbandmen of the first class supported nine individuals, and those ranking next to them supported eight. The [best] husbandmen of the second class supported seven men, and those ranking next to them supported six; while the lowest class [only] supported five.
>
> (p. 294)

In Mencius' view, it is these surpluses in agricultural production that form the basis for safeguarding people's lives and consolidating the emperor's rule. Similar views on the surplus production can be found everywhere in the book *Mencius* and could surely draw the attention of Du Halde and his contemporaries when it came to their detailed summaries. As an enthusiastic reader who focused on such records, Quesnay was certainly not an exception. In fact, such views helped him to create a unique theory of net product.

Mencius also emphasized the importance of land: "The precious things of the prince of a State are three;—the territory, the people, and the business of the government" (p. 378). He regarded "land" as the principal "precious thing" of the emperor's rule. This view is similar to that embodied in the relevant statements in *Da Xue* (*The Great Learning*) and *Zhong Yong* (*The Doctrine of the Mean*). In the former can be found the statement that "[p]ossessing the territory will give him its wealth" (Confucius, 1869, pp. 277–278); in the latter, it is held in the same way that heaven and earth are the roots of all things, and earth can especially reflect the role of natural forces (Ibid., pp. 284, 294, 307, 315, 317). Both books are considered to be close to *Mencius* in economic thinking, and had been circulated in Europe before the translation of *Mencius*. These Confucian classics view the influence of natural productivity on social and economic activities from the perspective of "land," and regard "land" as the source of wealth production. This is not only the classic basis for using "land" as the main focus of property throughout the whole feudal period of China, but also the powerful evidence of the special status given to the production factor of "land" in Quesnay's theory of net product.

In addition to the influence of the Confucian classics introduced into Europe, another very important factor is that the Jesuits having arrived in China since the late sixteenth century, when the Ming Dynasty was approaching its end, acquainted themselves with a large number of Chinese scholars and their works, which enabled them to learn and convey to European readers many Chinese cultural traditions and ideas, including Chinese agricultural thought. Among these Chinese people, the most prominent was Xü Guangqi (1562–1633). Since his conversion to Christianity in the early seventeenth century, Xü had strongly supported, by way of his profound knowledge and prominent position in the imperial court, the missionary activities of the Jesuits in China for thirty years. He is regarded as the joining point in the bridge of normal cultural connections between the East and the West. For our research, it is noteworthy that his concept of agricultural primacy and his masterpiece *Nong Zheng*

Quan Shu (*The Complete Treatise on Agriculture*) may have a special influence on the Physiocrats' establishment of their theory of net product.

Xü (1984) emphasized the fundamental principle that it is agriculture that ensures "nature's giving birth to wealth," believing that this principle is a must to understand the path of rich countries. This is closely related to his view of wealth: the currency is but the weights and measures of all wealth, instead of wealth itself, and for an ancient wise king, wealth is nothing but millet for food and silk for clothes, so only millet and silk are called wealth. Starting from such a concept of wealth, Xü studied the roots of wealth production, and his "argument for nature's giving birth to wealth" necessarily led him to the conclusion that agriculture is what produces wealth, that is, agriculture is the only source of wealth. Xü also held that the wealth that is born out of land is inexhaustible, which means that agriculture is the inexhaustible source of wealth production, and that industrial and commercial activities, in contrast, are derivatives of the agricultural field. Xü (1956) thought that commerce refers to the activity of trading agricultural products during the slack season.

Xü's thoughts on the importance of agriculture are fully reflected in his *Nong Zheng Quan Shu*. This masterpiece is a comprehensive summary of the past agronomic achievements in China, mainly consisting of 12 parts: agriculture, land, husbandry, hydraulics, agricultural implements, the art of planting, silkworms, silk production, trees, the breeding of animals, the manufacture of food, and provisions against famine. All of them are production issues that are related, directly or not, to the development of agriculture. It can thus be concluded that he was fully devoted to the study of production with agriculture as the core. Maverick (1946, p. 80), when talking about the fact that the Physiocrats informed the French that China was truly aware of the importance of agriculture and farmers, points out, "Though the Physiocrats did not know him (referring to Xü Guangqi) personally, Xü was nevertheless an important link in the chain that gave them their knowledge of China; for it was especially from him that the missionaries had received information about the Chinese attitude toward agriculture." Therefore, that Xü's thoughts of agricultural primacy and the Physiocrats' theory of net product are in some basic principles consistent with or similar to each other does point to the possibility that the latter absorbed certain elements from the former.

Xü's discussion of agriculture and its unique feature of productivity, as the product of the development of traditional Chinese thought of agricultural primacy at the end of the Ming Dynasty, reflects the common view among Chinese scholars during that period. A typical example is that contained in "On the Sacred King's Preferring Agriculture" by Zhuang Yuanchen, a scholar in the late Ming Dynasty (Tan, 1985b, p. 55). Zhuang (1939, pp. 88–90) said,

> Only agriculture can create the wealth unborn in heaven and earth while the other sectors cannot but engage in exchanging such wealth between human beings. It is the gift from nature that enables agriculture to lead to wealth; while it is the exchanges between human beings that make the other sectors lead to wealth. These other sectors lead to the redistribution of wealth, making one rich at the cost of another. This is like diverting the water from a pool to a pond: the pond will be full while the pool will be dry. But if you dig for a spring, the water

keeps pouring out with no end. The farmer digs for the source, while the merchant diverts water. This is why a wise king prefers agriculture to other sectors.

...

He who can create the wealth unborn in heaven and earth is a farmer; he who can make a product unborn in heaven and earth is a manufacturer; he who can distribute things left undistributed by heaven and earth is a merchant.

The above elaboration on the importance of agriculture, including its focus and conclusion, has striking similarities with the discussion by the Physiocrats. For example, agriculture is regarded as the only productive sector that creates wealth, while other economic sectors cannot produce wealth themselves. And the wealth from agriculture, different from that of other sectors, is purely what is bestowed by nature. Industry "makes a product," and commerce "distributes things," but agriculture "creates wealth." The former two only play the roles of changing the form of and circulating wealth produced by agriculture.

To summarize, the traditional Chinese thought of agricultural primacy is eligible, at least in the following aspects, to become the pioneering idea of Quesnay's doctrine of "net product." First, agriculture acts as the sole source of wealth production. Second, agriculture's "creating wealth" refers to its increasing the amount of material wealth in terms of use value. Third, industry and commerce do not create wealth, but, by means of "the exchanges between human beings," carry out the circulation of, or change the form of, material wealth produced by agriculture. Fourth, only agricultural production can provide surplus products, and the proportion of surplus agricultural products varies according to the local level of productivity. It is the foundation for the expenses of other non-agricultural workers and for the construction of "a rich country with a strong army." Fifth, different from other non-agricultural sectors that obtain wealth by means of human factors, that is, "the exchanges between human beings," only agriculture uses land as a means of creating wealth, or in other words, obtaining wealth as "the gift from nature."

In these ancient Chinese views on the primacy of agriculture, the discussion of agricultural surplus products was restricted to a general level, and there was still no specific explanation for their source in terms of the difference in the value of inputs and outputs in the agricultural production process. Yet, since agriculture was seen as the only production sector that created wealth, and commerce was seen as only being useful in terms of "diverting the water from a pool to a pond," that is, circulating wealth, we can be certain that the source of surplus "products" that ancient Chinese discussed can only be found in the field of production and not in circulation. Marx (1969) once claimed that it was the Physiocrats' "great merit"(p. 44) that they conceived the concepts of value and surplus-value as arising from production rather than circulation, and argued, "[I]f the creation of surplus-value in the sphere of production itself is what has to be established, it is necessary first of all to go back to that branch of production in which surplus-value is found independently of circulation—that is, agriculture. The initiative was therefore taken in a predominantly agricultural country" (p. 50). In Marx's analysis, however, it is only mentioned as an addition that the French pioneers preceding the Physiocrats could occasionally display ideas relevant to Physiocracy. What we need to add here is that China, as a country having been consistently dominated by agriculture, has produced and accumulated in its long history the thought of agricultural primacy, rich and refined enough to be an important reference for the Physiocrats to create their "epoch-making" (p. 50) theory of net product. What needs to be particularly pointed out is that, the above-mentioned ideas of China's emphasis on agriculture, including the concept of agricultural production surplus contained in Mencius' remarks, are all embodied in classic quotes or universally accepted principles that have been recited and upheld by Chinese intellectuals of all the following generations, which may well have been transferred to the West along with the spread of Chinese culture, so as to be borrowed and assimilated by the Physiocratic School led by Quesnay.

Furthermore, the West had had no concept of net product before the Physiocrats' time. When Mirabeau said that "[t]he discovery of the *net product*, which we owe to the venerable Confucius of Europe (referring to Quesnay), will one day change the face of the world" (Quoted in Meek, 1962, pp. 19–20), he already suggested that the creation of the theory of net product has a certain link with traditional Chinese thought represented by Confucius. It was also said that, a contemporary of Quesnay's once pointed out to him, "The doctrine you propound, namely, that agriculture is the sole source of wealth, was held already by Socrates, by Fu-hsi, by Yao, by Sung and by Confucius" (Quoted in Reichwein, 1925, 106). This is tantamount to announcing that ancient Chinese thought is a basic source for the theory of net product. Hudson (1931, p. 323), a modern academic, gives the following analysis:

> The doctrine that land is the source of all wealth belongs to the ideology of pure land-revenue economy untouched by city-state commercialism [...]. It is in fact ancient Chinese doctrine, and there can be little doubt that it was chiefly because of his admiration for Chinese philosophy that Quesnay, a scholar and a theorist and not a man of affairs, came to elaborate a theory which was really quite out of place in the world of already complex capitalist-commercial economy in which he lived.

This "doctrine" refers to Quesnay's theory of net product. True, Hudson's evaluation of the significance of the theory itself is not an issue of the most immediate relevance here, but the fact that he agrees with Chinese origin of the theory, and analyzes, from the unique perspective of social and economic bases, the reasons why Quesnay's theory is not completely a native growth in Europe but has its origin in China, is definitely of reference value to the present study in this book.

3 Attitudes Towards Industry and Commerce

In the previous section, when discussing the influence on the Physiocrats of ancient Chinese thinkers' agricultural primacy, we incidentally touch upon some similarities in their attitudes towards industry and commerce. Now we focus on such similarities.

In the history of ancient Chinese economic thought, the discussion of agricultural primacy was always inseparable from the view of industry and commerce, and, by and by, there emerged a unique couple of concepts—*nong ben* (the primary role of agriculture) versus *gong shang mo* (the secondary role of industry and commerce), which convey their basic attitudes towards the three sectors. Generally speaking, this order of priorities originating at the end of the Warring States Period had been in a process of continuous consolidation until the Tang Dynasty, when it occupied a dominant position in social ideology, and became a traditional dogma. Then, due to the slow development of the feudal commodity economy, the number of the viewpoints favoring or attaching importance to the role and status of industry and commerce was increasing. In the anti-traditional critical struggle that was continuously getting stronger, the traditional dogma was doubted and challenged, until it was shaken. When it came to the seventeenth and eighteenth centuries, there emerged a period of active cultural exchanges between China and the West, and in the process, though such a dogma still occupied the dominant position, the arguments for the suppression or despise of industry and commerce as well as their practitioners (Tan, 1985a, pp. 113–119) became far less strong than in the early feudal period. It was against this background that the information about Chinese industry and commerce was exposed to the Physiocrats through the reports that missionaries in China sent back to Europe at the time. According to the information currently available, ancient Chinese industrial and commercial thought and policies had in the following aspects a significant impact on the Physiocrats, which may constitute a direct source for some of their similar views.

Firstly, the Physiocrats divided into three classes the people engaged in economic activities, namely, agriculture, industry and commerce, which is also the traditional view of classifying social classes in ancient China.

This view circulated widely in Europe at that time. Maverick (1946, p. 14) quotes a book published in 1675, in which it is recorded that "[the Chinese] divide all their people into four States or Degrees, which are [...] Scholars, Husband-men, Handicrafts, and Merchants. The Husband-men of China are mighty numerous, and as to rank are prefer'd before Merchants and Mechanicks." Du Halde is quoted by Maverick (1938, p. 61) to have said, "The People [...] are distinguished into three sorts of Professions: that of the Husbandmen, which is in great esteem; that of Merchants [...] and that of Mechanics, who being constantly employed in the manual Arts, help these to supply Necessities and Conveniences of Life." Resorting to these materials many times, Quesnay (1946) mentioned that China's civilian class includes "husbandmen, merchants, artisans" (p. 172), and among the civilians, "the husbandmen hold first rank, then the merchants, and generally all the artisans" (pp. 174–175); and that "[f]armers rank higher than merchants and artisans in China" (p. 205), in contrast to the fact that "[t]here is a certain kingdom (France) in Europe that has not yet felt the importance of agriculture" (p. 205). Quesnay (1888) suggested to the rulers of Europe that farmers, due to the role and nature of their use of wealth, should be given much greater attention than businessmen. It can thus be seen that Quesnay's division of the people into three classes, of respectively agriculture, industry and commerce, and his use of this order as a criterion to indicate their different positions and roles in the social economy, are simply an application of traditional Chinese views to elaborate his own economic theory.

Secondly, the Physiocrats' understanding of the basic relationship between agriculture and industry and commerce absorbed ancient China's way of placing agriculture before industry and commerce.

China's traditional precept of "the priority of agriculture over industry and commerce" has always been regarded as the rule of a wise emperor. Its main purpose is to borrow the original meaning of the word *ben-mo* (the Fundamental and the Incidental), such as "root-branch," "priority-inferiority," and "first–second succession," and by extension, to distinguish or express the different economic nature of agriculture and industry and commerce, as well as the order of priorities in terms of their functions in economic activities. Starting from the point of view that commerce and industry cannot produce wealth, but agriculture is the only source of production, this precept advocates that "the people will be poor if they are made to pursue industry and commerce, but will become rich if they are allowed to pursue agriculture" (Yu, 2002, p. 82). It opposes the idea of prioritizing the end over the root by driving people away from agriculture. These Chinese arguments apparently provided nourishment for the Physiocratic School to elaborate on the relationship between agriculture and industry and commerce. Quesnay (1962) once said that manufacture and commerce, supported by disorderly luxury, and the concentration and accumulation of population and wealth in the metropolis, hinder the improvement of the countryside, make it desolate, give rise to contempt for agriculture, and thus bring the country to a state of exhaustion. How similar these arguments are to the ancient Chinese views of agriculture and industry!

The Physiocrats used the root of a tree to refer to agriculture and its branches and leaves for the other two—almost the same metaphor as China's term of "*ben-mo*"—to describe the relationship between agriculture and industry and commerce. Mirabeau (Quoted in Higgs, 1897, pp. 21–22) summarized the relationship in his work of 1756—*L'Ami des Hommes*—in the following way:

> The state is a tree, agriculture its roots, population its trunk, arts and commerce its leaves. From the roots come the vivifying sap drawn up by multitudinous fibres from the soil. The leaves, the most brilliant part of the tree, are the least enduring. A storm may destroy them. But the sap will soon renew them if the roots maintain their vigour. If, however, some unfriendly insect attack the roots, then in vain do we wait for the sun and the dew to reanimate the withered trunk. To the roots must the remedy go, to let them expand and recover. If not, the tree will perish.

By and by, this metaphor of regarding agriculture as the root and industry and commerce as leaves came to be a favorite one among all Physiocrats. Quesnay (1962) himself resorted frequently to this metaphor in his analysis of the relationship between agriculture and the other two, and once remarked in "Grains," "We must try to grow the root of a tree, rather than merely care about its branches and leaves; the latter two can be allowed to flourish freely while the former must always be carefully tended to draw and multiply the necessary sap from the earth." In "Impôts," considering whether it is necessary to stress agriculture, or as he called, "nature's productions" (Quoted in Schelle, 1908, p. 186), or to emphasize only handicrafts, Quesnay once again remarked, "The first is attached to the trunk of the tree, and the other only to a branch. The former resorts to the principles of the economic government of a great kingdom, bringing abundance and wealth back to the state, while the latter only looks at the industry of the small trading nations, making such abundance and wealth disappear" (p. 186). It can thus be concluded that both the theory and its linguistic form the Physiocrats employed to advocate the priority of agriculture over industry and commerce can find their origin in China's ancient thought of placing agriculture before the other two. For Quesnay, it was China that set for other "big" countries the exemplary role of adhering to agriculture as the economic foundation.

Thirdly, like ancient Chinese thinkers, the Physiocrats, while regarding industry and commerce as secondary to agriculture, did not deny the socio-economic functions of industry and commerce.

Agriculture had originally been strongly emphasized in traditional Chinese thought as above industry and commerce—the latter two had been even "despised"—especially in the early stage of feudal landlord economy. But for the Physiocratic School, Confucius, who was worshipped by them as a god, was different from the later Confucian scholars in the attitude towards business, and did not oppose Confucian scholars' conducting business. This is why Quesnay (1946) once listed having "reformed abuses which had crept in, and [...] re-established confidence in commerce" (p. 162) as one of the important achievements Confucius made when he was minister in the principality of Lu. In another place, Quesnay (p. 147) also mentioned that after Fu Xi's reign, Shen Nong (Shen Nung) was credited with having "promoted trade and established public markets." Besides, most of the Chinese industrial and commercial ideas acquainted by the Physiocrats, especially those about the real industrial and commercial situation in China, were from the Ming and Qing dynasties, in which the continued development of the feudal commodity economy had already nurtured and produced the germ of capitalist relations of production. This growing economic factor was reflected in the fact that the role of industry and commerce in social economy was increasingly recognized and affirmed by people, while the idea of "suppressing" or "belittling the end," that is, industry and commerce, gradually faded and entered a declining process. Such industrial and commercial ideology and reality in China, which were different from those of the pre-feudal period, were precisely what the Physiocrats saw and felt deeply from the descriptions of their contemporaries as well as the missionaries having been to China.

Louis Le Comte (Quoted in Maverick, 1946, p. 17) said,

> It is a maxim among the Chinese "to encourage trade as much as possible through the whole Empire. All the other Policy is conducive to the plenty or convenience of their Country; but this is concerned for the very lives of the People, who would be soon reduced to the last extremity if Trade should once fail."

Du Halde also reported that "[t]he amount of the domestic trade [...] exceeds the whole commerce of Europe" (p. 37). Silhouette referred to China as having "an enlightened council on commerce, which attends both to domestic and foreign trade" (p. 27). In the light of these sources and their underlying spirit, Quesnay (1946, pp. 207–209) published his views on Chinese commerce under the heading "Commerce viewed as serving agriculture" in Sect. 9, Chap. 2, of *Despotism in China*. The main thrust of his statement on Chinese domestic commerce is as follows:

> It has been seen that the Chinese Empire is very well provided with all kinds of products, and it is easy to presume from this that the commerce of this nation is quite flourishing. But as the Chinese find all the necessaries of life among themselves (and since the great population assures a market to consume all these commodities within the country itself), their foreign commerce is very limited in comparison with the size of the state. The principal trade is carried on within the empire, all of the parts of which are not equally provided with the same things. Inasmuch as each province has its needs and only its own particular products, all would lapse into poverty, were it not for the fact that they exchange with one another their useful products. An established circulation in a country eighteen hundred leagues in circumference obviously presents a very extensive commerce; moreover the historian says that the commerce carried on in the interior of China is so great that all Europe's commerce could not be compared to it. [...]
>
> The transportation of the various articles of merchandise is very easy in China due to the number of canals which cut through all the provinces. Traffic and marketing are very prompt; self-interest, which is the dominating passion of the Chinese people, holds them to continual activity; everything is in motion in the cities and in the country; the highways are as crowded as the streets of our commercial cities, and the whole empire seems to be nothing less than one vast fair.[7]

Quesnay (1946, pp. 210–211) not only depicted and praised the prosperity of Chinese commerce, but even argued against the rumor that Chinese merchants were adept at fraud:

> Those who have told these tales have certainly confounded the business carried on with Europeans in the port of Canton – they have, I say, confounded, this newly established business in which both sides try to cheat one another, with the commerce between subjects of the empire. The government, which has little interest in foreign trade, tolerates fraudulent practices there because it is difficult to discipline foreigners three thousand leagues from home, who disappear as soon as they have sold their merchandise. [We have many examples of very praiseworthy nations that have been corrupted by the contamination of foreign commerce.] It seems that in the contest the Chinese have become more skillful than the Europeans, and they practice this skill with much more equanimity; and they never expose themselves by coming to trade in our ports where the merchants call regularly, are well known, and where good faith is established. It is not conceivable that trade may be practiced among the inhabitants of a country with fraudulent practices going on reciprocally. What is gained by mutually cheating one another? This would only cause painful and very embarrassing disturbances which would make daily commerce very difficult, almost impossible. But this is even more inconceivable in a nation so civilized as China, where at all times good faith and rectitude in commerce have been noteworthy; this is one of the principal subjects of the ethics of Confucius, the ethics which amount to law in this empire.

Quesnay's defense, like the preceding praise, points to in the Chinese paradigm the indispensable function of "commerce viewed as serving agriculture," and the prosperity of commerce implies the development of agriculture. Quesnay (1888) clearly took this to heart, so he said that any assistance to rural trade is not excessive, as it facilitates the sale of agricultural products, and that the more active rural trade is, the more it helps agriculture, which is the source of the national income. He even paralleled "wealthy husbandmen and wealthy merchants engaged in rural trade" (Quesnay, 1962, p. 247), and thought they both, "after the proprietors [...], constitute

[7] "League" is a unit for measuring distance, equal to about 3 miles or 4000 m.

the most honourable, praiseworthy, and important order of citizens in the state" (p. 247).

Ancient Chinese thinkers generally treated industry and commerce as the counterparts of agriculture, always mentioning both industry and commerce or implicitly including one in their discussion of the other. They made a strict distinction between industry and commerce only when they were specifically devoted to the relative importance of each of the two. In his study of Chinese industry and commerce, Quesnay included his views on industry in the section on commerce, so there is no need for a separate section on industry. However, his overview of China is accompanied by a reference to the fact that artisans there ran around from morning till night to solicit business: they, like other people including farmers, ensure that "all the inventions that industry can discover, all the improvements that necessity brings to attention, all the resources that self-interest inspires, are here employed and used profitably" (Quesnay, 1946, p. 171). It is evident that he also saw in China an example of the full use of industry as a socio-economic necessity. In short, one of Baudeau's authoritative arguments for industry and commerce was the spread and prosperity of the two in China, when he claimed that "[f]ar from being useless, these (industry and commerce) are the arts that supply the luxuries as well as the necessaries of life, and upon these mankind is dependent both for its preservation and for its well-being" (Quoted in Gide & Rist, 1915, p. 13), and thus for the increase of agricultural productivity.

Of course, the Physiocrats' treatment of industry and commerce is to a certain extent similar to China's "suppressing" or "belittling" the two, as is reflected in Du Halde's introduction of Chinese emperors and sages to belittle other occupations in order to improve the status of agriculture, and Silhouette's statement of the Chinese people's view that those who were best at doing business were also best at deception. These arguments have left traces to varying degrees in Quesnay's view of industry and commerce. For example, Quesnay (1946, pp. 295–296) denounced the monopoly system by calling the privileges often devised by

> [t]he tradespeople, manufacturing entrepreneurs and artisan groups [. . .] the artifices of [the] usurpers who overcharge [the nation] for the commodities and merchandise. [...] [T]he purchases which [a nation] makes at a price forced by a voracious commerce, diminish consumption and population, and cause agriculture and revenue to dwindle away. [. . .] [E]ven commerce is destroyed by the avidity of the business men, who, in their artifice dare to avail themselves of the insidious pretext that they are making commerce flourish and enriching the nation by the growth of their fortunes.

The Physiocrats' opposition to the luxury crafts used by a few rulers was also in line with the traditional Chinese argument: if such expensive pursuit of "carving and engraving" techniques were not forbidden, claimed Liu Xiang (2019, p. 1105), a scholar of the Western Han Dynasty, "the state would be impoverished with a few of its people obsessed with luxury."

In any case, in the view of later generations of economists, the Physiocratic theory that industry and commerce are unproductive does not in the least mean to belittle the two. This tendency to affirm and value the role of industry and commerce in economy is in line with the trend that has become increasingly favorable to the two in China since the Ming and Qing dynasties.

Fourthly, the Physiocrats gave special attention to China's foreign trade.

In the late seventeenth century, Fernandez Navarrete (Quoted in Maverick, 1938, pp. 63–64), a Dominican missionary, "tells us that the Chinese Government opposes foreign trade, 'The Chineses say they want nothing that Foreign Countries afford, and they are in the right. This is a good piece of Policy. The same might be done in other Kingdoms, but they do it not, because they will not.'" In the eighteenth century, more Europeans were amazed at the fact that the Chinese were able to get by without foreign trade, especially since at that time Chinese exports had declined due to European imitation of the manufacture of Chinese industrial goods such as porcelain, lacquerware, and silk fabrics, without causing poverty within the Eastern country. This economic phenomenon naturally attracted the attention of the Physiocrats as well.

Quesnay (1946) once specifically analyzed the reasons why China's foreign trade was "very limited:"

> [...] But as the Chinese find all the necessaries of life among themselves (and since the great population assures a market to consume all these commodities within the country itself), their foreign commerce is very limited in comparison with the size of the state.
>
> (p. 208)
>
> Since the domestic commerce of China is flourishing, it is not surprising that the inhabitants take so few pains to extend it abroad, especially when one notes the scorn that they have for foreign nations. The foreign commerce is very limited; the maritime cities of Canton, Amoy, and Ningpo, are the only ports where cargoes may be loaded for abroad. Their voyages by sea are no longer very extensive; they scarcely pass the Straits of the Sound; their ordinary shipping runs to Japan, Siam, Manila and Batavia.
>
> Foreign commerce is perhaps more injurious than favorable to the prosperity of the nations that devote themselves to it, aside from the merchants, who can make great fortunes from it, in large measure at the expense of their fellow citizens. The commodities that they go so far to seek are seldom more than expensive frivolities which support an injurious luxury. A number of nations can be named that are much attached to this kind of commerce which they practice in all parts of the world, but, with the exception of the profits of their traders, these do not provide examples of prosperity.
>
> (p. 211)

In another place he added, "We have many examples of very praiseworthy nations that have been corrupted by the contamination of foreign commerce" (p. 210). In other words, only China's insistence on "very limited" foreign trade activity was the right way to avoid its damage and to maintain the country's prosperity.

Quesnay's particular emphasis on China's foreign trade policy and practice was not merely a matter of opinion, but had other plans. After examining the then state of Chinese commerce, which was conducted primarily within the country, he went on to make the following observation:

> A purely domestic commerce may seem quite inadequate to those who believe that nations must trade with foreigners in order to grow rich in money. They may not have noticed that the greatest opulence possible consists in the greatest consumption possible. This consumption

> has its source within the territory of every nation, and this territory is even the source of gold and silver, whether they are taken from mines, or purchased with other products. Those who own mines sell their gold and silver in order to extend their consumption, for which use the metals, in themselves, are useless; those who do not own this merchandise, buy it, simply to facilitate exchange in their trading, nor do they burden themselves with it beyond this usage, because gold and silver are purchased by riches that are more necessary than these metals, and because the more one buys of them the more he diminishes his consumption, which is true opulence. Moreover, the commerce of nations, which has no object other than consumption, is confused with the commerce of merchants, which is a service that they make pay very well, and all the more so when their commerce is extended afar. The more the nations can save the cost of this, even to the harm of the great fortunes of the merchants, the more they will gain for consumption and for the outlays necessary for the perpetual reproduction of the riches that spring from the earth and furnish the revenues of the nation and of the sovereign.
>
> (Quesnay, 1946, pp. 208–209)

In this way, Quesnay extracted a new economic theory from China's foreign trade, and used it to refute the old-fashioned European view that foreign trade is particularly important because wealth is generated in circulation. That is to say, the current state of China's foreign trade became, in Quesnay's hands, a powerful weapon against mercantilism.

In fact, the Physiocrats did not completely reject the role of foreign trade, and sometimes put it in a high position.[8] After all, the example of China's foreign trade impressed them in a way that is hard to imagine. According to their theory, foreign trade did not increase wealth and belonged to the unproductive sector, so they regarded it "merely as a *pis aller*" (Quoted in Gide & Rist, 1915, p. 28) even though they recognized its necessity. Quesnay argued,

> The settlement of international indebtedness by payment of money is a mere *pis aller* of foreign trade, adopted by those nations which are unable to give commodities in return for commodities according to custom. And foreign trade itself is a mere *pis aller* adopted by those nations whose home trade is insufficient to enable them to make the best use of their own productions. It is very strange that anyone should have laid such stress upon a mere *pis aller* of commerce.
>
> (p. 28 [Note 3])

His disciple Mercier de la Rivière thought that "it is a necessary evil" (p. 28). For much the same reason as Quesnay's treating it as "a *pis aller*," Mercier claimed, "A nation, once arrived at the best possible condition, has no more use for the help of foreign trade … its external trade diminishes in the same ratio as its internal trade increases" (Quoted in Ware, 1931, p. 607 [Note 1]). Both statements were obviously based on the ideal model of China's domestic commercial prosperity and its "limited" external

---

[8] Quesnay (1962) mentioned many times the need to stabilize the prices of Agricultural products: that there is the need to engage in "an import and export trade with other nations which is mutual, unobstructed, and perfectly free" (p. 94), and that "agriculture and foreign trade […] constitute the source of the renascent wealth and revenue of nations" (p. 89). In the Russian translation, a note is added to the above last quotation: "The view of foreign trade as a source of national wealth was not developed in Quesnay's later writings. Not only that, but he took the opposite view that trade was an unproductive endeavour" (Quted in Quesnay, 1979, p. 104 [Note 1]).

trade. In this sense, that the analysis of Quesnay's *Tableau Économique* leaves foreign trade aside is not only a theoretical hypothesis that abstractly examines bourgeois society, but also a result of the deep influence from China's foreign trade discussions and practice.

Fifthly, the traces of ancient Chinese economic thought can also be found in the monetary and price theories of the Physiocratic School.

It was popular in ancient China to say that gold and silver currencies "cannot ease hunger or prevent cold [...], so that it is necessary to value grain instead of gold and jade" (Chao, 1975). Xu Guangqi (1984), who was well known to Western missionaries, clearly stated that currency was the measure of wealth, not wealth itself. He distinguished currency from the labor products of grain, clothing and silk, and denied that currency was national wealth: If currency is used as wealth, then more currency will make one rich? This is so in one family, but not in a whole country. That is, if we study wealth from the perspective of the entire national economy, we should focus on the raw products of labor such as corn and silk, and monetary wealth can be disregarded. Similarly, Quesnay (1962) distinguished between monetary wealth and wealth in general, pointing out that currency itself was by no means consumable wealth, but only an instrument of trade, a measure of the value of the goods circulating in trade: "[I]t is not the greater or lesser quantity of monetary wealth which determines the wealth of a state" (p. 77). The similarity between Quesnay's view of money and the above views of ancient Chinese thinkers is readily apparent. We may well argue that he used the ancient Chinese view of money to counter the mercantilist arguments that placed too much emphasis on money.

Another example is the issue of price. A traditional Chinese maxim in ancient China is that "cheap grain hurts farmers, and expensive grain consumers" (Sima, 1993, p. 85),so for the benefit of farmers and consumers, two methods were adopted: (1) the feudal governments all adopted the policy of *ping di*, a way to stabilize grain prices at an appropriate level by buying up grain when it is very cheap during good harvests and selling grain when it is very expensive during famines, and (2) in the late feudal period, it was emphasized that the merchants should have the freedom of transshipment to stabilize the price of grain at a moderate level. Quesnay likewise attached great importance to the price of agricultural products, seeking, through the free export of agricultural products, especially cereals, to make their prices equal to the common prices of other countries and "always remain at an intermediate level" (p. 95), without being affected by the alternations of abundance and scarcity. However, the most immediate problem to be solved by the Physiocrats was the artificially low prices of agricultural products, which had been kept down by the neglect of agriculture under the long reign of the mercantilist policy. So Quesnay placed special emphasis on raising the prices of agricultural products, especially cereals, and put forward the following maxim: "Abundance plus valuelessness does not equal wealth. Scarcity plus dearness equals poverty. Abundance plus dearness equals opulence" (p. 235). Thus, in agricultural prices, Quesnay differs from the ancient Chinese thinkers who promoted the policy of "more grain but lower prices," which is a reflection of the demands of different ages.

Sixthly, "internationalism" was shared by the Physiocrats and ancient Chinese thinkers.

On the one hand, "the Physiocrats," Gide and Rist (1915, p. 37) state, "were wholehearted 'internationalists.' In this respect they differ from their prototypes, the Chinese." This is probably a reference to the closed China of the Ming and Qing dynasties. Actually, we may find that in this aspect, the Physiocratic School used China precisely as a model, if we look at its economic view on foreign trade, as mentioned earlier. On the other hand, the ancient Chinese rulers often claimed to be "the world," treating other countries as barbarian states and advocating civilizing these states with "the prudent virtue of the wise king." This was a kind of "China's arrogance," and there was no "internationalism." However, as Takamoto Seiichi (1931) says, this kind of thought preaches that barbarian countries, however far away they are, should enjoy the grace of kingliness (p. 38), and with the help of the Chinese Empire, can share peace with the Chinese. This Chinese kingliness, as was envied by Quesnay, does not contradict, but is in perfect harmony with, their internationalism (p. 39).

4 Additional Remarks

When European and American economists discuss the origins of Quesnay's Physiocratic system, they generally focus on two points. The first is his experience of growing up in a peasant family, as it is said that "Quesnay's peasant background led him to respect agriculture and those engaged in it" (Fox-Genovese, 1976, p. 93). The second is that he took the British economy as his object of study, which is why Fox-Genovese says that "he (Quesnay) selected as his model the most highly developed economy in the world" (p. 52), that his "economics owed much to English development" (p. 57), and that "he celebrated England as the home of a prosperous agriculture" (p. 124).

The first point is a fact that people do not deny, but it is only a secondary factor, because being born a farmer alone is far from enough to establish a system of economic doctrines. The second point is true, for we can find many examples in Quesnay's economic treatises, especially early ones like "Fermiers," where he described the British economy, or used England as a model. But it is worth pondering why Physiocracy arose in France and not in England, and why France gave birth to the most China-admiring Quesnay's group and not to others. Admittedly, the emergence of Physiocracy was due, first of all, to the specific historical conditions of France at that time, in particular the country's own socio-economic factors. At the same time, it must be acknowledged that Quesnay's exposure to a variety of sources was also crucial to the creation of a new doctrine that was completely different from the old mercantilist one. This is the focus of this book. It is clearly inadvisable to jump to a conclusion in examining the sources of Physiocracy on the basis of the mere mention of a country or a person by name in some of Quesnay's writings. Even so, the fact that Quesnay mainly mentioned England specifically in some of his earlier writings, but devoted to China in *Despotism in China*, one of his later writings, may as well lead us to the conclusion that China was more important to him than England.

Takimoto Seiichi (1931, p. 29), a Japanese economist, makes an attempt to delineate the trajectory of the Chinese influence on Quesnay's agricultural emphasis. He speculates that since Quesnay was the son of a farmer, it is conceivable that he was already interested in agriculture before he engaged in the study of China, and it was probably during his study of agriculture that he happened to read Du Halde's treatise on China and learned about the Chinese system, which he was to be deeply influenced by and which catered to his own intentions to form his later economic theory. Takimoto also specifically speculates that Quesnay's exposure to Du Halde's work began in the same year or the year after he published "Grains." As it turned out, on the basis of his lifelong ardent study of agriculture, Quesnay came into contact with Chinese culture that attached special importance to agriculture, which increased his confidence in his research, resulting in a doctrine emphasizing agriculture (p. 30). Therefore, Takimoto rises above different disputes, arguing that all other speculations about the origin of Quesnay's Physiocracy among Western economists were groundless, and that Quesnay's fundamental thought of agricultural preference "was so extreme because it was influenced by the system and doctrine of ancient China's kings" (p. 33).

Unfortunately, Takimoto's above assertions are based on speculations and are thus unconvincing. Our study in this chapter seeks to reveal, from within Quesnay's doctrine, how his extensive exposure to ancient Chinese materials about emphasizing agriculture influenced the elaboration of his own theory of agricultural primacy. This study shows that Quesnay not only strongly praised and advocated the emulation of Chinese agricultural thought and policy, but also put forward a number of theoretical views, that agriculture is the only sector of production, that land is the source of all wealth, that only agricultural production creates surpluses or "net products," that agriculture increased material wealth as a gift of nature, that society is divided into three classes engaged in economic activities—namely, agriculture, industry and commerce, that industry and commerce are unproductive sectors and depend on agriculture, that foreign trade is an expedient measure, that currency, different from consumption wealth, is only a tool of trade, that monetary wealth does not represent national wealth, and that agricultural prices need to be stabilized, to name only a few. All these views bear the marks of, or at least have a great similarity, with the ancient Chinese idea of emphasizing agriculture. As far as agricultural primacy alone is concerned, the Physiocratic School borrowed and absorbed Chinese ideas on a wide range of subjects, which is not the case when they talked about Britain. It is only because of this that Martin (1963, p. 235), a Western scholar, has remarked, "England seemed to the Physiocrats a model only less to be imitated than China." That is to say, Quesnay built up his system of prioritizing agriculture by resorting to models from countries other than his own, and among those foreign models, Britain included, China was the country that received the most attention.

Of course, Quesnay's theory of agricultural primacy is fundamentally different from the ancient Chinese idea of emphasizing agriculture. The former, "in its essence, proclaimed the rise of the bourgeois system of production on the ruins of the feudal"

(Marx, 1969, p. 53), while the latter was nothing less than a part of feudalism, at most with some new economic elements or the germ of capitalism after the Ming and Qing Dynasties. What Quesnay drew from the specimens of British agriculture were the purely capitalist economic elements, such as the adoption of large-scale agricultural operations by tenant farmers, which is incomparable to the traditional small land management of Chinese feudalism. In any case, as a kind of advanced ideological material, the ancient Chinese view of attaching importance to agriculture had a very significant influence on Quesnay's theory of agricultural primacy. No economist who discards the narrow prejudice of Eurocentrism will be blind to this influence.

Chapter 8
Single *Impôt Territorial*, Population, and Property Ownership

In addition to what is discussed above, the influence of ancient Chinese thought on the economic doctrines of the Physiocratic School is also prominently reflected, in varying degrees, in the theories of a single *impôt territorial* (the most prominent), population and property ownership, which are to be analyzed in this chapter.

1 Single *Impôt Territorial*

It has been noted among Western economists that a large part of the Physiocratic system, which is in fact the most characteristic, is devoted to the elaboration of a theory of taxation, that is, the theory of a single *impôt territorial*. The following analysis will show that this theory, like many of the Physiocrats' other important economic views, is partly based on China, their ideal country. Also discussed will be some relevant financial views of the Physiocratic School that are modelled on ancient Chinese thought and institutions.

I. The Westward transmission and influence of ancient Chinese taxation ideas

A large number of Chinese materials were brought to Europe in the seventeenth and eighteenth centuries, of which a considerable part is on taxation ideas and systems. Those that were widely spread, roughly speaking, have the following features.

First, in China, landlords paid taxes.

Fernandez Navarrete pointed out in his book on China published in 1675, "The Husband-men are generally poor People and have but a small parcel of Land they farm (i.e. rent) from others: the general Rule is that the Landlord pays Taxes and has half the Crop, the Husband-man tills the Ground and has the other half for his pains" (Quoted in Maverick, 1946, p. 15).

Second, the Chinese advocated a reasonable tax burden.

M. Tan, *The Chinese Origin of Physiocracy*,
https://doi.org/10.1007/978-981-97-9703-5_8

Confucius, noted Silhouette, a contemporary of the Physiocrats, had "taught that the prince who taxes the people too heavily impoverishes himself" (p. 33). Navarrete quoted the edict of Emperor Taizong of the Tang Dynasty to the effect that "it is but reasonable to lay a Burden upon him that has strength to bear it; but it is a madness to place the Weight upon him that is not able to carry himself" (p. 15). Le Comte, a missionary to China, recorded the reasoning of the Chinese against the oppression of harsh government: "[T]hey say [that the] proceeds [from harsh government comes] not from the absoluteness of the Princes' power, for they cannot be too much their subjects' masters; but from the Princes' own wildness, which neither the Voice of Nature nor the Laws of God can ever countenance" (p. 18). At the same time, Silhouette mentioned that, in China, "[t]he laws are so favorable to [the emperor] that he cannot violate them without injuring his own powers, nor can he change them without arousing the people to insurrection" (p. 30). The main purpose of these arguments was to prove that ancient Chinese had always opposed heavy taxation and advocated the reasonableness of tax burdens.

Third, many scholars believed that the Chinese tax law had many advantages, in terms of, for example, the institutions of tax collection.

Le Comte said,

> [O]f all their wholesome institutions, there is nothing which contributes so much to the keeping up Peace and Order, as does their method of Levying the Emperor's Revenue ... All the Estates there are measured, and all the Families registered, and whatsoever the Emperor is to have by Excise on Goods, or Tax upon Persons, is publickly known; every body brings in what is due from him ...
>
> (pp. 17-18)

Silhouette reported in a similar way,

> The raising of taxes is accomplished in an orderly manner and without need of employing a great number of special officers. ... Each brings in his contribution to the mandarin of the city. ... The local mandarin turns the taxes over to a higher officer who represents the province. Much of the tribute is consumed in the province; the remainder is sent to Peking.
>
> (pp. 30–31)

Marsy also mentioned,

> In China there are no "farmers" (contractors) of the tax, but the principal magistrate of the district collects the tax and forwards it to the provincial magistrate. The collection is admirably simple and orderly.
>
> Between the ages of twenty and sixty years, each citizen pays a tax proportioned to his actual ability to pay. All fields are measured annually before the harvest, and each husbandman is told what he must pay. All land is taxed, even that belonging to temples, for the gods are no more exempt than are men.
>
> Those slow in paying their taxes do not face the confiscation of their property, but are punished by the bastinado, by imprisonment, or by quartering beggars upon them.
>
> The Emperor rarely exercises his absolute power to increase taxes, but almost every year remits or reduces them for distressed districts or whole provinces.
>
> (pp. 36–37)

Quesnay (1946, p. 221) gave the following observation:

> [I]t is even [the emperor's] custom every year to exempt one or two provinces from providing their share, that is, provinces that have suffered, whether from pestilence or other distressing happening.

"Most of the practical difficulties of the French monarchy," some historians argue according to their analysis, "could be traced to its methods of raising revenue" (Palmer, Colton & Kramer, 2007, p. 312). Therefore, the above ideas and system of taxation from China were very timely for the French thinkers who had long been troubled by the problem of taxation, and became an important impetus for the advocates of tax reform. A famous one at that time was the French military engineer and economist Marshal Vauban (1633–1707), who published anonymously his *La Dîme Royale* in 1707. Taking as his guide the practice of regarding agriculture as the most important economic sector, Vauban (1888) described in the above work the miserable lives of the French farmers and criticized the system of tax farming. He believed that the main reason for the poverty of the farmers was the onerousness of various rents and taxes, so he strongly advocated reforming the tax system. He proposed the kingdom's tithe system, that is, a simple system of rent taxation for all classes and all incomes, to replace the harsh taxes imposed on the farmers. Of this proposal of tax reform, Quesnay (1888) later said that Vauban wanted to eliminate arbitrary taxation and worked out carefully for a long time the kingdom's system of one-tenth taxation. Vauban's taxation system, which aimed at making taxation simple, certain and universal, and especially at relieving the burden of farmers, is in principle an echo of the ancient Chinese idea of tax on rental income, which was popular in Europe during that period.

Vauban's so-called "dîme" differs from the type of religious tax levied on the population by Christian churches in Europe under the rubric of "tithe." In Maverick's (1946, p. 120) words, "Marshal Vauban had urged that the principal tax be made one tenth of the agricultural harvest and of industrial production. ... the proposal of the dîme, or tax of one-tenth, was quite in harmony with the practices reported from China." And Vauban's suggestion to adopt the Chinese system of village-25 families (Quoted in Geng, 1933, p. 21) is a testament to this. Maverick (1946, p. 120) also says that through the first half of the eighteenth century, many people, including the Abbé Baudeau, a later Physiocrat, "endorsed this suggestion as to the best method to reform the complex, corrupt, and harsh French system of taxation." Obviously, if Vauban's proposal had referred only to the traditional church tithe in Europe, it would not have been a tax reform at all, or have had to be published anonymously, not to say to have won the approval of many would-be reformers for nearly half a century. The allure of Vauban's proposal was that it was based on Chinese sources: the ancient principle of the "tax of one tenth," as a universally recognized political slogan of the various schools of thought in the pre-Qin period, had since then been frequently referred to in the more than 2000 years of feudalism. Once introduced to Europe, such an important idea of taxation, which was commonplace in China, easily attracted the attention of Westerners who were struggling to reform the tax system. In his *Questions*, Turgot specifically mentioned that he learned that "the dixme (the tax of one-tenth) of the crops from the land forms the principal revenue of the Emperor of China" (Quoted in Maverick, 1946, p. 55). Later Smith (1812, p. 664) also said in his *Wealth of Nations*, "In China, the principal revenue of the sovereign consists in a tenth part of the produce of all the lands of the empire." It was this Chinese ideal of tithing that Vauban used as a guiding principle in his reform of the tax system.

Neither Quesnay nor Turgot, however, was entirely in favor of Vauban's tithe scheme. Quesnay (1962) thought that the scheme, though it would increase the monarch's revenue and lighten the burden on the people more than the present system of tax farming, had the disadvantage of including both a single *impôt territorial* and a tax on industrial production, which turned out to be unsuitable for both. In particular, it seemed to him that those who proposed to replace the land tax by a tenth tax failed to examine the irregularities arising from the different methods of cultivation, and the changes connected with the replacement. To this latter point Turgot added a note: A tenth tax from the sterile land becomes a double tax compared with a tenth tax from the fertile land. Therefore, in the case of a tax on different yields, the tax of one tenth on grain is unfair in a proportional sense. It is, of course, proportional to the yield, yet disproportionate to the expenditure on land of different quality and to the value of the sowing material (Quoted in Quesnay, 1979).

In fact, none of these criticisms had anything to do with the Chinese example in the tithing scheme. Firstly, in ancient China, little thought was given to taxing industrial production, and agricultural taxation was always considered to be the most desirable tax system. Secondly, in addition to promoting the generally accepted tithe as the more reasonable rate of taxation, there was an idea of differential taxation in ancient China, which advocated different rates of taxation according to different regions or different lines of business.[1] This drew Turgot's attention: he once quoted in his *Questions* a note by Poivre on the Chinese tithe: "[T]his fraction, one-tenth, is not imposed equally on all lands; that on the best, it rises as high as one-tenth, and on the worst lands it falls to a thirtieth. Undoubtedly it has taken a long time to determine this fraction for each piece of land" (Quoted in Maverick, 1946, p. 55). Therefore, it was actually to correct Vauban's tithe scheme with the ancient Chinese idea of "tithe tax" that Turgot supported Quesnay's view on the one-tenth tax system.

Georges Weulersse, a French scholar, mentions in his 1910 book *Le Mouvement physiocratiqite en France (de 1756 a 1770)* that "[the Physiocrats'] advocacy of the single tax, to be imposed on the net product of the soil, and based in part upon reports on practices in China, met opposition from another group of reformers, following another morsel of wisdom from China, the followers of Vauban the advocate of the dixme royal" (Quoted in Maverick, 1940, p. 317). This argument, apart from the significance of its assertion that Vauban's view of tithing was derived from his Chinese knowledge, is inaccurate in its statement about the opposition between the tax system of Physiocracy and Vauban's tithe tax scheme. In fact, the tithe scheme

---

[1] It is stipulated, for example, in the section of *Zaishi* of *Zhou Li* (*Rites of Zhou*): "For land use, there is no levy on official residences. For gardens and ordinary people's residential buildings, the tax rate is one out of twenty; for urban suburbs, one out of ten; for outer suburbs, three out of twenty; for all the other areas, no more than two out of ten. Only the tax rate for lacquer forests is five out of twenty" (Yang, 2004).

informed later thinking about a single *impôt territorial* on a number of basic rent principles. In his *History of Economic Thought*, Haney (1911, p. 135) points out that Vauban, while recognizing income from official businesses, customs duties and excise taxes as the sources of the state's revenue, "on the whole may be regarded as a pioneer of the single tax;" or, as stated by Ji Taoda (1963, p. 22), "His [Vauban's] conception of this single tax system may be said to be the forerunner of the economic policy advocated by the later Physiocrats." It is not difficult to find a consistent source of Chinese knowledge in this succession of tax reform ideas.

After Vauban came other thinkers who advocated tax reform, based on the then prevalent situation in France, which continued to be very similar to the ancient Chinese taxation views transmitted to the West at that time. Boisguillebert, in his elaboration on the serious consequences brought by various heavy taxes, argued that the burden of taxation should be in line with the principle of justice; proposed to simplify and reduce the taxation of farmers; advocated direct taxation; and recognized that the increase in tax rates did not necessarily increase the revenue of the kingdom, and that an appropriate tax rate could make the kingdom very rich. More notably, Turgot's various reforms in Limoges, such as his commitment to land surveying and valuation in order to develop a kind of land survey inventory as a more rational basis for poll taxation, which was quite similar to the "equalization of fields and taxes" in the Song and Ming Dynasties or the land clearing for the purpose of equalizing the tax burden.[2] Turgot advocated the abolition of corvée, the hiring of workers to build roads, and making local taxpayers pay for the costs incurred, which was similar to the change of the feudal burden of labor into monetary payment, and the change of the compulsory labor levy into measures such as employment since the Tang and Song dynasties. After his appointment as chancellor of the exchequer, Turgot urged the king to lead by example a frugal life when he was in financial distress, which was in parallel with the traditional Chinese idea of favoring frugality.

In short, all the above discussions are important pavements for the following research into the influence of ancient Chinese taxation ideas and policies on the single land tax theory of the Physiocratic School.

II. **The Chinese origin of the theory of a single *impôt territorial***

Quesnay's theory of a single *impôt territorial* did not come into being all of a sudden. In his early years, "he [took] part in 1725 at a meeting for protesting against a new *taille*, and proposing an excise instead of it—an attitude very different from what might be expected from the author of the Single tax, but proving his early practical interest in the system of taxation" (Bauer, 1895, p. 661). Later, in his first treatise on economics, "Fermiers" (1756), he suggested that in order to secure the payment of the rent tax, and to protect the taxpayer from rent collectors' impropriety and miscalculation, the tax was to be levied on invariable principles; but he did not then know exactly what this invariable principle on which he was to rely, so he

[2] Turgot once asked "whether in each district [of China] there is a public table or register, in which each piece is entered, with a note as to the fraction according to which it must pay tax" (Quoted in Maverick, 1946, p. 55). This shows his interest in the subject in China, and it is likely that he was making further enquiries based on what he already knew.

still faltered in the face of the confusion of whether to share the tax proportionally. The best taxation method he could conceive of at that time was for people from all walks of life in agriculture, industry and commerce to declare their property on their own and subject themselves to public scrutiny, and then the tax was collected in proportion to the law according to the amount declared (Quesnay, 1962). That is why Higgs (1897, p. 29) says that, at that time, Quesnay's "*impôt unique* had not yet presented itself to him as the perfect solution of this problem." The following year, in his "Impôts" written for *l'Encyclopédie*, Quesnay developed a clear idea of a single *impôt territorial*. It was said to be in the course of writing his early economic works that Quesnay began to study Chinese culture extensively and systematically. Accordingly, the development of Quesnay's theory of a single *impôt territorial* was simultaneous with his exposure to ancient Chinese ideas and institutions of taxation.

The core of the theory is that the land owner in possession of the "net product" bore the full burden of the tax, while the tenant farmer and the industrialist were exempted from all taxation. In this regard, Adam Smith (1812) mentioned in *The Wealth of Nations*, "That system which represents the produce of land as the sole source of the revenue and wealth of every country has, so far as I know, never been adopted by any nation, and it at present exists only in the speculations of a few men of great learning and ingenuity in France" (pp. 524–525). He thus regarded the Physiocratic doctrine of taxation as "a system which never has done, and probably never will do, any harm in any part of the world" (p. 525), as well as a "very ingenious system" (p. 525). In fact, as early as 1770, six years before the publication of Smith's *Wealth of Nations*, the Duke of Baden in Germany had experimented with this single tax system in three selected villages in his dominions.[3] The late nineteenth century American economist Henry George publicly expressed his gratitude to the Physiocratic School for instilling in him the theory of a single *impôt territorial*, which was a remarkable event in the history of economic theory.[4]

The bourgeois economists have mixed feelings about this theory. Haney (1911, p. 149) claims, "Though the single-tax idea was based upon an erroneous notion of productivity, [...] it rendered a great service. Under the advocacy of it, the cumbersome, wasteful mass of taxes which prevailed was criticised; and the discussions to which it gave rise led to a better understanding of the principles of taxation." Higgs (1897, p. 144) argues, "Their *impôt unique* might have proved, as Voltaire said, an *impôt inique*; but in probity and honesty of purpose they fought earnestly against injustice and oppression." Schumpeter (1954a, p. 231), however, claims,

---

[3] The Duke is said to have appointed Johann August Schlettwein (1731–1802), known as "Germany's foremost Physiocrat," to be in charge of this experiment and to levy a "single tax" equivalent to 20% of the "net product" (Klippel, 1994).

[4] Henry George has "dedicate[ed] his *Protection or Free Trade?* (New York, 1891) 'to the memory of those illustrious Frenchmen of a century ago, Quesnay, Turgot, Mirabeau, Condorcet, Dupont and their fellows, who in the night of despotism foresaw the glories of the coming day'" (Quoted in Higgs, 1897, p. 135 [Note 2]). But he admitted that he had never read the Physiocrats' original writings. Besides, he argued that the increase in land rents due to social progress should be fully owned by the community through a single tax, in order to push further the nationalization of the land, which differed significantly from the Physiocrats' single *impôt territorial*.

"This theory may be untenable. Even if it were tenable as an abstract proposition, its application to the practical question of taxation would be indefensible." It was Marx (1969, p. 52) alone who penetrated deeply into the inner substance and real meaning of the single *impôt territorial*, when he argued,

> [I]n the conclusions which the Physiocrats themselves draw, the ostensible veneration of landed property becomes transformed into the economic negation of it and the affirmation of capitalist production. On the one hand, all taxes are put on rent, or in other words, landed property is in part confiscated, which is what the legislation of the French Revolution sought to carry through and which is the final conclusion of the fully developed Ricardian modern political economy.

As an important economic doctrine, the idea of a single *impôt territorial* is firmly connected with other economic theories within Physiocracy, especially the net product theory. We have already in the previous chapter analyzed in detail the influence of the ancient Chinese agriculture-oriented thought on the creation of the Physiocratic theory of net product, which lays the foundation for this section to study the Chinese origin of the theory of a single *impôt territorial*. In addition, the Physiocrats drew on many sources of Chinese taxation in elaborating their single land tax theory. In his *Despotism in China*, Quesnay devotes a whole chapter, namely Chap. 4, to the analysis of taxation in China, and elsewhere in the book, there are many references to rent-tax, such as Sect. 4 of Chap. 7, "Taxes other than on land," Sect. 7 of Chap. 8, "The right of taxation is securely founded," and Sect. 20 of Chap. 8, "Public revenue." The author quoted or copied in these parts a large number of accounts of that period on the subject of Chinese tax collection, which are in turn amply quoted above in this section. What's more important is that Quesnay, on the basis of his study of Chinese taxation, made comments and elaborated on the taxation of his own country.

This rich source of ideas is highly valuable for an in-depth discussion of the origin of Quesnay's theory of taxation in terms of the following four aspects.

Firstly, subjection of the tax system to the natural order.

"The great advantage of the Physiocratic *impôt* [...]," the two French economists Gide and Rist (1915) point out, "was that it was regulated by a natural norm, which gave the amount of the net product. Without this, taxation becomes arbitrary. At bottom the system affords a barrier against the autocracy of the sovereign" (pp. 43–44). This is the basic tax view that is derived from the Physiocrats' doctrine of natural order. Du Pont once stated, "The tax must never be assessed in accordance with individual caprice. The amount is determined by the natural order" (p. 44 [Note 1]); and, more specifically, "[i]f unfortunately it be true that three-tenths of the annual product is not sufficient to cover the ordinary expenditure, there is only one natural and reasonable conclusion to be drawn from this, namely, curtail the expenditure" (p. 44 [Note 1]). Quesnay (1962) also said that "[t]his tax ('a simple real tax') [...] is indicated by natural law" (p. 241), while "any other form of imposition would be contrary to the natural order, since it would be detrimental to reproduction and to taxation, and the taxes would fall on the taxes themselves" (p. 154); and that "[t]axation [...] is essentially determined by immutable laws and rules, from which the ruler and the subjects may not diverge except to their disadvantage" (1946, p. 278).

These "immutable laws and rules," that is, the laws of the natural order, are what Quesnay, in summing up the Chinese tax system, called the basis on which "The Right of Taxation is Securely Founded" (p. 278). In his view, "[e]very kingdom but China has been ignorant of the necessity for this provision [of teaching the positive laws], which is the basis of government" (p. 271), and therefore, "[t]he prime object of the administration of a prosperous and lasting government should then be, as in the Chinese Empire, the profound study and the continual and general teaching of the natural laws" (p. 281). It can be seen from the above that the insistence by Quesnay and other Physiocrats on the natural order to determine or direct taxation ultimately came from China's example.

Secondly, the use of land rent as the only object of taxation.

The Physiocrats believed that "net product" was the only possible source of taxation, and that, since "net product" boiled down to rent, rent was the only taxable income. They advocated a single tax system that only taxed the rent embodied in land income. Quesnay (1888) repeatedly illustrated this view in his "Impôts" to the effect that it is important that the whole system of taxation should be based on the taxation of the land, that it is important that only the income supplied by agriculture and the various kinds of work sustained by it should be taxed, and that all the results of taxation are borne by the income of the land. Turgot agreed with the above opinion, saying, "The revenues of the landowners are the only source from which the State can derive its own revenue. In what form soever taxes be imposed or collected they are always, in the last result, paid by the proprietors of the land, either by increase of their expenses or diminution of their receipts" (Quoted in Higgs, 1897, p. 93).

This peculiar view of taxation based solely on rent might well have been inspired by the reports circulated at the time that the produce of the land was divided 50–50 between Chinese landlords and tenant farmers, and that only the landlords were to pay the tax. To prove this, it may be useful to reproduce below a passage from Quesnay's (1946, p. 220) discussion of China's taxation:

> The amount that subjects of the empire must pay is regulated by the area of land they possess, an area that is allotted according to the fertility of the land. [...]
>
> [...] From spring until harvest time, peasants may not be molested; after this time a quota of produce is received from them in kind or in money; if they do not pay, the poor and the old people who are supported in each city by the charities of the sovereign, are sent into their houses to remain there until they have consumed the amount owed to the emperor. This arrangement only obtains for small proprietors who themselves cultivate some portion of the ground they own; for as we have just seen, farmers are not taxed on land that they cultivate, or if payment is demanded of them, from this payment is subtracted the cost of farming, as is practiced in France in the case of the vingtième (one-twentieth land tax) that is levied on the incomes of proprietors. Thus, this payment is made by the farmer; whether it is made in one manner or in the other is immaterial and does not expose him to the danger of being fined.

Thus, we can see that Quesnay particularly emphasized the following characteristics of the Chinese system of taxation. First, the tax was mainly on land. Second, the tax was based on the area and fertility of the land. Third, all taxes were borne by the landowners. Fourth, the tax was never levied on the peasants who rented the land.

Obviously, these four were also the basis of Quesnay's theory of a single *impôt territorial*. Quesnay (1888) talked more about the taxation of small landowners who earned their own living in China, which was in line with his assertion in "Grains" that the people who were taxed were all those who had small and medium-sized assets. That the large landowners were subject to taxation might well be self-evident to him, for when he emphasized that the Chinese tenant farmers should not be taxed, he already included the idea that the taxation was to be exclusively borne by the unproductive landowners who collected rent. Regardless of the category of landowners, however, what Quesnay saw from China was the fact that only landlords bore the burden of taxation, which interested him very much. For this reason, he gave a summary of the Chinese taxation system under the heading of "The Public Revenue" in his description of "the Chinese doctrine, worthy to be used as a model for all states" (1946, p. 264). The basic idea is as follows:

> [I]t is manifest that the tax necessary for the fund to satisfy the needs of the state cannot have, in an agricultural nation, any other source or any other origin than that which produces the goods necessary to satisfy the needs of men, and this source is the soil itself, made fertile by outlays and labor. Consequently, the annual tax necessary for the state cannot consist of anything but a portion of the annual produce of the soil, the ownership of which lies in those to whom this land was distributed; and, therefore, the tax can indeed be nothing else but a portion of the proceeds from the land, which belongs to the landowners -- of the proceeds, I say, that exceed the cost of the labor of cultivation, and the other advance expenditure necessary to prepare for that cultivation. All these expenses are repaid by the product to which they give rise, and the surplus is a net product, which forms the public revenue and the income of the proprietors.
>
> (pp. 289–290)

At this point, it is clear that Quesnay's theory of a single *impôt territorial* was based on the theory and practice of China as its model.

According to Oncken's research, Quesnay not only preached the land tax law prevalent in China of his age, but also highly praised the tax system recorded in *Zhou Li* (*Rites of Zhou*) (Quoted in Tang, 1936, pp. 50, 365–366). *Gong* (the production tax) and *Fu* (the extra military tribute, including manpower and supplies) stand at the core of the fiscal system of *Zhou Li*, both of which constitute the basic part of the financial revenue of feudal states, with *Fu* playing a more important role. In this book, there are nine items of tax to "collect money and property:" the first six include the payment of tax in kind based on land acreage and distance from the city center, and the remaining three are excise taxes, namely, *Guanshi* on tariff and trade, *Shanze* on mine, fishery and forestry, and *Biyu* on other taxable items. This tax system is mainly based on land tax. What's more, land is an object of tax in other pre-Qin classics, such as *Shang Shu* (*The Book of Documents*) and *Guo Yu* (*Discourses of the States*), in which the kinds and quantity of tax are also determined by the specific conditions of land (Legge, 1879, p. 64; Xü, 2002, p. 227).

However, in ancient Chinese classics, Mencius' (1875, pp. 172–173) proposal of a single tax on agriculture is particularly similar to Quesnay's idea of a single *impôt territorial*. Mencius argued that the ideal of taxation system at his time should be as follows:

> [I]n the market-places he levy a ground-rent on the shops but do not tax the goods, or enforce the [proper] regulations without levying a ground-rent. [...]
>
> [A]t the frontier-gates there be an inspection of the persons, but no charges levied. [...]
>
> [T]he husbandmen be required to give their material aid [in cultivating the public field], and no levies be made [of the produce of their own]. [...]
>
> [F]rom the [occupiers of the] people's dwellings he do not exact the cloth required from the individual [idler] or the quota for residences. [...]

We can see that "if the above items are exempted from taxation, the only source of revenue left will be agricultural production" (Hu, 1962, p. 247). The standard agricultural tax rate Mencius (1875, p. 204) advocated is embodied in the following: "I would ask you [the ruler], in the [purely] country districts, to observe the nine-squares division, having one square cultivated on the system of mutual aid; and in the central parts of the State, to levy a tenth, to be paid by the cultivators themselves." What is advocated here is in fact a single agricultural tax system.[5] As already mentioned, since *The Book of Mencius* was introduced to the West, it was likely that Quesnay absorbed some of its economic ideas. It was therefore not a coincidence that Quesnay and Mencius were similar in their thinking on the single tax. Moreover, for a long time in ancient China, the single agricultural tax was theoretically considered the ideal tax system, despite the fact that the collection of non-agricultural taxes, such as industrial and commercial taxes, was never stopped. This traditional idea had remained deeply rooted in the minds of Chinese scholars until the seventeenth and eighteenth centuries, so it could not but have an influence on Quesnay, who was a great admirer of Chinese culture. In short, both according to Quesnay's own description and summary of the Chinese taxation system, and according to the original outlook of the traditional Chinese taxation thought that he came across, the special theory of single taxation of land proposed by him, in addition to the socio-economic foundation on which it grew in France, could not be separated from the nourishment of China's fertile soil of agricultural thought.

Thirdly, the transfer and imputation of tax.

An important basis for Quesnay's theory of a single *impôt territorial* is his belief that even if the burden of taxation was not imposed directly on the rent of the landowners, but on the revenue of the non-landowners such as tenant farmers and industrialists, it would eventually be passed on indirectly to the landowner through tax transfer. It would therefore be better to abolish all miscellaneous taxes outright and levy a single tax instead. Quesnay repeatedly warned of the draconian consequences of taxing tenant farmers and industrialists. Taxing tenant farmers meant destroying the source of the country's annual reproduction of wealth. It was argued therefore that the cultivator should no longer bear taxes except the income paid to the landowner, whether directly or indirectly. The Abbé Baudeau was even more straightforward, arguing that "whoever hurts or degrades, attacks or robs them (the agriculturists)

[5] In his doctoral thesis, Ly Siou-Y (1938) also mentions that Mencius believed that good politics in a country is to reduce taxes as much as possible, and therefore suggested that only a single tax, that is, only the land tax, should be introduced and that all other taxes, such as commercial taxes or customs duties, should be abolished.

is the cruelest enemy of society" (Quoted in Gide & Rist, 1915, p. 26). The same was true of the industrialists. Quesnay (1888) argued that merchants, craftsmen and workers only paid in advance the taxes imposed on them, because they passed them on to their customers who bought goods or manufactures through prices, or were compensated when they received wages, so that the result was always a tax on the products of the land.

What is fascinating is that, among the above arguments Quesnay put forward, almost every point can be generalized from the Chinese examples or theories he cited. In arguing that tenant farmers could not be taxed, Quesnay (1946) repeatedly stated that in China, tenant "farmers are not taxed on land that they cultivate" (p. 220) and that no "farmers of the taxes [...] are known in that country" (p. 221). It has been said that when the Physiocrats talked about the rights of cultivators, they thought only of tenant farmers and small farmers, but never of hired agricultural laborers. When Quesnay talked about Chinese farmers, he only thought of those who rented land; and when he compared the French and Chinese tenant farmers, he used the same French term (Fermiers), even though this term actually represents two completely different concepts, namely, capitalist tenant agriculturists and feudal tenant peasants. Quesnay stated that the reason Chinese tenant farmers did not pay taxes was to ensure that the cost of farming was not compromised. A concept similar to his "prepayment" was almost immediately apparent in this account. He then gave a summary of the Chinese taxation, in which he wrote,

> Nor, it is evident, can that tax be placed upon the funds advanced to prepare the land for cultivation, for this would soon ruin the cultivation and all the goods necessary for men's subsistence. This, then, would not be a contribution toward the needs of the state, but a general devastation, which would destroy the state and the nation.
>
> (p. 293)

In this way he drew the conclusion that all tenant farmers should not be taxed, from the popular account that tenant farmers were not burdened with taxes in China.

Still in this summary, Quesnay went on to say,

> Nor should this tax, say the Chinese, be imposed upon commodities or merchandise destined for men's use. This would be subjecting the men themselves, their needs, and their labor, to taxation, and converting this tax, levied for the needs of the state, into devastation all the more rapid, because it would surrender the nation to the avidity of a horde of men or rather enemies engaged in the collection of this unfortunate tax, from which the sovereign himself would not obtain enough to cover the losses which it caused him on that portion of his revenue that he received (goods paid in kind) as his share of the net proceeds of the land.
>
> (p. 293)

Thus, his rejection of taxation on commodities is in accordance with what the Chinese said above. That taxing goods means taxing people themselves is another way of expressing the theory of tax transfer. In his view, people themselves are nothing but their needs and their capacity for labor, which in turn boil down to the cost of human labor. Such labor will be inconceivable without the necessary cost of maintaining people's means of subsistence. People themselves lose their wealth and gain only their needs. Therefore, taxes cannot be levied on them, nor on the wages of their labor. If such wages, which are necessary for the subsistence of the people themselves and their families, are taxed, a tax transfer is bound to take place. For unless their wages are raised, they will not be able to pay the tax. This raises the price of labor without increasing the productivity of labor, causing a loss on the part of those who pay the wages. Thus, the product of labor remains unchanged while wages are raised, necessarily resulting in a diminution of employment or production as well as of population. All this reasoning, which Quesnay considered to be incomprehensible to Europeans, came from the basic principles followed by the Chinese government. He said,

> These are the fundamental principles of the doctrine which has regulated the government of China so satisfactorily for many centuries. But the conclusions that the Chinese draw therefrom would be quite difficult to persuade Europeans to adopt.
>
> (p. 292)

To further explain these Chinese views to the Europeans, Quesnay added,

> [A] personal tax placed upon men or upon the payment received for their labor, is, they say, a tax that is necessarily disorderly and unjust, determined by nothing but caprice and an arbitrary estimation of the citizens' capacities. Thus, it is an unlimited and disastrous imposition.
>
> (p. 292)

The unreasonableness of this taxation, according to the Chinese opinion which he expounded, was also manifested as follows:

> All farm workers, artisans, traders – in short, all classes that earn wages or salaries – cannot, of themselves, contribute to a tax for the public revenue and the needs of the state, because this tax, in the reaction, would reduce the cultivation of the land, would doubly reduce the income from the land, and would destroy itself and ruin the nation. Here, then, is a natural law which may not be violated without incurring the punishment that is inseparable from that law, making the tax that seemed necessary to the needs of the state more formidable than those needs themselves.
>
> (pp. 292–293)

The above discussion and summary of Quesnay's views on the Chinese taxation are concentrated in the section of "The Public Revenue" in Chapter 8 of his *Despotism of China*. It seemed that he was still not satisfied after such an extensive exposition and summary there, so he added,

> In other works*, one may find discussions which support these opinions of the Chinese, with rules which should be followed in order to assure to the state the most extensive tax revenue possible, which would be completely to the advantage of the nation and would avoid the damage caused by other types of taxation.
>
> (p. 293).[6]

---

[6] Here, "other works," according to Maverick's footnote, refer to "Works of Queanay and Miraheau, and the book currently (1767) appearing by Mercier de la Riviere.".

These so-called "opinions of the Chinese" are obviously mixed with a lot of Quesnay's personal analysis and opinions. However, they do have their origin in China, such as paying land rent to landlords by farmers who rent land, and paying state taxes by landlords; objection to industrial and commercial tax; and opposition against heavy taxation in favor of light taxation. The idea of tax transfer, according to Liu Xu (1975), was clearly put forward by Li Jue at the end of the Tang Dynasty: heavy taxes on daily necessities would inevitably lead to price increases due to tax transfer. The first consequence was that the poor and the weak were harmed to the greatest extent. The second was that the higher the price, the fewer the buyers, so the heavy tax may not be able to increase revenue. This view of tax transfer was heard from time to time in the late feudal period of China, and was used as an important argument against levying or re-levying commercial tax. In short, Quesnay himself frankly stated that his idea of taxation was derived from Chinese views, and he repeatedly took Chinese views as a model, which is precisely the strongest evidence for the Chinese origin of his idea of taxation and even the whole doctrine of the Physiocratic School.

Of course, Quesnay also noticed from the materials about Chinese taxation that, in addition to land taxes, there were also a few "irregular" taxes, such as customs duties and tolls in some areas, as well as the imposition of taxes on individuals in the form of poll taxes. He argued that in an empire in which wealth was derived from the land, these non-land taxes undermined both the taxation itself and the national revenue. Although these "irregular" taxes in China did not have totally disastrous consequences because they were quite restrained, were almost always of a fixed amount, and did not incur huge collection costs, they were, after all, a cause of misfortune and a defect brought into the Chinese government. But, he added, this defect need not be attributed to the government itself, for it was only an error in execution, and could be corrected without involving any change in the system of the empire itself (Quesnay, 1946, pp. 259–260). In this way, certain defects in Chinese taxation did not prevent Quesnay from still considering China's taxation system as the one that should be emulated. In fact, his call for the abolition of all other taxes except the land tax was only an ideal. In reality, as an expedient measure, he agreed to keep some miscellaneous taxes, including the poll tax he opposed.[7] In this sense, Quesnay believed that the country with a taxation system closest to his ideal of a single *impôt territorial* in the real world was China, which was why he studied Chinese taxation ideas and systems with great interest and admiration.

Fourthly, some principles of taxation.

The preceding points have already involved the principles of taxation, among which the following ones are often emphasized by Quesnay, and are closely related to the ancient Chinese idea of taxation.

The first one is "rule-based" or "orderly" taxation. One of the main reasons for Quesnay's strong opposition to the French system of tax farming is that the tax farmers

[7] For example, in his "Impôts," Quesnay (1888) said that if it is necessary to increase the revenue of the sovereign progressively, the poll tax may be maintained, and that as the population increases with the wealth of the country, the revenue from the poll tax will also increase accordingly.

were qualified by "bribes" or "favors," and when they obtained the qualification, they could take advantage of the prescribed taxation by imposing heavier taxes on the taxpayers, thus making the amount of taxation payable by the people an arbitrary and uncertain factor. So Quesnay (1888) hoped that a prosperous nation would never resort to this dangerous source. This view was not only directed at the state of the French tax system but also benefited from the Chinese tax situation made public in Europe. Many Westerners of the time mentioned that there were no tax farmers in China, that taxation was "admirably" simple and orderly, that the taxes levied by the emperor were made public, that every taxpayer knew what he had to pay, etc. (Maverick, 1946, pp. 18, 30–31, 36). Quesnay (1946) himself quoted the sixteen maxims of Yong Zheng (from Kang Xi), which stated that the people should "pay punctually the established taxes" (p. 198). He added, "The emperor may increase the tax when the needs of the state require it, but with the exception of cases of pressing necessity he rarely makes use of this power" (p. 221). These were not entirely fictitious, for it was always the common aim of the successive Chinese supreme rulers to maintain their regime for a long period of time under a long-standing unified political structure, regardless of the evil or goodness of their personal will. In order to achieve this goal, as a "wet nurse" in feudal countries, taxation could not be levied arbitrarily according to the insatiable greed of the rulers, and sometimes there existed some reasonable taxation facilities that were conceived in the long run. The long-term accumulation of these reasonable facilities would gradually develop into a system of taxation, and the corresponding tax thoughts would emerge. Indeed, in ancient China, there were many arguments against heavy taxation, such as the following two: (1) "If one collects taxes and fees according to the regular levies, then the people may have expenditure but will suffer no damage" (Quoted in Knoblock & Riegel, 1995, p. 68); (2) Be regular in taxation and avoid arbitrary taxation, by not levying extraordinary taxes or paying extraordinary tribute (Fu, 1999). In summarizing the spirit of taxation in China, Quesnay (1946, p. 289) pointed out in particular, "One of the most terrible features in governments under the absolute authority of a prince, is the imposition upon the subjects of arbitrary taxes, which have appeared to have neither rules nor limits prescribed by the natural laws. However, the author of nature has decisively fixed the order of things in this respect." This order is the principle of tax "fixed" on the basis of the single *impôt territorial*.

The second is the simplification of tax agencies and the saving of collection costs. Another serious shortcoming of the French tax system at that time is that the cumbersome tax collection machinery caused huge collection fees, which was even more unbearable for the people. It was said that in the time of Louis XIV, two-thirds of the tax revenue was spent on levies. Quesnay identified eight main reasons for the reduction in the advances required for productive expenditure, among which the first two were: "1. A bad system of tax-assessment [...]. 2. An extra burden of taxation due to the costs of collection" (1962, p. 136). His maxim was that "*the administration of finance, whether in the collection of taxes or in the expenditure of the government, should not bring about the formation of monetary fortunes*" (p. 237). For this purpose, Quesnay (1888) advocated an extremely simple system of taxation or a simple, easy and reliable method of taxation, and one of his reasons for advocating a single *impôt territorial* was that it was a simpler and more convenient method. For this reason, Quesnay paid great attention to the reported "simplicity" of China's tax system, especially to the fact that "[t]he raising of taxes is accomplished in an orderly manner and without need of employing a great number of special officers" (Maverick, 1946, p. 30). He described the Chinese tax system in concrete terms:

> The second sovereign tribunal of Peking, called Hu Pu, has [...] direction over the finances; all the revenues of the state pass through its hands, and the care of the imperial treasury is entrusted to it. Neither farmers of the taxes nor special tax collectors are known in that country. In each city the chief magistrates are charged with the collection of taxes. These mandarins render an accounting to the treasurer-general, established in each province, who accounts to the Hu Pu, and this tribunal to the emperor.
>
> (Quesnay, 1946, p. 221)

Du Pont too opposed the system of tax farming, advocating in the spirit of the ancient Chinese tax system that "[i]t would be better for the landed proprietors to pay it (the tax) direct to the Treasury, and thus save the cost of collection" (Quoted in Gide & Rist, 1915, p. 42 [Note 1]). In the history of China, except for a few dynasties such as the Yuan Dynasty, the system of collecting taxes delegated to individuals by the state according to a certain amount was rarely as prevalent as in Europe since ancient Rome. The famous state tax reforms, ranging from the two tax laws of the Tang Dynasty, to the one whip law of the Ming Dynasty, and then to the unification of the land and clan system of the early Qing Dynasty, all embodied the basic spirit of simplifying the collection procedures. Such materials should have contributed to the development of Quesnay's later principles of "economy" and "convenience" in tax collection.

The third is a reasonable tax burden. Quesnay argued that taxation was necessary, and that this had been verified by the Chinese experience. What he wanted to demonstrate was the point that it is not the tax itself, but the manner in which it is levied that does the country great harm. Included here is a question of how to make the tax burden reasonable, and the maxim he proposed was "*[t]hat taxes should not be destructive or disproportionate to the mass of the nation's revenue; that their increase should follow the increase of the revenue*" (Quesnay, 1962, p. 232). This was also the conclusion he reached in his exposition of the principles of taxation in China: "the income of the state [is] always proportional to the increasing or decreasing income from the lands of the kingdom" (1946, p. 290). This emphasis on the reasonableness of the tax burden is consistent with Fu Xuan's (1999) principle of averaging the burden, which had been popular for a long time since the Western Zhou Dynasty in China, that is, equalizing the tax burden by taking into account the people's wealth and averaging it. The remark of Qiu Jun (1993), a scholar of the Ming Dynasty, may sum up Quesnay's original intention: "A ruler has to take something from the people, but he must not take too much. If he does not take something from the people, the state cannot go on; if he takes too much from the people, the people cannot go on." This principle can be seen in the Chinese tax materials available in Quesnay's time, such as the aforementioned requirement that Chinese citizens paid taxes commensurate with their actual ability to pay, and Emperor Taizong's statement that a reasonable tax burden should be borne by those who could afford it or else it was folly. Quesnay himself reveled in the fact that the share of tax paid by Chinese subjects was based on both the size of their estates and the quality of the land, and that the Chinese emperor, even as a matter of custom, exempted one or two disaster-stricken provinces from taxation every year. He also noted from Du Halde's report that "the annual tax total [in China] is a thousand millions of [French] money" (Quesnay, 1946, pp. 220–221), which was a small amount compared to the size of the country, thus proving that "property, though of high value, is taxed but little" (p. 221). This is apparently another example of the light taxation of China that he had in mind to substantiate his principle of a reasonable tax burden.

What's more, the Physiocrats' other principles of taxation, such as the argument for the superiority of direct over indirect taxation, can also be seen in the ancient Chinese idea of taxation. Even Montesquieu (1989, pp. 226–227) said, "In despotic states, where direct taxes are established, the peoples are infinitely happier: witness Persia and China." However, the so-called direct taxation of the Physiocrats only referred to the collection of the net products of the land, and all other taxation, according to their understanding, was included in the category of indirect taxation. This is different from the general concepts of direct and indirect taxation.

It should be noted that Quesnay always looked at all the materials of thought from China with rose-colored eyes, and likewise, he tried his best to embellish and exaggerate them when he quoted Chinese taxation materials. For example, the principles of "regular levy," "evenness" and simplicity in Chinese taxation thought originally imply, to a different extent, the serious shortcomings of Chinese feudal reality, such as abnormal taxation, arbitrary apportionment and numerous formalities. However, in Quesnay's eyes, everything in China's tax collection became a perfect example, which is obviously an illusion. It cannot be denied that the various ideas, policies and systems of taxation developed in ancient China, after thousands of years of accumulation and development, did give considerable impetus to Quesnay's creation of a theory of taxation that was new and unique to Europeans. This assertion, in the light of the materials cited above, can also be said to be the opinion of Quesnay himself. This is rare for an independent thinker, which shows all the more that he was greatly influenced by the Chinese idea of taxation.

This fact has been recognized by some Westerners. Weulersse pointed out as early as 1910 that the Physiocrats' "advocacy of the single tax [was] based in part upon reports on practices in China" (Quoted in Maverick, 1940, p. 317). Reichwein (1925) further asserts that "Quesnay's theory of taxation, which plays an important part in his system, had been worked out on the lines of old Chinese law" (p. 108), and that "the latter (Quesnay's theory of taxation) were taken from the former (the Chinese tax-regulations)" (p. 109). Takimoto Seiichi (1931, p. 37) affirms, too, that Quesnay's single tax is China's tribute law. Even some Western scholars who claim that Quesnay's single tax might be inspired by British economist John Locke[8] have to admit that "the analogy of China so forcibly impressed the Physiocrats that they were

[8] Higgs (1897, p. 134), for example, says, "The *impôt unique* [...] had possibly been suggested to Quesnay by a statement of Locke that all taxes fall ultimately upon the land." Haney (1911, p. 149), too, claims, "[T]hey (the Physiocrats) argued, as Locke and others before them, that all

seized with an enthusiasm even for the Celestial government" (Higgs, 1897, p. 140). This is tantamount to admitting that ancient China is the source of the Physiocrats' theory of a single *impôt territorial*. The analysis in this section is intended to put this assertion on a more substantial and convincing basis.

III. **Other fiscal views**

Besides the theory of a single *impôt territorial*, the most prominent in the fiscal thought of the Physiocrats and the most obviously influenced by ancient Chinese fiscal thought, some of their other fiscal views are also more or less borrowed and absorbed from ancient China. Two examples are noted below.

1. The relationship between finance and economy.

The Physiocrats are considered to have touched upon the root of the relationship between economy and finance, which is nothing but their recognition that tax collection must be conducive to social and economic consolidation and development. This viewpoint is based on their argument for the unity of the interest of the people and that of the monarchy. Quesnay (1946) held, when discussing China's despotic system, that "[the sovereign's] interest, when properly understood, always agrees with that of the nation" (p. 271), because "[t]he natural laws establish a bond between the sovereign and the nation" (p. 271). This statement was widely spread among the Physiocrats. The Abbé Baudeau said, "The people's interests and the sovereign's are [...] necessarily one" (Quoted in Gide & Rist, 1915, p. 41 [Note 1]). "All our interests and wills," Mercier de la Rivière remarked, "will be linked to the interest and will of the sovereign, forming for our common good a harmony" (p. 46 [Note 1]). Hence Quesnay's famous statement: "Pauvres paysans, pauvre royaume! Pauvre royaume, pauvre roi!" (p. 5) This thinking and even language form are almost identical to those of the people-oriented financial maxim of Chinese Confucianism: "If the people have plenty, their prince will not be left to want alone. If the people are in want, their prince cannot enjoy plenty alone" (Confucius, 1869, p. 195). The Confucian view of cultivating tax sources by keeping wealth in the people is everywhere in Chinese ancient books. Many advocators emerged after Confucius, such as Xunzi (1990, p. 135), who remarked in the late Warring States Period, "If the lower classes are poor, the ruler will be poor; if they are prosperous, then the ruler will be rich." Sima Guang (1965) stated that in the Tang Dynasty, as the number of households increased, the scope of tax collection would naturally widen, which was why Liu Yan, at the helm of the treasury, always took as his first priority the care of the people. In the Ming Dynasty, Qiu Jun (1993) argued that those who are good at enriching the country must manage well first the wealth of the people and then that of the country, and that the monarch controls the use of taxation, which seems to work for the benefit of the country, but actually serves the interest of the people. All these scholars advocated enriching the feudal state finance on the basis of making the people rich, which involves the understanding of the relationship between finance and economy, and could be used by the Physiocrats when expounding similar ideas.

---

taxes must fall on land ultimately." Here again, we may see the prejudice of some British and American economists who always refer to Britain as the authentic birthplace of economics.

2. The idea of fiscal expenditure.

Gide and Rist (1915, p. 43) point out that in terms of fiscal issues, "the most interesting point of all is that they (the Physiocrats) thought the State should adapt its needs to meet its revenue, and not vice versa." In our view, what is even more interesting is that this financial view of the Physiocrats is exactly the same as the general fiscal principle of "keeping expenditure within the limits of revenues," which has been upheld since the Western Zhou in China.[9] The Physiocrats' views on fiscal revenue are mainly included in their theory of a single *impôt territorial* (See the discussion above). Therefore, the focus here is on the influence of ancient Chinese thought on their fiscal expenditure.

The Physiocrats attached great importance to the system of fiscal expenditure in ancient China, and Quesnay described in great detail the expenditure principles and expenditure items of this system in his works on China:

> According to the ancient principles of the Chinese Government, which regard the sovereign as the head of a great family, the emperor provides for all the needs of his officers. Portions of the provincial contributions are consumed by the salaries of all varieties of magistrates and other stipendiaries, by the maintenance of the poor, the old, and the invalids; by the payment of the troops, by the expenses of public works, by the maintenance of the posts and all the highways of the empire; by the outlay for examinations, the expenses for the trips of applicants for degrees; by the revenues which support the princes and princesses of the imperial family, by the relief that the emperor grants to provinces afflicted by calamities, by the rewards he distributes to encourage excellence and to mark good examples; or in recognizing the good services of those who, of whatever kind they may be, have obtained some advantage for the state or who are distinguished by exceptional acts.
>
> (Quesnay, 1946, pp. 221–222)

Moreover, Quesnay specified some other items which were included in the fiscal expenditures of the country, such as the expenses of the travel, necessary vessels, and carriages of the officials and their attendants who were summoned to the court from the provinces, or sent by the court to the provinces; the expenses of the travel of foreign envoys from the first day of their arrival to the time of their departure, and the expenses of their accommodation in the palace. He illustrated the principle of expenditure of fiscal resources by citing the example of public buildings, where the astonishingly magnificent houses, built by the public authorities, were particularly noteworthy for the enormous expense of their construction and for their special maintenance, praiseworthy for the care taken for their solidity, and for the convenience and security afforded to passing travelers, merchants and coachmen. The same was true of the highways, with small gardens with benches at intervals as resting places providing comfortable and pleasant resting places for pedestrians, with roadside guard posts set up and soldiers stationed to protect the safety of travelers, provide

[9] In the middle of the Tang Dynasty, Yang Yan clearly stated, according to Liu Xu (1975), that the cost of all labor and the payment of taxes were calculated before they were collected from the people, and the revenue was determined according to the expenses. This view of "basing the revenue on the expenditure" can only be found in the history of financial thought in ancient China. However, it has always been the principle of keeping expenditures within the limit of income that occupied the dominant position in ancient China.

road guides, and serve as post stations for the transmission of letters between the court and the localities. In particular, Quesnay mentioned that after the founding of the capital of Peking by the first emperor Kublai Khan of the Yuan Dynasty, the emperor had the 300-league-long Grand Canal dredged, which became one of the miracles that connected China from north to south, regularly transporting to Peking all the supplies needed by the imperial court, the garrison and the inhabitants of the city in four to five thousand ships with a load of eight tons. In Quesnay's (1946, pp. 221–224) opinion, all these expenditures, together with the funds for the daily inspection of the Canal and for sending work to repair it, were indispensable.

Having learned about the above-mentioned Quesnay's (1962) understanding and propaganda of China's principle of fiscal expenditure, we will not feel surprised at his inclusion within the "General Maxims for the Economic Government of an Agricultural Kingdom" of the following: "*the marketing and transport of produce and manufactured commodities should be facilitated, through the repair of roads and the navigation of canals, rivers, and the sea*" (p. 235); and "*the government should trouble itself less with economizing than with the operations necessary for the prosperity of the kingdom*; for very high expenditure may cease to be excessive by virtue of the increase of wealth" (p. 237). In other words, Quesnay saw in the Chinese example the necessity that "taxes ought to be paid liberally, and not grudgingly" (Gide & Rist, 1915, p. 38) for "establishing public works, making roads, etc." (p. 38).[10]

In the last section of *Despotism in China*, entitled "Accounting for the Public Funds", Quesnay (1946) said, "The accounting for the expenditure of state funds is a very complicated branch of government and very susceptible to disorder" (p. 301). He thought that, "to throw light upon the confusion of governmental expenditures" (p. 301), it is necessary to "[subject] this accounting to forms and strict rules, to prevent the dissipation of the state funds and to suppress the ingenious avidity and the fraudulent practices of the majority of accountants" (p. 301). To do this, however, entails the need to "enlighten the nation" (p. 302), because "ignorance is always the principal cause of the most disastrous errors of government, of the ruin of nations, and of the decadence of empires" (pp. 302–303). At this point, Quesnay again turned to China for the solution. He argued,

> [F]rom [such ignorance] China has always been so securely preserved by the ministry of the scholars, who occupy the foremost rank in the nation and who are as attentive in guiding the people by the light of reason, as in subjecting the government clearly to the natural and immutable laws which constitute the essential order of nations.
>
> (p. 303)

He went on to say,

> "In that immense empire, all the errors and all the malversations of the leaders are continually divulged in a publication authorized by the government, in order to assure, in all the provinces of the great kingdom, the observance of the laws against the abuse of authority, and to assure

[10] Jean-François Gerbillon (1735), a Jesuit who had been to China, once said that the Kang Xi emperor was never stingy with his money, and that the emperor did not complain about the expense of doing things for the good of the country. The influence of such an account on Quesnay is clear.

> continual enlightenment by a free opposition, which is one of the essential conditions of a secure and unalterable government."
>
> (p. 303)

It can be seen that he found the fundamental way to solve the accounting problem of fiscal expenditure from ancient China's knowledge of natural laws and its concrete measures such as free reporting and government notification.

What we are talking about here is not simply the issue of fiscal expenditure, but, by extension, an attempt to refute the view that the state can only have temporary forms of rule so that "the irregularity of governments is [thus] attributed to the natural order" (p. 303). Quesnay's refutation of "this absurd fatalism" also took China as "an example of a stable, permanent and invariable government" (p. 304). He asserted that "the laws which constitute the natural order are perpetual and immutable laws, and that the irregularities of governments are only betrayals of these paternal laws" (p. 303). The chaos in fiscal expenditure was only a manifestation of the chaos in the rule. In Quesnay's view, the Chinese government could overcome all kinds of chaotic phenomena, including that of fiscal expenditure, and always remain stable and lasting, which gives people an important enlightenment:

> Does not this vast empire, subjected to the natural order, present an example of a stable, permanent and invariable government, proving that the inconstancy of transitory governments has no other basis or rule except the inconstancy of men themselves? But can it not be said that this happy and perpetual uniformity in the government of China, only exists because this empire is less exposed than other states to the encroachments of neighboring powers? No, for does not China have formidable neighboring powers? Has it not been conquered? Has not its vast expanse had to undergo divisions and formed many kingdoms? It is, then, not to special circumstances that one must attribute the perpetuity of its government, but to an inherently stable order.
>
> (p. 304)

It was with this firm belief in the Chinese government that Quesnay attempted to transplant the so-called "inherently stable order" embodied in China's long history to his time in France, to rescue the country from its desperate financial and economic woes.

2 Population

Population is another important issue in the economic doctrines of the Physiocratic School. Mirabeau's famous *L'ami des hommes* (1756), and Quesnay's unpublished "Hommes,"[11] written for *l'Encyclopédie* in 1757, are both treatises on the subject. Other economic works of this School also deal with population extensively. It is

[11] The article "Hommes" was delivered to *l'Encyclopédie* in 1757 and retrieved by Quesnay in the same year. It was later mentioned by Du Pont in 1769 to readers of *Ephémérides*, but was not published in the journal. It was not until 1908 that the article was first published by a later author in *The Journal of the History of Economic Sociology*.

noteworthy that Quesnay's account of population was from the outset illustrated with the aid of Chinese materials, unlike his early elaborations of other economic theories, where he was always very careful not to reveal the source of his ideas. Moreover, unlike some of his other economic theories, which were either short-lived, such as the single *impôt territorial*, or were only rediscovered after a long period of time, such as the *Tableau Économique*, Quesnay's basic population argument was inherited directly, exaggerated and mixed with other plagiarized elements by Malthus, resulting in the infamous Malthusian Theory of Population. Therefore, it is undoubtedly a worthy task to study how Quesnay discovered and derived a distinctive set of demographic views from Chinese population and how such views are connected with ancient Chinese population thought.

I. **Attention to China's population**

Quesnay's (1946) first impression of China's population was that it was large and dense, which he repeatedly mentioned in his discussion of the extent and prosperity of the Chinese empire. He pointed out that China was by far the "most densely populated, and the most flourishing kingdom known" (p. 165) in the world. He quoted Le Comte by saying,

> [Even China's] smallest province [...] is so fertile and so populous that it alone could form a considerable state. [...] The ruler who is master of it [...] will assuredly have enough wealth and enough subjects to satisfy any reasonable ambition.

(p. 165)

In particular, Le Comte's description of the number and size of Chinese cities based on his experiences in China gave Quesnay a deep appreciation of the large size of China's population. For example, Le Comte was quoted to have said,

> I have seen [...] seven or eight cities, all larger than Paris [...]. There are more than eighty cities of the first order, comparable to Lyons, Rouen, or Bordeaux. Among two hundred of the second order, there are more than a hundred like Orléans, and among about twelve hundred of the third order there are to be found five to six hundred as large as Dijon or la Rochelle, not to speak of a prodigious number of villages that surpass in grandeur and in the number of inhabitants the cities of Marennes and St. Jean-de-Lus.

(pp. 165–166)

Quesnay was convinced of these accounts and cited them as proofs of China's massive population.

Another impression, a more striking one, of China's population on Quesnay was the poverty of large numbers of inhabitants due to overpopulation. Many reports from China during that period attested to this. In a report, for example, Du Halde "admitted the great poverty, and told of the exposure of infants to death, and the fact, so strange to Europeans, that famines were endured without riots and violence" (Quoted in Maverick, 1946, p. 24). J. F. Melon analyzed the above report at the time and said,

[I]f the population are in greater numbers than the harvest which must feed them, there must naturally be continuous famine; but, if it be poor distribution which causes the starving of a portion of the population, this fault is a gross one, which dishonors the Chinese government.

(p. 34)

Here Melon seemed to attribute the poverty more to the misdistribution of the government. Herr Osbeck, a Swedish priest, "expressed concern about the great pressure of population in China, which holds the Chinese in poverty despite their remarkable industry and excellent institutions" (p. 37). All of these arguments linked China's overpopulation to poverty in China. But they were limited to an analysis of China's demographic situation and were far from a general population theory.

Quesnay (1946) also paid great attention to this demographic problem in China, noting,

[I]n spite of the industry and sobriety of the Chinese people, the fertility of the soil, and the abundance that reigns, there are few countries that have so much poverty among the humbler classes. However great that empire may be, it is too crowded for the multitude that inhabit it. All Europe combined would not number so many families.

(p. 168)

He spoke of the various evils which arose in China from overpopulation in the following way:

People may be seen (in China) so poor that, unable to provide their infants with food, they expose them in the streets.

...

Misery produces in China an enormous number of slaves, or persons who indenture themselves under the condition that they may some time redeem their freedom. A man sometimes sells his son or even himself and his family for a very small price.

(pp. 168–169)

However, he was strongly opposed to placing on the Chinese government the responsibility for these terrible disasters:

[W]e must not blame this calamity upon the very constitution of a good government; for a bad government that destroys men by the confiscation of the wealth of a kingdom, or by reason of continual unjust and absurd wars stirred up by an inordinate ambition or by the monopoly of foreign commerce, presents to observers a much more horrible spectacle.

(p. 261)

In refuting the criticism of Chinese despotism by his contemporary Montesquieu, he stated more clearly that "[a] large population can accumulate only under a good government, for bad governments destroy wealth and men" (p. 244); that "[a] prodigious people and a bad government can not be found together in any kingdom in the world" (p. 244); and that "this prodigious number of people can be only a result of good government in the empire" (p. 246).

On the one hand, Quesnay wanted to maintain the image of China's good governance, and to present the large population as an inevitable consequence of this governance. On the other hand, he could not avoid the fact that China was overpopulated and had a large number of poor inhabitants. How to explain this phenomenon became one of the basic issues for Quesnay's population theory, which provided him with inspiration and facts to break away from the prevailing European mercantilist view that the more people there are, the more wealth they produce.

II. Relationship between population and wealth: the case of China

As we know, there was an important event in the founding history of the Physiocratic School, that is, a debate between Quesnay and Mirabeau in July 1757. It was prompted by the arguments presented by Mirabeau in his *L'ami des hommes*, mainly involving the relationship between population and wealth. Mirabeau held a mercantilist view, particularly under the influence of Cantillon, that "the greater the population, the greater the quantity of labor; the greater the quantity of labor, the greater the wealth" (Quoted in Zhao, 1976, pp. 74–75). Quesnay opposed this view, arguing "that Cantillon had set the plough before the oxen,—that population was not a means to national wealth, but *vice versa*" (Quoted in Higgs, 1897, p. 23). As a result of the debate, Mirabeau renounced his views and became a devotee of Quesnay.

Fox-Genovese (1976, p. 162) comments on the debate in the following way:

> The gap between Quesnay's and Mirabeau's understanding of the function of labor can be seen clearly in their attitudes towards China. Where Quesnay saw only the piteous waste of millions of human beings eking out a scant livelihood from a disastrously labor-intensive culture, Mirabeau saw a wondrously wise people who [were] 'persuaded that from the use of land depends … the means of subsistence which one extracts from them, … and that population is the only true wealth of the State.'

This comment is a rather superficial estimate of the impact that the demographic phenomenon in China had on Quesnay. Mirabeau's praise of China's large population is easy to understand, since it was a popular belief among European thinkers of that time that the more people there are, the more wealth there is. Moreover, Europe was suffering from an insufficient working population, and it was difficult for Europeans to appreciate the problems that would arise from overpopulation. In this case, Quesnay's attention to the consequences of overpopulation in the context of the Chinese experience was truly remarkable. The point is that Quesnay's use of China as an example of good governance and his regarding China's large population as a consequence of that good governance remove the politics of attributing the poverty to the Chinese government from the causes of overpopulation, so that he could look directly to the economic sphere for the causes. It was in this new search that Quesnay formulated an important proposition that would later have considerable influence in shaping the Malthusian Theory of Population, which states that population increases faster than wealth, and that overpopulation leads to national poverty.

With regard to the first part of this proposition, Quesnay evidently drew his inspiration from the demographic situation in China, for at that time, Europeans were still addicted to the desire for the source of wealth in large populations. He said,

> This prodigious multiplication of people, regarded as so useful and desirable in the states of Europe, sometimes produces appalling results. In Europe it is thought that a large population is the source of wealth, but this is to take the effect for the cause, for population exceeds

> wealth everywhere; it is wealth that multiplies both wealth and men; but the propagation of men always exceeds the wealth.
>
> (Quesnay, 1946, p. 168)

He added in another place,

> Population always exceeds wealth in both good and bad governments, because propagation is limited by nothing but subsistence, and always tends to increase even further; there are poor people everywhere.
>
> (p. 261)

These two quotes are from his observation of the demographic situation in China, rather than from that in European countries at the time, including France.

The latter part of the proposition had already been more fully elaborated by Quesnay (1888) in his "Hommes:" he repeatedly affirmed that the growth of population depends entirely on the increase of wealth, that wealth and population can be maintained only in conditions of affluence caused by wealth itself, and that if, on the contrary, the proportion of wealth and population is destroyed and the population appears to be larger, such overpopulation will impoverish the country more and more, wages will fall in proportion to the increase of population, and consumption will fall in proportion to the fall of wages. In his later works, such as the "General Maxims for the Economic Government of an Agricultural Kingdom," Quesnay (1962) devoted himself to the general maxim "*[t]hat less attention should be paid to augmenting the population than to increasing the revenue*" (p. 237), arguing, "Some superficial thinkers imagine that great wealth in a state is obtained as a result of an abundance of men; but their view springs from the fact that they forget that men can obtain and perpetuate wealth only by means of wealth, and only to the extent that a proper proportion exists between men and wealth" (pp. 259–260). Since there was no overpopulation in Europe in Quesnay's time, it would be futile to uncover the intellectual roots of the above ideas in the context of Europe itself. It is best to look at Quesnay's own answer as to where his ideas came from.

In the same treatise on population, Quesnay (1888) began with the idea that when a country reaches a high level of prosperity, both in terms of population and products, people will benefit the country more with their wealth than with the size of their population. When wealth is great, people are prosperous, and their consumption, commensurate with their wealth, promotes the production of wealth and maintains the power of the state. On the contrary, if the size of the population is excessive in relation to the amount of wealth obtained from the land and from foreign trade, such an excessive population does not contribute to the increase of wealth, but rather to the rise in the prices of food products through its consumption. If the population is too large, then consumption is limited to the most urgent necessities. As a result, the country will go from prosperity to poverty. It will not be possible for people to cut back on their consumption in order to allocate a portion of it to the expenses of the government and the defense of the country. Such a country would be obliged to make the land produce the most necessary things, and thus limit its own consumption. And such is the condition of the population of China, which, though vast and rich in land, can only secure for its inhabitants rice and some other grains which serve as food. The Chinese are well managed, have no wars, and do not invade other countries, and their population has increased more than the means of subsistence which a vast and well cultivated country can supply, though this circumstance which impels the excessive growth of population is not found in other countries.

Since such overpopulation did not occur in other countries, when he made the proposition that overpopulation would lead to national poverty, he relied solely on the example of China. In his early economic writings, it was rare for him to state so openly that his theories were based on a single country.

Quesnay's admission that his population theory was inspired by China's demographic situation may have had something to do with the fact that China was then in the Qian Long era, a period of rapid population growth that lasted several decades. It was likely that he got this information from the reports of the Westerners who had been to China at that time. However, in describing China's population at considerable length, he did not mention whether he had access to information on ancient Chinese demographic thought. The exploration of this question is directly related to the sources of his unique population theory.

In ancient China, population issues received special attention. Official documents, historians' records, and private writings dealing with relevant issues throughout the ages have been voluminous, resulting in the preservation of an extremely rich collection of demographic statistics and ideas. One of the most interesting aspects is that ancient Chinese, when discussing the relationship between population and wealth, formed at a very early time some ideas similar to Quesnay's population proposition. For example, during the pre-Qin period, Guanzi and Shang Yang initially realized the relative surplus of population from the perspective of the comparative relationship between population and land. In *Guanzi* is recorded the following remark: "If [a state's] territory is extensive but not well managed, it is called being satisfied with [mere] land. If its population is large but not well ordered, it is called being satisfied with [merely] having people" (Guanzi, 2001, p. 360). This was the first time in Chinese history that the concept of relative overpopulation was put forward. And in *Book of Shang Yang—land calculation*, the so-called "limited land with numerous people" also refers to overpopulation; Shang Yang proposed a solution to the problem of large population, that is, to expand the cultivation of land when population is too big. At the end of the Warring States period, Han Fei Tzŭ (1959) raised the problem of population growth again, saying, "Nowadays, [...] people do not regard five children as many. Each child may in his or her turn beget five offspring, so that before the death of the grandfather there may be twenty-five grand-children" (pp. 276–277). What he meant is that the population had doubled over the past three generations, and that the large population was the source of chaos. His analysis in the chapter of "Five Vermin" in *The Complete Works of Han Fei Tzŭ* is as follows: "In olden times, [...] [a]s the people were few, their possessions were more than sufficient" (p. 276); but in his times, "people have become numerous and supplies scanty; toil has become hard and provisions meager. Therefore people quarrel" (p. 277). He noticed for the first time the inverse relationship between population and wealth, and was concerned about the rapid population growth. Here, he regarded the fact that "people have become numerous and supplies scanty" as the inevitable result of historical development and the social reality at that time, and argued that "though rewards are doubled and punishments repeated, disorder is inevitable" (p. 277). In fact, this population view already embodies the theoretical premise that the growth rate of the means of subsistence cannot keep up with the population reproduction speed that leads to overpopulation, that is, absolute surplus of population. In the Northern Song Dynasty, Su Shi (1935) believed that a large population is not only useless to the rich, but also is the source of trouble. Ma Duanlin (1986), a famous historian of the Song and Yuan Dynasties, studied the population quality, so as to prove that the number of people is not crucial to the prosperity or decline of a country, and reject the traditional view of the increase or decrease in the number of people as a measure of the prosperity or decline of a country. Xu Guangqi (1956) explicitly put forward at the end of the Ming Dynasty the concept of population growth rate, by stating that the birth rate is doubled in about 30 years and that it cannot be reduced unless there is a big war. And in the Qing dynasty of the late eighteenth century, Hong Liangji (1965), a famous scholar of the Qing Dynasty, put forward in the two sections entitled "Governance" and "Livelihood" of *Yi Yan* a very typical set of views on absolute overpopulation. His main points are as follows: the household in a hundred years increases in turn from five times, ten times to twenty times, while the cultivated land in the same period only gradually doubles, from one time, three times to five times, lagging far behind the growth rate of the household; and overpopulation is the cause of social poverty and unrest. The remedies he put forward are firstly "regulation by heaven and earth," which refers to the population reduction caused by floods, droughts and epidemics, and secondly "regulation by the monarch," which refers to emigration, reclamation, relief and tax reduction.

Among the above-mentioned representative views on population in ancient China, Xu Guangqi's argument, with the transmission of his agricultural ideas to the West, may have attracted Quesnay's attention, while Hong Liangji's writings were certainly not seen by Quesnay because of their late completion. It is still difficult to determine whether the views on population by the representative Legalists such as Han Fei Zi (Han Fei Tzŭ) were ever introduced to the West and understood by Quesnay. However, there is no doubt that Quesnay's new arguments on the relationship between population and wealth are unique and unprecedented among European scholars, and in the history of Chinese population thought, there have already been a number of very similar early ideas. It is also surprising that both Quesnay and Hong Liangji, within a gap of only thirty years, came to almost identical conclusions about absolute overpopulation based on their observations of the same demographic phenomenon in China. Therefore, there are only two possibilities about the origin of Quesnay's unique population theory: one is that he drew his inspiration from China and developed it through his own independent thinking; the other is that he not only drew his inspiration from China but also benefited from the influence of some similar early population views in ancient China. In whatever the case, Quesnay himself repeatedly showed the importance of the demographic situation in China as an inspiration for his new theory of population, which need not be repeated here. However, due to the limitation of the materials currently available, it is still not known for sure whether the above-mentioned population thought in ancient China really had an impact on him, which awaits further exploration in the future.

Moreover, Quesnay not only drew distinctive demographic propositions from the Chinese example he focused on, but also rejected the notion that the Chinese government was to blame for the poverty in ancient China. In the chapter under the title "Asserted Shortcomings of the Government of China," Quesnay (1946) devoted to the issue a whole section titled "Overpopulation and Unequal Distribution of Wealth," in which he stated,

> Perhaps it may better be said that [...] it is the inequality in the distribution of property that gives abundance to some and refuses necessaries to the others; that hence, the population of a kingdom would not exceed its wealth if the wealth of the nation were more equally distributed. This may be partly true in nations given to the plunder of irregular taxes or of monopolies in commerce and agriculture authorized through bad administration of the government. For these disorders form sudden hoards of wealth that are not distributed, but cause a void in the circulation that can only be filled at the cost of suffering. But wherever the status of the rich is founded upon the ownership of real property from which they draw a large annual income that they spend annually, the poverty of a number of inhabitants cannot be attributed to inequality in the distribution of wealth.
>
> (p. 261)

Government relief is also a redistribution of wealth, about which Quesnay, when discussing China's extent and prosperity, said,

> One might think that alms-giving is not encouraged enough by the government; but alms cannot adequately provide against this; for in the system of distribution of necessaries, the wages paid to men for their labor enable them to live. What is distributed as alms is a deduction from the amount distributed as wages, which make it possible for men without property to live.
>
> (p. 168)

He further argued,

> Alms are necessary to provide for the pressing needs of the indigent who are unable to provide for themselves; but they always involve a deflection to an equal extent from the system of labor and the circulation of wealth which recreates the wealth necessary for human subsistence. Thus, when population exceeds wealth, alms cannot provide against the inevitable poverty of the excess population.
>
> (p. 169)

The distribution of wealth, according to Quesnay, has nothing to do with the causes of people's poverty and can be redistributed by the consumption of the rich without government intervention. He pointed out,

> Those who have incomes can consume them only with the assistance of the labor and services of those who have no income; the outlay of the one is the income of the others. The proceeds from the consumption of high priced products are paid to those who created them, reimbursing them so that they can make the outlays needed to reproduce them. It is thus that disbursals multiply and perpetuate riches.
>
> (pp. 168–169)

Quesnay expressed the same opinion when he discussed the overpopulation and the unequal distribution of wealth in the Chinese empire:

> The rich, it is true, enjoy abundance and actually so much the more when they are effectively consuming their wealth; but they cannot consume their wealth without the services of other men, who profit by their expenditures, for it is impossible for men to spend without some profiting from others. This is what forms that constant circulation of wealth upon which all the inhabitants of a well-governed kingdom base their hopes. Thus, in effect, it is only the amount of the wealth which sets a limit to population.
>
> (p. 262)

These views, as developed in *Despotism in China*, were briefly summed up in Quesnay's (1888) early treatise on population in a passage underlined, which is to the effect that what men spend out of their own wages or earnings can be of benefit to others, and become again a source of producing and restoring wealth. It shows the importance he attached to this argument.

Coincidentally, in the ancient history of China, there were many arguments for such views or measures. For example, the concept of "luxury consumption" recorded in *Guanzi*, a classic from the pre-Qin period, stresses that in the economic downturn consumption should be encouraged: "Let the rich live in luxury and the poor do work for them" (Guanzi, 1998, p. 311). This means that the luxury consumption of the rich not only depends on the work of the poor, but also provides the poor with the opportunity to work, which is why consumption is stimulated to promote production. In the Western Han Dynasty, Sang Hongyang agreed with the idea from *Guanzi*, saying that the extravagant consumption of the rich can increase the livelihood of the poor, i.e. increasing consumption can expand exchanges to stimulate production (Huan, 1931, pp. 22–23). In the Northern Song Dynasty, Fan Zhongyan and Shen Kuo both believed that increasing consumption can stimulate production and increase employment, and Fan successfully used this measure to deal with the famine in Hangzhou (Shen, 2008, p. 359). In the Ming Dynasty, Lu Ji (1991) also said that the luxury consumption of the rich can make equally well-off all the people in the country. It is not known whether these views of extravagant consumption in ancient China had any influence on the same kind of ideas in Quesnay's population theory, but it is certain that the two are consistent in their basic arguments.

In short, Quesnay believed that the widespread poverty in China was due to overpopulation and could not be blamed on the Chinese government, whose good governance was impeccable. The point is that there is always an inherent tendency in society for population to reproduce more than wealth, and overpopulation inevitably leads to poverty. It was only because the population had grown to excess under the good rule of China that this tendency of population growth was made evident there. In other words, the conditions for the manifestation of this so-called population growth trend did not yet exist in the European demographic context.

This view of population is clearly wrong, both in theory and in practice. However, its uniqueness lies in the fact that Quesnay invented or created this population theory by observing and studying the demographic situation in China, which was thought to be unique at that time, or, as he said, not found in any other country. Malthus then put forward the so-called eternal "natural law of population" based on the principle that population grows geometrically, while the means of life grows arithmetically, which is just a mathematical expression of Quesnay's basic assertion that population always grows faster than wealth. This is why Higgs (1897, p. 136) points out, "Malthus (…) shows in his writings an affinity with the Physiocrats, which must undoubtedly be traced to their direct influence. Quesnay and Mirabeau had laid down propositions which contain the germ of his theory of population, though his views on this subject were probably arrived at independently." Schumpeter (1954a, p. 257) also says,

> [Quesnay] held not only that propagation has no other limits than those of subsistence but also that it tends *always* to go beyond them. The only justification he proffered for this dogmatic statement was that, always and everywhere, there are people who live in poverty or want (*indigence*). This overpopulation theory of poverty is of the essence of 'Malthusianism.'

Schumpeter's interpretation of Quesnay's "only justification" here is not entirely accurate. The above arguments make it abundantly clear that Quesnay was prompted to put forward a new view of population when he saw the poverty caused by overpopulation in China, his most admired example. That the poverty of the population in other regions or countries in general did not concern him as much as that of China was not denied by him, and therefore the example of China was his "only justification."

Whether Quesnay's population theory was based on ancient Chinese demographic views contained in the Chinese materials available to him still requires further research. An important basis for such a study is that, prior to Quesnay's population theory, there had been no similar theoretical viewpoint or "germ" in the West, while there had been no lack of the precursor ideas in ancient China.

III. **Solution to China's "overpopulation"**

Quesnay's interest in China's overpopulation can also be seen in his vision of finding a way out of the country's problem. He referred to the laws of the Incas that forbade marriage before the age of 20 for women and 25 for men, in order to ensure that children would offer services to their parents for a longer period of time and thereby increase their wealth. In his view, this law was equally applicable to China, where it also had the advantage of preventing an overpopulation which appeared unfavorable to the reputation of the government (Quesnay, 1946, p. 263). This approach, which envisioned a ban on early marriage as a means of curbing population growth, is somewhat akin to what was in the later Malthusian Theory of Population called preventive "moral restraint," i.e., preventing from getting married poor, working people who were unable to support their families. Quesnay did not push further this line of thought, however, but turned to another approach, namely the opening of foreign colonies.

This approach had already been mentioned by J. F. Melon in his *Essai Politique sur le Commerce*, the first edition of which was published in Paris in 1734 and the second in 1736. He stated that in 4,000 years, China had not had a man of genius who had thought deeply enough about colonization as a way out of overpopulation, and that China could easily reach the large islands off its coast, and would see in them an opportunity to get rid of overpopulation (Maverick, 1946, p. 34). Quesnay

(1946, pp. 262–263), as can be seen below, is said to have "borrowed" Melon's views without acknowledging them:

> In order to prevent overcrowding, in a well-governed nation, there is no other recourse but that of colonies, which can be established under the auspices of a good administration. The colonial communities founded by emigration of excess population, drawn by the fertility of a new territory, relieve the nation of a multitude of poor who require much attention and special protection on the part of the government. In this respect one may find in the administration of the government and in the inhabitants of China a clearly reprehensible fault.
>
> In the vicinity of this empire there are many large islands, deserted or partially desert, of which some time ago, Europeans took possession. Could not these lands have been a great outlet for the surplus population of China? True, nostratism, or love of country, is so strong among the Chinese that they cannot bring themselves to leave their own country. But it also appears that they are not led in that direction by the administration, since it tolerates the exposure of infants and the slavery of many subjects reduced to extremities, rather than encouraging the founding of settlements outside the country that would tie entirely to the benefit of the population and would thereby relieve overcrowding in the kingdom. This is to fail in a duty that humanity and religion prescribe, which would provide opportunities for all, and is well worthy of the attention of those charged by providence with the government of nations. In fulfilling this duty they would re-establish their dominion and promote the propagation of the human race.

Here, Quesnay saw emigration to establish colonies as the only solution to China's overpopulation, and it was on this issue that he was critical of the inaction of the Chinese government, which was so careful in other affairs but was helpless in the face of a large number of slaves caused by overpopulation (pp. 262–263). This was a rare view for someone who was always a great admirer of China, and it further demonstrated Quesnay's eagerness to solve China's overpopulation problem. However, it was rather absurd of him to propose, on the basis of Westerners' logic, colonization as a solution to China's overpopulation—absolute overpopulation in his view: this was far beyond the policy of pioneering land by emigrants and settlers, advocated and implemented by many generations of Chinese rulers in the past. But it is a clear fact that his effort to take China as the research object, and devote himself to exploring and summarizing the population situation in China (probably directly inspired by the ancient Chinese population thought), though rarely understood by Europeans at that time, had an important influence on later economists.

To sum up, we can find that, first, Quesnay paid great attention to China's population problem, exploring and putting forward a set of demographic views that are completely different from those by European mercantilists. Second, he took the demographic situation of China as the only basis for the basic proposition that population growth is faster than the growth of wealth, and that overpopulation will impoverish the country. This proposition was later elaborated and publicized by Malthus, and had a great influence on Western economic theorists. Third, guided by his China-admiring mentality, he took the population growth in China as a result of its good governance, so that the poverty caused by overpopulation must not be attributed to the improper distribution of the Chinese government and the government's mistake lay only in its failure to evacuate these surplus population by opening up foreign colonies. Fourth, in European history, his theory of population is distinctive and unsupported because it has no precedent or origin, but there is no lack of similar population views in ancient China. All these findings show that Quesnay's population theories, especially those unique ideas, whether correct or not, are to a large extent the product of his diligent study of the population problem in China, a country he set as a model. Although he was exposed to a large number of Chinese population data, in the vogue for China then prevalent in France and even in the whole of Europe, it remains to be further investigated whether he was directly inspired or influenced by the ancient Chinese thought on population. Still, the fact that his population theories are outside the European tradition and close to certain population ideas of ancient China is enough to show that the source of his ideas is not confined to the European tradition, but may have been enriched by the ancient Chinese thought transmitted to the West.

3 Property Ownership

The Physiocrats attached great importance to property ownership and repeatedly stressed that private ownership is in line with the natural order.

One of the general guidelines proposed by Quesnay is that the rightful ownership of immovable and movable property must be guaranteed: "The safety of private property is the real basis of the economic order of society" (Quoted in Gide & Rist, 1915, p. 25). Mercier de la Rivière also said, "It is impossible not to recognise the right of property as a divine institution, for it has been ordained that this should be the indirect means of perpetuating the work of creation" (p. 21 [Note 2]). In his view, property can be likened to a tree, and all kinds of social systems are branches growing from the trunk (p. 25). On this issue, the Physiocrats again actively looked for the basis to support their argument from Chinese examples. A typical case is Quesnay's *Despotism in China*, in which he devoted a special section to the ownership of wealth and classified it into the category of China's fundamental laws. Quesnay (1946) pointed out in this section,

> The ownership of wealth is quite secure in China; we have previously seen that the right of property is extended even to slaves or bonded domestics, and throughout the empire children inherit the wealth of their parents and of relatives according to the natural order of the right of succession.
>
> (p. 203)

In particular, he described the inheritance of assets under the Chinese concubinage system as follows:

> Although by their laws a Chinese may not have more than one legitimate wife, [...] nevertheless having several concubines is permitted. [...] These second wives are definitely inferior to the legitimate wife and they must respect her as the mistress of the home. Their children are regarded as belonging to the first wife [...]. These children have the right, [...] to inherit from the father along with children of the legitimate wife, if there are any, which shows the extent of the right of inheritance and the security of the right of property in this empire.
>
> (pp. 203–204)

It was from the fact that the inheritance tradition of common Chinese families differs from the European tradition of primogeniture, that he tended to feel that the property ownership in China was more secure.

He also spoke of the special protection of property ownership in China from a different perspective. He noted, for example, that "[s]eizure [of land] is not practiced upon those who are slow in paying; for that would ruin the families, who would then become charges of the state" (p. 220). Here, the confiscation of property was for him an infringement of the sacred right to private property. When describing Chinese public revenue, he further argued that such punishment would be detrimental to the production of wealth:

> If there were no possessors of the lands, to whom the ownership was assured, and if the lands were common, they would be neglected, for none would wish to assume the expense of improvement or maintenance, if his profit were not assured.
>
> (p. 291)

He justified the Chinese Government's failure to address poverty through wealth distribution: "[W]herever the status of the rich is founded upon the ownership of real property [...], the poverty of a number of inhabitants cannot be attributed to inequality in the distribution of wealth" (p. 261). This means that the Chinese Government's practice is motivated by the belief in the protection of property ownership. He admitted that a farmer in China "spends whole days digging or ploughing by hand. ... This peasant, however, has his liberty and property assured; there is no chance of his being despoiled by arbitrary impositions, nor by exactions of tax collectors" (p. 170). It was under this protection of property ownership in China that "[m]en are very hardworking, wherever they are assured the benefits of their labor. However small the earning may be, it is the more precious to them, because it is their sole resource to provide for their needs" (p. 170). Even the Chinese slave-servants, in his view, enjoyed the protection of private property:

> The authority of masters over slaves is limited to ordinary duties, and they treat them like their own children; also, the slaves' loyalty to their masters is inviolable. If any slave acquires money by his own industry the master has no right to take the slave's wealth, and the slave may buy back his freedom if his master consents, or if he has retained the right to do so in his indenture.
>
> (pp. 169–170)

Thus, Quesnay, to characterize the Chinese system, specially foregrounded "Personal Liberty" and "Ownership of the Necessaries Produced Daily." The specific explanation is as follows:

> [Nature] has decreed that the right of each individual is limited, in the natural order, to what he can obtain by his own labor. Thus, the right of everyone to everything is an idle fancy. Liberty of the person, and property, or the assurance of enjoying the products that each procures primarily through looking out for his own needs, are thus henceforth guaranteed to man by the natural laws which constitute the essential order of properly regulated societies.
>
> (pp. 283–284)

Of course, Quesnay did not have to derive entirely from the Chinese system his concept of property ownership, but his assumption that the Chinese system of private ownership was secure and consistent with the natural order did contribute positively to his emphasis on the concept of private ownership of property.

Of all property ownership, the most important, both for Quesnay himself and for the social realities of China, which he revered, was land ownership. Quesnay described the existence of the proprietors as what the "order of society presupposes" (Quoted in Gide & Rist, 1915, p. 21 [Note 2]). Mercier de la Rivière called the landed proprietor the "foremost and most essential agent of production" (p. 22 [Note 4]). "The *class of proprietors*," according to Quesnay's (1962, p. 150) definition in his "Analysis of the Arithmetical Formula of the *Tableau Économique* of the Distribution of Annual Expenditure in an agricultural Nation," "includes the sovereign, the owners of land, and the tithe-owners," all of whom are considered to have contributed to social production. The contribution of the landowner is the investment in land, i.e., the advance payment of the cost of preparing the land for cultivation and thus for the production of net products. The sovereign's is the so-called "investment of the monarchy," i.e., the building of roads, canals and other public facilities, as well as the enforcement of laws to ensure the security of property, the maintenance of the balance of the economic system, the proper functioning of the social and natural order, etc. (pp. 150–202). In this regard, Gide and Rist (1915, pp. 19–20) say that the Physiocratic School divided society into three classes—the productive, proprietary and sterile classes and that "[t]he singular position which the proprietors [held] in this tripartite division of society is one of the most curious features of the system" (p. 21). In fact, this feature can be analyzed by a correct understanding of the feudalistic appearance that the Physiocratic system gave. What is worth mentioning is why the Physiocrats placed so much emphasis on the role of monarchical investment in the social economy of the landowning class and included it in their famous theory of prepayment, that is, the theory of capital. If we see Quesnay talking about the Chinese emperors' unstinting investment in various public works such as roads and canals, and his praise of the Chinese monarchy as "perfect government" and "protective power," we will not find it difficult to understand why his economic theory carries the Chinese "feudal signboard" (Marx, 1992, p. 436), in addition to its French counterpart, everywhere in his fervor to follow the Chinese example.

Finally, it should be noted that the Physiocrats also drew on or referred to Chinese sources to varying degrees in their discussion of other economic issues such as distribution, consumption, and wages. The economic theory of Quesnay, according to Takimoto Seiichi (1931, p. 37), lays special emphasis on distribution, which is no different from Confucius' saying—"Do not worry about scarcity but unequal distribution"—and the statement that "distribution should be equal for the benefit of the people" in *The Book of Yi Zhou*. These issues have been touched upon, though not discussed in detail, in the different places of the previous chapters and does not have to be repeated here.

Chapter 9
Conclusion

Now the conclusion of the whole book: first a general picture of the Westward spread of Chinese culture in the seventeenth and eighteenth centuries, and then a chapter-by-chapter summary of the seven key aspects of Physiocracy that have been greatly influenced by ancient Chinese thought.

1 The Westward Spread of Chinese Culture

From the sixteenth century onwards, the works of various pre-Qin scholars represented by Confucianists, together with the Neo-Confucianists of the Song Dynasties, and the reports on China's laws and systems, were successively introduced into Europe by Jesuit priests to China. Especially since the beginning of the seventeenth century, the century-long controversy within the European Church over the Chinese rites gave a great impetus to the spread of ancient Chinese thought in the West. At the same time, the massive trafficking of Chinese artifacts and specialties to Europe had a profound impact on the Rococo cultural movement in that period. Under the influence of these important factors, the vogue for China spread throughout Europe and reached its climax in the first half of the eighteenth century.[1]

The eighteenth century in Europe was an era of Greek and Chinese philosophical thought paralleling each other. Europe had been deeply influenced by Greek culture in the Renaissance, but in the Enlightenment, Greek influence was replaced by that of Chinese culture (Zhu, 1957, p. 49). Even among European scholars, it

[1] Maverick (1946, p. 124) says, "The vogue [for China and Chinese objects] had begun a half -century earlier under Louis XIV, and was revived at intervals, until in the middle of the century under Louis XV it reached a high pitch."

M. Tan, *The Chinese Origin of Physiocracy*,
https://doi.org/10.1007/978-981-97-9703-5_9

was proposed that the ancient Greek civilization originated from China.[2] Most of the famous European thinkers in the period from the sixteenth to eighteenth century studied Chinese philosophy, to facilitate their long-term debate on Chinese culture, whether as proponents or as opponents of the culture. As a result, just as Reichwein (1925, pp. 88–89) says, "[a] more or less generally accepted conception of the Chinese had gradually formed itself in the European mind, and this was continually being held up as a model."[3] This image of China as a "model" was infatuated and worshipped by Europeans at that time, which is hardly imaginable to the modern mind. Indeed, "[i]n the eighteenth century it was China that fascinated" (Hudson, 1931, p. 25), both in general fashion, where "everything Chinese was in fashion and indiscriminately admired" (p. 286), and in the educated class, of which every intellectual was "better informed about China" (p. 327).

At the end of the seventeenth century, France came to be the center and origin of spreading Chinese culture in Europe. Important eighteenth-century French thinkers, such as Voltaire, Rousseau, Montesquieu, Diderot, and Holbach, all expressed admiration for Chinese culture to varying degrees. Voltaire, the greatest authority of the Enlightenment, was so enamored of Chinese culture that he advocated "complete sinicization." "Many minds," Reichwein (1925, p. 92) claims, "were possessed by the notion that the salvation of France depended on its permeation with the ennobling spirit of China." Indeed, the French interest in Chinese cultural civilization, at least among art lovers, had been preserved for a long time. This interest continued into the nineteenth century.

Many scholars have explored from various angles the reasons for the great repercussion of the spread of Chinese culture in Europe. Zhu Qianzhi (2005b, p. 266) argues that the impact was due to the qualities of Chinese philosophy, and strengthens his point by quoting Du Halde's (1741, p. 39) observation: "[T]he Moral Philosophy of the Chinese is of a Popular Nature, tending rather to reform the Manners of Mankind than to increase the Number of its own Disciples. Tho' among their Philosophers there was not the same Glow of Wit which distinguish'd those of Greece and Rome, it is easy to perceive that their Discourses are accommodated to the Capacities of the Vulgar." The introduction of this Chinese philosophy coincided with or advanced the European Enlightenment, which called for a popular and practical

[2] The ritual objects of the ancient Greek gods, according to a French scholar, were introduced to the West from China. This view was influenced by the popular Chinese culture in Europe in the first half of the eighteenth century.

[3] Many Western scholars support this view. Joseph Needham (1956, p. 496), for example, who has a favorite view of China, says that in the seventeenth and eighteenth centuries, "[s]ome of the best minds of Europe gave themselves in due course to the study of Chinese philosophy by means of the Jesuit despatches." Even those who were prejudiced against China, such as Heinz Gollwitzer (1962), the author of *Die Gelbe Gefahr: Geschichte eines Schlagworts, Studien zum Imperialistischen Denken*, admitted that from the sixteenth to eighteenth century, according to the Jesuit missionaries, there were many in Europe who found the Chinese moral and social system ideal, the social philosophy of the state of Confucius even superior to those of some European traditions, and the Chinese literature and art works fascinating. The Enlightenment scholars, such as Leibniz, Wolff, Voltaire to the Physiocrats, made frequent warm and friendly comments on the Far East.

philosophy, and was therefore welcomed and acclaimed at the time. Hudson (1931, pp. 309–310) points out, "In comparing Chinese with European thought during the seventeenth and eighteenth centuries [...], account must also be taken of the extraordinary social and political success of Chinese culture under the conditions it had so far had to meet. ... In China the traditional system was so successful in practice that there was little disposition to tamper with its theoretical presuppositions." This is regarded as another important reason why Chinese thought had a great influence on Europe at that time. Zhu Jieqin (2005a, p. 3) states more clearly in his preface to Zhu Qianzhi's book, "Facts have proved that China outperformed Europe in many aspects of the material and cultural civilization in the eighteenth century [...]. The Age of Enlightenment was not only the heyday when Chinese culture was introduced into Europe, but also a crucial link between the past and the future in the history of cultural exchanges between China and the West." These opinions can be summarized as follows. First, the Westward spread of Chinese culture provided a medium for Western Enlightenment scholars and reformers to realize or repose their ideals. Second, European thinkers did find much new to draw from Chinese culture. In both respects, the Physiocrats, Quesnay in particular, were the primary figures linking Chinese culture closely to the establishment of their own doctrines.

Known at that time as "the Confucius of Europe," Quesnay advocated Chinese philosophy, held Confucius' virtues and teachings in high esteem, used *The Analects of Confucius* as a bible, established an organization of "economists" following the example of the Confucian school, and formulated on the basis of the maxims of Confucius his own "General Maxims for the Economic Government of an Agricultural Kingdom." Even the eulogy delivered by his disciples after his death described his life's main achievements as the implementation of Confucius' teachings. Quesnay's enthusiasm for Chinese philosophy, particularly Confucianism, was partly due to the fact that it was the fashion of the time and partly to the circumstances of his life. That Quesnay was the imperial physician to the Marquise de Pompadour, the mistress of Louis XV, who was very fond of and devoted to the study of Chinese relics, naturally added to Quesnay's love of Chinese culture. It was through Pompadour's persuasion that Louis XV later held the ceremony of "ploughing the land" in imitation of that practiced by the emperors in ancient China.

Quesnay seldom mentioned the source of his ideas in his early economic writings, but even so, his unpublished early treatise, "Hommes," revealed his admiration for China as a "well managed" and "well cultivated" country. He ingeniously revealed the source of his real thoughts, however, when he, in the first chapter of *Philosophie Rurale*, which he co-authored with Mirabeau, printed a picture of the Chinese emperor in a farming procession, and when he instructed Du Pont to mark as "Peking" the address of the first edition of this Physiocratic monograph. The most representative of all is his last book, *Despotism in China* (1769), which consists of eight chapters (with altogether forty-nine sections): the first chapter, "Introduction," includes an overview of China's origin, territory, prosperity, social hierarchy, military power, etc.; the other chapters respectively discuss "Fundamental Laws of the Empire," "Positive Legislation," "Taxation," "Authority," "Administration," "Asserted Shortcomings of the Government of China," and "Comparison of Chinese

Laws with the Natural Principles Underlying Prosperous Governments" (in the last chapter as the conclusion). Such an exhaustive treatise devoted to the praise of the Chinese monarchy is clearly a culmination of his many years of extensive collection and systematic study of Chinese materials. This achievement of Quesnay's later years reflects his strong desire to seek from the Chinese model answers to the real problems in France, which in fact reveals the Chinese origin of his economic doctrines. He had been exploring this important source relentlessly for more than ten years, providing us with valuable first-hand information.

Another important representative advocator of Physiocracy is Turgot, once the Chancellor of the Exchequer, who worked hard to promote the policy of the Physiocrats. He was at the forefront of advocating China at the time, making the Physiocratic School more prominent, and some of his close associates, like Voltaire and Poivre, were famous for their advocacy of learning from China. He had direct contact with two Chinese students, called *les Chinois de Turgot*, and played an active role in extending the two's studies in France. In particular, while studying economics with the two Chinese students, Turgot wrote his famous book on economics, *Réflexions*, which has become a great episode in the history of economic theory. Turgot himself publicly stated several times that this work was addressed to the two Chinese students as a "preface" to help them understand his *Questions*. *Réflexions* and *Questions* supplement each other, from which we can find that many economic theoretical problems investigated by Turgot are, to varying degrees, related to his knowledge of Chinese thought. These economic theories were expected to be confirmed by Chinese examples, were inspired by Chinese materials, were directly nourished by ancient Chinese thoughts, or at least are quite similar to Chinese traditional doctrines. At the same time, there are some similarities between his economic policies and ancient Chinese economic measures, although the two embodied very different spirits of the times. It is noteworthy that Turgot, who was already of high political and academic standing at that time, posed dozens of questions for two little-known Chinese students and wrote a special book for them called *Réflexions*, and the King of France answered the appeals of Turgot and others and specially approved financial support for the two students. This shows that in the minds of the French people at that time, the spread of Chinese thought was already very influential, and they wanted to continue to strengthen this Chinese influence. Whether the Chinese students had much effect after their return was, however, irrelevant to China and of little concern to France.

As economists, Quesnay and Turgot are considered to have occupied different positions in the admiration of China, with the former above the latter. Maverick's (1946, pp. 113–114) reason is as follows: "Most French scholars think of Turgot as primarily a statesman and political thinker, and only secondarily an economist; and of Quesnay as primarily an economist, who also presented important ideas in the political field." In fact, this argument is inaccurate. Our research shows that both Quesnay and Turgot took a very positive attitude towards the Chinese culture that was introduced to Europe at that time, but each had his own specific characteristics in the way of absorbing this foreign culture, and it is difficult to distinguish who is higher or lower. In terms of only economics, Quesnay is the founder of Physiocracy, and according to Marx's (1969, p. 54) evaluation, Turgot's thought is the culmination of the Physiocratic system, and both have made significant contributions to the independence of economics as a science, leaving us no clues to distinguish between their advantages and disadvantages of spreading Chinese culture in economics. Their social relations and personal experiences show that their economic theories were deeply influenced by ancient Chinese economic thought, which was determined by their social settings. Just as the French scholar Weulersse (Quoted in Maverick, 1946, pp. 124–125) says, "in the eighteenth century the remote Empire of China served as an ideal to many French reformers, and this general sentiment predisposed the economists to admire the economic and political institutions of China." As far as our research is concerned, the only difference between Quesnay and Turgot lies in that Quesnay expressed his systematic understanding of ancient Chinese thoughts and systems more deeply and more meticulously in his later years, and many of his disciples put forward various explanatory opinions on their master's views of understanding China, which provides us with more data and clues, in comparison with the similar contents in Turgot's economic theory, to explore the relationship between Physiocracy and ancient Chinese economic thoughts.

2 The Chinese Origin of Physiocracy

The Chinese origin is visible in almost every aspect of the economic doctrines of the Physiocratic School. The following is an overview of some very important aspects.

1. The natural order.

The natural order, as the philosophical foundation of Physiocracy, is generally believed to have developed under the influence of the French Enlightenment School in the eighteenth century, inheriting the traditional Western conception of natural law. However, our analysis shows that there is an extraordinary connection between the Physiocratic doctrine of natural order and the ancient Chinese thought they had at their disposal, and that the close connection goes even beyond its inheritance of the Western concept of natural law. As the basis of this Physiocratic doctrine, universal laws or natural laws have boasted lively and in-depth discussions by both Chinese and Western scholars, which are sufficient for the Physiocratic School to draw on. And the emphasis on rationality can also be drawn from both ancient China and ancient Greece, but the view of rationality from Chinese origins, in terms of its emphasis on understanding natural laws through learning and education, and its rejection of religious revelation, is more thorough and stronger than the similar concepts from ancient Greece. In terms of other claims that the observance of the laws of nature will lead to the highest welfare, although similar views can be found in the ancient thoughts of both China and the West, the Physiocrats attached more importance to the intellectual sources from China, and even the purely Western argument that the natural order had been created by a supreme deity, they believed, can be based on the classical concepts of "heaven" and "God" in the ancient Chinese texts.

More significantly, Quesnay, inspired by the moral doctrine of Confucius, proposed a definition of moral law or moral order and included it, along with the physical order, in the category of the natural order. The so-called moral doctrine in the Age of Enlightenment refers to the doctrine of human society, which recognizes and explores the law and order in morality, indicating that human society, like the entire material world, has objective laws that are not subject to people's will, and that the natural order is immutable and should be distinguished from the positive order that varies from time to time and from place to place. This specialty is obviously not a characteristic of the traditional Western system of thought, but has an extremely rich source of ideas in Confucian moral doctrine. In addition, the natural order of the Physiocrats is organic in nature, that is, it argues for the interdependence of various factors, which is again a unique difference from the mainstream Western thought, but is in line with the basic characteristics of ancient Chinese thought. These two important aspects of the Physiocratic doctrine of natural order, which are alien to the Western tradition, are both products of the absorption of ancient Chinese thought. Their significance lies in the fact that they recognize for the first time the existence of objective laws inherent in the organism of human society, and thus set forth the task of understanding objective laws for political economy. The theoretical assertions are, for example, that social economy is restricted by certain objective laws, that there are internal relations among economic categories, and that the development of the world is theoretically predictable. The basis was thus laid down for the tradition of bourgeois classical political economy.

2. The *Tableau Économique*.

The *Tableau* is an ingenious work of political economy in its infancy. Significantly, since Quesnay's creation of the *Tableau*, both its admirers and detractors had invariably explored its origin from the Chinese knowledge that was widespread in Europe at the time. For this, three explanations are the most representative. The first is that the *Tableau* is a specification and systematization of the Chinese principle of natural order. As we know, Quesnay's doctrine of natural order, as the cornerstone of his *Tableau*, draws on or even derives entirely from ancient Chinese thought in many important aspects. In fact, Quesnay regarded the whole social and economic life as an organically connected whole and explored the objective economic laws that exist in it, which reflects in a concrete and systematic way the requirement of the principle of natural order that contains many elements of Chinese thought. Therefore, this first view is by no means fictitious. The second view compares the *Tableau* to the 64 hexagrams—drawn by Fu Xi, as the legend has it—of the *I-Ching*. Here it is not only definitely concluded that it was Quesnay who first described social and economic activities in the form of charts, which was inspired by the line description of the hexagrams in the *I-Ching*, but through in-depth study it is found that the principles of keeping simplicity and controlling complexity, macro or overall analysis methods, system concepts, equilibrium theory, and explanation of the organic system of the whole economic life, which are embodied in the *Tableau*, are in terms of the germination or preceding materials of the *Tableau* all rare in the Western traditional economic viewpoints, but abundant in the ancient Chinese culture represented by the *I-Ching*. The third associates the *Tableau* with the Chinese hieroglyphic or ideographic script. Here, Chinese characters are regarded as a multi-functional writing system with mathematical quality. This unique quality enlightened Quesnay to use precise mathematical formulas to demonstrate his argumentation in the *Tableau*, which actually gave birth to his method of mathematical analysis. Thus, we do not feel surprised at all at the fact that modern scholars still consider the characteristic of pictographs being irrelevant to their pronunciation as "the 'mathematical' quality in language," and summarize from the hexagrams in the *I-Ching*, which was regarded as the origin of Chinese characters at that time, the complicated and rigorous structure of mathematical logic.

Generally speaking, the closer Western scholars get to Quesnay's time, the more they notice the connection between the *Tableau* and Chinese cultural tradition. As time goes on, the connection fades, blurs and is even forgotten in the Western academic circle. At present, the discussion of the sources of the *Tableau* in the history of economic theory is basically confined to the West's own inheritance system. In particular, the concept of circulatory flow in the *Tableau*, the most prominent and important one, is held to be inspired by the discovery of blood circulation in the human body by the European scientific community. However, if we compare the cultural traditions of the East and the West, we will find that the dominant viewpoint put forward by economists in studying the origin of the *Tableau* has never been outside the traditional vision of the West. This confinement makes their studies far from convincing. The reason is that the concept of circulation was always a very popular and important idea in ancient China. The origin of Chinese circulation thought, the scope of its application, its position in people's consciousness, and especially the use of abstract circulation concepts or the metaphor of the blood-vitality cycle for direct economic analysis had all been unattainable by Westerners before the Physiocratic School. Therefore, this Chinese concept of circulation, when it was brought to the European intellectual world as a basic category of thought along with the transmission of Chinese culture to the West, attracted the attention of Quesnay, always a China admirer, who added to his creation of the concept of circulation flow in the *Tableau* a Chinese source of thought that is no less important than the Western scientific discoveries. It is true that in Western writings, some principles of the *Tableau* are traced back to a few pioneers of the Physiocratic School, but it should be pointed out that, on the one hand, these pioneers were all from the era when Chinese cultural artifacts were in vogue, and since they could not trace their ideas to Western antiquity, the possibility that they themselves were influenced in some way by Chinese cultural traditions that have similar intellectual prototypes should not be overlooked; on the other hand, Quesnay, as a European, retained a certain amount of Western tradition as a matter of course, but this did not prevent him from drawing from the East many of the important ideas in the creation of the *Tableau*.

3. *Laissez faire*.

In China, since the pre-Qin period, "leaving the people alone" has always been believed to be the ideal state of adapting to nature, while State intervention, although often utilized in practice, has generally been regarded in theory as an activity only of necessity. A representative viewpoint is embodied in the so-called *wu wei er zhi* ("ruling by doing nothing"), a concept that did not exist in the ancient West. Significantly, the Physiocrats derived economic liberalism from the natural order and put forward the slogan of *laissez faire*, which is very similar to the ancient Chinese notions of "obeying the way of heaven" (Guanzi, 2001, p. 85) and "deriv[ing] rules (…) from the heavens" (Legge, 1885, p. 425), both advocating the principle of "mak[ing] more beneficial to the people the things from which they naturally derive benefit" (Confucius, 1869, p. 262), and the maxim of governance that "Tao never does; [y]et through it all things are done" (Lao Zi, 1994, p. 188). Moreover, the slogan of *laissez faire* embodies many other dimensions, such as the naturalistic view of individual self-interest, the principle of free passage in trade, the opposition to government interference, and the function of government that is mainly to know, abide by and instill the laws of the natural order in its citizens, all of which can be derived from China's intellectual tradition since the pre-Qin period that emphasizes "ruling by doing nothing" embodied in the view of self-interest, the practice of levying no taxes at the passes and in the markets (Mencius, 1875, pp. 147–148), the advocacy that "the highest type of ruler accepts the nature of the people" (Sima, 1993, p. 434), and Confucius' thought of "exercis[ing] government by means of […] virtue" (Confucius, 1869, p. 121), or its interpretation that "the virtuous do nothing."

The Physiocrats advocated *laissez faire*, using China's "enlightened" despotic monarchy as its ideal model. By "enlightened," they meant that the Chinese monarch recognized the natural order and used it to guide the making of the positive order, thus keeping society in a healthy state. This is in line with their view that French society at that time was in a state of sickness because its positive order violated the natural order. That's why they advocated emulation of the Chinese despotism as a prescription against the ills of French society. At first glance, it may seem a contradiction to link enlightened despotism with *laissez faire*. But in the eyes of the Physiocrats, only by implementing enlightened despotism could the *laissez-faire* spirit be truly adopted, because they found in China that the monarchy was based on the laws of nature, that the relationship between ruler and vassal was like that between father and son, that the rule was maintained by moral and ethical norms, that scholars were selected according to merit and ability, that there was a supervisory system to prevent the monarch from abusing his power, and that the enlightened monarch led by example. This understanding of the Physiocrats is reflected in some popular sayings of ancient China: "So long as I work after sunrise and rest after sunset, digging wells for water, and ploughing the fields for food, the power of the emperor means nothing to me" (Huangfu, 2010); "So long as the emperor governs the country by virtue, he needs to do nothing and the world belongs to him" (Quoted in Zhu, 1992); and "Heaven sees as my people see, Heaven hears as my people hear" (Mencius, 1875, p. 281). These views are all typical of the *laissez-faire* state under an enlightened dictatorship, which was unique to China and was never found in the West. Therefore, we can be sure that the *laissez faire* advocated by the Physiocrats is closely related to their ideal of an enlightened and despotic China, which upheld the principle of "ruling by doing nothing." In particular, the juxtaposition of *laissez faire* and enlightened despotism, which seems to be difficult to explain today, was at that time the most important evidence for Quesnay's admiration and adoption of Chinese thought.

4. Agricultural primacy.

The remarks of the Physiocrats praising China's agricultural thought and policies are very prominent, especially in showing a keen interest in the great ceremony of "ploughing the field" held by the Chinese emperor as the key way to show his emphasis on agriculture. Not only did they openly affirm China as a model for emphasizing agriculture, but their doctrine advocating the importance of agriculture was also permeated with the theoretical views similar to those of ancient China's agricultural primacy. The pre-Qin Confucian scholars, who were highly respected by the Physiocrats, and the Ming scholars, who had a direct influence on the missionaries who spread Chinese culture in Europe, elaborated on the importance of agriculture in a variety of ways. Their representative viewpoints are as follows: "Only agriculture can create the wealth unborn in heaven and earth" (Zhuang, 1939, p. 88), that is, agriculture is the only source of wealth production; agriculture's "creating" wealth means creating surplus production, which is manifested as surplus agricultural products in terms of use value; the proportion of surplus agricultural products differs from place to place depending on the level of agricultural productivity, and such products form the material basis of the entire social life and national prosperity; different from other non-agricultural sectors that lead to wealth by human factors, agriculture creates wealth, i.e., the land is the source of producing wealth, and is enriched by "the gift from nature;" industry and commerce come from agriculture and are unproductive, either contributing to the wealth creation of agriculture, or only taking the wealth produced by agriculture and performing the function of "distributing" it. Obviously, Quesnay's so-called doctrine of "net product" is based on theoretical views similar to these ancient Chinese agricultural ideas. In particular, since the concept of "net product" had no precedent in the West, it is all the more worthwhile to investigate the source of this doctrine from the traditional Chinese concept of emphasizing agriculture. The doctrine is the core, around which the entire Physiocratic system revolves, and on which all Physiocracy-related policies are based. Quesnay's contemporaries clearly hinted that there is a certain relationship between this core theory and ancient Chinese agricultural thought, and our study provides a richer and more solid historical basis for the interpretation and confirmation of this hint.

Led by the common emphasis on agriculture, the Physiocrats and the Chinese ancients are similar in many aspects in their treatment of industry and commerce. Firstly, the Physiocrats divided society into three classes engaged in economic activities: agriculture, industry and commerce, which is the same as that in ancient China. Secondly, their understanding of the basic relationship between agriculture and industry and commerce is based on the ancient Chinese principle of putting agriculture before industry and commerce. Thirdly, like the Confucian scholars of the pre-Qin period, and especially the thinkers of the Ming and Qing dynasties, the Physiocrats believed that, commerce and industry, though of secondary importance to agriculture, have a necessary socio-economic function. Fourthly, they attached particular importance to China's foreign trade policy and practice, and refuted the view that foreign trade is the real source of wealth, on the basis of the fact that China was prosperous but its foreign trade was "very limited," which was used as a powerful weapon against mercantilism. Fifthly, those ancient Chinese views that had been introduced to Europe added some oriental colors to the money and price theories of the Physiocratic School, such as the popular maxims that gold and silver currencies "cannot ease hunger or prevent cold [...], so that it is necessary to value grain instead of gold and jade" (Chao, 1975), and that because "cheap grain hurts farmers, and expensive grain consumers" (Sima, 1993, p. 85), it is necessary for the state to stabilize grain prices at an appropriate level by buying up grain when it is very cheap or by encouraging free transit by merchants.

5. Single *impôt territorial*, population and property ownership.

The Westward transmission of ancient Chinese taxation ideas and systems had a catalytic effect on the tax reform in France in the seventeenth and eighteenth centuries. One notable example is the Chinese tithe scheme advocated by Vauban, the pioneer of the Physiocratic School. The influence of Chinese taxation views on the Physiocrats, in terms of Quesnay's own understanding and interpretation of Chinese materials, is displayed at least in the following aspects. First, taxation is directed and determined by the natural order. Second, land revenue or rent is the only object of taxation. Third, levies other than land rent will eventually be passed on to the landlord indirectly through tax transfer. Fourth, taxation should be carried out according to "rules" or in an "orderly" way, that is, tax agencies should be simplified, tax collection fees should be saved, and the principle of reasonable tax burden should be implemented. In almost every one of these arguments, Quesnay cited Chinese examples or ideas as the basis, with the doctrine of a single *impôt territorial* being the most prominent. In other fiscal issues, such as the relationship between finance and economy, the general principle of keeping expenditure within the limits of revenues, the establishment of standards for fiscal expenditure, and the accounting of state funds, the Physiocrats all took China as a model, and tried to discover from Chinese ideas and institutions a general fiscal code sufficient for French rulers to follow.

Population is another focus of the Physiocrats' study of Chinese materials. According to his observation of China's population, Quesnay put forward the proposition that population grows faster than wealth, and overpopulation makes a country poor. This is also the basic proposition and theoretical prelude of the famous Malthusian Theory of Population. It should be pointed out that Quesnay did not criticize the Chinese government for the country's widespread poverty because of its large number of people. On the contrary, he thought that the large population was the result and symbol of the good rule of the government, and it was only in China that the natural trend of population reproduction exceeding wealth growth was revealed, which was not available in Europe at that time. His unique population theory is quite different from the traditional thought in the European mercantilist era, but many similar population views can be found in ancient China. He also defended the Chinese government's behavior of not relying on wealth redistribution or relief to save the poor, and his defense is very similar to the view of "luxury consumption" in ancient China that goes as follows: "Let the rich live in luxury and the poor do work for them" (Guanzi, 1998, p. 311). Quesnay discovered the so-called population growth trend from the example of China that he thought was the only one in the world, so he actively sought to solve China's overpopulation problem: he envisioned a solution through overseas emigration and colonization. In his view, the Chinese government's blunder lay only in its failure to guide its people to expand overseas. This absurd suggestion reflected the great expectations he had for China.

In the aspect of property ownership, the Physiocrats still believed that the security of China's system of private ownership and its conformity to the natural order constituted the foundations of a sound society's basic institutions. Their concept of prepayment, with its unique emphasis on investment in the land by the landowner and investment in the monarchy by the monarch, was also influenced and inspired by relevant Chinese materials. In addition, their emphasis on distribution is seen as not dissimilar to the Confucian view of distribution in the pre-Qin period: "[R]ulers of states and chiefs of families are not troubled lest their people should be few, but are troubled lest they should not keep their several places" (Confucius, 1869, p. 232).

The above comprehensive analysis reveals that the economic doctrines of the Physiocrats were influenced by ancient Chinese economic thought. This influence is by no means shallow and narrow, but broad and deep. Almost all the important aspects of Physiocracy have retained the mark of Chinese thought in varying degrees. Among these marks, some are completely based on the inspiration from Chinese thought; some are mainly based on Chinese ideas and supplemented by some Western arguments; Some use Chinese examples to strengthen and enrich the original arguments of the Physiocrats; some are based on the Western tradition and supplemented by similar materials in China as evidence; Others resort purely to the ancient Chinese tradition by "conjur[ing] up the spirits of the past to their service and borrow[ing] from them names, battle cries and costumes in order to present the new scene of world history in this time-honoured disguise and this borrowed language" (Marx, 1966, p. 398). This generalization, based on the different situations in which Physiocracy was influenced by Chinese thought, allows us to see the following.

On the one hand, the spread of Chinese academic thought had different levels or types of influence on the Physiocrats. Those aspects that can be said to have basically come from China include the following: the moral order and organicity in the Physiocratic doctrine of natural order, the emphasis on learning and propagating natural laws through universal education, the principle of mastering complexity by simplicity in the *Tableau Économique*, the research method of focusing on macroscopic or overall explanation and using diagrams to show the organic system of the whole economic life, and the *laissez-faire* principle drawn from enlightened despotism. Others have their origins in both China and the West, referring to both traditions but in general making more use of the Chinese banner, such as the concept of universal laws of nature, the idea of circular flow, the thought that agriculture is the only source of productive wealth, and some theoretical premises of the single *impôt territorial*. Still some others are mainly based on Chinese materials rather than the similar views directly or indirectly derived from China as mentioned above, such as the view on foreign trade, the idea of land ownership, and the arguments on the principle of fiscal expenditure. In addition, views like God's creation of the natural order seek to be confirmed in Chinese thought purely from the perspective of Western tradition. As for celebrating the enlightened monarchs in China, the purpose is to put a layer of Chinese-style costumes on their "feudal signboard" (Marx, 1992, p. 436). Of course, there are also some Physiocratic theories with unclear origins that need further discussion, so as to determine whether they come from the West or the East.

On the other hand, it proves all the more how eagerly the Physiocrats absorbed the nourishment of economic thoughts from ancient Chinese culture that they labeled their theoretical viewpoints as Chinese at different levels, whether such views were derived from non-Western foreign thoughts, followed the original European traditions, or came out of their own independent opinions. By the time of the Physiocratic School, China was a feudal empire with a vast territory, whose social and economic prosperity had been maintained for thousands of years, long enough to be the envy of the Physiocrats. Moreover, until the seventeenth century, the development of ancient Chinese economic thought had been at the forefront of economic thought in the world, providing enough rich and glorious achievements of economic thought for the Physiocrats to draw from.

Of course, the development of Physiocracy cannot be separated from its Western origin. As a Frenchman, Quesnay could hardly accept Chinese thought 100%, and his doctrine must have its Western origin. Up to now, many works on the history of economic thought have recorded in-depth research into this origin, only to arrive at the conclusion that Quesnay's natural order can be traced all the way back from Quesnay's age of Enlightenment, through the Middle Ages, to ancient Rome, and last to ancient Greece. Another conclusion from the research is that there are certain elements of the intellectual origin, which are mainly attributed to some French pioneers who were earlier than, or contemporary with, Quesnay. But the question is why Quesnay took China as an example in everything, and quoted from Greece only in a few places. Moreover, many doctrines of the Physiocratic system, especially those that are recognized as novel and unique, can almost always find their preceding materials in ancient China. It is very difficult, in contrast, to find the overall inheritance relationship in the Western traditional thought. All these facts prove convincingly that the Physiocrats took China as an extremely important source of their economic theories.

It is true that the influence of the Physiocrats declined rapidly in history with the ebb of the Chinese vogue in Europe, but their positive influence on economics cannot be thus ignored. If Physiocracy had not contributed to the development of economic theory, the importance attached to it in recent decades (including that by Marx more than 100 years ago) would have been pointless. Although the economic science after the Physiocratic School basically developed along the Western track, various unique theories formed by this school on the basis of digesting Chinese traditional culture have deeply penetrated into the evolution of Western economics.

Reichwein (1925, p. 149), a Western scholar, after studying the general cultural contacts between China and Europe in the eighteenth century, concludes that "the Physiocrats had taken their theory of the economic basis of the State mainly from the conditions of ancient China." And Heinz Gollwitzer (1962), the author of *Die Gelbe Gefahr: Geschichte eines Schlagworts, Studien zum Imperialistischen Denken,* affirms on the basis of the often warm and friendly appraisal of Far Eastern China by the Physiocrats that these economic thinkers learned a great deal by comparing their world with that of the Far East. But most Western scholars, including those who have discussed China's influence on European culture, have failed to appreciate the significant contribution of ancient Chinese economic thought to Physiocracy, just as they have neglected the full significance of China's philosophical contributions. What is even more arrogant and ignorant is the Eurocentric view held by Taylor (1956, p. 414), an American scholar, who claims, "Probably none of the old Eastern cultures ever contained, even, anything comparable to those good beginnings of economic analysis produced in the medieval West by its scholastic doctors." The author of this book endeavors to prove systematically, by means of solid facts and a large amount of data, the Chinese origin of the economic doctrine of Physiocracy and Western economics at large, and to outline concretely the rich nourishment that the Physiocrats received from China when they created their theoretical system and the influence of Physiocracy on future generations of economists, so as to demonstrate the great significance of cultural exchanges between China and the West for the development of economics in the eighteenth century, refute those absurd remarks that ignore the contribution and influence of Eastern economic thought on that of the world, and carry forward the brilliant achievements of ancient Chinese economic thought.

Joseph Needham, a famous Western scientist, has devoted his life to the study of ancient Chinese science and civilization. What he has realized is as follows: "He (the citizen of the world) can only give them (citizens of another nation) the understanding and appreciation which they deserve if he knows the achievements of the sages and precursors of their culture as well as of his own" (Needham, 1954, p. 9). He thus recommends that one see for oneself the great classics of Chinese philosophy and the history of Chinese technological development:

> I would very much recommend to anyone the experience of having a closer look at the great classics of Chinese philosophy, as well as the parallel course of technology in China. It is so exciting because Chinese culture is really the only other great body of thought of equal complexity and depth to our own—at least equal, perhaps more, but certainly of equal complexity; [...] Chinese civilization has the overpowering beauty of the wholly other, and only the wholly other can inspire the deepest love and the profoundest desire to learn.
>
> (1947, p. 19)

He concludes after decades of research that "her (China's) legacy joined with those of all the other cultures in a process which is palpably bringing into being the world co-operative commonwealth" (1964, p. 308).

These arguments do not take into account the glorious economic thought of ancient China, which Needham only refers to as "philosophy" in a general way. In fact, they apply not only to China's philosophy and natural sciences, but also to its economic science. The study of the Chinese origin of the Physiocrats' economic doctrine shows us a way to combine the "heritage" of ancient Chinese economic thought with that of the Physiocrats. On the one hand, in the history of economic theory, Physiocracy has through Adam Smith exerted great influence on the establishment of the theoretical system of bourgeois classical political economy. On the other hand, nearly a hundred years of sorting out and exploring the relevant economic materials by economists has continuously added new theoretical vitality to the development of economics for future generations. Both of the above illustrate the important position of Physiocracy in the establishment and development of modern political economy. In short, the Physiocrats are "the true fathers of modern political economy" (Marx, 1969, p. 44), and "the Physiocratic system is the first systematic conception of capitalist production" (1992, p. 436). Indeed, since Physiocracy is so significant to the economic science, we can well see the great influence of ancient Chinese economic thought on the world economic science. Therefore, China's ancient economic thought should be recorded in the annals of the world economic thought not only by its brilliant achievements, but also by its being one of the direct origins of modern political economy.

Postscript to the Second Reprint

The Chinese Origin of Physiocracy has been sold out in China since its first Chinese edition was published in 1992, for which I am filled with gratitude to my academic colleagues. Now that Shanghai People's Publishing House has decided to reprint the work, memories come flooding back—the challenges of selecting this research topic, the scholarly rewards, and above all, the decade of mentorship from my teacher Hu Jichuang.

I

There may be three reasons for the rareness of Chinese scholars' exploring the origin of Physiocracy from a Chinese perspective.

First, China's humiliating weakness and backwardness in the second half of the nineteenth century and the first half of the twentieth century have nurtured among some Chinese scholars the disregard for their own country's glorious past achievements, its cultural heritage in particular. These scholars have been turning to the West and Japan, especially various Western economic theories, for effective ways to strengthen the country and enrich the people. It is a pity that they have never thought independently that their own motherland's cultural inheritance may have had some influence on the origin of those great economic theories from the West. This mentality, once taking form under special historical conditions, is more often than not deep-rooted and hard to change.

Second, the difficulty in discovering the data about the influence and the insufficiency of accumulated results make it difficult to turn this topic into a hotspot of research. Chinese scholars have obviously learned about this connection from the research Western scholars did in the late nineteenth and early twentieth centuries, which is however difficult to specify, not to say to verify, since the proof materials for further exploration either are mainly concentrated in the West, or have to be sorted out from the great variety of writings scattered in various Western languages. No wonder, it is still not clear to what extent the representatives of the Physiocratic

M. Tan, *The Chinese Origin of Physiocracy*, https://doi.org/10.1007/978-981-97-9703-5

School and traditional Chinese culture are connected, especially how the latter influenced the establishment of the Physiocratic system. The majority of Chinese scholars who have occasionally come across this topic over the past seventy years or so have thus categorically denied that this connection has any theoretical significance, simply paraphrased the views of Western scholars for the sake of curiosity, or drawn inferences from the available information and opinions, so that few discoveries have been made on the basis of credible materials.

Third, different from ancient China's much-acclaimed achievements in philosophy, literature, as well as science and technology, its progress in economic thought has long been unknown, even to the majority of China's economists. This may be because ancient economic thought had always been embedded in other ancient fields of study, philosophy and ethics in particular, and had never achieved its own independent status until modern times. But when people came to realize that ancient economic thought can be studied independently of other dominant disciplines, China's economic studies were already dominated by imported economics that was Eurocentric. That is why ancient Chinese economic thoughts were abandoned, enjoyed as an antique, or even dismissed as evidence to prove that it had "no value at all when compared with modern European and American economic science" (Zhao, 1933, p. i), and to make Chinese people "realize their own inadequacy" (Gan, 1926, p. 16). Such a prejudice still lingers in the minds of many people today.

Choosing such an obscure topic, though appearing as if I asked for trouble, has been a good opportunity to improve my research capability. It was Mr. Hu Jichuang who finally prompted me to make this hard choice, which had been fostered by his years of guidance.

I still remember that Mr. Hu had a long encouraging talk with me when I was admitted to his 1980 program of the Master of Arts in Economics—I was the only candidate at the time. One of his remarks has left the deepest impression on me: "If your goal is to teach, I can enable you to stand on the podium in one year; if you want to climb to the top of the academic ladder, you must be prepared for a lifetime of hard work." This statement has been imprinted onto my mind, though it did not sink in at the time. With the passage of time, I admired more and more his great knowledge of both the East and the West, and his inspiring persistence in developing his scholarly career, even at the age of eighty.

Hu's research may be roughly divided into the following stages. Before the liberation of China in 1949, after his return from the London School of Economics in the late 1930s, he was mainly engaged in the teaching and research of the history of Western economics, and accumulated some data on ancient Chinese economic thought. After the founding of the People's Republic of China (PRC), he was mainly occupied with the study of the history of economic thought in ancient China until the mid-1960s, and established a complete theoretical system of economic thought for thousands of years from the pre-Qin period to the eve of the Opium War (1840–1842). Despite all kinds of persecution and restrictions during the Cultural Revolution, he still diligently studied the history of modern Chinese economic thought in the latter half of the Revolution. Since the reform and opening up of China in the late 1970s, he rejuvenated his academic career, and made a series of groundbreaking contributions in the comparative study of Chinese and foreign economic thought, the study of the history of Chinese economic thought (expanded from 1919 to 1949, and even well beyond), and the history of foreign economic theories. In other words, when I started to study under his supervision, it was the turning point when he was ready to leap from one academic peak to another one. It was thus quite meaningful that he, at the beginning of my enrollment, instructed me to "climb to the academic peak." It was his encouragement that spurred me to choose research topics that others were reluctant to venture into.

I first learned about the influence of pre-Qin economic thought on that of Europe, Physiocracy in particular, from the last chapter of Hu's *History of Chinese Economic Thought* (Vol. I). This short discussion, consisting of only two thousand characters, arrives at a positive conclusion, striking and inspiring, based on some of the research available at the time. Of course, such a brief discussion is not enough for a detailed and in-depth research of historical materials, and some conclusions are based on speculation. Later, Hu shifted his focus to the comparative study of Chinese and foreign economic thought, and devoted himself to introducing to foreign countries the glorious achievements of China's ancient economic thought, producing a number of works in Chinese and English, such as *Chinese Economic Thought Before the Seventeenth Century*, *A Concise History of Chinese Economic Thought*, and *Prehistory of Political Economy*. Once, I asked him why he did not specially turn to the influence of ancient Chinese economic thought on the economic theories of Europe, since it occupied such a significant place in the comparison of Chinese and foreign economic thought. He answered, surprisingly but reasonably, that the economic scholars of his generation had already completed the collation and summary of thousands of years of Chinese economic thought, and was still capable of comparing the unearthed heritage of Chinese and foreign economic thought and translating the result into English, but found it hard to make further investigation of how ancient Chinese economic thought influenced the economic theories of the West, due to the particularity and complexity of the materials. The work had to be left to the younger generation. This remark has ever since kept lingering in my mind.

It was two years after I finished my MA degree that I put this topic on my research agenda. I was working at the time as both Hu's research assistant and the deputy chair of the Department of Economics. Around the first half of 1985, I expressed my intention to apply for Hu's doctoral supervision. Unexpectedly, he put forward a seemingly simple but quite stringent prerequisite, that is, I had to submit in advance a topic that was likely to later develop into a doctoral dissertation. So I submitted to him many topics within my research scope of the history of Chinese economic thought, only to find them all rejected. Hu, who was always amiable, showed such a serious attitude towards this issue, that I felt as if I had been hit with a baton, and sobered up a lot. In the following year, after a careful review of a lot of materials, I formulated two preliminary topics. One was the present topic, but I still had doubts about whether I could do it well. The other was "the history of China's Modern fiscal thought," to be a sequel to *The History of China's Fiscal Thought*, a book that I was at the time co-authoring with Hu. A lot of new materials had been collected about China's fiscal thought after 1919, which, except for those that were used in the co-authored book, might well be used for my doctoral dissertation. I thus felt very confident. In the entrance examination for doctoral students in 1986, however, in addition to the normal examination subjects, Hu added a new subject for me, the only applicant, namely, the proposal for my doctoral dissertation. The examination panel consisted of three senior professors with him acting as the leader. The interview lasted half a day. After I explained in detail my two topics and consciously indicated that I was more confident about the latter one, the three professors asked me a succession of questions and gave me a lot of insightful guidance, so that I confidently chose the former one instead.

Mr. Hu attached great importance to my dissertation and looked forward to my success. He would question me about the progress of the dissertation, including new ideas, materials or difficulties, encouraged me and provided me with detailed guidance. For me, choosing this topic was like stepping into purgatory. It took more than four years just to find, collect and accumulate relevant domestic and international data. Since 1988, my work as an assistant to the university president had greatly reduced my time for research and writing. In particular, in 1989, when the writing of my dissertation began, I had to spend a lot of time on my administrative work because of some unexpected events. It can be said that the entire first draft was completed in a stitch-by-stitch manner. However, the progress was supported by all sides, which sometimes led to unexpected discoveries. For example, at the Fourth Annual Conference on the History of Chinese Economic Thought held at Peking University in 1988, Mr. Wu Baosan mentioned that during his visit abroad, he came across a French doctoral dissertation written in 1936 by a Chinese student studying at the University of Dijon, France, which elaborated on the influence of ancient Chinese economic thought on the formation of Physiocracy. This was a wonderful clue to me. Following the direction, I immediately wrote to ask for a copy, and soon received a reply from Mr. Schmitt, the director of the library of the University of Dijon, saying that this unpublished doctoral thesis was quite old and had few copies available, but that since I as a Chinese scholar was so interested in it, they were willing to give a copy. And along with the letter, he sent a photocopy of the original printed version, whose name can be translated as "The Main Schools of Ancient Chinese Economic Thought and their Influence on the Formation of the Theory of the Physiocratic School." The name of the author was translated into French, called Ly Siou y, which was unknown at the time. Coincidentally, when I was looking at the bibliographies of old periodicals and papers before the founding of the PRC, I happened to find an article signed by Ly Siou-Y, entitled "L'Influence de la Pensée Économico-Politique de la Chine Ancienne sur la Doctrine Physiocratique" in Vol. 1, No. 3, 1938, *Social Research* of Sun Yat-sen University. Later, I asked Tang Zhaolian, a teacher from Sun Yat-sen University, to find and photocopy it for me. When I got a copy of the article, it turned out that, apart from the title being translated into Chinese, the original French text of the second part of Ly Siou Y's doctoral thesis was entirely reproduced. Only then did it come to me that Ly Siou Y and Li Zhaoyi actually refer to the same person. Gains like this in the process often gave me a lot of excitement.

The first draft of my dissertation, once completed, was sent to many experts for comments. Their feedback, though not unanimously positive, was encouraging and enlightening, and was received with gratitude. In particular, Mr. Chen Daisun wrote a letter to Mr. Hu on October 16, 1989, expressing his opinion after reading this draft twice, which consists of nearly 300,000 characters. On the one hand, he affirmed that the work had entailed "a great effort ... I hope and believe that it will be published in the future to fill in the gaps that have always been the concern of Chinese scholars." On the other hand, he put forward in as many as seven pages "a few small questions," which, divided into four categories and thirteen items, are all actually very important and not "small" at all. They cover mainly the following four aspects. First comes the common tendency that must be avoided in the study, that is, "after studying a topic in depth for a long time, one tends to develop a preference for the people and things in it, and to make unconscious exaggerations," so that the arguments should be more rigorous to make the "concluding remarks more concrete and clearer." The second is about the analysis of the evolution of the *Tableau Économique* in the manuscript, for which he raised eight to nine questions in succession for my consideration, and recommended me to refer to *Quesnay's Tableau Economique* (1972), co-edited by Marguerite Kuczynski and Ronald L. Meek, because he thought that "this book provides a reliable description of the development of the first versions of the *Tableau*." The third is about academic norms, for which he stated that, for the convenience of the reader, the year of publication is indispensable for the literature cited, whether in the footnotes, in the bibliography, or in the first mention in both when the same one is cited in a succession. Last but not least, he took pains to point out some errors in the use of Chinese characters, including explaining the differences between Chinese characters, such as that between *jin-luan* (exclusive domain) and *jin-qu* (forbidden area): the former figuratively "refers to exclusive interests that are not allowed to be infringed by others," while the latter "refers to areas that are forbidden to enter." These opinions are very instructive. He added that he would like to provide the author with these questions directly for reference, but he was afraid that he might be too blunt and offensive, so he asked Hu to make a decision for him and forward them when convenient. He stressed in particular that the purpose of putting forward these questions was only to improve the dissertation. I am indeed grateful to him, a highly honorable scholar, for his taking a fledgling's work so seriously by giving it such a careful evaluation and taking such a prudent attitude to protect and stimulate the enthusiasm of young students.

My thankfulness goes, too, to Wu Baoshan, Zhao Jing, Ye Shichang, Zhu Jiazhen, Wang Tongxun and a dozen other experts and professors, for their valuable comments on this work. It was on the basis of their great help that the present manuscript was revised and supplemented. The original doctoral dissertation was titled "The Chinese Origin of the Economic Doctrine of the Physiocratic School." Later, in view of the fact that the Chinese translation of the name of the Physiocratic School as a specific concept already highlights the disciplinary nature of economics, and in order to mark the territorial characteristics of this school, I changed the title to, literally, "The Chinese Origin of the Doctrine of the French Physiocratic School." Hu paid close attention to the publication of this manuscript, and wrote a preface for it. After the publication, he submitted a review for it to *Economic Research Journal*, a top journal of economics in China. For me, Hu's effort has been both an invaluable help and a great encouragement. He expressed his great expectations for the future development of Chinese economic thought. When the first edition of this work was published, Hu suggested that I translate it into English, and for this purpose he specially contacted Foreign Languages Press in Beijing. He told me that this book might be more meaningful to foreign academics than to domestic ones. It is a pity that this suggestion has not been adopted for various reasons.

The above memories, still vivid in my mind, seem to have happened only yesterday. They convey my nostalgia for my mentor Hu Jichuang, and my deep gratitude to my predecessors for their strong support. What's more, throughout the whole course of preparing this dissertation, it was my wife's considerateness that prevented me from the distractions of trivial matters, and it was the innocence of my young son that brought me great solace. The reprinting of this book provides an opportunity for me to express to them my heartfelt thankfulness.

II

The editors of Shanghai People's Publishing House, when informing me of the reasons for reprinting my book, mentioned that it had caused a stir in academic circles and aroused the interest of some researchers. They asked me whether any changes would be needed in the reprinting. Since I have done my best in conforming to the academic norms and all my viewpoints in the book are based on the materials I have collected, I feel that there is no need to make significant revisions except for a few misprints. In addition, the focus of my research has been shifted elsewhere, leaving me no time for such revisions. The growing recognition of my modest research in academic circles may be attributed to China's rapid development in recent years, which has fostered a strong sense of intellectual confidence among Chinese scholars in the field of economic thought. This in turn highlights the importance of this work. Thus, I find it necessary to add a few points here.

1. Exploring the influence of traditional Chinese thought on the creation of Physiocracy may be an important breakthrough in clarifying the historical interpenetration between Chinese and Western economic thought.

The interpenetration, following the consensus in modern times that clearly rejects the one-way relationship in which the West exerts influence on China, focuses on the two-way relationship in which China has also exerted influence on the West, or at least on certain important schools of thought in the West, in a way that cannot be ignored, although the degree or scope of this mutual influence may vary. The question is not an empty one. In general, before the modern era, although ancient China mainly pursued a policy of isolation and self-defense, boasting such a vast territory, and maintaining relatively friendly relations with its neighbors, the country found it practically impossible to break off all official and private contacts with other countries. In fact, China always maintained such contacts with the outside in a close or loose way since ancient times, especially the non-official contacts with European countries, which reached a climax in the seventeenth and eighteenth centuries. Since ancient China had been for a long time in the ranks of the advanced countries, both in terms of economic strength and cultural accumulation, from a global perspective, it is impossible to exclude the possibility that in the cultural exchanges between China and the European countries, Chinese culture, which is typical of the Eastern culture, may have had a profound influence on the precursor ideas of Western economic theories. Specifically, many Western scholars have been aware of this obvious influence from the East and have made various useful explorations in this regard, and the Physiocrats, in particular, have provided direct evidence by openly or implicitly admitting that some of their important ideas were derived from China. Of course, as far as economic thought is concerned, the Chinese influence on the West may not stop at the Physiocratic School, but according to the historical materials we have so far, the data involving the Physiocratic School are the most concentrated and clear, and this School has played a special role in the formation and evolution of modern Western economic doctrines. Therefore, we regard the investigation of the Chinese origin of Physiocracy as an important means to clarify the penetration of Chinese traditional thoughts into Western economic theories.

This investigation, based on the findings of previous research, seeks to contribute to the relevant research more abundant materials, more effective research ideas, more colorful presentation, and more convincing examples and perspectives. However, it is not easy to accomplish this task. In addition to the specific difficulties listed in the fourth section of the introduction to this book, there may be some problems that are more difficult to grasp. For example, economic thought had always been one of the main components of philosophy before economics became an independent discipline, which was true in both China and the West. Then, in the process of the Westward transmission of Chinese culture, it is still a question to be sorted out how to separate from philosophy the economic thought, especially the ancient Chinese economic thought that may have its unique influence on Western economic theories, including Physiocracy. Western scholars generally recognize that Chinese philosophy has its own unique significance and attach great importance to it. The philosophical writings of Hegel (1770–1831), born only four years before Quesnay's death (1774), may be cited here as an example.

In Hegel's time, Europeans were not as keen to pay homage to what was spread from China as Quesnay had earlier been. However, in Hegel's (1899b) writings, even though he views Chinese philosophy with the harshness of a Westerner, there is a strong sense of the deep influence that traditional Chinese culture had on the West. In his *Philosophy of History*, he describes China as "an empire possessing one (a history) so remarkable, one going back to the most ancient times" (p. 61). In his view, "[t]he Chinese morality—since Europeans have become acquainted with it and with the writings of Confucius—has obtained the greatest praise and proportionate attention from those who are familiar with the Christian morality" (pp. 70–71). Yet, "[t]o the Chinese their [those Christian and Indian nations'] moral laws are just like natural laws [...]. Morality is a political affair [in those Christian and Indian nations] [...];

while the conception of an abstract subject, 'a wise man' forms the culminating point among the Chinese" (p. 71). He advocates what he calls "the Geographical Basis" (p. 79) for distinguishing between Eastern and Western thought forms, and thinks that, as a country with plains and valleys, China boasts the following geographical features:

> In these regions (such as China) extensive Kingdoms arise, and the foundation of great States begins. For agriculture, which prevails here as the primary principle of subsistence for individuals, is assisted by the regularity of seasons [...]; property in land commences, and the consequent legal relations;—that is to say, the basis and foundation of the State.
>
> (p. 89)

Therefore, at that time, the people were closed to themselves and could not share the maritime civilization of the West (pp. 88–91). Another geographical feature is as follows:

> *Asia* (including China) is, characteristically, the *Orient* quarter of the globe—the region of origination. [...] [B]ut as Europe presents on the whole, the centre and end of the old world, and is absolutely the *West*—so Asia is absolutely the *East*.
>
> In Asia arose the Light of Spirit, and therefore the history of the World.
>
> (p. 99)
>
> Anterior Asia [...] has, consequently, a relation to Europe; for what is most remarkable in it, this land has not kept for itself, but sent over to Europe. It presents the origination of all religious and political principles, but Europe has been the scene of their development.
>
> (p. 101)

Thus, "[t]he History of the World travels from East to West, for Europe is absolutely the end of History, Asia the beginning" (p. 103). Hegel divides the development of human consciousness into four historical phases: the ancient Eastern world is in the "childhood" (the East) or "boyhood" (Central Asia) of spiritual history, the ancient Greek world in the "adolescence," the ancient Roman world in "the *Manhood*," and the German world in the "*Old Age*" (pp. 103–110).

After the above division, Hegel devotes the first part of the book to a discussion of "the Oriental World." In particular, he mentions that "[w]ith China [...]—the realm of theocratic despotism—History begins" (p. 112); that "[i]n China the Monarch is Chief as Patriarch" (p. 112); that China's "moral laws are treated as legislative enactments, and law on its part has an ethical aspect" (pp. 112-113); that China is characterized by "the immovable unity" (p. 113); that China is "shut up within itself, abstract and calm" (p. 114); and that, in particular, "[i]f we compare these kingdoms in the light of their various fates, we find the empire of the two Chinese rivers the only durable kingdom in the World. Conquests cannot affect such an empire" (p. 115).

Hegel then devotes to China an entire section of 23 pages (pp. 116–138). "With the Empire of China," Hegel claims, "History has to begin, for it is the oldest, as far as history gives us any information; and its *principle* has such substantiality, that for the empire in question it is at once the oldest and the newest" (p. 116). What Hegel means is: "Early do we see China advancing to the condition in which it is found at this day; [but] [...] every change is excluded, and the fixedness of a character which recurs perpetually, takes the place of what we should call the truly historical" (p. 116).

Hegel mainly introduces the following aspects of China:

(1) "No People has a so strictly continuous series of Writers of History as the Chinese. [...] [S]uch a constitution exists in China, and that in a distinct and prominent form. [...] The Chinese have certain ancient canonical documents, from which their history, constitution, and religion can be gathered" (pp. 116-117). These classics include *Shang Shu* (*The Book of Documents*), the *I-Ching* (*The Book of Changes*), *Shi Jing* (*The Book of Odes*), *Li Ji* (*The Book of Rites*), and *Chun Qiu* (*Spring and Autumn Annals*).

(2) "The population and the thoroughly organized State-arrangements, descending even to the minutest details, have astonished Europeans; and a matter of especial astonishment is the accuracy with which their historical works are executed" (p. 118).

(3) China's course of history is said to have begun with the southward advance of the culture of the Fu Xi culture at the earliest. Since then, the dynasties have repeatedly changed, but the new ones must still abide by Chinese laws and study Chinese academics (pp. 118–120).

(4) "[T]he *Spirit* of the constitution [...] has always remained the same. We can deduce it from the general principle, which is [...] the Spirit of the Family. [...] On this form of moral union alone rests the Chinese State, and it is objective Family Piety that characterizes it" (pp. 120–121).

(5) "The Emperor claims the deepest reverence. [...] [T]he Emperor is the head of the State and therefore must appear as the first and best in everything. [...] China has therefore succeeded in getting the greatest and best governors, to whom the expression 'Solomonian Wisdom' might be applied [...]. All the (European) ideals of princes and of princely education which have been so numerous and varied [...] are realized here. [...] Besides the imperial dignity there is properly no elevated rank, no nobility among the Chinese; [...] all are equal, [...] Official stations are [...] occupied by men of the greatest intellect and education. The Chinese State has consequently been often set up as an Ideal which may serve even us for a model" (pp. 123–124).

(6) Within the legal relationship of the Chinese people, the change of ownership follows the order that first takes the land as the property of the State, then the land becomes private property, and the inhabitants of the land become serfs, but since all the people are equal and humble before the emperor, there is little difference between the free people and the lowly, and there is no such thing as an individual right between men (pp. 130–131).

(7) "[T]he religious exaltation of man has merely a human reference—simple morality and right-doing. [...] In China the individual [...] is [...] dependent on objects of nature, of which the most exalted is the material heaven. [...] The Chinese religion involves that primitive element of magical influence over nature" (pp. 131–132).

(8) "In mentioning Chinese sciences we encounter a considerable clamor about their perfection and antiquity. [...] [However,] there are wanting to them [...] that free ground of subjectivity [...]. A free, ideal, spiritual kingdom has here no place. What may be called scientific is of a merely empirical nature, and is made absolutely subservient to the Useful on behalf of the State" (p. 134).

(9) "The Chinese have [...] a *Philosophy*, whose elementary principles are of great antiquity" (p. 136). The *I-Ching*, in which the "lines are the foundation of their characters as also of their philosophy" (Hegel, 1892, p. 121), "treats of Origination and Destruction. In this book are found the purely abstract ideas of Unity and Duality" (Hegel, 1899b, p. 136), as well as the discussion of the existence of substance attached to these abstract forms of thought. "The fundamental principle recognized is *Reason— Tao* [...]. To become acquainted with its forms is regarded among the Chinese also as the highest science; yet this has no connection with the educational pursuits which more nearly concern the State. The works of Lao-tse, and especially his work 'Tao-te-King,' are celebrated. [...] With the works of Confucius we have become more intimately acquainted [...], which form the basis of the customs and conduct of the Chinese. In the principal work of Confucius [...] are found correct moral apophthegms; but there is a circumlocution, a reflex character, and circuitousness in the thought, which prevents it from rising above mediocrity" (p. 136).

(10) "The Chinese are far behind in Mathematics, Physics, and Astronomy, notwithstanding their quondam reputation in regard to them. They knew many things at a time when Europeans had not discovered them, but they have not understood how to apply their knowledge: as *e.g.* the Magnet, and the Art of Printing" (pp. 136-137).

In short, "[i]n China the patriarchal principle rules a people in a condition of nonage, the part of whose moral resolution is occupied by the regulating law, and the moral oversight of the Emperor" (p. 139).

"Hegel's Lectures on the Philosophy of History," claims Sibree (1899, p. iii), "are recognized in Germany as a popular introduction to his system." These lectures are intended to express how philosophical ideas have become the true core of history and the soul of the historical nations of the world. Charles Hegel (1899a, p. xi) remarks, "In proceeding to treat of China [...], he (G. W. F. Hegel) wished, as he said himself, only to show by example how philosophy ought to comprehend the character of a nation; and this could be done more easily in the case of the stationary nations of the East, than in that of peoples which have a *bonâ fide* history and a historical development of character." In other words, G. W. F. Hegel (1899b, p. 330) thinks that China does not yet have a true history of character, i.e. a history of spiritual concepts, and at the same time he admits that "the Spirit of the East [has spread] over the West." This arrogance in speaking of China, and of the East in general, may have something to do with him as a European scholar, who "always felt a youthful enthusiasm" (Hegel, 1899a, p. xi) for the Greeks.

These views on Eastern philosophy, Chinese philosophy in particular, are equally, and in some respects perhaps more clearly, expressed in his *Lectures on the History of Philosophy* (abbreviated as *Lectures*). His basic view remains that the Chinese people's "intellectual activities as a whole [...] are at a standstill. [...] [T]he Chinese [...] may have been as far advanced in every respect two thousand years ago as now" (Hegel, 1892, p. 3).The "Oriental Philosophy" in *Lectures* is placed in the opening section before the main text to show that it "does not enter into the substance or range of our subject as represented here. Its position is preliminary, and we only deal with it at all in order to account for not treating of it at greater length" (p. 117). This is because, in contrast to that of the West, "[i]n the case of Eastern Religion, [...] we are much more directly reminded of the philosophic conception, for since in the East the element of subjectivity has not come forth" (p. 118). It is true that in certain "period in which this great universal Oriental conception aroused the East—the land of circumscription and of limitation, where the spirit of subjectivity reigns. More particularly in the first centuries of Christendom [...] did these great Oriental ideas penetrate into Italy (broadly speaking, the West); and in the Gnostic philosophy they began to force the idea of the illimitable into the Western mind" (p. 117). But Eastern Philosophy is after all different from the Western counterpart. In fact, the real reason is most clearly expressed in the opening paragraph of the first part of the text, "Greek Philosophy:"

> The name of Greece strikes home to the hearts of men of education in Europe, and more particularly is this so with us Germans. Europeans have taken their religion [...] from a point somewhat further off than Greece—they took it from the East [...]. But the here, the present, art and science, that which in giving liberty to our spiritual life, gives it dignity as it likewise bestows upon it ornament, we know to have proceeded from Greece either directly or indirectly.
>
> (p. 149)

With this stance in the leading position, Hegel's lectures still devote a large space to Chinese philosophy. The following points are the most talked about. First, the philosophy of Confucius. "The first subject of remark with regard to the Chinese," Hegel," Hegel claims, "respects the teaching of Confucius (500 years before Christ) which made a great sensation in Liebnitz's time; this teaching is a moral philosophy [...] and [...] is the authority most esteemed in China" (p. 120). He thinks that it is a national philosophy, constituting the foundation of Chinese education, culture and practical activities, and says that Confucius talked about "nothing definite further than a commonplace moral [...], which may be found as well expressed and better, in every place and amongst every people. [...] He is hence only a man who has a certain amount of practical and worldly wisdom—one with whom there is no speculative philosophy" (p. 121). Second, the philosophy of the *I-Ching*. This ancient classic embodies Fu Xi philosophy. Here Hegel claims, "[T]he Chinese have also taken up their attention with abstract thoughts and with pure categories. The old book Y-king, or the Book of Principles, serves as the foundation for such; it contains the wisdom of the Chinese, [...]. [...] These symbols are quite abstract categories, and consequently the most superficial determinations of the understanding. It must certainly be considered that pure thoughts are brought to consciousness, but in this case we make no advance, merely remaining stationary so far as they are concerned" (pp. 121–122). Third, Daoist (Taoist) philosophy. *Tao Te Ching* is the main work of this sect, a book about reason and morality, and its philosophical thought does not go beyond the abstract beginning of "nothing," and still stays at the primary stage (pp. 124–125). Therefore, according to Hegel, the philosophy of Chinese religion is abstract, and its content is incapable of creating a category (-prescribed) kingdom for thought.

The reasons for quoting in detail Hegel's account of Chinese and Eastern philosophy is that it can shed light in the following aspects on the choice of the Physiocratic School as the key object of our study on the influence that ancient Chinese economic thought had on the creation of modern economic science in the West.

First, the changing attitudes of Quesnay, Smith and Hegel towards ancient Chinese philosophy are in line with the choice of the Physiocrats as our focus, reflecting the deep influence of ancient Chinese thought on that of the West, its economic thought in particular. Hegel's account of Chinese philosophy is in its basic conclusions very similar to Adam Smith's (1812, pp. 88–89) discussion of China's economic problems in his 1776 *Wealth of Nations*, in that both judge China to be in a state of long-term stagnation. However, Smith does not argue that this state was immutable. In his view, China had always been the richest country in the world, but its development had reached the limits allowed by the state's legal system due to its disdain for foreign trade and lack of capital accumulation. Therefore, only by getting rid of the shackles of this feudal system could it embark on the road of economic growth again. In contrast, Hegel (1892, p. 3) argues that Chinese philosophy had long since entered a fixed state of termination, that is, the entire intellectual activity of the Chinese had been stagnant almost from the beginning. Smith's and especially Hegel's historical data on China coincide with, and probably come from the same source as, the data on China cited by Quesnay in his work of 1767 *Despotism in China*. However, it is intriguing to note the respective attitudes of these three prominent Western scholars towards roughly the same Chinese historical material. Quesnay is all praise; Smith, a little later, has some reservations about such praise and begins to make economic criticisms; and Hegel, who is active in the first three decades of the nineteenth century, places Chinese philosophy in the infantile position of spiritual history. In other words, with the passage of time, that is, with the ebbing of the Chinese vogue in Europe, the trajectory of the three scholars in their view of China shifts from glorification to criticism and then to a more derogatory evaluation. Pointing out this trajectory does not mean that the influence of traditional Chinese culture on Western economic thought has disappeared. On the contrary, this shows that it is more advantageous to examine this influence by focusing on the Physiocratic School than on Smith and Hegel in a later time. At the same time, this shows that, regardless of Smith, ancient Chinese philosophy must have been introduced to the West in large quantities and have left a deep impression on the Western philosophical community long before Hegel, which is why it attracted such attention and interest from Hegel, thus opening up the possibility for the then-forming Western independent economic theory to draw on, via the Western philosophical community, the imported Chinese economic thought.

Second, Hegel's careful study of ancient Chinese philosophy has, in a way, benefited his research of both Western philosophy and the difference between the ancient thought of the East and that of the West. Hegel (1899b), though stating in his discussion of Eastern philosophy that its spiritual representative, that is, the oldest Chinese thought, only reflects the "childhood" (p. 105) of the spirit in the development of human consciousness, makes an in-depth study on the thoughts of pre-Qin scholars, especially those of Confucius, the *I-Ching* and Lao Zi. Only in this way does he establish his philosophy of history by taking China as an empire in his retrospective discussion of ancient history, or as the starting point of the world's spiritual history, and describe, with the judgment that "[w]ith China [...] History begins" (p. 112), the stages of development that "[i]n Asia arose the Light of Spirit" (p. 99) and then spread from the East to the West. Undoubtedly, he makes a unique analysis (Hou, et al., 1957, pp. 302–308) of ancient Chinese thought, especially that of Lao Zi, and highlights what the ancient thought of the East differs from that of the West. In fact, it was this difference that aroused Hegel's great interest in the study of the philosophy of the Ancient East, China in particular, which in turn led to his discovery of the "flash of truth" in the philosophy; it was also this difference that led his study, to a certain extent, to his own theoretical system or his formation of certain basic philosophical categories. It is a pity that he was so excessively preoccupied with the homeland feelings about ancient Greek thought, that he did not discuss the scope and degree of the influence which this philosophical "spirit" had on the development of Western philosophy, but merely dismissed ancient Chinese philosophy as an impoverished and infantile theory that never changes. This attitude is in sharp contrast to that of the Physiocrats active in the half century before him, who openly advocated that Europe should follow the example of the East. The two are obviously based on different historical conditions.

Third, Hegel's study of ancient Chinese philosophy draws our attention to the interpenetration between philosophy and economics, which may shed light on the birth of some economic concepts, such as equilibrium. Hegel's discussion on oriental philosophy does indeed touch upon the Chinese economy, but the whole of it is based on philosophical thought. Of course, some concepts of oriental philosophy can be used directly as theoretical categories of economics. However, it is difficult to find similar ideas in Hegel's discussion of China. For example, the concept of equilibrium, which is now common in Western economics, was probably preceded by philosophical ideas. But whether it originated from the West's own tradition or from an Eastern culture is a mystery. Western economists have seldom traced the origins of this concept, and trace, even when they do, at most back to the days of the Physiocratic School. It is the same case with the field of philosophy. Thus, due to the lack of direct and reliable proof materials, we can only start our analysis by examining the time-honored traditions of China and the West. The latter is accustomed to discussing individual problems on a case-by-case basis, and does not advocate overall equilibrium, while the former precisely emphasizes the mutual coordination among different things and even the organic connection between man and nature. Considering that Westerners regard the Physiocratic School as the pioneer of the equilibrium analysis, and the Physiocratic School respected the ideas from China, we may well conclude that the Physiocratic thought of equilibrium may have originated from China. This conclusion, reasonable as it is, is not free of speculation, and still awaits more convincing evidence.

Indeed, Hegel's discussion of Chinese philosophy gives us an increasing sense of the influence of ancient China on Western thought. At the same time, his bias against Chinese philosophy shows that, even if we focus on the Physiocratic School for a breakthrough in the search for the influence of ancient China on the birth of Western economics, we still need the joint efforts of academic colleagues, including the interdisciplinary cooperation between economists and philosophers, to fundamentally clarify the infiltration of Chinese traditional thoughts into Western modern economic theories.

2. In the comparison of Chinese and Western economic thought, the unique parts of the former are often found to be the most influential on the latter.

According to the author's research, the parts of ancient Chinese thought introduced to the West that were most valued and absorbed by the Physiocratic School are precisely those that have the most traditional or unique characteristics of China. In other words, those aspects of Physiocracy that are unique according to Western scholars and whose sources are not easily found in the Western tradition demonstrate striking similarities to the distinctive features of traditional Chinese thought. Numerous examples have been given in this book, which are open to comments. Here, suffice it to add just one example.

During my visit to Columbia University in New York, USA, in 1993, I found in its famous East Asian Library the long-heard doctoral dissertation, *The Economic Principles of Confucius and His School*, by Chen Huan-chang (1881–1933), a student of the university. Chen was a native of Gaoyao County, Guangdong Province, and his father was an alternate inspector in the Qing Dynasty. On the eve of the Reform Movement of 1898, when Kang Yu-wei gave lectures at Wanmu Caotang in Guangzhou, he joined in the studies under the guidance of Kang, set up the National Confucian Association in his hometown by following Kang's idea of establishing Confucianism in the form of Christianity, and offered a memorial tablet of Confucius in the Chen clan's ancestral hall. In 1904, he went to Beijing to take a special examination and was awarded the title of *Jinshi* (or *Chin Shih*, advanced scholar), and in 1907, he was sent to the United States to study economics in the Political Science Department of Columbia University. He received his doctorate in early 1911. He translated the title of his doctoral dissertation into a flexible Chinese version, literally meaning "Financial Management of Confucius." The dissertation, which enjoyed the distinction of being published under the auspices of the University, was compiled into a two-volume, 756-page book in the STUDIES IN HISTORY, ECONOMICS AND PUBLIC LAW series edited by the Faculty of Political Science of Columbia University. Since its publication, the book has been sold around the world and has been widely acclaimed among Western scholars. What is intriguing is that Chen's dissertation has attracted the attention of the Western academic circles precisely because it deals with the part of Chinese economic thought that is the richest in its own characteristics.

In the "AUTHOR'S PREFACE," Chen (1911, pp. xi–xii) states,

> THE following treatise includes a discussion of the economic principles of the chief disciples of Confucius in successive dynasties, as well as of the teachings of the Master himself, and, briefly for purposes of comparison, of the leaders of other schools, e. g., those of Kuan Tzü, Lao Tzü, Mo Tzü, Shang Yang, and Hsü Hsing. It was deemed best to combine with the discussion of economic theory some consideration of economic history. Consequently the conditions out of which the theories arose and to which they were to be applied have usually been described. The canonical writings were taken as primary sources, and the historical writings as secondary. In connection with every theory and institution considered, the attempt has been made to throw light upon its origin and earliest development. Because of the wealth of material, only the most important or most interesting historical facts since the Han dynasty have received attention. Although some information in regard to conditions in China to-day is given, it was not thought desirable to go very much into detail, because these conditions are in process of revolutionary change and many questions are still unsettled.
>
> The treatise is, therefore, essentially a study of the old régime in China. It is a survey of the Chinese thought and Chinese institutions which developed independently of the Occident. Although my arrangement of the material follows that which has become conventional among western writers and my understanding of the old texts was greatly helped by western thinkers, I have been very careful not to read into the writings of the ancient Chinese ideas drawn from modern western economists. All my statements are based upon the words or the spirit of the words of the original texts, and are in harmony with the whole system of Confucius as revealed by a comparative study of the various sources. In support of my interpretation numerous quotations and references are given. The Confucian writings may be compared to a great mountain containing rich mineral resources. I am in the position of a miner, extracting a particular ore and contributing it to the world's production. As the miner does not create the ore itself, but through his labor in exploring, digging and refining makes it available for human use, so I have tried to add something to human knowledge.

Thus, the author repeatedly emphasizes that this dissertation is based on the doctrine of Confucius, a typical representative of traditional Chinese thought, which is completely independent of the West, and excludes the transformative influence that "conditions in China to-day" may have on this traditional thought, which alone can better reflect the contribution of traditional Chinese thought to human knowledge as part of "the world's production." Interestingly, the author, in order to identify himself as a unique researcher, has written in the author's column on the book's title page the following:

> **CHEN HUAN-CHANG, Ph.D.,**
>
> ***Chin Shih of 2455 A. K. (1904, A. D.)***
>
> ***Former Secretary of the Grand Secretariat,***
>
> ***Peking, China***

Moreover, Chen Huan-chang (p. xii) is very confident about his research, claiming,

> My task has been so great that I have doubtless made some mistakes, but I have earnestly tried to be accurate in all my statements. This is the first attempt to present the economic principles of Confucius and his school in a systematic form in any language. At some future time I intend to translate this book into Chinese.

However, later he did not fulfill his promise of translation, but in the process of advocating Confucianism,, he only mentioned in passing that the purpose of this treatise was to talk about Confucianism in the context of wealth management, so that the people of the world will know that Confucianism is as practical and feasible as the inseparability of cloth, silk, beans and grain (Chen, 1919), that is, this doctoral thesis was meant as a tool to promote Confucianism. In the "AUTHOR'S PREFACE," he expresses his gratitude to his former teacher, Kang Yu-wei, from whom he believes he has "obtained a general view of Confucianism" (Chen, 1911, p. xii), and to several professors and scholars at Columbia University. Finally, the date at the end of the preface is peculiarly inscribed as "*the seventh day of the seventh month, two thousand four hundred and sixty-two years after Confucius, (August 30, 1911 A. D.)*" (p. xii), as a mark of reverence for Confucius' teachings in the form of a Confucian chronology.

Maybe, because Chen Huan-chang had always been interested in preaching Confucianism, after his return to China, he even intensified his efforts to use Confucianism, to counter the spread of new ideas in China. Some people thus describe his book as a "patchwork in English" that "uses the reactionary theories of bourgeois vulgar economics and pragmatic philosophy popular in American society at that time to supplement the Confucian and Mencian doctrines in China" (Zheng, 1980, p. 393). This view, however, seems to be somewhat radical. After all, this treatise is an extraordinary effort to discover, organize and summarize Confucian economic thought as represented by Confucius, and to introduce and publicize these economic achievements directly to the international academic community.

The whole treatise is divided into five parts, with altogether nine books and thirty-six chapters.

Part I Introduction consists of three books. The first book is on "Confucius and his school," introducing the life of Confucius, his basic ideas, his writings, his disciples, and the historical evolution of his doctrines. The second is about the relationship between economics and other sciences, or more specifically, the relations of economics to respectively other sciences in general, sociology, politics, and ethics. The third, titled "General Economic Principles," deals with economic development as the main cause of progress, economic organization, economic policies and the divisions of economics.

Part II Consumption, consisting of only the fourth book, mainly deals with the general principles of consumption, the happiness of the rich and the poor, different ways of getting pleasure, general standard of expenditure and particular expenditures.

Part III Production contains Books V, VI, VII and VIII. Book V is about the three factors of production, labor-population, nature and capital. Book VI deals with the branches of production in general, agriculture, industry and commerce. Book VII turns to distribution, mainly its general principles and the reflection in rent, interest, profit, and wages. Book VIII elaborates on "socialistic policies," relating to the Jing Tian (Tsing Tien) system, monopoly, the exclusion of the ruling class from the economic field, government control of demand and supply, government control of grain, government loans, and public relief.

Part IV Public Finance, including only one book, mainly covers public expenditures, taxation in general, and direct and indirect taxes.

Part V is the conclusion of the whole treatise.

The above list of contents, even from today's point of view, basically covers the main economic ideas of Confucius' doctrine. It is obvious that Chen's treatise adopts as a basis for analysis the prevailing theoretical system of Western economics of the time. The most striking effect of its publication, as can be seen below, has been the special attention it has drawn to Confucius and China's Confucian economic thought among Western scholars, especially Western economists.

Friedrich Hirth (1911, p. vii), a professor of Chinese at Columbia University, states in his "FOREWORD" to the book,

> DR. CHEN HUAN-CHANG [...] has seen some service as a mandarin in one of the metropolitan offices in Peking; he is deeply versed in his native literature, of which the so-called Confucian classics have occupied him for many years; he is a personal friend and has been a pupil of Kang Yu-wei, one of the originators of the modern Chinese reform movement and himself a profound connoisseur of Chinese literature. Thus armed, he came to New York about five years ago to study English and take courses in political economy at Columbia University. [...] Dr. Chen proves a disciple worthy of his great teacher. His enthusiasm for the great sage and his doctrine could not be surpassed; western readers will find in his book the representation of Confucianism from the purely Confucianist point of view by an author who is a Confucianist himself and has had the advantage of sifting his ideas through the methods of western science.

Seager (1911, p. ix), a professor of political economy at the same university, comments in his "PREFACE" in a more professional way,

> In presenting the economic teachings of Confucianism, Dr. Chen has adopted the same order of arrangement that has become usual in English treatises on political economy. [...] [This] enables the author, with his wide acquaintance with the best English economic literature, to bring out many interesting contrasts between Chinese civilization and the civilization of the Occident. His discussions of such institutions as the family, marriage, private property and the position of woman have an interest and value quite apart from their relation to the main purpose of his study.
>
> No one can read these pages without becoming convinced that Confucianism is a great economic, as well as a great moral and religious, system and that it contains most, if not all, of the elements necessary to the solution of the serious problems that confront China to-day. That these problems may be speedily and happily solved and that Dr. Chen may take the prominent and distinguished part in the reformation of his country for which his high character and unusual attainments so well fit him is the earnest hope of his American friends.

It is easy to see from the above two quotations the deep impression made on American scholars by Chen's doctoral dissertation, which is devoted to the economic thought of Confucius and his school of thought. That is why the dissertation was published and then reprinted in 1930. It was said to have been praised at that time in *The American Historical Review* as an unprecedented achievement, and then in various English-language newspapers and magazines in China. Edwin R. A. Seligma, a professor of economics at Columbia University, even cited it as an authoritative work for questioning Chinese students in their dissertation defenses (Hu, 1984b, p. 476).

Schumpeter (1954a, p. 53) also mentions Chen's book when he traces the earliest origins of economic analysis worldwide, that is, the so-called "trace of analytic effort:"

> More than anywhere else we might expect to find such traces in ancient China, the home of the oldest literary culture of which we know. We find in fact a highly developed public administration that dealt currently with agrarian, commercial, and financial problems. These problems are frequently touched upon, mainly from an ethical standpoint, in the remains of Chinese classical literature, for instance in the teaching of Kung Fu Tse (551-478 B.C.), who was himself at two stages of his life a practical administrator and reformer, and of Mêng Tsù (Mencius, 372-288 B.C. ...), from whose works it is possible to compile a comprehensive system of economic policy. Moreover, there were methods of monetary management and of exchange control that seem to presuppose a certain amount of analysis. The phenomena incident to the recurrent inflations were no doubt observed and discussed by men much superior to us in cultural refinement.

Although he still maintains that there is no ancient Chinese work that can be characterized by what he calls "scientific" and that has been handed down to reason about strictly economic subjects, he adds with great caution, "The obvious inference is of course highly uncertain. There may have been analytic work, the records of which failed to survive" (p. 53). Schumpeter's main bases for looking to ancient China for the origins of economic analysis, and for guessing that traces of such analytical efforts are most likely to be found there, according to his own notes, are the work of Chen Huan-chang, the aforementioned 1936 doctoral dissertation in French by Ly Siou-Y, and the work of another Western scholar E. D. Thomas's *Chinese Political Thought* (1927) (p. 53 [Note 3]).[1] In particular, it is clearly under the influence of Chen Huan-chang's work that Schumpeter emphasizes the works of Confucius and Mencius, arguing that a complete system of economic policy can be compiled from such works.

The main reason why Chen Huan-chang's doctoral dissertation is discussed in detail above is that "it is the first famous work of Chinese economic thought published in the West by China's scholars in the early twentieth century, and one of the earliest works of the economic science published by Chinese people in the West" (Hu, 1984b, p. 476), which may more convincingly explain how the ancient economic thought with Chinese characteristics can have a unique influence in the Western world. As a matter of fact, the richness and variety of the world's academic achievements come from the contributions of all countries, each with its own characteristics, and the mutual influence and integration of each country's unique academics have promoted the development of the world's academics. In this light, it does not have to make people feel incredible that the Physiocrats drew nourishment from the traditional Chinese culture transmitted from the West at that time as one of the direct and important intellectual origins of its theoretical system, which is in fact a reflection of the internal driving force for the development of the world economic theory at that historical stage. At the same time, Chen Huan-chang's doctoral dissertation is known to Chinese scholars only by name, for there is still no Chinese translation, which partly accounts for the above brief explanation.

---

[1] By the way, the famous name Chen Huan-chang seems to be unfamiliar to the Chinese translators of *History of Economic Analysis*, who translated it as "Huang Changchen." They were even more ignorant of the obscure name Ly Siou-Y, so they retained only the Chinese translation of "S. Y. Li." Schumpeter (1991, p. 86) abbreviated the long title of Ly Siou-Y's book to *Les grands courants de la pensée économique chinoise dans l'antiquité*.

3. The study of the Chinese origin of Physiocracy can not only prompt us to re-examine the historical position of Chinese economic thought in the world, but also push us to investigate its relevance for today's world.

In his review of Chen Huan-chang's doctoral dissertation, Hu Jichuang (1984b, p. 476) laments the fact that "in China, the economists who are early to emerge in the international arena are those specializing in the part of Chinese economic thought that has attracted little attention at home for a long time," which refers to the situation in the first half of the twentieth century. Later, in his "Preface" to this book, he changes the tone, arguing that the message of this book is that "China, having been known as 'the sleeping lion of East Asia' for more than two centuries, will certainly make its own new contribution to world economics in the near future." Either way, we can see that Hu, who as an octogenarian has worked hard for decades on the history of Chinese economic thought, has a firm belief in the development prospect of this field, in spite of his slight regret at its being neglected in China.

Chinese economic thought had its own brilliance in the past. Things changed only when China's feudal economic system, rigid and solidified, could not withstand the impact of foreign powers relying on their strength of ships and guns, and once the country's door was opened, gradually disintegrated in the face of the invasion of Western capitalist economy from Japan and the West. If the skin doesn't exist, how can the hair be attached? Its dominant position was then gradually replaced by that of the imported Western bourgeois economic theories. At the beginning of the twentieth century, in the unprecedented upsurge of studying abroad in Japan, the theoretical system of modern economics, together with a large number of new terms, was translated and processed first in Japan and then introduced into China in a rush. Since then, the economic thoughts popular in China, in terms of both theoretical or logical reasoning, and expressions and special terms, are almost all imported from Japan and the West, and China's own economic ideas seem to have disappeared. Under such circumstances, talking about or sorting out Chinese economic thoughts is often regarded as an outdated fascination for useless old things. In fact, this is a misunderstanding.

Chinese economic thought is a historical category full of vitality, constantly supplementing and developing itself. It is rooted in China's own economic practice, not only drawing on all valuable foreign economic theoretical achievements, just as Physiocracy once drew nourishment from Chinese economic thought, but also generalizing or reflecting the increasingly deep exploration and creation of Chinese scholars in their economic studies. It is thus not a stagnant concept. It had been in a leading position in the history of the world, and was then stuck in a downturn and backward state. However, its development has not come to a standstill, nor will it ever be in the future, but keeps moving on all the time. It is not an outmoded concept, either. It had its glory in ancient times, is now experiencing the nourishment and accumulation of a new source of life, and will certainly reproduce its glory in the future. Last but not least, it is far from a closed concept. It was forced to learn from the West in a humiliating environment, but now, with China's opening-up, it embraces the world and the future with confidence.

The economic rise of some East Asian countries in the 1970s led many European and American scholars to examine the mysteries of such economic achievements from the perspective of economic thoughts. At last, they all attributed the rise to the influence of Confucian culture. This conclusion, whether correct or not, is a question worth pondering. Why does only the modern influence of traditional Confucian culture draw the attention of Western scholars? Perhaps it can be said that, when a country is weak and backward, even its cultural tradition is often despised, and that, when it becomes strong and advanced, it tends to make people more respectful of, or appreciate, the things that are precious in its cultural traditions. China has in recent years made great economic achievements that attract the world's attention. At the same time, China's economists have begun to put forward or brew the so-called Chinese school of economics and even Chinese economics. This is a natural development. Its starting point is that China's unique great practice must be guided by its own economic theory, and the economic theories summarized from this practice are bound to have their own distinctive features. Based on this, the inheritance of its tradition of economic thought will naturally be highlighted, because China's present cannot be severed from its past. Some people are worried that this formulation may give rise to the so-called "cult of the ancients." In fact, this worry is still tainted by the above-mentioned misunderstanding. The economic thought of the past has left to the modern times not only feudal and backward economic concepts such as the closed-mindedness and the mentality of small-farm agriculture, but also the values, ethical norms, modes of thinking and rich achievements in economic thoughts that are integrated with the extensive and profound traditional Chinese culture. True that China's traditional economic thought had a strong and profound influence on the Physiocratic School, but this heritage, after several millennia of critical evolution and organic integration, has transcended its historical origins to constitute the DNA of Chinese economic thinking. Far from being eclipsed in the current trajectory of China's economic theorization, it will certainly flourish with the country's economic take-off and the progress of the times.

It has been more than four years since the first edition of this book was published. Busy with so many things every day, I have gradually forgotten the various experiences and feelings I had while I was immersed in this research. Now, when I write this postscript for its reprinting, I suddenly fall into a reverie about the past: I have so many fresh and grateful memories of my mentor Hu Jichuang, my seniors and relatives, and so many thoughts and expectations about this work! Last but not least, I would like to express my gratitude to Mr. Chen Xin, President of Shanghai People's Publishing House, and Mr. Shi Hongjun, Editor in charge of this book, for their enthusiastic academic spirit in proposing to reprint this book.

November 1997

References

Americana Corporation (Ed.) (1957). *The Encyclopedia Americana* (Vol. 23). Americana Corp.

Anikin, A. V. (1979). *A Science in its youth: Pre-marxian political economy* (K. M. Cook, Trans.). International Publishers.

Aquinas, T. (1959). Summa Theologica. In A. P. D'Entrèves (Ed.) (J. G. Dawson, Trans.), *Aquinas selected political writings* (pp. 102–179). Basil Blackwell.

Ashley, W. J. (1898). Introduction. In A. R. J. Turgot, *Reflections on the formation and the distribution of riches* (W. J. Ashley, Trans.) (pp. v–xiii). The Macmillan Co.

Barna, T. (1975). Quesnay's tableau in modern guise. *The Economic Journal, 85*(339), 485–496.

Bary, W. T. (1983). *The liberal tradition in China.* Columbia University Press.

Bauer, S. (1895). The biography of Quesnay. *The Economic Journal, 5*(20), 660–661.

Beijing Sino-French Sinology Institute (Ed.) (1943). *Sinology in eighteenth- and nineteenth-century France.*

Bernard, H. (1936). *Aux Portes de la Chine. Les Missionaires du Seizième Siècle 1514–1588* (R. Xiao, Trans. into Chinese). The Commercial Press.

Bhatia, H. L. (1978). *History of economic thought.* Vikas Pub. House.

Blaug, M. (1985). *Economic theory in retrospect* (4th ed.). Cambridge University Press.

Bloomfield, A. I. (1938). The foreign-trade doctrines of the physiocrats. *The American Economic Review, 28*(4), 716–735.

Bouvet, J. (1699) *The history of Cang-Hy, the Present Emperour of China Pesented to the Most Christian King.* Printed for F. Coggan.

Cantillon, R. (2017). *On the nature of commerce in general* (H. Higgs, Trans.). Routledge.

Capra, F. (1975). *The Tao of physics.* Shambhala.

Chang, J. L. Y. (1986). Chinese economic thought before the seventeenth century: a review. *History of Political Economy, 18*(1), 180–182.

Chao, C. (1975). *On the importance of grain.* Zhonghua Book Company.

Chen, D. (1981). *From the classical school of economics to Marx.* Shanghai People's Publishing House.

Chen, D. (1988a). François Quesnay. In *Encyclopedia of China—Economics* (Vol. II). Encyclopedia of China Publishing House.

Chen, D. (1988b). Laissez faire. In *Encyclopedia of China—Economics* (Vol. III). Encyclopedia of China Publishing House.

Chen, H. (1911) *The economic principles of confucius and his school.* Longmans, Green & Co.

Chen, H. (1919). *On the religion of Confucianism.* The Commercial Press.

Ch'ên, S. (1935a). The jesuitical views of Confucianism and their repercussions in China's academia at the end of the Ming dynasty and the beginning of the Qing dynasty. In *National Peking University Studies of Traditional Chinese Culture* (Vol. 5, No. 2, pp. 1–64).

M. Tan, *The Chinese Origin of Physiocracy*, https://doi.org/10.1007/978-981-97-9703-5

Ch'ên, S. (1935b). Sino-European cultural contacts since the discovery of the sea route: A bibliographical note. *Nankai Social & Economic Quarterly* (Vol. 8, No. 1, pp. 44–74).

Ch'ên, S. (1946). Foreword. In L. A. Maverick, *China: A model for Europe* (pp. v–vii). Paul Anderson Company

Cheng, Y., & Zheng, R. (1989). *Chen Yi's annotation of the book of changes*. Shanghai Chinese Classics Publishing House.

Ching, J. (1983). Leibniz and Chinese neo-confucianism. *Research into the History of Chinese Philosophy, 4*(4), 114–118.

Clark, T. B. (1939). *Oriental England: A study of oriental influences in eighteenth century England as reflected in the drama*. Kelly and Walsh, Limited.

Clerc, N. G. (1769). *Yu le Grand et Confucius*. Ponce Courtois.

Condorcet, J. A. N. (1787). *The Life of M. Turgot, controller-general of the finances of France in the years 1774, 1775 and 1776* (Translator unidentified). J. Johnson

Confucius. (1869). The Classics. In J. Legge (Trans.), *The life and teachings of confucius* (2nd ed.) (pp. 116–320). N. Trübner

Daire, E. (Ed.). (1846). *Physiocrates*. Librairie de Guillaumin.

de Clavijo, R. G. (1859). *Narrative of the embassy of Ruy Gonzalez de Clavijo to the court of Timour at Samarcand, A.D. 1403–6* (C. R. Markham, Trans.). The Hakluyt society.

de Sacy, J. S. (1970). *Henri Bertin dans le sillage de la Chine: 1720–1792*. Éditions Cathasia.

Diderot, D. (1975). *Œuvres complètes* (H. Dieckmann & J. Varloot, Eds.). Hermann.

Dong, G. (1987). *The mathematical structure of Yi diagrams*. Shanghai People's Publishing House.

Dong, Z. (1975). *Chunqiu Fanlu (Luxuriant dew of the spring and autumn annals)*, Annotated by Ling Shu. Zhonghua Book Company, 1975.

Du Halde, J. B. (1741). *A description of the empire of China and Chinese-tartary, together with the kingdoms of Korea, and Tibet* (Vol. 2, English Translation). J. Thomas for E. Cave.

Durant, W., & Durant, A. (1963). *The story of civilization: Part VIII the age of Louis XIV*. Simon and Schuster.

Durrant, S., Li, W., & Schaberg, D. (2016). (Trs.), *Zuo tradition / Zuozhuan: Commentary on the "spring and autumn annals"*. University of Washington Press.

Einaudi, L. (1958). *François Quesnay et la physiocratie*. Institut National d'Études Démographiques.

Einaudi, M. (1938). *The physiocratic doctrine of judicial control, Cambridge*. Harvard University Press.

Eltis, W. A. (1975). *François Quesnay: A reinterpretation 1. The Tableau Économique* (Vol. 27, No. 2, pp. 167–200). Oxford Economic Papers, New Series.

Engels, F. (1966). Karl Marx, A contribution to the critique of political economy. In K. Marx, & F. Engels, *Selected works* (Vol. 1, pp. 507–516) (the Institute of Marxism-Leninism, Trans.). Progress Publishers.

Engels, F. (1977). *Anti-Dühring* (Emile Burns Trans.). Progress Publishers.

Fan, C. (1931). Dr. Johnson, Goldsmith and Chinese culture. *Nanking Journal, 1*(2), 389–406.

Fan, C. (1943a). Chinese thought and English deism. *The Journal of Literature, History, and Philosophy* (I), *1*(1), 1–21.

Fan, C. (1943b). Chinese thought and English deism. *The Journal of Literature, History, and Philosophy* (II), *1*(2), 111–137.

Fan, C. (1981). Chinese humanism and the English enlightenment. *Literary Heritage, 15*(4), 1–13.

Fan, C. (2015). *Essays on Chinese and western culture*. Yilin Press.

Fang, H. (1947). *History of catholicism in China* (Vol. I). The Commercial Press.

Fang, H. (1987). *A history of the relationship between China and the West* (Vols. I & II). Yuelu Press.

Fang, R. C. (1931). China in eighteenth-century English literature (To be continued). *Quarterly Journal of Liberal Arts, Wuhan University, 2*(1), 15–35.

Feng, Z. (Ed.). (1979). *The complete history of the West* (Vol. XII). Yanjing Cultural Enterprise Co., Ltd.

Fox-Genovese, E. (1976). *The origins of physiocracy: Economic revolution and social order in eighteenth-century France.* Cornell University Press.
Fu, X. (1999). Fuzi: Fair allocation of taxes and forced labor. In K. Yan (Ed.), *The complete works of the Jin dynasty* (Vol. 48). The Commercial Press.
Fung, Y. (1948). *A short history of Chinese philosophy.* The Macmillan Company.
Gan, N. (1926). *History of pre-qin economic thought in China.* The Commercial Press.
Geng, D. (1933). On Montesquieu's elaboration of chinese political system in his L'Esprit des Lois. *Guanghua University Semi-Monthly, 2*(4), 20–23.
Geng, D. (1934). Voltaire and confucius. *Guanghua University Semi-Monthly, 3*(3), 10–13.
Geng, S. (1987). Recent French studies of the Jesuits in China. *Trends of Recent Researches on the History of China, 9*(7), 20–27.
Gerbillon, J. F. (1735). Relations de huit voyages dans la Grande Tartarie de 1688 a 1699. In J. B. du Halde, *Description Geographique, Historique, Chronologique, Politique, et Physique de l'Empire de la Chine et de la Tartarie Chinoise* (Vol. 4, pp. 87–422). P.G. le Mercier.
Gide, C., & Rist, C. (1915). *A history of economic doctrines* (W. Smart and R. Richards, Trans.). George G. Harrop & Company.
Gollwitzer, H. (1962). *Die Gelbe Gefahr: Geschichte eines Schlagworts, Studien zum Imperialistischen Denken.* Vandenhoeck & Ruprecht.
Gorai, K. (1938). *The impact of confucianism on german political thought* (B. Liu, & Y. Liu, Trs. into Chinese). The Commercial Press.
Gordon, H. S. (1968). Laissez-Faire. In D. L. Sills (Ed.), *International encyclopedia of the social sciences* (Vol. 8, pp. 546–549). The Macmillan Company & The Free Press.
Goto, S. (1956). *The westward spread of China's thought in France.* Japan Yōtoku Press.
Gray, A. (1931). *The development of economic doctrine, London.* Longmans, Green and Co.
Gu, X., et al. (Trs.) (1986). *The continental states of Europe in the Seventeenth and eighteenth centuries*, Revised Ed.. The Commercial Press.
Gu, Y. (1924). *Gu Yanwu's collected writings* (Vol. 1, p. 10). Changming Book Co.
Guanzi. (1998). *Guanzi: Political, economic, and philosophical essays from early China* (Vol. 2, Chapters XII, 35–XXIV, 86) (W. Allyn Rickett, Trans.). Princeton University Press.
Guanzi. (2001). *Guanzi: Political, economic, and philosophical essays from early China* (Vol. 1, Chapters I, 1–XI, 34, and XX, 64-XXI, pp. 65–66) (1st revised ed., W. Allyn Rickett, Trans.). Cheng & Tsui Company.
Guo, Y. (1934). Interpreting the physiocrats' economic doctrines. *Chinese Economy, 2*(8), 1–10.
Han Fei Tzŭ (1939). *The complete works of Han Fei Tzŭ* (Vol. 1) (W. K. Liao, Trans.). Arthur Probsthain.
Han Fei Tzŭ (1959). *The complete works of Han Fei Tzŭ* (Vol. 2) (W. K., Liao, Trans.). Arthur Probsthain.
Handman, M., et al. (1931). Economic history—The decline of Laissez Faire. *The American Economic Review, 21*(1), 3–10.
Haney, L. H. (1911). *History of economic thought.* The MacMillan Company.
He, B. (1935). A study of the spread of Chinese culture to the West. *The China New Critic. 1*(3), 59–80.
He, Z. (1988). Chinese Confucianism and the enlightenment in western Europe. *Chinese Literature and History, 8*(6), 110–115.
Heckscher, E. F. (1936). Revisions in economic history: V. mercantilism. *The Economic History Review, 7*(1), 44–54.
Hegel, C. (1899a). Charles Hegel's preface. In G. W. F. Hegel, *The philosophy of history* (J. Sibree, Trans.). The Colonial Press.
Hegel, G. W. F. (1892). *Lectures on the history of philosophy* (Vol. 1) (E. S. Haldane, Trans.). Kegan Paul, Trench, Trübner & Co. LTD.
Hegel, G. W. F. (1899b). *The philosophy of history* (J. Sibree, Trans.). The Colonial Press.
Higgs, H. (1897). *The physiocrats.* The Macmillan Company.

Hirth, F. (1911). Foreword. In H. C. Chen, *The economic principles of confucius and his school* (Vol. 1). Longmans, Green & Co.
Hong, L. (1965). *Collection of Hong Liangji's works*. The Commercial Press.
Hou, W., Zhao, J., & Du, G. (1957). *General history of Chinese thought* (Vol. One). People's Publishing House.
Hou, J. (1982). *History of Chinese economic thought*. Central Supplier of Cultural Relics.
Hu, J. (1962). *A history of Chinese economic thought* (Vol. 1). Shanghai People's Publishing House.
Hu, J. (1984). *An outline of the history of modern Chinese economic thought*. China Social Sciences Press.
Hu, J. (1963). *A history of Chinese economic thought* (Vol. 2). Shanghai People's Publishing House.
Hu, J. (1984a). *Chinese economic thought before the seventeenth century*. Foreign Languages Press.
Hu, J. (1988). *Prehistory of political economy*. Liaoning People's Publishing House.
Huan, K. (1931). *Discourses on salt and iron*, Chaps. I-XIX (E. M. Gale (Trans.). Brill.
Huan, K. (1934). *Discourses on salt and iron*, Chaps. XX-XVIII (Vol. LXV, pp. 73–110) (Z. Lin Trans.). *Journal of the North China Branch of the Royal Asiatic Society*. http://www2.iath.virginia.edu/saxon/servlet/SaxonServlet?source=xwomen/texts/yantie.xml&style=xwomen/xsl/dynaxml.xsl&chunk.id=d1.6&toc.depth=1&toc.id=d2.24&doc.lang=english
Huan, K. (2016). *Discourses on salt and iron*. Sunshine Press.
Huang, S. (1991). *Han Shu: Shi Huo Zhi—The first work of China's economic history*. Economic Press China.
Huang, T. [Tsung-hsi, or Zongxi] (1993). *Waiting for the dawn: A plan for the prince* (W. T. De Bary, Trans.). Columbia University Press.
Huangfu, M. (2010). *The emperor's time in China*. Qilu Press.
Hudson, G. F. (1931). *Europe & China: A survey of their relations from the earliest times to 1800*. Edward Arnold & Co.
Hume, D. (1779). *Essays and treatises on several subjects* (Vol. 1). J. Williams.
Idei, S. (1929). *History of economic thought* (J. Liu, Tr. into Chinese). Shanghai United Bookstore.
Ishida, M. (1941). *Cultural exchanges between China and the West* (H. Zhang, Tr. into Chinese). The Commercial Press.
Ji, T. (1963). *Physiocracy*. The Commercial Press.
Keynes, J. M. (1964). *The general theory of employment, interest, and money*. Harcourt Brace Jovanovic.
Klippel, D. (1994). Johann august Schlettwein and the economic faculty at the university of Gießen. *History of Political Thought, 15*(2), 203–227.
Knoblock, J., & Riegel, J. (1995). *Mozi: A study and translation of the ethical and political writings*. Institute of East Asian Studies.
Krader, L. (1974). *The ethnological notebooks of Karl Marx*. International Institute of Social History.
Landreth, H. (1976). *History of economic theory: Scope, method and content*. Houghton Mifflin Company.
Lao Zi (Lao Tzu) (1994). *Tao Tê Ching*. In A. Waley, *The way and its power: Lao Tzu's Tao Tê Ching and its place in Chinese thought* (pp. 141–243). Grove Press.
Legge, J. (Tr.) (1879). The Shû King. In F. M. Müller (Ed.), *The sacred books of China: The texts of confucianism Part I* (pp. 1–272). The Clarendon Press.
Legge, J. (Tr.) (1885). The Lî Kî, I-X. In F. M. Müller (Ed.), *The sacred books of China: the texts of confucianism Part III* (pp. 61–480). The Clarendon Press.
Legge, J. (Tr.) (1963). *The sacred books of China: The I Ching*, F. M. Müller (Ed.). Dover Publications.
Leibniz, G. W. (1994). *Writings on China*, translated, with an introduction, notes, and commentaries by Daniel J. Cook and Henry Rosemont Jr., Open Court Publishing Company.
Lekachman, R. (1959). *A history of economic ideas*. Harper & Row.
Lenin, V. I. (1976). *Collected works* (Vol. 38) (Philosophical Notebooks, Clemence Dutt, Trans.). Progress Publishers.
Leontief, W. (1951). *The structure of American economy, 1919–1939*. Oxford University Press.

Lévy-Bruhl, L. (1899). *History of modern philosophy in France.* The Open Court Publishing Co.
Lewiński, J. S. (1931). *The founders of political economy.* P. S. King & Son Ltd.
Li, G. (1931). On the relationship between the French physiocrats and Chinese political and economic thoughts. *The Student Monthly of Peking National University, 1*(3), 1–15.
Li, G., et al. (Eds.). (1959). *The continental states of Europe in the seventeenth and eighteenth centuries.* The Sanlian Press.
Li, J. (Ed.). (1986). *Dialogues between Zhu Xi and his disciples.* Zhonghua Book Company.
Li, J. (1979). On the introduction of western bourgeois economics into China at the end of the Qing dynasty. *Economic Research Journal, 14*(4), 68–75.
Li, W. (Ed.). (1957). *History of modern agriculture in China* (Vol. 1, pp. 71–72). The Sanlian Press.
Li, Y. (1922). The relationship between the economist Turgot and two young Chinese scholars. *National Peking University Social Sciences Quarterly, 1*(1), 166–180.
Li, Z. (1961). *Fen Shu (A book to burn).* Zhonghua Book Company.
Li, Z. (1974). *Cang Shu (A book to keep)* (Vol. 24). Zhonghua Book Company.
Lin, Z. (1979). *History of the Western economic thought.* San Min Book Co., Ltd.
Liu, A. (2010). *The Huainanzi: A guide to the theory and practice of government in early Han China* (J. S. Major, S. A. Queen, A. S. Meyer, & H. D. Roth, Trans.). Columbia University Press.
Liu, B. (1990). *Lun Yu Zheng Yi.* Zhonghua Book Company.
Liu, T. (2014). *Sketches of the imperial capital* (Vol. 5). Chinese Bookshop.
Liu, X. (2019). *Shuo Yuan*, 2 Vols. Annotated and translated (into modern Chinese) by Wang Tianhai and Yang Xiulan (p. 1105). Zhonghua Book Company.
Liu, X. (1975). *Jiu Tang Shu.* Zhonghua Book Company.
Lu, J. (1991). *Excerpts from the miscellaneous writings in the Jianjia Hall.* Zhonghua Book Company.
Lu, J. (1935). *Xin Yu.* Zhonghua Book Company.
Lundbeck, C. (1988). The spread of neo-confucianism in Europe (G. Sheng, Tr. into Chinese), *Trends of Recent Researches on the History of China* (Vol. 10, No. 7, pp. 15–20).
Lü, B. (Ed.). (2000).*The annals of Lü Buwei*, John Knoblock and Jeffrey Riegel (Trans.). Stanford University Press.
Ly, S. (1936). *Les Grands Courants de la Pensée Économique Chinoise dans L'Antiquité (du Vie au IIIe siècle avant J.-C.) et leur Influence sur la Formation de la Doctrine Physiocratique* [Doctoral dissertation, the Law School of Dijon University].
Ly, S. (1938). L'Influence de la Pensée Économico-Politique de la Chine Ancienne sur la Doctrine Physiocratique. *Social Research 1*(3), 1–30.
Ma, D. (1986). *Wen Xian Tong Kao.* Zhonghua Book Company.
Malebranche, N. (1980). *Dialogue between a christian philosopher and a Chinese philosopher on the existence and nature of god* (D. A. Iorio, Trans.). Catholic University Press.
Maritain, J. (1951). *Man and the state.* The University of Chicago Press.
Martin, K. (1963). *French liberal thought in the eighteenth century: a study of political ideas from Bayle to Condorcet, New York.* Harper and Row.
Marx, K. (1913). *The poverty of philosophy* (H. Quelch, Trans.). Charles H. Kerr & Company.
Marx, K. (1966). The eighteenth Brumaire of Louis Bonaparte. In K. Marx, & F. Engels, *Selected works* (Vol. 1, pp. 394–487, the Institute of Marxism-Leninism Trans.). Progress Publishers.
Marx, K. (1969). *Theories of surplus-value*, Part I (Emile Burns Trans.). Progress Publishers.
Marx, K. (1990). *Capital* (Vol. 1) (B. Fowkes, Trans.). Penguin Books.
Marx, K. (1991). *Capital* (Vol. 3) (D. Fernbach, Trans.). Penguin Books.
Marx, K. (1992). *Capital* (Vol. 2) (D. Fernbach, Trans.). Penguin Books.
Mason, S. F. (1962). *A history of the sciences.* Collier Books.
Maverick, L. A. (1938). Chinese influences upon the physiocrats. *Economic History, 3*(13), 54–67.
Maverick, L. A. (1940). The Chinese and the physiocrats: A supplement. *Economic History, 4*(15), 312–318.
Maverick, L. A. (1946). *China: A model for Europe.* Paul Anderson Company.

Meek, R. L. (1962). *The economics of physiocracy: Essays and translations*. George Allen & Unwin Ltd.
Meek, R. L. (1973). *Precursors of Adam Smith*. J. M. Dent & Sons Ltd.
Mencius. (1875). *The works of Mencius* (L. James, Trans.). In L. James, *The life and teachings of Mencius* (pp. 123–385). N. Trübner.
Mercier de la Rivière, P. P. (1846). *L'Ordre Naturel et Essentiel des Sociétés Politiques*, In: Eugène Daire (Ed.), *Physiocrates* (pp. 445–641). Librairie de Guillaumin.
Mirabeau, V. de R., & Quesnay, F. (1764). *Philosophie rurale* (Vol. 3). Libraires Associés.
Montesquieu, C. de (1989). *The Spirit of the Laws*, Anne M. Cohler, Basia C. Miller & Harold S. Stone (Trs.). Cambridge University Press.
Morley, J. (1886). *Diderot and the encyclopedists* (Vol. 1). Macmillan and Co.
Mourant, J. A. (1949). Discussion. Mr. Neill and physiocracy. *Journal of the History of Ideas, 10*(1), 130–134.
Mungello, D. E. (1977). *Leibniz and confucianism: The search for accord*. The University Press of Hawaii.
Needham, J. (1946). On science and social change. *Science & Society, 10*(3), 225–251.
Needham, J. (1947). *Science and society in ancient China*. Watts & Co.
Needham, J. (1954). *Science and civilisation in China* (Vol. 1). Cambridge University Press.
Needham, J. (1956). *Science and civilisation in China* (Vol. 2). Cambridge University Press.
Needham, J. (1963). Poverties and Triumphs of the Chinese Scientific Tradition. In A. C. Crombie (Ed.), *Scientific change: Historical studies in the intellectual* (pp. 117–153). Heinemann.
Needham, J. (1964). Science and China's influence on the world. In R. Dawson (Ed.) *The legacy of China* (pp. 234–308). Oxford University Press.
Needham, J. (1966). Time and knowledge in China and the West. In J. T. Fraser (Ed.), *The Voices of Time* (pp. 92–135). G. Braziller.
Needham, J. (1969). *The grand titration: Science and society in East and West*. Routledge.
Needham, J. (2004). *Science and civilisation in China*. Part II: General conclusions and reflections (Vol. 7). Cambridge University Press.
Neill, T. P. (1948). Quesnay and physiocracy. *Journal of the History of Ideas, 9*(2), 153–173.
Neill, T. P. (1949). The physiocrats' concept of economics. *The Quarterly Journal of Economics, 63*(4), 532–553.
Newman, P. C. (1952). *The development of economic thought*. Prentice-Hall.
Palmer, R. R., Colton, J., & Kramer, L. (2007). *A history of the modern world: To 1815* (10th Ed.). McGraw-Hill Companies.
Peking University's Department of Philosophy (Ed.). (1979). *Philosophy in eighteenth-century France*. The Commercial Press.
Petty, W. (1690). *Political Arithmetick*. Robert Clavel.
Pfeil, S. (1957). Laissez-Faire. In A. Corporation (Ed.), *The encyclopedia Americana* (Vol. 16, pp. 655–656). Americana Corp.
Phillips, A. (1955). The tableau économique as a simple Leontief model. *The Quarterly Journal of Economics, 69*(1), 137–144.
Pinot, V. (1906–1907). Les physiocrates et la chine au XVIIIe Siècle. *Revue d'Histoire Moderne et Contemporaine* (Vol. VIII, pp. 200–214).
Pont, D. (1767). *Physiocratie, ou constitution naturelle du gouvernement le plus avantageux au genre humain*. Leyden/Paris.
Pont, D. (1898). Introductory note. In A. R. J. Turgot, *Reflections on the formation and the distribution of riches* (W. J. Ashley Trans.) (p. 1). The Macmillan Co.
Qiu, J. (1993). *The derivation of the great learning: A supplement* (Vols. 20–22). Zhongzhou Chinese Classics Publishing House.
Quesnay, F. (1888) *Œuvres Économiques et Philosophiques de F. Quesnay*. Jules Peelman & CIE.
Quesnay, F. (1946). *Despotism in China* (L. A. Maverick, Trans.). In Maverick, L. A., *China: A model for Europe*. Paul Anderson Company (pp. 139–304).

Quesnay, F. (1962). Part one: Translations. In Meek, R. L., *The economics of physiocracy: Essays and translations* (pp. 43–262). George Allen & Unwin Ltd.

Quesnay, F. (1972). *Quesnay's Tableau Economique* (M. Kuczynski & R. L. Meek, Trs.). Palgrave Macmillan.

Quesnay, F. (1979). *Selected economic works*. (F. Wu, & C. Zhang, Tr. into Chinese). The Commercial Press.

Rae, J. (1895). *Life of Adam Smith*. Macmillan & Co.

Raleigh, W. (1910). *The English voyages of the sixteenth century*. James MacLehose and Sons.

Reichwein, A. (1925). *China and Europe: Intellectual and artistic contacts in the eighteenth century* (J. C. Powell, Trans.). Kegan Paul, Trench, Trubner & Co., Ltd.

Reichwein, A. (1962). *China and Europe: Intellectual and artistic contacts in the eighteenth century*. (J. Zhu Tr. into Chinese). The Commercial Press.

Ren, J. (Ed.). (1983). *History of the development of Chinese philosophy*. People's Publishing House.

Ricci, M. (2016). *The true meaning of the lord of heaven*, Revised Ed., Douglas Lancashire and Peter Hu Kuo-chen (Tr.). Institute of Jesuit Sources, Boston College.

Rima, I. H. (2001). *Development of economic analysis* (6th ed.). Routledge.

Roll, E. (1923). *A history of economic thought*. Faber and Faber Ltd.

Rotelle, J. E., et al. (eds.). (1991–2019). *The works of Saint Augustine. A translation for the 21st Century* (Vol. 46). New City Press.

Rousseau, J. J. (1997). *The social contract and other later political writings*, Victor Gourevitch (ed.). Cambridge University Press.

Rozenberg, D. I. (1934–1936). *Istoriia Politicheskoi Ekonomii*, Parts. 1–3. Leningrad.

Roy, O. (1972). *Leibniz et La Chine*. Vrin.

Rubin, I. I. (1932) *François Quesnay* (T. Da, Tr. into chinese). Han Wei Publishing House.

Rubin, I. I. (1979). *A history of economic thought, translated and edited by Donald Filtzer from 2nd revised* (Russian). Inklinks.

Rule, P. A. (1972). *K'ung-tzu or Confucius? The Jesuit Interpretation of Confucius* [Ph. D thesis of Australian National University].

Samuels, W. J. (1962). The physiocratic theory of economic policy. *The Quarterly Journal of Economics, 76*(1), 145–162.

Samuelson, P. A. (1962). Economists and the history of ideas. *The American Economic Review, 52*(1), 1–18.

Samuelson, P. A. (1982). Quesnay's 'tableau Economique' as a theorist would formulare it today. In I. Bradley & M. Howard (Eds.), *Classical and Marxian political economy* (pp. 45–78). The Macmillan Press Ltd.

Say, L. (1888). *Turgot* (M. B. Anderson, Trans.). A. C. McClurg and Company.

Schelle, G. (Ed.) (1908). Impôts par QUESNAY. article inédit avec notes de Torgot. *Revue d'histoire des doctrines économiques et socials 1*, 137–186.

Schumpeter, J. A. (1954a). *History of economic analysis*. George Allen and Unwin Ltd.

Schumpeter, J. A. (1954b). *Economic doctrine and method*. (R. Aris, Trans.). Oxford University Press.

Schumpeter, J. A. (1991). *History of economic analysis* (Vol. 1). (Zhu Yang et al., Trans. into Chinese). The Commercial Press.

Seager, H. R. (1911). Preface. In H. C., Chen, *The economic principles of confucius and his school* (Vol. 1). Longmans, Green & Co.

Semmel, B. (1965). Malthus: 'Physiocracy' and the commercial system. *The Economic History Review, 17*(3), 522–535.

Shanghai Bookstore Publishing House (Ed.) (1988). *Dao Zang (A Complete Collection of Daoist Scriptures)* (Vol. 1–36). Cultural Relics Press, Shanghai Bookstore, Tianjing Chinese Classics Publishing House.

Shao, Y. (2016). *Huang Ji Jing Shi Shu (Book of Supreme World Ordering Principles)*. Annotated by Y. Guo & T. Yu. Shanghai Chinese Classics Publishing House.

Shen, D. (2002). *Shenzi*. Zhonghua Book Company.

Shen, F. (2017). *A history of cultural exchange between China and the West*. Shanghai People's Publishing House.

Shen, K. (2008). *Brush talks from dream brook* (Vol. I) (H. Wang, & Z. Zhao Trans.). Sichuan People's Publishing House.

Shen, Z. (1983). *Modern western legal philosophy*. Law Press.

Sibree, J. (1899). Translator's introduction. In G. W. F. Hegel, *The philosophy of history*, J. Sibree (Tr.). The Colonial Press.

Sima, G. (1965). *Zizhi Tongjian* (Vol. 20). Zhonghua Book Company.

Sima, Q. (1971). *Records of the grand historian of China* (Vol. I) (B. Watson, Trans.). Columbia Unversity Press.

Sima, Q. (1993). *Records of the grand historian: Han Dynasty II*. Revised Ed. (B. Watson, Trans.). Columbia Unversity Press.

Smith, A. (1812). *An inquiry into the nature and causes of the wealth of nations*. Ward, Lock, and Tyler.

Smith, A. (1937). *An inquiry into the nature and causes of the wealth of nations*, Edward Cannan (Ed.). The Modern Library.

Spann, O. (1930). *Types of economic theory*. George Allen & Unwin Ltd.

Spengler, J. J. (1945). The physiocrats and say's law of markets. II. *Journal of Political Economy, 53*(4), 317–347.

Spengler, J. J. (1968). Economic thought: Physiocratic thought. In D. L. Sills (Ed.), *International encyclopedia of the social sciences* (Vol. 4, pp. 443–446). The Macmillan Company & The Free Press.

Stewart, D. (1811). Account of the life and writings of Adam Smith, LL.D. In D. Stewart, (Ed.), *The works of Adam Smith, LL.D.* (Vol. V, pp. 401–552). T. Cadell.

Stollberg, R. (1960). *Geschichte der Bürgerlichen Politischen Ökonomie - Eine Allgemeinverständliche Einführung*. Die Wirtschaft.

Su, S. (1935). *A complete collection of Su Shi's works* (Vol. 22). The Commercial Press.

Sun, Y. (1982). *The complete works of Sun Yat-sen* (Vol. 2). Zhonghua Book Company.

Takimoto, S. (1931). The source of the fundamental thoughts of the physiocrats. *Reading Magazine, 1*(6), 1–39.

Tan, M. (1985a). The historical evolution of the thought of China's agricultural primacy over that of industry and commerce. *Quarterly Journal of Shanghai Academy of Social Sciences, 1*(4), 113–119.

Tan, M. (1985b). Zhuang Yuanchen's economic thoughts. *Inquiry into Economic Problems, 6*(9), 52–55.

Tang, Q. (1936). *History of Chinese economic thought* (Vol. 1). The Commercial Press.

Tang, Z. (1955). *Qian Shu*. Shanghai Ancient Books Publishing House.

Taylor, O. H. (1955). *Economics and liberalism, Cambridge*. Harvard University Press.

Taylor, O. H., & Clark, J. M. (1956). Discussion. *The American Economic Review 46*(2), 413–418.

Temple, W. (1770). *Works* (Vol. 3). J. Brotherton and W. Sewell, etc.

The Editorial Board of the History of Western Legal Thought (Ed.) (1983). *Selected sources on the history of western legal thought*. Beijing University Press.

Turgot, A. R. J. (1844). Questions sur la Chine. In A. R. J. Turgot (Ed.), *Œuvres de Turgot* (pp. 310–321). Guillaumin.

Turgot, A. R. J. (1898). *Reflections on the formation and the distribution of riches* (W. J. Ashley, Trans.). The Macmillan Co.

Uritam, R. A. (1975). Physics and the view of nature in traditional China. *American Journal of Physics, 43*(2), 136–152.

Viner, J. (1865). Guide to John Rae's life of Adam Smith. In J. Rae, *Life of Adam Smith* (pp. 1–145). A.M. Kelley, bookseller.

Vauban, S. Le P. (1888). *La Dîme royale*. Guillaumin.

Volgin, V. P. (1983). *The development of social thought in eighteenth-century France*, (M. Yang & Y. Jin, Trs into Chinese). The Commercial Press.

Voltaire (1829). *Dictionnaire Philosophique*. Lequien Fils.

Voltaire. (1901). *The works of voltaire: A contemporary version* (Vols. II, IV (Part I), V (Part I) and XIII (Part I)) J. Morley et al. (Eds.) (W. F. Fleming, Trans.). E. R. DuMont.

Wan, Q., & Wu, Y. (1986). *Adam Smith and the wealth of nations*. Jilin University Press.

Wang, Y. (1957). *A study of China's semi-feudal and semi-colonial economy*. People's Publishing House.

Wang, Y. (1979). *The spread of Chinese culture to the West in the Ming and Qing dynasties*. The Commercial Press.

Wang, Z. (1981). The influence of Chinese culture on the world. In X. Qin (Ed.), *A history of the cultural development of the republic of China* (Vol. 1). Modern China Press.

Ware, N. J. (1931). The physiocrats: A study in economic rationlization. *The American Economic Review, 21*(4), 607–619.

Weber, M. (2005). *The protestant ethic and the spirit of capitalism* (Talcott Parsons, Trans.). Routledge Classics.

Whittaker, E. (1960). *Schools and streams of economic thought*. Rand Mcnally & Company.

Wu, B. (1989). An examination of the influence of ancient Chinese economic thought on the economic doctrines of the physiocratic school. *Researches in Chinese Economic History, 4*(1), 143–156.

Wu, E. (1982). On the origin of an illustration of Taiji. *Social Science Front, 5*(2), 13–20.

Xiu, R. (1987). Microcirculation and traditional chinese medicine. *Xinhua Wenzhai, 9*(10), 183.

Xü, G. (1956). *Nong Zheng Quan Shu*. Zhonghua Book Company.

Xü, G. (1984). *Collection of Xü Guangqi's works*. Shanghai Classics Publishing House.

Xü, Y. (2002). *Guo Yu Ji Jie*. Zhonghua Book Company.

Xu, Z., & Chang, P. (Ed.) (2014). *Zhou Li* (Vol. 2), Annotated and translated into modern Chinese by Z. Xu and P. Chang. Zhonghua Book Company.

Xü, Z. (1982). On the hexagrams of the I-Ching. *Social Science Front, 5*(1), 46–54.

Xun Zi (Xunzi) (1990). *Xunzi: A Translation and Study of the Complete Works*, Vol. II, John Knoblock (Tr.). Stanford University Press.

Xun Zi (Xunzi) (1994). *Xunzi: A Translation and Study of the Complete Works*, Vol. III, John Knoblock (Tr.). Stanford University Press.

Yang, R. (1945). *Saint-just*. The Commercial Press.

Yang, T. (Ed.) (2004). *Zhou Li: An Annotation and A Translation*, Yang Tianyu (Tr. into modern Chinese). Shanghai Classics Publishing House.

Yu, Z. (2002). *Jia Yi's Xin Shu: Annotated and translated into modern Chinese*. Heilongjiang People's Publishing House.

Yu, Z. (Ed.) (1986). *Encyclopedia of economics II history of economic thought*. Taiwan Linking Publishing Co., Ltd.

Yuan, M. (1988). *Collected works of Yuan Mei*. Annotated by B. Zhou. Shanghai Chinese Classics Publishing House.

Yuan, X. (1930). China's contribution to Western economic thought. *Commercial Studies, 2*(4), 1–9.

Zempliner, A. (1962). Die chinesische Philosophie und J. Ch. Wolff. *Deutsche Zeitschrift Für Philosophie, 10*(6), 758–778.

Zhang, B. (1994). *Xu Jin Si Lu* (Vol. 1). Shanghai Chinese Classics Publishing House.

Zhang, D. (1934). A western philosophical view of Lao Zi and Zhuang Zi. *Yanjing University Journal, 8*(16), 133–160.

Zhang, H. (Ed.). (1983a). *History of western legal thought*. Beijing University Press.

Zhang, P. (1983b). Chinese cultural fever in France two hundred years ago. *History of Foreign Countries, 3*(8), 32–33.

Zhang, Z. (1966). *Quotations of Zhang Zai*. The Commercial Press.

Zhao, J. (1986). *Speeches on the history of ancient chinese economic thought*. People's Publishing House.

Zhao, L. (1933). *The economic theories of modern Europe*. The Commercial Press.

Zhao, N. (1976). *History of European and American economic theories*. Zhengzhong Book Company.

Zheng, Z. (1980). *Chen Huan-chang*. Zhonghua Book Company.

Zhu, J. (1962). Translator's Preface. In A. Reichwein, *China and Europe: Intellectual and artistic contacts in the eighteenth century* (J. Zhu, Trans.). The Commercial Press.

Zhu, J. (2005a). Preface I. In Q. Zhu (Ed.), *The influence of Chinese philosophy on Europe* (pp. 1–4). Shanghai People's Press.

Zhu, Q. (1957). The influence of Chinese philosophy on European philosophy in the eighteenth century. *Philosophical Research, 3*(4), 48–57.

Zhu, Q. (2005b). *The influence of Chinese philosophy on Europe*. Shanghai People's Press.

Zhu, Q. (2014). *The influence of Chinese thought on European culture*. Shanxi People's Publishing House.

Zhu, X. (1992). *Annotations of confucius' analects* (Vol. 1). Qilu Press.

Zhu, X. (2006). *The complete works of Zhu Xi*. National Library of China Publishing House.

Zhu, X. (2016). *Commentaries on the four books*. The Commercial Press.

Zhuang, Y. (1939). *Shu Jü Zi Nei Wai Pian (Shu Jü Zi on Personal and National Affairs)*. The Commercial Press.

Zhuang Zi (Chuang Tzu). (1891). The writings of Kwang Tzu. In F. M. Müller (Ed.). *The sacred books of China: The texts of Taoism* (L. James Trans.) (pp. 127–392). The Clarendon Press.

Zilsel, E. (1942). The genesis of the concept of physical law. *The Philosophical Review, 51*(3), 245–279.

Index

M. Tan, *The Chinese Origin of Physiocracy*, https://doi.org/10.1007/978-981-97-9703-5

The manufacturer's authorised representative in the EU is Springer Nature Customer Service Centre GmbH, Europaplatz 3, 69115 Heidelberg, Germany. If you have any concerns regarding our products, please contact ProductSafety@springernature.com

Printed and bound by CPI Group (UK) Ltd, Croydon, CR0 4YY
01/10/2026
02225925-0017